The United States
15th Infantry Regiment
in China, 1912–1938

The United States 15th Infantry Regiment in China, 1912–1938

ALFRED EMILE CORNEBISE

McFarland & Company, Inc., Publishers
Jefferson, North Carolina, and London

ALSO BY ALFRED EMILE CORNEBISE

*The CCC Chronicles: Camp Newspapers of the
Civilian Conservation Corps, 1933–1942*
(McFarland, 2004)

LIBRARY OF CONGRESS CATALOGUING-IN-PUBLICATION DATA

Cornebise, Alfred E.
    The United States 15th Infantry Regiment in China,
1912–1938 / Alfred Emile Cornebise.
       p.   cm.
    Includes bibliographical references and index.

    ISBN 0-7864-1988-1 (softcover : 50# alkaline paper) ∞

    1. United States. Army. Infantry Regiment, 15th — History — 20th
century.   2. United States. Army — Foreign service — China.
3. China — History, Military — 20th century.   4. China — History —
1912–1928.   5. China — History — 1928–1937.   I. Title.
UA2915th .C67   2004
356'.113'0973 — dc22   2004021872

British Library cataloguing data are available

©2004 Alfred Emile Cornebise. All rights reserved

*No part of this book may be reproduced or transmitted in any form
or by any means, electronic or mechanical, including photocopying
or recording, or by any information storage and retrieval system,
without permission in writing from the publisher.*

On the cover: the 15th Infantry's band on parade in the American
Compound, 1927 (*Ntaional Archives 111-SC-106231*); the regimental
coat of arms

Manufactured in the United States of America

*McFarland & Company, Inc., Publishers
    Box 611, Jefferson, North Carolina 28640
    www.mcfarlandpub.com*

For Trevyn Gard Cornebise and
Samuel Alfred Alan Cornebise

Acknowledgments

As always, the interlibrary loan office at the Michener Library at the University of Northern Colorado, ably presided over by Lois Leffler, has been most helpful in getting materials to me, sometimes when they were seemingly unobtainable. Ann Squier and Joyce Ehlert at the General Forrest Harding Memorial Museum in Franklin, Ohio, one rainy April afternoon opened up to me many of the treasures there that gave some insight into what service in China was like for the officers and men of the 15th Infantry Regiment. The halls of the George C. Marshall Foundation's Library in Lexington, Virginia, are graced by Joanne D. Hartog, the director of the library and archives, who located some of the most useful sources that I consulted in my research for this study. At Archives II in College Park, Maryland, Mitchell Yockelson and Timothy Nenninger, as always, most ably assisted me in locating numerous relevant materials, as did Trevor Plante at Archives I in Washington.

I wish to acknowledge the assistance and close interest in this study of Dagmar K. Getz, archivist at the Kautz Family YMCA Archives at the Elmer L. Andersen Library on the University of Minnesota campus. Her deep knowledge of the sources on YMCA history materially assisted me in pursuing useful documents pertaining to China during the decades between the world wars.

Alan Archambault and Greg Hagge, at the Fort Lewis Military Museum, provided me with useful information regarding the return of the 15th Infantry to the United States in March 1938.

I must recognize the encouragement and insights of my colleague in the department of history at the University of Northern Colorado, Professor Ronald Edgerton, whose knowledge of Chinese and Far Eastern history has proved most helpful.

Many thanks also to Michael Cornebise for his assistance with the map of North China and to Jason Schlueter for redrawing it.

Finally, to my wife Jan Miller Cornebise, my warmest thanks for her unending tolerance and support of my research projects and her assistance with the illustrations. To all of my efforts she brings a fine knowledge of the English language and how the written page should appear. Her careful reading and critiques of my work remain central to the final outcome.

Alfred E. Cornebise
Greeley, Colorado
Fall 2004

Table of Contents

Acknowledgments	vii
Map of North China	x
Preface	1
I. The Setting	7
II. The 15th Marches onto the Chinese Stage	21
III. History and Organization	51
IV. Leadership	61
V. The Officer Corps and the Rank and File	76
VI. *The Sentinel*	96
VII. Attitudes, Morale and the Daily Round	111
VIII. The Training Cycle	137
IX. Athletes, Thespians and Musicians	153
X. The Chinese Land, History and People	166
XI. Les Femmes	188
XII. The Regulars, Horses and Other Matters	197
XIII. Withdrawal of the 15th from China	210
XIV. The Regiment's Chinese Legacy	217
Chapter Notes	229
Selected Bibliography	259
Index	263

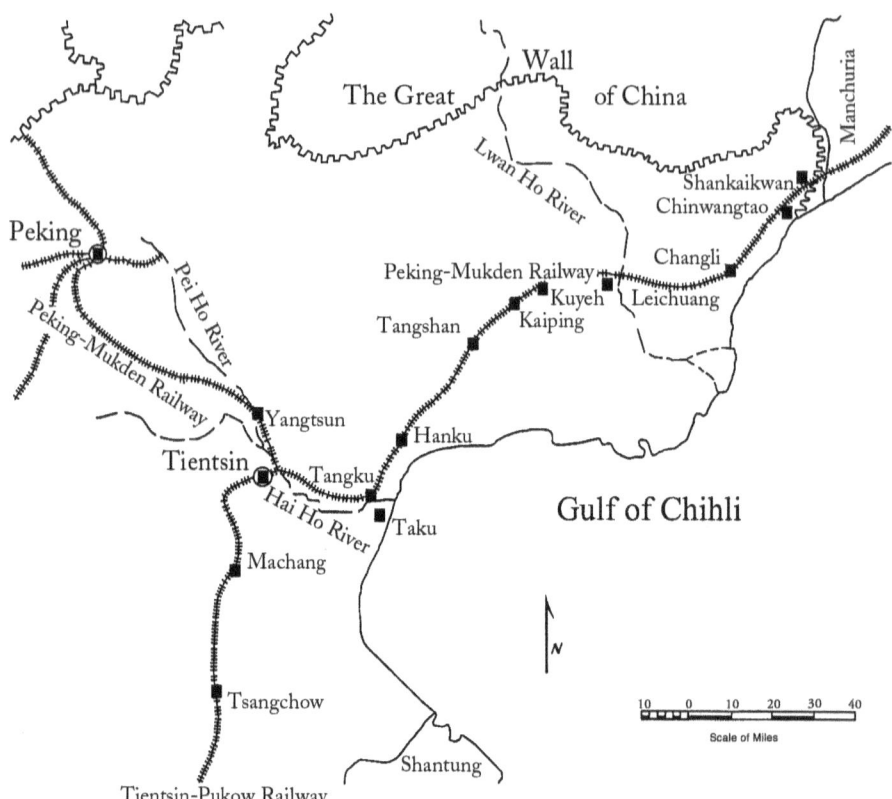

Map of North China by Jason Schlueter

Preface

To one veteran of the U.S. Army's 15th Infantry Regiment, which was stationed in China from 1912 to 1938 — Private Charles Grandison Finney, who served in the late 1920s— it remained a mystery why the outfit's history in the Orient was not better known. He found it odd that more people had not written about those days, but surmised that perhaps too much background had to be introduced "to make any sense out of it"—certainly a sound observation and one with which this study has had to contend. He added, perhaps more significantly, "With a couple of wars in between I suppose it sizes up as very small beer."[1]

Indeed, in relation to the numbers of books pertaining to all aspects of both world wars, comparatively little has been written about peacetime service in the U.S. Army between them, though this can be instructive and useful. Accounts of the deployment of its units in foreign lands during those same years are scarcer still but are also of interest. In some small measure, this narrative seeks to address both of these subjects.

The 15th Regiment initially served in China as part of the relief expedition that ended the siege of foreigners in Peking during the Boxer Uprising (1899–1900).[2] Withdrawn after these events, it was ordered back to China following the collapse of the Manchu (Qing) Dynasty (1644–1912) in 1912.[3] Placed under the control of the State Department, it was headquartered at Tientsin (Tianjin) in northern China, 65 miles southeast of Peking (Beijing). Taking up its position astride the Peking-Mukden (Beijing-Shenyang) railway in January 1912, the 1,000-man force was engaged in protecting American interests in China during those tumultuous years; they were especially challenged in the 1920s, when warlords struggled to gain ascendency in the Chinese Republic. When Chiang Kai-shek established a measure of control in China by 1928, the regiment remained in China, partially to counter Japan's increasingly aggressive actions, despite considerable misgivings within and outside of the Army as to the feasibility, desirability, and ethical appropriateness of the policy retaining it there. The success of the Japanese in conquering much of eastern China by 1938 finally compelled Washington to withdraw the 15th in March of that year.

The regiment was in China in support of what some citizens—though hardly all—considered the nation's best interests. This was certainly true of American businessmen and missionaries who thought that they had the right to be in China in the first place and to claim protection of their government while there. The State Department sought to accommodate them. The War Department acquiesced but was never comfortable with the notion that its forces in China were mainly being utilized for diplomatic or political purposes, desiring for the most part to get its men in that increasingly exposed quarter safely home. The 15th emerged as the U.S. Army's counterpart of the U.S. Navy's "Sand Pebble" establishment, i.e., those ships engaged in gunboat and other naval operations, and its history in China provides a means of assessing certain developments in American foreign, domestic and military policy between the world wars.[4]

The troops sent to China found various attractions there. There was, for one, the "lure of the East"—a way for soldiers to seek adventure in conditions tinted with more than a hint of danger. When Prohibition came to America, some sought a refuge where liquor was plentiful, either in Germany, or failing that—the Americans withdrew from the Rhine in 1923—China. Tientsin likewise seemed a desirable place of escape when the Depression came. There are always women present where soldiers are stationed and those in China seemed especially alluring, exotic—and numerous.

Families of military personnel, for their own reasons, found China every bit as enticing. To be sure, there were dangers to life, limb and health, but there were all of those wonderful servants who could be hired for a pittance, those marvelous shopping opportunities, and a generally privileged position, all enhanced by a favorable monetary exchange rate. For the more refined and astute there was contact with the ancient and impressive culture of China. Service there was all the more fascinating for China was a beautiful, if sometimes harsh, land with a myriad of unforgettable sights, sounds and smells.

In addition, for the Army officers and men fortunate to serve in China, professional skills could be honed in one of the few places on the globe where conflict involving American troops seemed a distinct possibility, with all of its opportunities for military attainment, preferment and promotion. Perhaps some glory awaited. Why not, then, serve in a crack regiment—which some regarded the 15th to be—that seemed to meet the hopes, aspirations, and requirements of many concerned?

In a study of these events, one also encounters elements in the American deployment that evince various concerns. While the United States was often ambivalent about being a colonial power, it nonetheless revealed certain attributes of imperialism in its deployment in China. Attitudes developed during the nation's involvement in the Philippines also poured over into the Chinese setting. Accordingly, the United States was regarded in China as simply another Western power and as such was tarred with the same brush used in limning other foreigners. In the text that follows, the reader will encounter indications of some enlightenment on the part of the American troops as to China and the Chinese. For instance, there was an effort at the regiment's command levels to foster an appreciation for things Chinese even to the extent of requiring officers to study the Chinese language.

Nonetheless, Americans often judged the Chinese by superficial appearances and the sights, sounds, smells, and much else that led to an inability to appreciate the long history of Chinese civilization and its high cultural attainments. The rank and file were much more involved in their own creature comforts, which could be met in China as at few other stations in the Army's establishment. American judgments of the Chinese were compounded by characteristic notions that all things Western were inherently superior. Such prejudices, evidences of racism, and limitations of the typical American point of view of that era offend the sensibilities of many observers of a later age, particularly those with deep knowledge and appreciation of things Chinese. Still, the historian of the American involvement in China must be guided by the demands of close and accurate reporting of what occurred, as well as depicting prevailing attitudes, to the end of presenting a true bill of particulars reflecting those times.

Naturally, American aspirations and endeavors encountered, and sometimes confronted, those of China, Britain, France, fascist Italy and, more importantly, imperial Japan. These rounded out the mosiac of the often momentous occurrences that transpired in that fateful period between the world wars. There emerged from this cockpit a remarkable group of American Army officers—known informally in some circles as that "Damned China Crowd"—dozens of whom attained the rank of general and who later served in key leadership roles for America and much of the free world in World War II and beyond. Indeed, this development concerning the regiment remains more important to American history than its contacts with the Chinese and other nations in the Far East in those years.

Throughout the course of its deployment in the Orient, however, only a few Americans were aware of the 15th's presence there. By contrast, from the writings of Rudyard Kipling to Winston Churchill, the British were well-informed of their nation's colonial and foreign ventures and wars. Correspondingly little has been written about the American troops abroad in similar circumstances, though there are some references in memoirs and biographies and in a few other studies. The official documentation for studying the 15th's China deployment is substantial and is located in major record collections in the National Archives in Washington, D.C., and in Maryland; the U.S. Army Military History Institute at Carlisle Barracks, Pennsylvania; the George C. Marshall Foundation in Lexington, Virginia; and other sites.

There is also an as yet insufficiently utilized source ready at hand. Throughout much of its career in China, the regiment produced a regimental newspaper-cum-magazine, *The Sentinel*, under the general supervision of the education and recreation officer. Founded in 1919, the paper was supported by subscriptions and advertising. It was published every Friday — later Saturday — by *The Tientsin Press*, a local Chinese English-language journal. Averaging about 28 pages, by 1921 *The Sentinel*'s circulation was around 1,450 copies, some 500 of which were mailed to the United States "as a letter to home folks and others interested in any of us in far away 'heathen' China." This collective memoir of the regiment has been extensively drawn upon for this study, complementing the considerable body of other primary sources also utilized.[5]

Although Kipling maintained of the East and West that the twain never meet — at least not meaningfully — for a few thousand Americans associated with the U.S. Army's 15th Infantry Regiment there were just such contacts. The story that follows recounts and assesses some aspects of the involvement and service of that organization during the fateful quarter of a century in the Orient between the world wars. The study can inform those wishing to understand something about U.S. Army operations in China — as well as details of Army service in those years in general — and on occasion reveals self-perceptions of a key generation of U.S. military personnel deployed there. The reader will not find in the pages of this book, however, a detailed consideration and analysis of either American foreign or military policy for the Orient during that period — both already considered in numerous able accounts — though they are given some attention so as to make the account intelligible. Nor is this primarily a history of China. Rather, herein one can learn something of the metes and bounds of U.S. Army service in China, grasp what it was like to be there, and encounter a delineation of some who served, with some notion of what this duty entailed.

A Note on Romanization

Principal Chinese personal and place names in the text have been rendered in the Wade-Giles system so as to conform to the spelling in use at the time of the 15th's deployment in China. For the convenience of those more familiar with the Pinyin system, I have indicated these spellings in parentheses when the word is first employed. I have spelled "Peking" as "Peiping" for sources and accounts generated after that form was introduced in 1928.

Chapter I

The Setting

1912

Have all the wars you want to; do as you have always did
But keep 'em rolling to the ocean, and listen, Yeller Kid
That damn old Peking-Mukden's got to run![1]

East of Suez

For I've been East of Suez.
And I've seen them fish at play:
There's nothing to it, I tell a man,
To come such a long, long way.[2]

On September 25, 1924, Private Otto Beinke, a soldier in the United States Regular Army, found himself on the gangplank of the U.S. Army Transport (USAT) *Chateau Thierry*, moored at the Brooklyn docks.[3] Though the passengers were mainly U.S. Army personnel, civilians also streamed aboard. Beinke's final destination was the American Barracks, Tientsin, China, the home of the U.S. Army's 15th Infantry Regiment, the main unit of the United States Army Forces in China (USAFC). A long blast of the ship's whistle brought an end to farewell handshakes, hugs, and the hasty drying of tears, while the soldiers manifested an exuberant "three year spirit" of their upcoming term of foreign service as they got underway.

The long voyage first proceeded along the Eastern Seaboard, encountering the gales that frequently lashed famous maritime sites in the region, such as Cape Hatteras, North Carolina. The subsequent more leisurely cruise under clear skies, through warmer weather and the stunning blue water of the Caribbean, ended at the Panama Canal Zone.[4] After a brief stop for the passengers to see the sights at Panama City, the ship continued to Los Angeles and then San Francisco, where Beinke and his China-bound buddies boarded the "doughboy special," the U.S. Army Transport *Thomas*, a veteran of many transpacific runs. A layover in Honolulu enabled the troops to appreciate the "Hula-Hula Janes" doing their stuff, but these pleasures were short-lived, and the ship, on the twenty-third of October, 1924, departed for the Philippines. Following a brief stop at Guam, the ship entered Manila Bay on November 8. The troops left the ship for sightseeing in Manila, being temporarily based at nearby Fort McKinley. Once more underway, the *Thomas* proceeded northward, sailing by Formosa. The weather became much colder and heavier clothing was required as the ship entered the Yellow Sea. On November 21, the ship anchored at Chinwangtao (CWT for short, now Qinhuangdao), the major northern Chinese port on the Gulf of Chihli (Zhili) serving much of northern China, including Peking and Tientsin, and through which ran the Peking-Mukden railroad. There was snow on the piers as the men disembarked, and the distant mountains were covered in white. Had the men arrived in the spring, they might have been met by the harsh reality of the Mongolian desert to the north of Peking, whose raging dust storms, accompanied by an intense cold, often enveloped the city in a blanket of yellow powder, turning the light of day into a gloomy twilight. As one anonymous soldier-poet expressed it, "Not many drops of water / But lots of grains of sand / Makes this mighty country / A very unpleasant land."[5]

Leaving the ship, the new arrivals climbed aboard rail cars for the six-hour trip to Tientsin, 167 miles to the southwest. The local scene was dismal. The men beheld large areas of small one-story shacks made of mud and straw, and only the railway station buildings and the Standard Oil Company's tanks and warehouses were of more substantial construction. As the train departed the station, they saw mile after mile of graves in countless numbers dotting the landscape, the coffins having been placed above ground and covered with humps of dirt. Attesting to the long history of the ancient land, the mounds reminded some observers of ant hills or "Eskimo's igloos—except that they were made of mud," and were only the first of many depressing sights that the troops beheld in China.[6]

Another traveller's first impression was that "yellow is the predominant color in China. The people are yellow in complexion. Before one reaches the China coast, even the ocean is seen to be yellow. The rivers are the same color, and when one lands, and takes a train journey of any appreciable length, almost all of the landscape is noticed to be of the same identical yellow." It was perhaps not surprising that even "the Imperial Dragon of past days was yellow, as also were the tiles upon the roofs of the Forbidden City, and other places of the former royalty."[7]

There were not only exotic sights but other assaults on the senses, described by one soldier as "obnoxious odors, unseemly sights, atrocious noises, itchy feeling, dung-like taste." His observations were echoed by an anonymous soldier in his evocative "An Idyll of the East":

> . . . .
> Ah! See how the smoky rickshaw lantern
> Gives off the sensuous scent of burning oil!
> All mingled with the virile tinge of garlic
> From Ta Ts'ao's humble supper, as with laboured breath
> He draws me past the garbage dump on Pei Tsung
> And home at last to dream.
> Ah! Never-fading romance of the East! Ah, me![8]

Beinke would no doubt have appreciated the observations of another 15th Regiment soldier, Private Knud Olsen, who by his own reckoning had been in almost every country in the world, "but never [before] in [the] land of two thousand years ago, where misery is contentment. The land of tea houses and temples, of palaces and hovels of famine and pestilence, of history and antiquity, of hairless men and toeless women, of the finest lamps and incense burners, the home of Mah Jongg and chop sticks. Where [there] are educated and ignorant, rich, beggar, and slave. A land of a hundred tongues and a thousand religions. A country that neither Volsted nor women can rule, where every general owns an army and his own ricksha.... Where every one just works, works, works, with the crudest of crude implements." Yet, as many observers noted, in spite of adversities, the people on the whole were a cheery lot, as the rickshaw boys, for example, almost invariably were. They seem to "grin and bear it," and go on with their work, all days of the week except for a spell of idleness over the Chinese New Year.[9]

Beinke's contingent arrived at Tientsin's East Station to find the regiment's Service Company patiently waiting with teams of horses and baggage wagons. They were soon marching along Victoria and Meadows Roads bound for the American compound. Beinke observed that proceeding through the heart of the city at 2 A.M. was noteworthy only for the stillness. The city of a million Chinese and 4,000 foreigners seemed to him "the deadest town in the world—even deader than Kansas City since women got into politics."

Had the new men arrived at the train station in the daytime, the scene would have been markedly different. Then the quiet would have given way to bedlam: men, baggage, wagons and horses, and a mass of "near-humanity" in the form of "babbling Chinese coolies" seeking to carry their luggage or take them aboard their rickshaws, all desperate to earn a few coppers so as to survive another day. Often the pressing masses were held off by the menacing clubs of the Chinese police: "There they were, fifty or more — held as hounds at bay, their eyes glued on the soldiers— all ready to dash forward the minute they were called. Now and then one would step forward a little — to gain a start — only to be beaten mercilessly by the police." When the signal was made to the waiting coolies, a seething mass of rickshaw men, "a dirty, excited mongrelity," swooped down on the soldiers, running into each other in their eagerness to gain trade, all mingled with strange cries and entreaties: "Me fast," "Me ding-how," "Compound," and other idioms common in coolie circles. There were "tall coolies, small coolies, lean coolies, fat coolies, coolies with 'Qs,' others with heads shaved bald; coolies with long noses, short noses, flat noses; coolies of all ages from ten to sixty." Occasionally, a rickshaw driver would die while running between his vehicle's shafts, the incident being placed in the hands of a "shimbo"—a Chinese policeman—who would give the body to other coolies to dispose of. One newly-arrived soldier, involved in such an event, feared that he would be charged with murder but was told that it was a common occurrence which should simply be forgotten. As to the rickshaws, one soldier recounted in *The Sentinel* that "for pure, unadulterated cussedness and recklessness, let me recommend you to the average ricksha coolie," thereby introducing readers to "the Garlic Motor that provided the thrills."[10]

Elsewhere throughout the city, the population — at least as perceived by the soldiers—seemed to consist largely of masses of dirty, crippled, stinking, terrible-looking beings. The half-clothed coolies, some mere boys, were often shivering. Some were carrying and drawing huge boxes, heavy loads of iron and wares "like beasts of burden," while others were loading and unloading coal and other cargo from ships and barges. The sight of such suffering and abject poverty was always appalling, especially to newcomers and more thoughtful observers, who were usually admonished to reject any idealistic views that they had earlier entertained regarding the equality of humankind. When in China, they were advised to "do as the Chinese did," which meant to "take life as it is," and "live today — let tomorrow take care of itself." In reality, Tientsin's social and business strata, among both Chinese and foreigners, were quite complex, with almost infinite gradations and levels of influence, wealth and poverty.[11]

By the end of 1917, the 15th was headquartered in the American compound — in Chinese, *Mei-Kuo Ying-P'an* — a city block in the former German concession. After the Germans were forced to withdraw in 1917 in the midst of World War I, the Chinese took over the territory, naming it the "First Special Area." In that year, the Oriental Real Estate Company — which, because of its lapses in maintaining reliable services, was

I. The Setting

The 15th Infantry on parade in the American Compound (*Mei-Kuo Ying-P'an*), Tientsin, China, 1927. Courtesy the National Archives, Washington, D.C. (111-SC-106241).

often referred to as the "Old, Rotten Extinct Company"—constructed three lines of buildings running east and west, with some detached structures. These were leased to the American command by the firm which maintained, heated, lighted and provided water for the establishment. The arrangement of the buildings subdivided the compound into three parallel courtyards, the largest of which, being 260 by 90 feet, was used for regimental ceremonies. One drawback was that the buildings were based upon plans that would permit them to be turned into apartment houses when the Americans departed. They therefore lacked storage space and other desirable facilities and were rather unsuited for barracks. Nearly all of the structures were three to four stories high, with finished basements. Constructed of brick covered with plaster or stucco, all had electricity and running water on each floor. Two companies were housed in each barracks building, and kitchens, storerooms and mess halls were in the basements. The hospital building was constructed specifically for that purpose, as was a large building known as Recreation Hall, which had a stage and was utilized for indoor athletic games, theatricals and movies. The guardhouse and the bathing facilities—certainly an inconvenience often complained about because the individual barracks lacked them—were in the basement of the Hall. To correct this, showers were later installed in each barracks. On the west side of the compound and across Shansi Road in an adjoining area were the stables, the corral, various sheds, the wagon park, an ice plant which also furnished distilled water, a bakery, the veterinary hospital, the post exchange and a blacksmith shop. The buildings were poorly constructed and difficult to maintain, but they provided a fairly satisfactory barracks, though "of course, not to be compared with permanent barracks in the United States."[12]

A visiting soldier of the 18th U.S. Infantry from Manila on temporary assignment with the 15th, however, saw the location and conditions in a more favorable light. "We are barracked in huge, old gray buildings—majestic—with more of an academic air than military one," he wrote. "The mess hall is like a hotel as to decoration, service and food. There are only 10 men to a squad room. Each room has its own servant; he makes the beds, shines the shoes, polishes the equipment and keeps things clean. For a dollar a month I get a shave every day and a hair cut every two weeks. We drill a little in the morning and a little in the afternoon. After that—a rickshaw and Tientsin." The men of the regiment were "immaculate as to bearing and appearance," and he thought them the "finest looking soldiers in this place of many soldiers."[13]

By 1926, the Tientsin garrison totalled 47 officers and 798 men of the regiment's Second and Third Battalions—the First was in Manila. In addition, a rifle company was stationed at Tongshan (sometimes spelled as it is at present, Tangshan) 85 miles east of Tientsin, a Chinese city of 50,000 with a foreign settlement of about 65 English and Belgian families. There, a subpost was located, and the normal tour of duty guarding the railroad shops of the Peking-Mukden railroad was for six months, when the company was replaced by another from Tientsin. Industrial Tongshan, the "Smoky City," or the "City of Black Diamonds," with its freight yards and coaling facilities, was not regarded as a good duty station, and the men always rejoiced when they could return to the amenities of the compound. One soldier, however, in his "Ode to Tongshan," perhaps ironically, saw the city in a rather different light: "Tongshan awake! bestir thyself, and listen to my lay / Fair mistress of the freight-yard and the coal."[14]

The nexus of the outfit's bailiwick was Tientsin, astride the Peking-Mukden railway. (Present-day Tientsin is a city of over 10 million inhabitants.) Its Chinese name meant "The Ford of Heaven," i.e., the ford that had to be taken by officials and embassies on their way from the south to Peking, the "Northern Capital." Sometimes called the Panorama City, Tientsin was about 65 miles by rail southeast of Peking, which had been the capital of China since 1421 under the Ming Dynasty (1368–1644). The city lay on a vast alluvial plain extending beyond Peking to the Gulf of Chihli on the Yellow Sea some 40 miles to the east. More specifically, it was located in the southeastern part of the province of Chihli (now Hebei) at the head of the Hai Ho, a short river formed by the confluence of the Grand Canal entering Tientsin from the west and the Pei Ho River. flowing from the direction of Peking to the northwest, as well as four other streams. The Hai Ho — the "Sea River" — was about 300 feet wide at Tientsin, from whence it proceeded 40 miles southeast to the coast, where its mouth at Tangku (Tanggu) was guarded by the Taku (Dagu) forts. A waterway of great commercial importance, it was navigable by small steamers, seagoing junks, and gunboats of the international concessionary powers.[15]

As far as the eye could see, the surrounding country was absolutely flat, dotted with small villages, brick kilns and the mounds of countless native graves, an astonishing sight often remarked upon by newcomers to the region. Complaints were often made about the climate and prevailing weather conditions. If not located in the Yangtze valley with China's three infamous so-called furnace cities — Nanking (Nanjing), Wuhan (still Wuhan) and Chungking (Chongqing) — summers were nonetheless often enervatingly hot and morbidly humid, contrasting sharply with the bitter cold of winter. In addition, its location on the banks about ten feet above the level of the river sometimes subjected the city to floods, especially in the summers, though an effective dike system helped to control the menace except in times of occasional extraordinary rainfall. In the spring, as has already been described, northeast China was often obscured under a choking veil of dust originating in the Gobi Desert to the north of Peking. Consequently, in the dwellings of the foreigners the windows were double sealed; nonetheless, after major storms, mementoes of [the] Gobi covered everything. The result was that everyone had some form of throat, nose, or sinus trouble, atomizers were standard equipment in every home, and persons having no resistance to respiratory diseases were advised not to seek service in China.

By the middle of the seventeenth century, when the Manchus came to the throne in China (1644), Tientsin became recognized as one of the greatest seaports in the nation. The city was a natural hub for imports and exports for much of northeastern China, serving as the axis of water and rail transportation, and its obvious communications center. Famous for its salt industry, the city was also known for its rice market and as an exporter of Siberian tea. Business interests in Tientsin were in the hands of both Chinese entrepreneurs, capitalists and industrialists, and a variety of foreign enterprises, as well as mixed entities with both foreign and native Chinese investors, staff and managers. Organizationally, it was divided into a large native Chinese city as well as the concessions administered separately by various foreigners, supplemented by various Chinese officials. The concessions were the abode of all outsiders as well as of many well-to-do Chinese.

By a Convention of Peace between France and China, signed in 1860, Tientsin was made a treaty port. Other agreements made at the same time extended concession rights to the United States and Britain, though the United States did not take up its options, and its concession was only informally recognized. In 1880, the Americans returned their concession to its former status "with the understanding that if at some future time it shall become desirable to establish suitable municipal regulation therein it shall be competent for the Consular authorities to do so." The Americans formally ended their concession in 1896, but in 1901, after their involvement in the Boxer Uprising, they attempted to revive it, to no avail. It was formally stipulated on October 23, 1902, that the British would assume control over any American interests in the concession with the understanding that the Americans could have the rights of asylum for troops and American residents "in case of trouble," i.e., if any military necessity in the future might so dictate.

Meanwhile, a bund was constructed, though hardly equalling Shanghai's famous concourse. In addition, the Tientsin-Tongshan section of what was to be the Peking-Mukden railway, built by the British, was opened in 1888. In 1895, the railway was extended from Tientsin to near Peking and then, in the other direction, towards Manchuria, reaching Shankaikwan (Shanhaiguan) in 1894, and by 1899, Chin Chow. The British also negotiated with allied governments the control of the railway from Peking to Shankaikwan in February 1901.

In 1895, a German concession was ceded in the city; a Japanese one in 1896. Because of their substantial involvement in the Boxer Uprising in Tientsin, on November 6, 1900, the Russians formally established a concession for themselves, consisting of about 1,000 acres with river frontage, despite opposition from other powers including the United States. A Belgian concession was announced on November 7, 1900, near the Russian site, consisting of 238 acres, also along the river. The French claimed an extension, as did the Italians and the Austrians. The Japanese added more land to their original territory and in 1901, the German and British holdings were expanded.[16]

I. The Setting

In 1917, as a result of the Great War, the Chinese took over the Austrian and German concessions, and after the Russian Revolution of 1917, the Chinese government occupied the Russian claim in 1920, holding it "in trust" for the eventual Russian government then struggling to become established as the Soviet Union. In 1924, the Soviet Union voluntarily surrendered the Russian concession. Belgium relinquished its holdings in 1929. By the end of the Great War, Tientsin was garrisoned only by British, French, Italian, Japanese and American troops, maintained under the Protocol of September 7, 1901. Having no concession, the Americans were housed in various buildings around town until after 1917, when they moved into the compound.

In the period between the world wars, Tientsin had a native population of almost a million. There were about 4,400 foreigners, half of whom were Japanese. Of the remaining, 1,200 were British and 700 were Americans. The foreign business sections of the city had the appearance of a typical American city of from 80,000 to a 100,000 in population. There were wide, paved streets flanked with stores whose show windows displayed as varied an assortment of familiar articles as one would find in any thriving Western metropolis. To be sure, there were differences: for one, there was the absence of the familiar red-front five- and ten-cent store common in the United States, and there was also "the presence of an occasional window display of bottled goods carrying more than one half of one percent alcoholic contents," certainly not prominent in Prohibition America. One American finding himself on Victoria Road bordering Victoria Park, the city's "Broadway," thought that he might as well be on Bond Street, London, or Fifth Avenue, New York. A visiting soldier on temporary assignment with the 15th was quite impressed. "The glamor of the place is beyond my power of exposition," he declared, asserting that it was "the most cosmopolitan place I, in my limited experience, have ever seen. In one block one may see an English, a French, and Italian soldier, a dozen Jap soldiers, a Jew drummer, an American expatriot [sic], a Russian ... of the lower class and a Capuchin monk."

An American officer stationed in Tientsin remembered that "life there was mighty pleasant" and "the foreign Concessions were like dream cities to a Westerner." They were "oases of homelands in a jungle of poverty and filth." In the concessions area, for instance, there was the long, curving, tree-lined Race Course Road running through a residential neighborhood near the American compound. It was divided by parks of green grass and small shrubs with foreign children playing in the shade of trees, while groups and couples, young and old alike, strolled along the boulevard. By way of contrast, on nearby Taku Road where "East met West," Chinese

Street scene, Tientsin, China. Cover of *The Sentinel*, March 23, 1929, by Private First Class L.M. Healy of the 15th Infantry.

and Russian shops abounded. There, autos and rickshaws vied for space along the narrow, dirty and crowded street; and noisy vendors, including barbers with their travelling shops and doughball sellers—peddling one of China's staffs of life—scrambled for trade.[17]

Indeed, it was good living at Tientsin during these years for both the officers and the rank and file of the U.S. Army. Pay was in gold with a favorable exchange rate, and "fine liquor and women were cheap and plentiful." "As for society's upper crust, with the military and diplomatic backdrop, flavored by the delights of the Tientsin Town and Race clubs, there was never a dull moment." There was the other side of the coin: foreigners living in Tientsin—as elsewhere in China—had to take "what at home would be unreasonable health precautions ... for there lurked disease in its most virulent forms." These conditions resulted in part because for centuries "night soil" had been used for fertilizer. Ordinary small-pox vaccine was not adequate; it had to be of the triple-strength "camel variety." Malaria was also prevalent during the late summer and early fall months. Drinking tap water "was an open invitation to the agonies of amoebic dysentery." All locally grown vegetables had to be boiled before eating, and the "beautiful native melons were habitually 'plugged' and contaminated water injected to give added weight."[18]

Some measure of that "good life" as experienced by the 15th's men can be ascertained in an anonymous trooper's poem, "Tientsin":

> Millions of sparkling, colorful lights,
> Thousands of girls and wonderful sights,
> Hundreds of night clubs, dozens of fights,
>   — Tientsin, China.
>
> Plenty of kisses, bottles of gin,
> Heartaches and sorrows lost in its din,
> Happiness, whoopee, laughter and sin
>   — Tientsin, China
>
> Rivers and rickshaws seeking the dawn,
> Skinfuls and sinfuls, headaches and yawns,
> Little lost dreams and each of them gone.
>   Tientsin, China[19]

The city boasted many amenities for foreign families, such as large modern hotels: the Astor House, the Court Hotel, and in the French concession, the Imperial Hotel. Sometimes the Army YMCA had rooms for rent on a monthly basis, usually used temporarily by families seeking permanent housing. Normally, officers and their families resided in the same areas of the city as the enlisted men did.[20]

Banks, credit and the fluctuating rate of exchange were common topics for discussion, and if military service in China was mysterious, "in China money could be as mysterious as anything else," as one sailor noted. Indeed, the Chinese seemed to Westerners "in their incessant chatter" to be mainly discussing one topic: money — about which they were canny, clever and devious, compelling one soldier-poet to lament in a prayer, "Oh love and protect us while in this Chinese Land / Shield and shelter us from this carnivorous band."[21]

In the early twentieth century, much of the silver currency in the form of *sycee*—bulk silver molded in different shapes and weights—had been replaced by the Mexican silver dollar. In turn, by the 1920s, the Mexican dollar was superseded by the Chinese silver dollar—or *yuan*, meaning literally "round one"—which was still nonetheless universally referred to as the "Mex." As the 1930s rolled around, the exchange rate was on the order of three or four "Mex" dollars, or "local currency," to one American gold one—which soldiers were paid in—making service in China even more desirable.[22]

One of the eagerly anticipated and greatly appreciated features of military service in China was the employment of servants in relatively large numbers. But while plentiful in quantity, they were not "always efficient in quality." The average family employed five, headed by the "Number One Boy" who was paid from 15 to 20 dollars a month, local currency. His duties were supervision of housekeeping, cleaning and cooking. Most of the actual fatigue work was done by a coolie whose monthly compensation was from nine to 12 dollars. The cook was a manservant paid from 15 to 20 dollars. In addition to cooking, he developed his own menus and did most of the marketing. A chauffeur's services for those possessing an automobile could be obtained for a monthly charge of 30 to 40 dollars. Some families purchased a rickshaw and hired a coolie to pull it. Others rode in public rickshaws available at nominal rates. "Their disadvantage [was] that they [were] frequently dirty," one report noted. The only Chinese female servants were the amahs who washed, did sewing and minded babies. The two former categories received from 12 to 16 dollars a month. Those who cared for the babies were paid 18 to 20 dollars monthly.

It was generally conceded that "as a general proposition the average Chinese servant is fairly honest." That is, they would not steal articles of value. But, "according to their code of ethics, it is no offense to take small articles of little value; items such as soap, needles, pins, socks, handkerchiefs, food and coal disappear with great regularity." In addition, there were the notorious "hidden charges," the consequence of all servants being "endowed with the Oriental 'squeeze' tradition"; that is, the commission the cook got on everything he bought and that which the Number One Boy got on everything the employer bought, making their total cost quite high. Indeed, as one American army officer noted, "unless an employer watched his coal, food and liquor, he would find himself 'squeezed' out of house and home."[23]

Another pleasure looked forward to by foreigners was shopping. Normally, one reporter wryly observed, in the course of a tour in China one's wife "invariably accumulated a rather impressive store of rugs, silver, linen, lingerie, embroideries and other impedimenta that would be utterly beyond his means if priced on Fifth Avenue." Also, the ladies "could enjoy shopping for such treasures as convent table cloths, camphorwood and Shansi chests, Chinese rugs and numerous other items at dirt cheap prices and easy credit." Chinese merchants usually accepted without hesitation the signatures of officers on chits for merchandise.[24] And shop they did, an activity amusingly described in "Farewell to the Jordans":

> The Jordans are leaving old China,
> They are saying good-bye to its shores;
> They are leaving the slant eyed celestials
> To their squeeze, revolutions and wars.
> But they don't return home empty handed
> From their three years purchasing toot
> For they're leaving the land of Confucius
> With at least half a ship load of loot. I say,
> With the *Thomas* half full of their loot....
> They have taken the gods from their niches
> They have scrolls that date back to Ming
> They have stripped all the screens from the Shansi
> And bought out the shops of Peking."[25]

The cost of food products ready for consumption was relatively high. There also tended to be considerable wastage in that there was invariably more food cooked than eaten. However, the American Barracks possessed a substantial post exchange and commissary from which staples could be bought at reasonable prices.[26]

As to clothing, there were numerous well-stocked, modern stores, many of which handled some American goods, though most products were manufactured in England or France. The latest fashions were not as stylish as in America, but China was famous for its tailors, which were numerous and efficient, and good shoes were made to order by Chinese or Russian shops. The services of a sewing amah was a good value for repair of clothing.

One of the advantages Tientsin had to offer service families was good schools. One was the well-staffed, relatively inexpensive American School near the compound. There was also the Tientsin Grammar School, founded in 1905 by the Tientsin School Association. Operated on the British form system, it was difficult for American students to fit into. For older students another option was the North China American School, a rather expensive boarding high school founded in 1913. Located in Tunghsien, in Chihli Province, it was about 15 miles from Peking and 65 from Tientsin.

In sum, Beinke and his buddies could look forward to an interesting stretch of service in "The Land of the Pagoda," as Captain A.S. Ander, of the American Red Cross called it in his Kiplingesque poem:

> Now this is the story of China, fair China 'cross the bay
> The land of the Pagoda, and the coolie's song they say.
> But the pig-tail is fast going, — romance I fear is dead
> For the Mandarin is wearing now — a plug-hat on his head.
> . . . .[27]

CHAPTER II

The 15th Marches onto the Chinese Stage

> China, however, is not an easy country to understand, and those who are best acquainted with it are puzzled to trace its sequence of thought or interpret its public opinion.[1]

In some respects, the 15th's history in China might be entitled "A Regiment in Search of a Viable Policy," though earlier in its career in China there was an appreciation of its need and utility. As one account has it, "every command is assigned a mission" to guide and control "all those acts and efforts which a command is expected or destined to accomplish." It consisted "of one or several tasks each imposed by higher authority, or required by force of circumstances." But the USATC's (United States Army Troops in China) agenda was "nowhere succinctly prescribed in orders or clearly enunciated by superior military authority." The ambivalent condition had always existed and the reasons were twofold: First, the isolated position of the garrison in a foreign country characterized by "constantly changing local conditions—political, military, and international," made it "impracticable and undesirable for our own military superiors to prescribe a line of action beyond their knowledge or control." Second, the Army's forces in China were subordinate, with respect to their mission, to the American minister in Peking and his superiors at the State Department in Washington. As time went on, the lines of any apprehendable policy became increasingly blurred because of the complex course of events in China; by the end of its deployment in 1938, the 15th had been reduced to an exposed, encircled pawn in a far greater game directed largely by the Japanese.[2]

In the main, the history of the 15th in China corresponded with Chinese history from 1900 on, though with a gap in the first decade. In later years, its presence paralleled the Chinese march through the years of the warlords, the triumph of Chiang Kai-shek and the establishment of a unified nation, though this was never fully attained. There then intruded the vicissitudes culminating in the fateful emergence and dominance of the Japanese in much of East Asia by the early 1930s. This ended with the withdrawal of the 15th in March of 1938 and America's generally leaving China and Japan to fight it out until Pearl Harbor effectively forced American intervention once again.

The regiment's deployment in China, beginning in 1900, was intertwined with important aspects of China's evolvement, especially regarding relations between East and West. The arrival of foreigners in China by the nineteenth century led to major depredations, incursions, and encroachments on Chinese rights and sensibilities. The first significant contacts began with the Opium War, "one of the cruelest chapters in China's degradation at the hands of the West." As one scholar has noted, "although small quantities of opium had been used medicinally in China since ancient times, the first large quantities were brought to China by Portugal at the beginning of the eighteenth century. In later years, opium poppies were grown in India, where, under careful and efficient British management, large quantities of the drug were harvested and shipped under the protection of the British navy to seaports in Southern China." Alarmed by the enormously damaging effects of opium on the minds and bodies of his subjects, the Manchu emperor Tao Kuang "strove to break 'the British Connection' in 1838 by ordering one of his ablest servants, Lin Tse-hsu, to put an end to the import of opium. After arriving in Canton [Guangzhou], Lin confiscated all the opium in the possession of foreign traders and had it publicly burned." But he was unable to extract a pledge that no future shipments of the drug would be made, and angered by the traders' arrogant refusal, he threatened to ban all foreign commercial traffic. Britain had long planned a war against China in order to gain more trade concessions, and Lin's actions gave them a pretext "to fire the first shot." The Opium War was over quickly, "for China had no defense against British guns." It formally ended with the Treaty of Nanking in 1842, which forced China to open five ports to British trade, cede the island of Hong Kong to Great Britain, and pay an indemnity for the opium confiscated. The opium trade also continued, bringing with it the destruction of human life on a huge scale.[3]

Subsequently, further gains were wrung from the Chinese, usually by military force or its threat, by the French, Germans, Russians, Japanese, Italians and even the Belgians and Austro-Hungarians, initiating the "century of unequal treaties." Within the treaty ports, certain areas called concessions were reserved for the use of the foreign residents, though foreigners were also allowed to reside among the Chinese. Within the concessions, the foreigners carried on business and trade, entirely governing themselves while being protected by their own military detachments.

Americans, although arriving later than most other Westerners, were not exempt from Chinese hostility or mere impatient tolerance by those who saw no choice but to accept the "Red Hairs"—foreigners—in their midst. Though the Americans had no formal concessions in China, they did demand certain rights that had been obtained by treaty. Chief among these were those following the Boxer Uprising, mainly the Boxer Protocols of September 7, 1901.[4]

The Chinese had numerous reasons to detest foreigners. Their position has been ably analyzed by a Britisher, Sir Robert Hart, who perhaps understood the Chinese as well as any Westerner ever has. Beginning his career in 1854 in the British Consular Service in China as an interpreter, in 1863 he became the inspector general of Chinese Imperial Customs, serving the Chinese government until 1908. It was no wonder, he wrote, that the Chinese should take a negative attitude: "'We did not invite you foreigners here,' they say; 'you crossed the seas of your own accord and more or less forced yourselves on us.'" Furthermore, "Chinese were accustomed to considering theirs the chief of kingdoms and all others tributaries," and they expected from all who approached them "an acknowledgment of superiority and a submissive tone and attitude." When, on the contrary, "men of the West ... laugh at their pretensions, question their superiority, refuse them obedience, and make them accept dictation," the Chinese are profoundly shocked. This attitude was reinforced by their "innate pride— pride of race, pride of intellect, pride of civilization, [and] pride of supremacy," which had been so hurt "by the manner of foreign impact that the other good points of Chinese character have, as it were, been stunned and cannot respond." Therefore, the Chinese, "an intelligent, cultivated race, sober, industrious, and on its own lines civilized, homogeneous in language, thought, and feeling, ... after thousands of years of haughty seclusion and exclusiveness," had been pushed "by the force of circumstances and by the superior strength of assailants into treaty relations with the rest of the world." While some Western wise men might be tolerated, none were loved, and the Chinese were determined to end the foreign presence, "their minds full of the memories of the good old times when for thousands of years China had lived her own life and been untroubled by the intrusion and restless competition of aliens and barbarians." As Hart concluded, "just as one can paralyse the body or corrupt the soul of a human being, so too it is possible to outrage the spirit and antagonise the nature of a people."[5]

There were specific affronts which were especially detested. Key among these was "the principle which underlies every treaty and runs through every treaty stipulation, and which unhappily is at the bottom of all the mischief," i.e., extraterritoriality—"extrality" for short—which even today deeply rankles the Chinese psyche. This formulation, which placed all foreign residents under the extraterritorial criminal and civil jurisdiction of consular and mixed courts, was formally introduced into China by the Treaty of Nanking between Britain and China in 1842. It was extended to include the United States by the Treaty of Wanghsia of July 3, 1844. In this doctrine what the West was saying and what came across to the Chinese was that "your laws are not our laws—your judges are corrupt—injustice prevails—torture is practised—punishments are barbarous—jails are hells—and we therefore withdraw our people from your jurisdiction." Far outweighing even the aggressive, sharp commercial practices and Christianity, it was the *imperium in imperio* which simply had far too much of that which "humiliates and disintegrates." Hart counseled that "could we but give up this ... relations would at once right themselves, rancour disappear, and friendliness rule instead."⁶

Almost as hated was the presence of Christian missionaries. There was a long tradition of Christian involvement in China, dating perhaps to the early 500s with the coming of the heretical Nestorians. The Catholics were present by the late 1200s, the Jesuits by the mid–1500s. The first Protestant missionary was the Reverend Robert Morrison, who arrived in China in 1807. From their earliest appearance, Christians often enjoyed success, but they were periodically persecuted as waves of antiforeign fervor, often fomented by Chinese intellectuals and Confucianists, gripped China. With the signing of the Treaty of Whampoa on October 24, 1844, between the French and the Chinese, Catholicism was officially tolerated, a provision extended to Protestants the following year. Subsequently, hand in hand with the development of the foreign concessions in the treaty ports, Christianity flourished. But there was always dissent. The devotion, zeal, and good works of the missionaries were widely recognized, and they had "everywhere been teaching good lessons, and benevolently opening hospitals and dispensing medicine for the relief of the sick and the afflicted, but wherever they go trouble goes with them, and instead of the welcome their good intentions merit, localities and officials turn against them." The reasons were many. Most importantly, their presence was considered a standing insult, "for does it not tell the Chinese their conduct is bad and requires change, their cult inadequate and wants addition, their gods despicable and to be cast into the gutter, their forefathers lost and themselves only to be saved by accepting the missionary's teaching?" The Chinese found all of this reprehensible and could not willingly assent to it.

In short, foreigners established effective control over much of China's territory, governmental functions and affairs in general, greatly influencing a checkered history—the long unraveling and reknitting of Chinese life—extending to after World War II.[7] The Chinese at length responded to the oppressive foreign presence in a series of uprisings—often erroneously labeled "rebellions"—such as the extensive, convulsive Taiping Uprising (1850–64) and the Boxer Uprising of 1899–1900. At this time, the Chinese regime, nominally in the hands of the empress dowager, Tz'u-hsi—ruling in the place of the emperor, Kuang-hsu—sought to drive foreigners from her land. To these ends, she found a Chinese patriotic society, the "Righteous and Harmonious Fists," called the Boxers by Westerners, ready at hand. Stridently determined to free China from alien control, by 1899. they openly attacked Westerners and threatened the capital city of Peking. This firestorm led to the death of many foreigners, especially missionaries, as well as their Chinese converts, while others fled to legations in Peking where they were defended by guards of the concessionary powers. Consequently, in early June 1900, a foreign international relief force of about 2,300 troops landed in China, intent upon defending their nationals and protecting their usurped commercial rights and privileges. On June 13, the empress dowager ordered the imperial troops to resist the allied forces advancing on Peking, which, with Boxer support, they did, momentarily forcing them to retreat to Tientsin. By June 20, 1900, the foreigners were besieged in their legations in Peking.

For their rescue, a second international force, this one numbering about 19,000 men, consisting of British, French, German, Russian and Japanese troops, and including American regular army units, was speedily deployed, and succeeded in raising the siege of Peking on August 14, 1900. As part of these endeavors, on July 7, 1900, the War Department ordered the 15th Regiment to prepare for foreign service, and the First Battalion was recruited to full strength from its other two battalions. Sailing for China on July 17, 1900, it arrived on August 16 off the Taku forts in China and by August 19 was in Tientsin. That same day, the Boxers were engaged by other Allied forces nearby, and the battalion was called to arms and held in reserve. The Boxers were repulsed and several hundred were captured and turned over to the battalion as prisoners of war.

Afterwards, in late August, the battalion continually reconnoitered and skirmished, and in September assumed the duty of guarding the supply junks transporting supplies up the Pei Ho River to the United States troops at Peking. From September, battalion troops took up station at Tientsin and Tangku, a supply depot on the coast.[8]

Meanwhile, following the capture of Peking, the empress dowager and her court, conceding defeat, fled to Sian (now Xi'an) while foreign troops looted the capital. A peace protocol was signed on September 7, 1901, which, among other things, allowed foreigners to establish a large permanent military force in Peking and elsewhere, and forced payment of a huge indemnity. The Legation Quarter was put into a state of permanent defense, the Taku forts on the coast were razed and Chinese troops were forbidden to be stationed anywhere near Tientsin. Shortly thereafter, the nations involved decided that to implement the Protocol, an international force consisting of American, British, French, German, Russian and Japanese troops would be permanently stationed in China to guard their vital lifeline, the Peking-Mukden railway, and to protect the lives and commercial enterprises of foreigners.[9]

There were other noteworthy results of the Boxer Uprising. Though the Chinese were not successful against the foreign powers—even failing to capture the legations in Peking—"still they [had] shown the world that they appreciate and are acquiring the best weapons; they are evidently learning the use of both rifle and gun; they are improving their military method, and the idea of strategy, though still in embryo, is taking shape and hardening; and they are henceforth more likely to go on developing might ... [rather] than return to their old and time-honoured belief in reasonable action and right." While many Chinese excoriated Boxer excesses, "the Chinese world may possibly have only one fault to find with them— that they did not succeed." Therefore, dead Boxers might well be considered as martyrs, and the question was "is there not a Phoenix-like power in the blood of martyrdom?" To many Chinese not part of the Boxer crowd, the foreigners were simply a large band of brigands who killed, burned, ravished, and looted and who would one day disappear, as brigands had disappeared before, leaving the Chinese once more to themselves. Certainly, the legacy of the Boxers would be a major factor in later Chinese development, especially as advanced by the Communists.[10]

As to the consequences of the encroachments of the Westerners and their prevailing attitudes, one Chinese official prophetically observed, "You are all too anxious to awake us and start us on a new road, and you will do it; but you will all regret it, for, once awaking and started, we shall go fast and far—farther than you think—much farther than you want!" Indeed, as one often heard among the citizenry, "Really you [Westerners] are too short-sighted, and you are forcing us to arm in self-defence, and giving us grudges to pay off instead of benefits to requite!"[11]

Many in the West failed to draw some of these obvious conclusions from the Boxer Uprising, principally regarding the appearance on the battlefield of modern weapons employed by soldiers becoming increasingly professional. The Chinese did not press the foreigners as they could have done. They were to learn that they could do this with success.

Clearly, the Boxer Uprising initiated a pivotal phase in the history of Chinese-Western relations. It also marked the beginning of the end of the Chinese Empire, which hung on until 1911 when new unrest unseated the boy emperor, P'u-i, paving the way for the proclamation of the Chinese Republic by Dr. Sun Yat-sen in January 1912. (P'u-i formally abdicated on February 12, 1912.) These events impelled the international community to reinforce their armed contingents, raising their numbers to over 10,000 troops.

These decisions once more involved the 15th Regiment, then stationed at Fort Douglas, Utah; they were ordered to the Philippines, arriving in Manila on December 3, 1911. There, the First Battalion was equipped and brought up to war strength and prepared to sail for China. Designated the China Expedition and led by the First Battalion's commander, Major James M. Arrasmith, the contingent departed Fort McKinley on January 11, 1912, and arrived at Chinwangtao, the major port city of the region, on January 18, 1912. According to the Boxer Protocol of September 7, 1901, which permitted the international powers to maintain forces in China, the regiment's aims were the protection of American citizens, business interests and missionaries and more specifically "to keep open railway communication between Peking and the sea." There were also political aims: to maintain American prestige and uphold "the commitment of the United States government to share with other powers the burden of stabilizing China."[12]

In Chinwangtao, the American China Expedition received more specific instructions from the American minister in Peking, W.A. Calhoun. He informed the troops that they were under his orders, thereby placing them under the control of the State Department, though they remained operationally under the War Department and the Philippines Division — later called the Philippine Department.[13]

From the outset, therefore, tensions existed between the Department of State and the War Department as well as the Philippines Division as to how best to accomplish the 15th's mission. While acknowledging the primacy of the diplomats, the technical and military considerations of the American deployment placed much discretion in the hands of the commanding officer of the 15th, and the possibility of conflicting interpretations of policy was always present. Given the perpetually uncertain conditions prevailing in China, the situation was ever fraught with difficulties for all concerned.[14]

A few days later, at 7:30 A.M. on January 22, the China Expedition departed the port and made its way inland, dropping off detachments to guard the railway along the way at Leichuang, Tangshan, Wali, Linsi and Kaiping. The main body of the unit arrived in Tientsin at 5:30 P.M. on the same day. They were met by a detachment and band of the Royal Tunskilling Fusiliers, British troops then stationed at Tientsin, and escorted to a barracks on Rue Dillon in the city's French concession.[15]

Soon the men saw some limited action. Following instructions from Calhoun in Peking, who feared a developing situation reminiscent of the Boxer Uprising days, a detachment of six officers and 221 enlisted men left Tientsin on March 3, 1912, for the purpose of reinforcing the Legation Guard in the capital. But the Chinese government soon had the situation in hand and the 15th's detachment returned to Tientsin on March 11. Simultaneously, the turmoil of the Chinese Revolution engulfed Tientsin, and the entire native Chinese city was burned and looted by revolutionists, though the foreign concessions were spared, no doubt because of the presence of foreign troops.

Shortly after the men returned from Peking, the China Expedition was joined by the regiment's Third Battalion. Under the command of Lieutenant Colonel Edwin A. Root, the regiment's executive officer, this contingent departed Fort McKinley on March 9, 1912, arriving in Tientsin on the seventeenth, when Root relieved Major Arrasmith as the expedition's commander. In this fashion, as one analyst has noted, "with a political purpose and little military value, the 15th Infantry settled into its barracks at Tientsin for a tour that lasted more than a quarter of a century."[16]

For many years following, China strove in vain to stabilize itself in vastly changed circumstances, seeking to modernize and unify the nation and simultaneously to end the hated foreign presence. But numerous shocks ensued. In particular, political chaos reigned in China from 1911 on. As one American observer noted, "The Republic was a joke. Warlords, by courtesy called 'Military Governors,' controlled every province, each with his own army of conscripts, or brigands, and civil war went blithely on. When a warlord began to feel his oats he attacked his next door neighbor if he thought he could get away with it. No one suffered much except the peasants.... Usually such inter-provincial affairs were settled by double-crossing or buying off the other fellow." In these circumstances, "armies were bought and sold like merchandise [and] the central government in Peking was a farce yet it continued to function in a way which only an Oriental could understand."[17]

In September of 1914, immediately after the outbreak of the Great War, the regiment, then commanded by Colonel J.C.F. Tillson, expanded its role. It was feared that the possible withdrawal of British, French and Japanese troops would leave the foreign settlements unprotected except by the American forces. The American vice consul general in Tientsin, G.C. Hanson, addressed notes to the Austrian, Belgian, German, British, French, Italian, Japanese and Russian consulates in Tientsin, requesting concurrence in the idea that American forces, in cases of emergency, might take such steps in their respective concessions "as were necessary adequately to suppress any uprising or riot." The Austrians, Germans and Belgians agreed; the others demurred pending further instructions from their governments. In any event, subsequently the American presence loomed larger in Tientsin.[18]

One immediate effect of the Great War on China was the ending of the involvement of two foreign nations, Germany and Austria-Hungary, whose nationals were temporarily interned in a hotel outside Peking not far from the Summer Palace and prudently surrounded by a wire enclosure. One observer of the Chinese scene asserted that this action was a milestone in modern Chinese history in that "it marked the beginning of the end of the foreigner's domination in the Far East." Gaped at by the Chinese, "for the first time in a generation, white men were completely at the mercy of the Chinese. Their superiority gained by guns, not culture, was gone."[19]

Other shocks of the Great War to the Chinese were more debilitating, one being the "Twenty-One Demands" made by Japan on China. One of these granted to the Japanese the former German rights in Shantung (Shandong) while another extended the Japanese leases in southern Manchuria to 99 years. At the Versailles Conference, which brought a formal end to the Great War, the Chinese failed to secure their goals of negating Japan's claims made in the Twenty-One Demands; obtaining an amelioration of the Chinese situation vis-à-vis foreign nations; and formally liquidating the interests that Austria, Hungary and Germany had held in China. When the Versailles Conference awarded the former German holdings in Shantung to Japan, large student-led uprisings, especially intense in Shanghai and Peking (in the latter location resulting in the turmoil occurring on May 4, 1919, subsequently referred to as the May Fourth Movement) revealed a sensitized and mobilized Chinese public opinion demanding the ouster of foreigners and a return of full sovereignty to their nation. The matter of the former holdings of the Central European nations ended more favorably by the signing of the Treaties of Versailles, St. Germaine and Trianon; all formally recognized the end of their concessions in China. In addition, the Russians independently agreed in July 1919, in return for the recognition of the Soviet government, to abandon all concessions and treaty rights in China including those of extraterritoriality.[20]

At the Washington Conference of 1920–21, convened to consider naval armaments and Far Eastern questions, the Chinese again sought to advance their case requesting that Articles VII and IX of the 1901 Protocol be cancelled. In addition, Chinese delegates asked for the restoring to China of full control over its own internal affairs. In response, the Conference, partly because of the uncertain political situation then existing in China, agreed only in principal to "respect the sovereignty, the independence, and the territorial and administrative integrity of China." A commission was set up to survey the existing situation and recommend measures of reform that, if undertaken by the Chinese government, would "warrant the several Powers in relinquishing, either progressively or otherwise, their respective rights of extraterritoriality."

At the Conference, the Chinese government additionally contended that the presence of Allied troops in China was no longer necessary, and that they should be recalled. The foreign governments had long maintained, as *The Sentinel* rather pointedly reported it, that their troops did not pose any threat to China, serving merely to remind the Chinese that "there are limits to the affronts that foreigners will tolerate at their hands." Also, the Legation Quarter at Peking, the foreign concessions at Tientsin, and the Peking-Mukden railway owed their comparative security to the presence of foreign garrisons "capable of dealing very effectively with five to ten times their own number of ill-disciplined armed coolies." In response to the Chinese request, the Conference asserted that the troops would be withdrawn when China "possesse[d] a Government wielding sufficient authority, through properly disciplined military forces, to assume the responsibilities now shouldered by the foreign garrisons in North China." Since that prospect seemed unlikely in the near future, the international troops, including the 15th, together with soldiers of Britain, France, Italy and Japan, would remain in situ.[21]

The 15th's sojourn in China also corresponds with the evolving warlordism in China, which dominated Chinese affairs from 1916 to 1928, when a national force under Chiang Kai-shek emerged and succeeded — to a degree — in unifying China. The period was characterized by regional armies forged by strong military commanders challenging the Chinese government at Peking and each other. These clashes were especially numerous in northern China.[22]

In those unsettled times in China, the 15th found itself closely enmeshed in turmoil as in 1920, for example. One *Sentinel* account noted that "our way was very rudely interrupted last summer [1920] right in the

II. The 15th Marches onto the Chinese Stage

middle of the hottest weather we experienced by one of the perennial Chinese 'wars.' Of course it appeared to us to be only a poor imitation for imposing an extravagant Broadway production of 'opera' bouffe, but as all foreigners long resident in the land know, one never can tell just what the Celestials will do, especially when almost driven mad by the extreme heat." The opposing generals issued manifestos, edicts, threats, and counterthreats, ignoring completely the central government at Peking. Soldiers were mobilized, recruits were rapidly inducted into service, and rolling stock of the government railways was commandeered, bringing transportation to an almost complete standstill. Overnight, "the peaceful and socially concerned duties of the Adjutant were ... whisked into the warlike activities of an Operations section, the wires and wireless were heated up, our camp at Chinwangtao-by-the-Sea, was broken into under cover of darkness, the troops in training in musketry at Leichuang were ordered held in readiness to move anywhere, everything and everybody buzzed with excitement." The end was an anticlimax, sputtering out as seemed often to be the case, but "even now the skies darken and we feel that back of the scenes the same old forces of Graft, Threat and Bluff are setting the stage and await only the warm sun rays of the summer to pull back the curtains." 1921 would once more see turmoil in China.[23]

These events resulted in a flurry of demands, which periodically surfaced in certain quarters in the United States, that American troops be withdrawn from China. Someone signing himself "A.C.S.," in an article in *The Sentinel*, argued that the American presence in China was too slight to prevent war or a new Boxer Rebellion, and indeed might incite these eventualities. The few hundred troops available in Tientsin were insufficient to make any difference, as hundreds of thousands would be required. In fact, China, "we are safe in saying, is no worse off in respect of internal chaos, than is Mexico, and Americans live there quite well." Besides, turmoil there was no new thing: "China ... has always been chaotic, at least ever since the advent of Europeans." Perhaps even more reprehensible, in his view, was that American soldiers were exposed to a "very evil invironment [*sic*]." If American mothers were fully informed as to the present state of the Chinese Republic, and the plight "into which their sons have fallen," he declared, they would put forth every effort to save them.[24]

The immediate reaction in the Army regarding the Chinese situation was to decide that the 31st and 15th infantries would remain in the Philippines and China but would be combined to form the 24th Infantry Brigade, headquartered in Manila. Talk of withdrawal of troops from China was not seriously entertained because the secretary of state "has been quite insistent that this force will remain in that country to discharge treaty obligations imposed on the United States."[25]

Almost on schedule, therefore, in late spring and on into the summer of 1922, a major contretemps known as the First Chihli-Fengtien War (Chih-Feng War for short; in Pinyin: Zhili-Fengtian War) broke out. Two dominant warlords, Chang Tso-lin (Zhang Zuolin), the main leader of a Manchurian army — known as the Fengtien Army — and the leader of the Chihli armies under Marshal Wu Pei-fu (Wu Peifu) clashed, with Wu winning. Though Wu had prevailed, Chang was able to retreat to his Manchurian stronghold and prepare for another attempt. The next round, called the Second Chihli-Fengtien War, would come two years later in the autumn of 1924; in this the 15th was to be more actively engaged.[26]

Meanwhile, because of the continuing Chinese civil wars, the War Department decided to detach the 15th from the Philippines Department and establish a separate force directly under the War Department. Brigadier General William Durward Connor was appointed to command the new entity, which was designated the "American Forces in China" (AFC). This reorganization better positioned the forces in China. An editorial in the *North China Star* explained Connor's importance, noting that the many problems faced by American soldiers stationed so far from home in a foreign country would be better served "by a general officer who has that freedom of action which belongs to his higher rank." Thus Connor had to be "a soldier in the true sense of the word and a diplomatic politician in the better sense of the term." On both counts, Connor measured up, bringing a broader vision into Chinese affairs than theretofore had been the case among American commanders in China.[27]

The State Department, however, had some apprehensions that with Connor's appointment, the War Department was contemplating a more independent stance in China. These concerns prompted Secretary of State Charles Evans Hughes to send a confidential note to the secretary of war, John W. Weeks, on November 8, 1922. Therein, Hughes made it plain that he recognized the "anomalous situation" of the AFC, noting that there might well be difficulties in determining their "freedom of military action" as well as in external relations with the Chinese and with the military authorities of other countries cooperating "in the safeguarding of the foreign Legations." But he hoped that Connor's instructions from the War Department would "assure a more effective cooperation with the aims of the Department of State and of its representative in China than has existed in the past." While not "assuming for the diplomatic representative any measure of authority in purely military matters," he insisted that Connor acknowledge that his forces were "ancillary to the Legation," and "maintained in China solely for the purpose of assuring the safety of the diplomatic mission at Peking." Hughes also wanted Connor to recognize that it was "no part of this Government's purpose to impress upon the Chinese government or people the military power or prestige of this country," and America had no intention of entering "into rivalry with such other countries as may deem it to their interest to make such a display of military power." This must have seemed to Connor to be a far too limited construing of the Regiment's mission, ignoring some of its goals.[28]

Connor, in his first annual report, duly noted that after his arrival in China on April 12, 1923, he took early opportunity "to visit the American Minister in Peking and to ascertain the aims and policies of the Legation, in order to insure thorough co-operation therewith." Nonetheless, the relations between the soldiers and the diplomats were never altogether smooth.

By early 1924, the threats posed by warring Chinese factions in 1922 having been safely passed through, the commandants of the foreign contingents in Tientsin — the French, British, Italian, Americans and Japanese — concluded that they could perhaps manage their stated missions reasonably well. Elaborate contingency plans were drafted and frequently revised by conferences of the foreign commandants, which seemed to make it possible for the time being, at least, to contend with China's continuing chaotic state. The plans were still based on Article IX of the Protocol of September 7, 1901, together with additional agreements of the Allied Diplomatic Body with the Chinese Government of 1912, which gave the right to signatory powers to occupy certain designated points between Peking and the sea. Also, according to the these, the focus was to avoid a siege of the legations similar to that of 1900 and to this end early evacuation plans were approved. It was recognized that the existing forces might not be adequate to implement the plans, and accordingly, provisions were drawn up for a rapid reinforcement if needed. In this regard, the security of Tientsin was vital because it was the most important strategic point of support for any reinforcements that might eventually arrive, and its defense could not be endangered by "unnecessary dispersion of forces."[29]

Much more astute and prescient were the views Connor had, in the meantime, matured. In a confidential communication transmitted in August of 1924 to the American minister to China, Dr. Jacob Gould Schurman, he indicated that any probability of China's establishing a firm footing, as the Washington Treaty specified, was remote. It had been in such a state of chaos since the overthrow of the monarchy that there was no opportunity for any leader to form anything like a stable foreign policy, and therefore Chinese leaders were driven mainly by expediency and opportunism.

Connor also emphasized that during the past decade, a persistent national consciousness had emerged. Though some analysts were certain that this was the same spirit that had brought about the Boxer troubles, Connor insisted that the new attitude was fundamentally "not anti-foreign but rather pro–Chinese." Extreme nationalistic views aimed at driving foreigners out by force or exterminating them, but the more moderate stance then prevailing was to "squeeze them out economically and politically." In any case, all Chinese nationalists of whatever hue particularly resented extraterritoriality rights, a feeling that was growing stronger, especially among returned students, many of whom — educated in Western countries including the United States — were "certainly the most intelligent among the younger element." Indeed, it was obvious to Connor that "there [was now] none of the quietism of old China, but something that might be taken for the alertness of Young China," as *The China Review*, published in New York, asserted in a perceptive article. Thomas Grant Springer, an American poet, playwright and novelist, similarly warned in his poem "Cathay Today" that there was truly new life then stirring in the East that was as formidable as any flood of the Yellow River — "China's Sorrow" — "a fierce torrent naught can dam or stay."[30]

As to Chinese tactics, Connor was of the opinion that the more conservative, far-seeing Chinese had embarked upon a policy of "nibbling away at foreigners' treaty rights" that encroached upon their sovereignty. They "seem to be feeling their way softly to see how far they can go without serious trouble," which they did not want because a more radical policy might invite foreign intervention. This was "the nearest approach to a national policy that the Chinese have evolved since the revolution," summarized as a "China for the Chinese" policy. On the whole, it was popular and warmly embraced by many Chinese of varying political leanings. A similar and related view, "Asia for the Asiatics," which the Japanese would later advance with a vengeance, was also in vogue.

Surveying the whole panoply of their nation's enemies, many Chinese recognized that they stood fundamentally alone but put their faith in China's "enormous territory and dense population, whose characteristics of industry and inertia are traditional." They were convinced that no nation "could seriously attack and physically occupy China." Even Japan, "favorably located as she is, cannot successfully subdue them either from a military or an economic point of view." Even if Japan inflicted severe military defeats on China, without a successful occupation which would be almost impossible to attain, it could only gain a momentary advantage. The Chinese therefore believed, characteristically taking the long view, that "in a century they will dominate this part of the world," a view with which Connor concurred.[31]

II. The 15th Marches onto the Chinese Stage

Though unable to convince the other allied commandants that their contingency plans were based on outmoded assumptions, Connor had a breathing space in which to orient himself before the Chinese campaigning season of 1924 began. The resulting struggle, the Second Chihli-Fengtien War, began on September 8 and continued to November 20, 1924. Despite the complexity of the Chinese tableau, the main lines were clear. There was the anomaly in China of a central government at Peking — ostensibly headed by the president of the Chinese Republic, Tso Kuhn (Cao Kun) — which supposedly controlled all of China. The government's control was, however, by no means a lasting nor a far-reaching one. The most important supporter of Kuhn was Marshal Wu Pei-fu, the inspector general of Shantung, Chihli and Hunan provinces, who also commanded the combined military and naval forces of the Republic of China. He was opposed by various powerful warlords, the most important of whom was Chang Tso-lin, who controlled most of Manchuria, i.e., the Fengtien forces from his headquarters in Mukden. An unknown quantity was the powerful figure of Feng Yu-shiang (Feng Yuxiang) — another colorful character as many of the warlords seemed to be — whose troops controlled Peking though he was ostensibly a supporter of Wu.[32]

But as always in this game of "3 Card Monte of the East," "Mr. Coolie Pays" while seeking to profit, *The Sentinel* explained, noting that the rank and file, if not gaining a fortune, certainly was attracted to the war for financial reasons. "There is no such thing in China as National Unity," the paper went on. "The average Chinaman does very little thinking and if he thinks at all he is concerned only with three meals a day and a few coppers. The army therefore is a popular occupation as it provides a means of getting something to eat and even if pay is seldom forthcoming there is always the chance of a victory and the subsequent looting." Accordingly, "to the average soldier, the General is everything, the Government nothing," and changes of sides were frequent as all involved continually assessed the probability of success of any force at any given time. Therefore, "the soldier as well as the General is on the side where the coppers are the most plentiful." While the article correctly identified some aspects of China's struggle, it was titled "Batteries for Today's Game," revealing the paper's persistence in seeing the Chinese civil war as essentially a sporting event or, in other presentations, as a mere card game. Such observations bear out the serious limitations of men of the 15th Regiment — and Westerners in general — as observers of the Chinese scene, which was far more complex than their insubstantial discussions reveal.[33]

Initially, the 1924 war focused on Peking, and in October, Marshal Feng Yu-shiang, the famous so-called Christian General, of much interest to the Americans in China, made an unexpected thrust, taking possession of the capital. Feng's forces, so Marshal Wu had thought, were to have formed the western reach of his line arrayed against Chang. In Peking, Feng dictated terms to President Tso Kuhn and called for the resignation of Marshal Wu, his ostensible ally.[34]

Meanwhile, Marshal Chang Tso-lin's forces, streaming down from Manchuria, moved swiftly against Wu's troops. Originally planning to invade Manchuria, Wu's men were concentrated along the Peking-Mukden railway at Shankaikwan, with reserve forces in and around Tientsin. Chang was successful in breaking the Great Wall line, using combined arms, including shock troops, aviation and artillery often manned by former Russian White Army soldiers. After a few engagements with Feng's troops near Tientsin and elsewhere, Wu fled to the Yangtze.[35]

In the meantime, on November 2, 1924, Tso Kuhn quit the presidency, being replaced by Tuan Chi-jui (Duan Qirui), who was named the new head of the Chinese Republic on November 24. At the same time, the disarmament of all of Wu's Chihli troops ensued. The 15th played a role in this operation, cooperating with others in persuading the defeated forces at Tientsin to surrender their arms in exchange for food, a ticklish situation which could have plunged the Americans into armed conflict.[36]

Shortly thereafter, on November 25, Marshal Feng bid farewell to his victorious army, urging them to be loyal to the new government, stating facetiously that "he would rather resign than incur jealousy of other militarists." Momentarily stepping off of the political stage, Feng turned his attention to strengthening his forces for the next round in China's recurring civil wars. It was surmised that in any future encounter, the main antagonists would surely be Feng and Chang.[37]

The 1924 conflict had closely involved the men of the 15th Regiment, which during this time was temporarily under the command of Lieutenant Colonel George Marshall. Their role in the disarmament of Wu's forces has been noted, but there were other important operations. The struggle threatened the Peking-Mukden railway, thereby bringing the Allied military forces at Tientsin into action. On the twelfth of September, 1924, the first of Wu Pei-fu's troops were moved toward Shankaikwan, and the foreign armies would soon be called upon to carry out their primary mission of maintaining open communication between Peking and the sea. On October 14, when civil passenger rail traffic ceased and the sector of the line between Tientsin and Peking became congested by the warring Chinese, the foreign commandants began operating regularly-scheduled international trains between Tientsin and Shankaikwan. These were maintained with only a few short interruptions until the end of the war. The trains

II. The 15th Marches onto the Chinese Stage

included separate cars for each armed train guard of the specific international garrisons assigned to that particular train and were commanded by an officer of one or another of the international garrisons.

In addition, the defense plan for Tientsin worked out by the foreign garrisons was successfully put into operation together with the stationing of detachments at strategic points along the railway. As a matter of course, the 15th Regiment's permanent detachment at Tangshan was involved. (It was during the struggle in and around Tientsin that the 15th earned the thanks of Chinese villagers, leading to the presentation of the marble gateway now adorning Fort Benning. This will be discussed later.)[38]

The AFC's high command also cannily used the situation to help attain the year's training goals. As General Connor noted, "the regiment received actual field training during this period." Specifically, "all organizations were placed on outpost duty and were given a thorough course ... in scouting and patrolling, establishment and operation of outposts, position in readiness, supply of troops on outposts and reliefs." Throughout, he went on, "the manner in which the troops functioned on the outguards in directing the Chinese around our sector of the foreign concessions was considered most satisfactory."[39]

On the diplomatic front, Connor perceived that a sound spirit of cooperation existed among the Allied forces and in addition the American Forces in China enjoyed close ties with the American diplomats in Peking. Similarly, close cooperation existed between the American Forces in China and the competent, knowledgeable American consul-general in Tientsin, Clarence E. Gauss. Because the Americans had practiced a strict neutrality during the civil war, cordial relations were maintained with those Chinese who had gained power no matter what their political orientation might be.[40]

By the end of 1924, the 15th had demonstrated its ability still to justify the avowed official reasons for its being initially stationed in China, i.e., to support the provisions of the Protocol of 1901. By December, *The Sentinel*'s editor guardedly hoped that China was perhaps at last on the verge of creating an effective government. But 1925 was to be another phase in China's continuing chaotic state with a considerably different outcome for the Americans. In fact, it was to be a turning point in the 15th's employment in China and in Chinese history as well.

Meanwhile, the end of the Chinese campaigning in 1924 resulting in Wu's defeat led to an uneasy truce, though turmoil continued in many parts of China as various leaders and factions strove to establish a new modus vivendi. Marshal Feng Yu-shiang had left the victorious Marshal Chang Tso-lin to his knitting while he took up his position as *Tupan* (military governor) of Northwestern Defense, a large territory of which he assumed control. There, he took advantage of the proximity to the Soviet Union to establish contact with Moscow, obtaining considerable support and military aid in exchange for moving closer to the Soviet orbit. This enabled him to resist the Japanese influence increasingly apparent in east and northeast China. He also adopted a stance that was much more nationalistic and anti-foreigner. This reflected his closer contact with the Russians and also with the Kuomintang Party, the burgeoning center of power in south China centered in Canton. His anti-foreigner bias was fueled by the events of May 30, 1925, when Shanghai police under an English officer fired on a crowd of demonstrators, resulting in a massive resurgence of anti-imperialism and xenophobia, especially among China's student population; this would thenceforth be known as the May Thirtieth Movement.

Soon, Feng's attention was drawn to developments involving Chang Tso-lin's Fengtien forces. These had been consolidated in northeast China, creating a loyal bloc of provinces as well as drawing upon support from the Japanese. These events triggered the renewed struggle which began in the autumn of 1925 and which once again closely involved the 15th Infantry. When Li Ching-lin (Lin Jinglin), one of Chang's supporters, entered Tientsin, Feng began massing substantial forces to drive him out. These impending actions threatened the 15th and the other international garrisons based there.[41]

In response to these moves, the 15th took steps to carry out its mission as in 1924: that of keeping the Peking-Mukden railway open. In October 1925, as a precaution in light of the increasingly tense situation, troops were kept constantly on duty at each railway station in Tientsin to obtain whatever information they could. By the end of November the struggles were growing more intense in Chihli and international trains were set in motion to ensure the continuance of rail traffic.

In early December, the conflict was centered around Tientsin. As the action began to swirl around them, the Allied garrisons on the one hand sought to contain the troops of Li Ching-lin while on the other planned how to deal with the advancing troops of Feng Yu-shiang. Feng's troops were rumored to entertain strong antiforeign tendencies and were expected to be difficult to handle.

At the same time, several successful international train runs were made. But momentous events surrounded the trip of one on December 9, 1925, when Captain Jesse D. Cope ran a train up to Peking. Attempting to return to Tientsin the following day, it reached Yangtsun where, because of fighting between armored trains of Feng and troops of Li Ching-lin, the train was held up until December 11. The train then departed for Tientsin, but shortly after leaving Yangtsun, it was fired upon by Li's artillery. There were no casualties, but windows were shattered and other damage was done to the train, which steamed back to Peking. A relief train commanded by Italians, which included a detachment of men from the 15th, attempted to rescue Cope but was forced back to Tientsin. This venture was the first instance of an international train's failing to accomplish its mission because of hostile fire.[42]

Another soon followed. On December 22, a train from Tientsin commanded by the Japanese, with First Lieutenant Philip E. Gallagher in charge of the 15th's 12-man train guard, failed to arrive at Shankaikwan, its destination. The train was stopped by rifle and machine gun fire. After repeated attempts, contact was made with Feng's commander but he refused passage for the train, forcing it to return to Tientsin. The allied forces suffered no casualties, though many windows on the train were broken and many of the coaches were struck by bullets.

In the meantime, on December 5, the 15th established a system of mounted patrols which continued until December 31. These covered the general area to the south and southwest of Tientsin within a six-mile radius. All Chinese troop movements were observed and wherever possible, personal contact with the commanders of these troops was established. The value of a working knowledge of the Chinese language by officers of the regiment "was proved beyond doubt and in more than one instance situations that might have resulted in a serious issue were handled successfully due largely to the ability of the officer concerned to explain the reasons for his actions."[43]

With the intensification of the Chinese struggle in and around Tientsin, commencing on December 13 the number of mounted patrols, supplemented by dismounted patrols, increased, and the troops in the compound were placed on alert, ready to "start a little fun." An outpost was established at Tu-Cheng covering the main avenue of approach into the American sector. The post was to prevent armed Chinese troops from advancing north and it was also to give timely warning in case of trouble. Commanded by noncommissioned officers, it daily came into contact with many bodies of Chinese troops, and "without exception the man in charge handled all situations in a highly satisfactory manner."[44]

At the most critical period of these events, from December 23 to 31, the regiment was once again temporarily commanded by Lieutenant Colonel George C. Marshall. During the period of December 24–26, when Tientsin was being evacuated by Li Ching-lin's troops which Feng had defeated, Feng's troops moved into the American sector, occupying the police barracks and municipal headquarters. General Connor ordered

Marshall, heading up a platoon, to demand that the Chinese troops evacuate the American area. In a confrontation in the police headquarters, the Chinese were informed that they must leave or turn over their arms. They elected to leave, and another possible armed clash was avoided.

In another instance, a body of about 5,000 men of Feng's Fifth Division entered the American sector on the road on the north side of the dike that marked the south boundary of the sector. Under the command of Captain William B. Tuttle, then the regimental adjutant, a detachment of nine enlisted men in a truck met the point guard of this column. The Chinese positioned themselves across the road and continued to advance with fixed bayonets. The American detachment also fixed bayonets and deployed. Tuttle advanced and ordered the Chinese to halt. After considerable argument, a Chinese officer agreed to withdraw his men from the American sector. "This situation was pregnant with grave possibilities, but was ably handled and Captain Tuttle received commendation from the Regimental Commander for his own conduct and that of his men."[45]

Subsequently, Feng was almost immediately defeated in Tientsin, mainly by troops raised by Marshal Wu Pei-fu — who had arrived once more front and center on the Chinese stage — and forced to depart the city. In the course of 1926, Feng's troops were forced back into western and northwestern China. Resigning as *Tupan* on January 1, 1926, he subsequently decamped for the Soviet Union, where he lived for many months. Feng also embarked upon another course, having at last been persuaded by his Soviet friends to join the Kuomintang a, fateful development for Feng and his nation in the months to come.

By the last day of December 1925, conditions around Tientsin were stabilized and the 15th discontinued its patrols and withdrew its outpost. While the international garrisons had escaped without injury or serious damage, there were major casualties of another kind: the legal, diplomatic and moral foundations upon which their presence in China rested.[46]

In fact, the event that Harding had commemorated in his poem "Casey Cope" (see note 42), though he was no doubt unaware of it, was a watershed of considerable importance in the history of the 15th Regiment. General Connor, however, well understood the gravity of the situation that had dawned with the new year of 1926. This he explained in a secret *tour d'horizon de la situation* to the American minister to China, John Van Antwerp MacMurray.[47]

The basic reason for the 15th's involvement in China in the first place had been to prevent a repetition of the Boxer Uprising. Things had fundamentally changed, however. Indeed, Chinese armed conflicts had gone well beyond mere set pieces of opéra bouffe, as *The Sentinel* had contemptuously labeled them as recently as 1921. The far-ranging, modern, well-armed and increasingly efficiently led Chinese armies of the warlords were unlike the antiforeign rabble contemplated in the Protocol of 1901. Furthermore, the Chinese had now turned their characteristics "of industry, patience, ingenuity, physical endurance, lack of nerves and materialism" toward military endeavors. Fifteen years earlier, Connor noted, "the military man and the profession of arms were despicable in Chinese eyes. A knowledge of the Classics was the highest attainment and was the key that opened the door to success." Entire families "would starve and freeze themselves so that one of their number might study ... and get his start on the ladder to official position." But classical studies were "as dead as the Dodo. Almost overnight the Chinese decided that they did not pay, and, with the materialism that marks the nation, they consigned the Classics to the scrap heap without hesitation." Militarism was the profession that now paid, and because "the genius of the Chinese people is materialism," they had adapted their "most ancient and sacred customs to the ways and means that pay them best."

In addition, the new armies were undergirded by a growing spirit of national consciousness which was the heart of any army anywhere, and if it continued to develop as it apparently would, "one of the greatest military deficiencies of the Chinese people will have been made up."

Consequently, while the international forces were still charged with the same mission, the conditions had entirely altered. "Heretofore," Connor went on, "we have been able to keep up communications, even against armed forces, by our moral ascendancy or by bluff, but this year our bluff was called and to avoid bloodshed we had to back down." What had just occurred was the "total failure of the last two or three international trains that we tried to run." Therefore, the last vestige "of our pretense to 'maintain open communications' disappeared during this last war when both combatants flatly refused to allow our International trains to pass and even fired upon them when they tried to [do so], and cooly [*sic*] marched thousands of troops through parts of our Defense Area without opposition." In short, the Protocol of 1901 and its related documents now had "very little if any binding force." Nor could the former conditions be restored short of a major war. This being the case, Connor believed that the foreign garrisons were a handicap rather than a help to the diplomatic representatives of their countries in Peking.

Regarding the Americans, Connor went on, there was a further serious consideration. All of the other international forces had concessions, which according to the Note of July 15, 1902, gave them the right to defend them and to exclude Chinese troops from their defense lines. Americans had none and used only land leased from the Chinese including the American compound; further, they could claim only certain rights essential to defending their status in Tientsin, which had no legal basis. If worse came to worse, the American garrison could only retire to the United States. In the circumstances, Washington had but three viable options: it could withdraw the garrison on the "grounds that no repetition of the Boxer Incident is probable." Or, the Chinese could be served notice that "hereafter we intend to enforce the provisions of the Protocol regardless of consequences." Finally, America could give up all the rights under the Protocol and keep the garrisons in Tientsin for the sole purpose of forestalling the effects of another Boxer Rebellion, paying no attention to violations occurring during the recent civil wars. The latter solution appeared to be the one that the other Allied governments were intent upon. Connor argued for withdrawal, the only prudent course, he maintained, because, barring the regularizing of the American position by diplomacy, "we cannot possibly remain in China under existing conditions." Indeed, "during the recent war we escaped conflict by as narrow a margin as I consider possible, and by one far too narrow for comfort."

If no decision were made to withdraw, Connor favored another alternative. The Americans could seek friendship with the Chinese, hoping to maintain good relations with the leaders who emerged from time to time in the perpetual conflicts and maneuverings that continued even when warfare was in abeyance. While the Chinese language, dress and customs were very different from those of the Occident, Connor recognized that "all human beings are very much alike in many traits," and Westerners who "go their way in China with an air of superior detachment," greatly affronted Chinese pride. Given the precarious position of the regiment, Connor recognized that "friendship with the Chinese is even a greater asset than [it] ordinarily is in a foreign land." The greatest bar to friendly relations was the difference in language, Connor observed, and even months before he reached China he began to study Chinese "so that to the surprise of the Chinese officials, I had a few simple phrases at my command when I first met them." These successes led Connor to make the study of colloquial Chinese compulsory for all officers of the American garrison. "This was a departure from any previous custom either in our own or any other garrison, and the reaction amongst the Chinese was instant and favorable."[48]

The response in Washington to the new conditions analyzed by Connor, far from contemplating a U.S. withdrawal, simply reiterated the position established from the outset of the regiment's deployment to China.[49]

II. The 15th Marches onto the Chinese Stage   43

Accordingly, the War Department continued, however reluctantly, to fall in line with the views of the State Department that "the activities of the U.S. Army Forces in China in all matters external to their administration, should be that determined by the State Department and expressed to the commanding general of those forces by the American Minister at Peking." Nonetheless, had the decision been up to the War Department, the 15th would have been withdrawn from China at this time. But American policy continued as before partially in response to the demands of spokesmen in Washington representing American business interests in Asia, such as the Standard Oil Company, as well as missionary organizations and relief agencies including the YMCA and the Red Cross. Aware of the importance of "face" in the East, its strictures seemed also apropos for Americans. At this juncture, to many it did not seem expedient to "cut and run." Only when there was agreement between the State Department and the War Department a decade later in far more threatening conditions would the withdrawal of the 15th be effected.

In the meantime, by 1926, major Chinese evolutions and continued turmoil underscored Connor's analysis. The next notable appearance on the Chinese stage that had a measurable effect on the regiment was that of the Kuomintang — the KMT or Nationalist Party. It was formed in 1912 by Sun Yat-sen's revolutionary faction, which played a role in ending the Manchu dynasty. But it was not until the successful Bolshevik revolution in the Soviet Union that the Kuomintang emerged as a major political party also with its own army. Advisers from the Communist International (the Comintern), especially Mikhail Borodin, infused the party with discipline and an organizational framework. Conditions in China also greatly facilitated the Kuomintang's development and, capitalizing on such events as the May 30, 1925, incident in Shanghai, became a significant force in Chinese politics. With the death of Sun Yat-sen on March 12, 1925, the rising leader Chiang Kai-shek took charge of the National Revolutionary government in Canton and in July 1926 launched the Northern Expedition, a military invasion of central and northern China. His chief goals were to subdue the warlords, unify the country and end foreign imperialism. To these ends he also harnessed the strong feelings against foreigners then rampant in China. Indeed, as Roy Chapman Andrews has remarked, the years 1926–1927 marked a turning point in the history of modern China. "Anti-foreignism burst into flame out of the still smoldering fires of the Boxer Rebellion of 1900. Foreign concessions, extra-territoriality, and the domination of the white man had been endured by the Chinese only because they could not resist." This they could now do.[50]

As time went on, two opposing factions dominated the Kuomintang:

the Communists and proponents of Chiang's more moderate program. The Communists stirred up the populace, and their agitation and propaganda demanded sweeping reforms and an end to the numerous "unequal treaties" that the Chinese had signed with foreigners. They established a center of power in Wuhan when this city fell to the Northern Expedition's forces. Meanwhile, on April 18, 1927, Chiang set up a new government at Nanking, the "Southern Capital." Foreigners in China grew alarmed, especially by the Communist activities but also unsure of Chiang, and poured thousands of additional troops into eastern and northern China. Pausing in his successful conquest of territories to the south of the Yangtze, on April 12, 1927 — assisted by such organized crime organizations as the notorious "Green Gang" (Ch'ing-pang) — Chiang crushed Communist activity in Shanghai and elsewhere, forcing a curtailment of their activities in Wuhan. At the same time, Chiang's main Chinese enemy, the Peking national government of Japanese client Chang Tso-lin raided the Soviet embassy in Peking on April 6, 1927, reducing Soviet influence considerably. This double blow brought an end to Soviet operations in China, and Borodin and others departed for Moscow. The Kuomintang, now rid of its left extremists, was free to continue the Northern Expedition. Military operations thereupon shifted north to the Tientsin-Peking area.

A few weeks earlier, when Chiang Kai-shek regained the Hankow (Wuhan) concessions and on March 24, 1927, moved into Nanking, several consulates had been attacked by his troops, the cities looted and many foreigners slain. The relative ease of these operations convinced the Kuomintang leaders that the foreign powers would not use force to defend their nationals and that the opportunity had arrived to drive them from the country. The Kuomintang thereupon demanded the return of the Tientsin and Shanghai concessions and the Legation Quarter in Peking. As some Westerners saw it, these events foreshadowed the Boxer situation all over again. But the Chinese overplayed their hand; the foreign powers had been driven too far. When Shanghai was threatened, they reacted immediately. Foreign nationals were called in from the interior of China, and Shanghai was strongly reinforced, the British bringing an entire division, including the Coldstream Guards, into the embattled city.

Initially, the American State Department hesitated to send in American forces when the situation in China became more threatening, but the men on the ground, principally the United States minister in Peking, John Van Antwerp MacMurray, and Rear Admiral Clarence S. Williams, the commander in chief of the Asiatic Fleet, convinced Washington to act more decisively. Consequently, substantial reinforcements were ordered to Shanghai. The first to be tapped were men of the Marine Corps' Fourth

Regiment, then in San Diego. Boarding the USS *Chaumont* on February 3, 1927, they were soon on the high seas bound for the Orient. When these seemed inadequate, additional Marines were summoned and the Third Brigade under the command of the redoubtable, controversial Brigadier General Smedley Darlington Butler was formed. Butler, a wounded veteran of the Boxer Uprising, was in journalistic hyperbole sometimes styled "Old Gimlet Eye." The Third Brigade consisted of the Fourth Regiment — to be stationed in Shanghai — the Sixth Regiment, a battery of artillery and a tank platoon from the Tenth Regiment, the Fifth Engineer Company, and later the 12th Regiment. These troops were supported by two U.S. Marine flying squadrons, Fighter Squadron Three and Scouting Squadron One. The aircraft were stationed ten miles from the mouth of the Hai Ho River (25 miles downstream from Tientsin near Tongku) at the village of Hsin Ho, alongside a Standard Oil compound located there.

When Chiang's forces swept northward from Shanghai, it was decided to send most of the marine brigade to Tientsin so as to provide support for any withdrawal of Americans in Peking to the sea if this proved necessary. These troops began arriving on the night of June 4, 1927, initially straining the accommodations in the city. Eventually, suitable quarters were found, many consisting of godowns (warehouses), private dwellings and other buildings; one encampment was set up on Woodrow Wilson Field and another in the vicinity of the Race Course.[51]

By February 1928, at the height of its strength, the brigade included 3,372 officers and men in Tientsin, and the 1,226 troops of the Fourth Regiment in Shanghai, for a total of 4,598. To these were added the 500-man Marine Legation Guard in Peking and, nominally, the 900 men of the 15th Regiment.[52]

The arrival of the marines made an immediate impression on the Chinese as well as the men of the 15th Regiment. As to the Chinese, one marine writing in *The Sentinel* noted that their "tractors and 75's sure startled old John Chinaman. They kinda look business like."[53]

The impact on the 15th was a mixed one. For one thing, the regiment was demoted from its usual rather prominent position in Tientsin to being subordinate to the larger Marine Corps outfit. Butler also outranked Brigadier General Joseph C. Castner, who had replaced Connor in May of 1926, and "there was a covert understanding whereby the Fifteenth would abandon the treaty commitment and obey Butler in any crisis." Significantly, *The Sentinel* maintained a studied silence regarding most Marine operations over the 18 months that they shared the city with the Leathernecks, though athletic contests and competitions on the firing ranges continued. The 15th was also challenged in an area where it had always excelled in Tientsin: its famous "spit and polish" parades and ceremonies, though here, as one observer has noted, the 15th maintained its pride of place.[54]

As to weightier matters, Butler steadfastly recognized the Army only as "protocol troops," with their own distinct mission in China, and while cooperating with the 15th, saw to it that his forces remained officially aloof. Indeed, "Butler was careful to disassociate himself and the marines from the Fifteenth," and could not emphasize strongly enough that his outfit was "an independent Brigade" whose commanding general "was responsible only to the Commander in Chief, Asiatic Fleet," and that no marine was in any sense "under the command of any military officers other than a United States Marine Officer." As one scholar has noted, "the marines thus remained independent of the whole treaty structure and free to ignore treaty stipulations such as defense of the neutral zones around the city and railway line to the sea — and to effectively thwart allied initiatives by simply refusing to cooperate."[55]

Vis-à-vis the other allied commandants in Tientsin, which were usually headed by a Japanese lieutenant general, Butler, though second highest in rank and commander of the largest contingent in Tientsin, remained detached and generally refrained from joining in any of the allied plans and actions. He refused to act in concert with the Japanese on several occasions, and regarded this as an effective means of limiting Japanese actions, benefiting both Americans and Chinese. As one scholar has suggested, Butler's 1927–29 stint in Tientsin marked the last time when the United States could function as a restraint on Japan in China.[56]

As to his own nation's policies, Butler, adopting a "hard-headed, skeptical prognosis," emerged among the more liberal of the Americans in China. While his arrival on the scene seemed a sop to American hawks (i.e., American business interests and the American minister to China, John MacMurray), he interpreted his orders as encompassing primarily the necessity of the "protecting of American lives," rather than employing the usual imperialistic "lives and property" phraseology. Dismissing his opponents as "self-serving troublemakers," he thereby placed himself in the camp of President Calvin Coolidge and the American secretary of state, Frank B. Kellogg. While recognizing the need for American intervention, the Coolidge administration evinced a pro–Chinese stance. Butler concurred, often expressing sympathy for the long-suffering Chinese and their "overriding cause of self determination." He noted in his final report that he hoped to refrain from harming the Chinese and refused to go along with desires of other foreign nations to adopt a belligerent stance against them, especially schemes emanating from the British and Japanese camps. In short, as Butler expressed it, "the fewer marks or scars of violence we make on China or the Chinese people, the fewer wounds we leave to heal."[57]

Accordingly, in opposition to MacMurray's persistent views that America must employ much more substantial military force against the Chinese, seeking to maintain at least the status quo, Butler and the leadership in Washington opted for conciliating them. To these ends, Butler was determined to "avoid all unnecessary conflicts or collisions with the Chinese," while maintaining "strict neutrality in relation to their armed civil war." Instead, Butler focused on what he perceived as more serious: the growing Japanese threat.[58]

MacMurray was thus frustrated, grumbling that Washington seemed bent upon throwing in their hand completely "even over such things as extraterritoriality." At this juncture, clearly the military emerged as the more moderate of the two centers of American power: on the one hand, the civilian diplomats on the scene in Peking, and on the other, the Marines in Tientsin commanded by Butler. The marine commander was often supported by the resident naval commanders of the Asiatic Fleet, first Admiral Clarence S. Williams and after September, 1927, Admiral Mark L. Bristol.[59]

Meanwhile, Chiang resumed his northward march, and by military operations, buying off warlords, and the widespread use of propaganda, swept into Peking on June 8, 1928, renaming the city Peiping ("Northern Peace") and moving the nation's capital south to Nanking. Chihli Province was renamed Hopei — now Hebei. Subsequently, it became clear that Chiang would succeed in overrunning most of northeastern China, and establishing a viable government in a more-or-less unified nation with its capital in Nanking. At the same time, it seemed evident that Japanese troops were not, for a time at least, posing threats to American lives and property. Consequently, the American commander in chief of the Asiatic Fleet, Rear Admiral Mark Bristol — who had relieved Admiral Williams on September 9, 1927 — decided "to make a friendly gesture towards the Chinese by reducing the number of Marines in North China." Accordingly, in the summer of 1928, the Third Brigade began to withdraw, and on January 20, 1929, the remaining marines had departed China with the exception of the Fourth Regiment, which remained in Shanghai. The prominent Tientsin newspaper *The Peking and Tientsin Times* mourned their passing, noting that "they were among us during one of the most critical periods in North China since 1900" and "their mere presence as a part of the international garrison had a steadying and reassuring effect during a time of very grave emergency."[60]

By the end of 1928, Chiang had completed the unification of China though on a shaky foundation that would never be secure. Conflict with Japan also had occurred during the Northern Expedition's operations, which set the stage for the next major events in Chinese history: the conquest of Manchuria and other areas by Japan, and the coming of the Sino-Japanese War in the 1930s. Meanwhile, Chiang's Nanking government entered into treaties with many states from July 25 to December 22, 1928, which formally recognized the Nanking government and its right to complete tariff autonomy. In further agreements in 1929 and 1930, nine nations gave up extraterritorial privileges in China, though France, Great Britain, the United States and Japan retained theirs until later, the British and Americans only formally ending extraterritoriality on January 11, 1943.[61]

As General Connor had earlier foreseen, a new era dawned, though with the Allied and American governments remaining in China. Regarding the 15th Regiment, MacMurray in Peiping at last conceded that the internal developments in China had "virtually relegated to abeyance what was, under the Protocol of 1901, the primary mission of the United States Army Forces—namely, the maintenance of open communication between Peiping and the sea," though the right under the Protocol was neither surrendered nor waived. Nevertheless, given the "present-day military and political conditions in China," it would be impossible successfully to assert this right and the present U.S. policy was "not to attempt ... any such assertion of it, which would be merely provocative and abortive and humiliating to [the nation's] prestige." In other words, keeping open communications from Peiping and the sea had "ceased to be the primary mission of the United States Army Forces, and [had] become a merely contingent mission, secondary to the protection of American life in the Tientisn area."

The new position adopted by MacMurray therefore required a new orientation for the American forces. In a communication to General Castner dated June 2, 1928, MacMurray set forth the new posture. In the first place, what was contemplated was "not conditions of organized warfare, but, at the worst, such as might arise out of mob action or sporadic and desultory attack by Chinese armed forces of one or another faction." That being the case, Castner should not contemplate such actions as certain other commandants are disposed to do which might "be merely provocative and tend to bring on unnecessarily conflicts which might create a situation actually serious." As to the Chinese, the American forces should "act impartially," and as was compatible with the needs to protect American citizens, "avoid any interference with the operations of Chinese military forces," or movements of the Chinese people, also avoiding "anything needlessly offensive or provocative to Chinese sensibilities." American

II. The 15th Marches onto the Chinese Stage

troops were only to hold their assigned sectors of the defense lines agreed to in the Combined Plan of Defense of Tientsin, rejecting any establishment of new outer lines "within which the movement of Chinese soldiers or civilians would be arbitrarily restricted," as some Allied commandants wanted to create. Castner was ordered to maintain an aloof stance and if necessary to adopt "one of definite opposition" to any proposal that might involve American forces in action resulting from "the provocative or impetuous action of other national forces."[62]

At the headquarters of the 15th, in response to the minister's letter, the troop detachment that had been long maintained at Tangshan to guard the railroad shops was recalled shortly thereafter, concentrating all of the regiment at Tientsin with the exception of a small permanent detachment at the firing range at Chinwangtao to guard the installation and keep it in good repair.

These developments had a further impact on the 15th Infantry. Its status in China would thenceforth appear increasingly superfluous, and ultimately, with the growing power of Japan, much more dangerous.

In the larger picture, Japan's rise to prominence dated to the initiation of the Meiji Period initiated in 1868 under the emperor Mutshuhito who, moving Japan's capital from Kyoto to Tokyo, ruled from 1867 to 1912. At this time, Japan began a period of rapid industrialization and modernization along Western lines. This course was highlighted by the Sino-Japanese War of 1894-1895, resulting in substantial Japanese gains at Chinese expense. Japan began to dominate Manchuria and Korea, annexing the latter in 1910. Meanwhile, the Russo-Japanese War of 1904-1905 further consolidated Japan's dominant position in much of northern Asia. In 1912, the Taisho Period began under the rule of the Emperor Yoshihito, who continued to 1926. During his tenure, further enhancement followed Japan's entry into World War I on the Allied side, which resulted in her "Twenty-One Demands" to China, initiating a policy of subordinating China and establishing Japanese preponderance in the Far East. Japan also temporarily gained control over former German holdings in China, notably in the Shantung peninsula.

Under the emperor Hirohito the Showa Period, which began in 1926, was characterized by militaristic and imperialistic policies that were a reaction against the relative liberalism and internationalism of the Taisho era. There was also a partial repudiation of the intellectual and cultural aspects of Western civilization and a revival of older Japanese ideologies. The army and navy came to dominate the government at the expense of civilian politicians. As a consequence, in the steadily worsening conditions, the 15th's eventual withdrawal from China seemed to be only a matter of time.

As has been noted, Butler's 1927–29 stint in Tientsin perhaps marked the last time when the United States could function as a restraint on Japan in China — barring a most unlikely much more substantial intervention — and from that time on, the Pacific War, integral to the massive cataclysm of World War II, was almost a foregone conclusion. As Roy Andrews, the American explorer, observed, "Like all others who knew the Orient, I was sure Japan would lift the curtain when the stage was set."[63]

CHAPTER III

History and Organization

> I yell, I bawl, I weep alone,
> I shout, I whoop, I long for home,
> For I have been "Oriented."[1]

By the 1920s, the 15th Infantry Regiment — sometimes playfully called the 15th Hoof, or more fancifully, the Dragon Regiment — had "more foreign service than any other Regiment in the service." It was more "talked about — written about — swore about — and wondered about" than any other, as one rather colorful account had it, and the only one "where a Doughboy can get a bottle of beer without stealing it." It was also the regiment in the Army where there was "more discipline required, more dynashine required, more linseed and elbow grease, more jewelry polish and ornamental jewelry, more made-to-order clothes and tailor bills, more chiropractic and manicure bills, more company bills and JAW-BONE [credit] than anywhere in the world."[2]

The history of the 15th is closely intertwined with that of the American republic. It was first organized on July 16, 1798, in the "Quasi War" with France.[3] Seeing little action, it was demobilized in 1800. It was resurrected on January 11, 1812, during the War of 1812. Following this conflict, it was again dissolved in May 1815, conforming with an act of Congress reducing the Army to 10,000 men.

The regiment reappeared in April 1847, during the war with Mexico. First sent to Vera Cruz to join the forces of General Winfield Scott, it participated in the march on Mexico City and took part in the attacks there, notably the assault on Chapultepec. The outfit was once more disbanded in August of 1848. Despite its earlier actions, because the 15th was a volunteer unit, the War Department did not regard these deployments, impressive as some of them were, as belonging legitimately to the history of the Regular Army. It was not until the Civil War that the regiment was officially recognized.

In May and July of 1861, in response to the pressing need for armed forces when the Civil War broke out, Congress gave President Lincoln the authority to increase the Regular Army by nine regiments of infantry and one each of artillery and cavalry. It was under this legislation that the 15th Infantry was organized as a Regular Army Regiment on May 4, 1861, by direction of the President, his action being confirmed by act of Congress on July 29, 1861. Initially, the First Battalion, formed on May 3, 1861, began training at Newport, Kentucky, where it remained until early in 1862. Then, ready for action, it marched into Tennessee, participating in the campaigns in the western theater, including the Battle of Shiloh in Tennessee on April 7, 1862. Other skirmishes and activities involved marching, countermarching and fighting through Tennessee, Alabama, and Kentucky. This led to the Battle of Chickamauga, near Chattanooga in September 1863, the heroics there providing the regiment with one of its banners proudly carried ever after. In November, the 15th took part in the successful Federal assault on Missionary Ridge, near Chattanooga. It was also present at the Battle of Kenesaw Mountain (June 27, 1864) near Atlanta, where the Federal forces were defeated by the Confederates. Undaunted, the 15th was ordered to take up positions around Atlanta, participating in operations in the area. These culminated in the general assault on the Confederate works at Jonesborough near Atlanta on September 1, resulting in Atlanta's fall. The 15th was then ordered to Chattanooga to occupy Lookout Mountain, where it remained until the end of the war. Later, the regiment was reorganized by an act of Congress on July 28, 1866, though it only became a full-fledged Regular outfit when it was consolidated with the 35th Infantry Regiment on March 3, 1869, by another Congressional act.

Following the Civil War, the regiment was engaged in garrison duty at various locations, including the District of Alabama from 1865 to 1868, and then in the West, involved in campaigns against the Ute Indians in Colorado and Utah, and the Mescalero Apaches in New Mexico and Arizona, serving in the District of New Mexico from 1869 to 1882; the Department of Dakota, 1882 to 1891; that of Missouri, 1891 to 1896; and finally the Department of Colorado, 1896 to 1898.

Then, 33 years after the close of the Civil War, the United States was again at war, with only 15,000 regular troops available for service. As a consequence of the tensions between the United States and Spain over Cuba, the American Congress passed a resolution on April 19, 1898, declaring "that the people of the Island of Cuba are, and of right ought to be, free and independent." This document also authorized the President to use land and naval forces to implement the resolution. In response, Spain formally initiated hostilities on April 24, and on the following day, Congress declared that a state of war existed between the United States and Spain.

The Spanish forces in Cuba numbered approximately 40,000 men. Consequently, America had promptly to raise an army, and a bill was passed authorizing a strength of 62,597 men for the Regular Army, and, in addition, called for 200,000 volunteers. In the meantime, the Regular forces were concentrated and started on the road to Cuba. The call found the 15th scattered over the Southwest, in New Mexico, Arizona, and Colorado, and the four-month war was over before it could be rallied (the armistice with Spain was signed on August 12, 1898). Nevertheless, not knowing how many additional forces might be required to keep the peace, the 15th was ordered to Huntsville, Alabama, the last units arriving on October 12, 1898. Following a short but intensive training period at Camp A.G. Force, Alabama, the 15th was dispatched by rail on November 23 to Savannah, Georgia, en route to Neuvitas, Cuba. Reaching there on December 4, the regiment proceeded to Puerto Principe, taking up quarters at Camp Allyn Capron. From there the troops marched to put down Cuban insurgent activity at Ciego de Avila. In late 1899, the regiment was ordered home, arriving in New York on January 9, 1900. Dispatched to various bases in northern New York and Vermont, the regiment soon regained its health and strength after its debilitating Cuban venture.

Shortly after the regiment's return to the United States, in 1900, another foreign upheaval ensued: the Boxer Uprising. The regiment's role therein has been discussed in chapter II.

Following its involvement in the Boxer Uprising, on November 25, 1900, with attention of the United States primarily focused on the continuing difficulties in the Philippines where Filipino insurrectionists such as Emilio Aquinaldo—freedom fighters to today's Filipinos—defied pacification (i.e., resisted American imperialism following the war with Spain), the regiment's First Battalion was relieved from duty in China and ordered to Manila. From there, units were dispatched to Legaspi, Tobacco, and Mauban for patrol duty. In the meantime, the regiment's Second and Third battalions sailed for the Philippines, serving there until the entire regiment was returned to the United States in July 1902, taking up garrison duties at Monterey, California.

Three years later, the 15th was once more ordered to the Philippines, arriving there on December 3, 1905, and remaining until late in 1907. Returning to the United States, it proceeded to Fort Douglas, Utah, where it was engaged in garrison duty until November 3, 1911.

As China settled down after the Boxer Uprising, the number of foreign troops was reduced to slightly over 4,000 and certain military posts along the Peking to Shankaikwan railway were closed. But with further convulsions in China in 1911, leading to the deposition of the Manchu dynasty — China's last — and the proclamation of the Chinese Republic by Dr. Sun Yat-sen in January 1912, foreign nations once again reinforced their contingents. These included men from the 15th Infantry as has been recounted in chapter II.

Subsequently, when the Great War came in 1914, many of the railway posts were again evacuated and the Russian detachments were withdrawn from China early in the year, in hope that this proof of the tsar's friendship would allay the hostility aroused by Russian action in Mongolia. The British and part of the India forces left immediately for active service. German troops and reservists were concentrated in Tsingtao (Qingdao) where, now as enemies, they were captured by Japanese and British forces. With the internment of the Austrian Legation Guard, the foreign garrisons in northern China once more were reduced to about 5,000 men. As to the men of the 15th, their attention became focused on the war in Europe rather than in China, which was regarded as a stultifying backwater, and numerous officers and men eagerly sought and obtained transfers to combat units in France.

Meanwhile, the 15th soldiered on, engaged in its routine garrison activities which also involved the coming and going of various commanding officers. In July of 1913, Colonel Jones was transferred to the Eighth Infantry, trading places with that outfit's colonel, John C.F. Tillson, who assumed command of the 15th on September 9, 1913. Just over two years later, on October 26, 1915, Colonel John F. Morrison took over the 15th in place of the ailing Tillson, who left the regiment in September bound for Letterman General Hospital in the States. The new commander, however, was on duty for less than a month. Appointed a brigadier general on November 21, he was replaced by Colonel Harry C. Hale, who took up his post in Tientsin on February 26, 1916.

Under Hale's command significant events occurred with consequences for the 15th. In the United States the National Defense Act of June 3, 1916, allowed various expedients to be taken to revamp and revitalize the nation's armed forces. Accordingly, it was ordered as of August 1, 1916, that the enlisted personnel of the 15th's absent Second Battalion in Manila was to form the First Battalion of the Philippine-based 31st Infantry — the "Polar Bears," so named because in 1919, the outfit had served with the American Expeditionary Force in Siberia. Sent to China by paper transfer, the Second was then reorganized, its Companies E, F, G, and H being recreated by absorbing enlisted personnel from the First and Third battalions in Tientsin. In addition, Machine Gun, Headquarters and Supply companies were established. By September 1916, the 15th was at last based at one place for the first time in several years.[4]

After a stint of command of about 18 months in China, Colonel Hale was appointed brigadier general and returned to the States on August 14, 1917. He was relieved by Colonel Walter H. Gordon who, reflecting the quickening pace in the U.S. Army after America entered the Great War, was also appointed a brigadier and consequently commanded the regiment for only a few weeks. He was replaced by Colonel Edward F. Sigerfoos who continued only to November 20, 1917, when Colonel William T. Wilder assumed command. Wilder stayed longer, about 18 months, until June 11, 1919. His replacement was Colonel William Meade Morrow, who took command on July 11, 1919, remaining until May of 1921 when he was succeeded by Colonel William F. Martin.[5]

Organizationally, the 15th emerged in China intact from the Great War's dislocations but in new quarters in the American compound in the former German concession. As of early 1921, numbering about 1,000 officers and men, the regiment consisted of three infantry battalions, each of four companies—A through M, with exception of J—and also a Headquarters Company, a Machine Gun Company, Supply Company, Quartermaster Department, the Medical Department and a Signal Corps unit. Another change in the organization occurred on March 11, 1921, when the principal weapons of companies H and M were changed from rifles and bayonets to pistols and machine guns bolstering the firepower of the regiment and eliminating the regimental Machine Gun Company.[6]

In 1920, after the Great War, to enhance regimental esprit de corps, the War Department issued Circular No. 19 ordering commanding officers to select and designate as Organization Day a date which "would be an annual holiday devoted to proper exercises in commemoration of the history and traditions of the regiment." In response, the 15th selected September 13, the day in 1847 when the fortress of Chapultepec in Mexico City fell to the arms of the 15th and the Ninth Infantry. This date was, however, disallowed by the War Department because it held that the regiment had only officially existed since May 4, 1861, when it was created early in the Civil War, and that regiments known as the 15th prior to that time had no relation to the contemporary organization. Therefore, May 4 was subsequently celebrated annually with impressive reviews and ceremonies.[7]

To further deepen the regiment's sense of history and its pride, in 1921 a regimental coat of arms was designed by a board of the 15th's officers in compliance with War Department's instructions. Featuring a pagoda indicative of the unit's China service, its motto was "We Will Keep Faith," a rather insipid borrowing of the Marines' more vigorous "Semper Fidelis." Forwarded to the War Department for approval, it was disallowed because once again it took credit for the regiment's service in the War of 1812 and the Mexican War of 1847. Men in the regiment grumbled that significant parts of regimental history were thereby "wiped out," and thus was relegated "into something next to oblivion the history of one of our best early regiments."[8]

Subsequently, a new coat of arms was designed and a new motto, the more robust "Can Do," was devised. This watchword, in pidgin English, derived from the laconic expression of the "honest Chinaman," and commemorated the regiment's long service in China. The shield of the new coat of arms was blue and white, the infantry colors, and featured a five-toed imperial Chinese dragon, as well as four red acorns, symbols of major Civil War battles, and a rock standing for the Battle of Chickamauga, "where the regiment fought and held so gallantly." The crest above the shield featured the Katipunan flag of the Philippine Insurrection. A distinctive insignia was also approved, consisting of a metal shield and motto; it was worn on the collar or shoulder straps of the uniform.[9]

Further regarding regimental pride, the men of the 15th notoriously paid especial attention to their uniforms and equipment, officers and men alike becoming fussy fashion plates. It became customary for the men to order tailor-made uniforms of "golden Hong Kong khaki" with its distinctive brownish-yellow tint. On garrison duty, officers and first sergeants carried swords, and leather garrison belts and swagger sticks were part of the off-duty uniform for officers and men alike. When the "tin hat" was worn on parade or for special inspections, it was buffed, shellacked and stenciled with the "Can Do" insignia. Each soldier was issued two stocks for his Springfield rifle: "One had the standard issue finish and was used for training and qualification firing. The second was for ceremonial use only, and was kept in [pristine] condition by being kept wrapped in linseed oil-soaked rags; to maintain this stock in top condition, it was given a treatment of equal parts of linseed oil, boning, and elbow grease." One officer in the regiment in the early 1930s, Captain Charles L. Bolte, recalled that when the men were standing inspection formations, "coolies would scurry about ... dusting off the shoes of the men in ranks. Officers and soldiers who would normally be armed with Cal. .45 pistols wore exact wooden replicas instead to prevent their belts from sagging. One battalion even put stovepipe in the blanket rolls instead of blankets." When Major General Eli A. Helmick, inspector general of the U.S. Army, inspected the 15th in the autumn of 1925, he was duly impressed with the high soldierly standards displayed and concurred with one of his officers who remarked that the 15th's was "the best exhibition of marching that he had seen since his Cadet days at the Military Academy." In addition, Helmick declared, their fine appearance was partly a consequence of their inclination to buy their own uniforms rather than wear "the cheap, shoddy [issue] clothing," with which, because its colors were not fast, it was difficult to equip a unit with uniforms of the same hue. The uniformity in colors enhanced the military appearance of the soldiers and was plainly "a great morale builder." He concluded that "I have not seen anywhere a finer looking body of American soldiers than those in the Fifteenth Infantry in China."[10]

In 1930, soldiers could also purchase the older traditional blue uniforms under the proviso of "authorized but not required." Ever interested in matters sartorial, many men of the 15th were soon sporting dress blues, and an officer from the individual's organization personally inspected each fitting to insure that the soldier was properly turned out. In addition, good-conduct men were authorized to wear civvies—the Americans being the only troops in China permitted to wear them—but these were also closely supervised by individual organizations so that only a well-dressed soldier would make an appearance on the street.

In 1931, snappy new band uniforms were ordered for the 15th and even the coolie work force was outfitted in new blue uniforms with an overseas cap sporting their company's letters as well as blue armbands designating the outfit to which they belonged. Then, perhaps partially to curtail too much distinction being accorded to the men of the 15th, in 1932, the War Department adopted a new shade of khaki and ordered all U.S. Army units to be dressed in this material, though the undaunted Can-Doers continued to tailor their uniforms.[11]

Further enhancements to the uniform were allowed. The 15th's headquarters passed on War Department directives that recognized the right of veterans of the Great War to wear the French fourragère—usually the colorful red and green cord of the Croix de Guerre—which some of the men of the 15th were soon sporting about the Compound adding luster to their already natty appearance. In addition, a regimental memo dated November 23, 1927, provided that a cloth arm patch was to be issued to all men who attained a suitable proficiency in the Chinese spoken language. Called a "Chung" ("Chinese"), it was to be worn on the outer side of the left sleeve of the coat, eight inches above the edge of the cuff. In 1930, the 15th was authorized to wear the rampant sea lion insignia of the Philippine Department—called the "wampus fish"—as a shoulder patch on the left shoulder of uniforms.[12]

Indeed, the regiment was never allowed to forget that it should aspire to be the best such organization in the Army. The presence of the Marine Corps Legation Guard in Peking helped keep the men up to the mark and the competition between the two services, manifested in sports and in performance on the firing ranges, constantly highlighted this state of affairs, as did the ever-present threat of military action that their position in China entailed. Sometimes even the marines were favorably impressed with the regiment. A certain Captain Wilson, who commanded a marine detachment of about 76 attached to the 15th Infantry during a period of unrest in China late in 1925, once remarked that he had often served with Regular Army units but "that the 15th Infantry [was] beyond doubt the finest Regular Army Regiment that he [had] ever seen." He thought particularly, that the "fine appearance, dress and bearing of the enlisted men" was first class. He was further "greatly impressed with the punctilious manner in which the enlisted men saluted and with the snap and precision shown in their training, especially in their close order drill."[13]

When the Marine Corps Third Brigade arrived in Tientsin during a time of heightened tension in 1927, however, the 15th was challenged by men unquestionably much more inclined to showmanship than any other in the history of the U.S. armed forces. Commanded by the redoubtable, controversial Brigadier General Smedley Darlington "Old Gimlet Eye" Butler, "the battle of the parade grounds" was duly joined. The marines knew full well what was at stake even before the outfit sailed from San Diego in mid–February 1927. This particular China expeditionary force was soon nicknamed the "exhibition force," and "its quartermaster later reminisced that the outfit was equipped more for parade competition with international units garrisoning China's treaty ports—[including the 15th]—than for fighting." He remembered that "all machine guns were nickel plated, our mortars were nickel plated and the 37 millimeter tank guns ... were also nickel plated." The arrival of the marines in Tientsin undoubtedly ushered in an uncomfortable 18 months for men of the 15th forced to share the turf of "their Tientsin" (i.e., "their women; their bars") with the preening interlopers. Butler wisely drew demarcation lines between off-duty areas of his marines and men of the 15th within the city.[14]

There was also much competition between and among the foreign contingents stationed in Tientsin, a "place of many soldiers." To military personnel, uniforms certainly matter, and some part of the military mind always clicks into place regarding them.[15] Because one of the 15th's roles was to assert America's presence in a demanding foreign environment, a snappy appearance counted for something. In this situation, the band likewise figured prominently. It certainly must have quickened the steps of those on parade in Tientsin to hear the warm acclaim of the members of the international community, which was often forthcoming, ringing in their ears.[16]

In light of the developments and innovations in the organization of the U.S. Army, as well as the needs and requirements for China service as perceived by Washington, the 15th was repeatedly altered organizationally in the decades following the Great War. In September of 1921, Major Noble J. Wiley, the commander of the regiment's First Battalion, which was then with the regiment in Tientsin, was ordered to move his outfit to Camp Eldridge, at Los Banos on Laguna de Bay in the Philippines, and it sailed on October 26. Late in 1923, the battalion moved to Fort William McKinley, Rizal, about nine miles from Manila. There, it was garrisoned with troops of the 57th and 45th Infantry regiments, both Philippine Scout regiments, and brigaded with the 31st Infantry as a part of the 24th Infantry Brigade, of the Philippines Division. Calling itself the Lost Battalion, condemned to "eating our bread among strangers," nonetheless service at McKinley was "most pleasant," one soldier admitted. In addition, the First Battalion served the 15th in useful ways, one being that men assigned to China often passed through its ranks for training and classification. Recently-arrived officers and men were placed on probation for three months, and those failing to measure up to the desired standards were not sent on to Tientsin.[17]

A more profound transformation came to the 15th in 1923, when, as of April 1, the separate command designated the American Forces in China (AFC) was created. Headquartered at Tientsin, it consisted of all troops and agencies of the U.S. Army then serving in China and it reported directly to the War Department instead of the Philippine Department — as it was then called. Accordingly, a general officer was designated to head up the new entity, the first being Brigadier General William Durward Connor.[18]

Further developments came on June 23, 1924, when War Department General Order 16 redesignated these troops as the United States Army Forces in China (USAFC). Then, with the success of Chiang Kai-shek in unifying China to a certain extent, Washington chose to tailor its forces in China to the new situation. Accordingly, War Department General Order 5, dated February 11, 1929, stipulated that the United States Army Forces in China would once more revert — as of midnight, March 16/17, 1929 — to the situation before 1923, i.e., to the control of the commanding general of the Philippine Department. Thereafter, the personnel of 15th Regiment were known as United States Army Troops in China

(USATC). This designation continued to the end of the 15th's service in China. Brigadier General Joseph C. Castner, who replaced Connor in 1926, was the last army general to command U.S. Army forces in China, departing Tientsin on March 10, 1929. The colonel commanding the 15th Infantry, with its 850 men and 56 officers, thereupon resumed command of the U.S. Army forces in China. Simultaneously, in a further reduction of the Army's presence in China, the 15th's First Battalion, then at Fort McKinley in the Philippines, was deactivated on April 1, 1929. All officers and men were reassigned to other organizations such as the 59th and 60th Coast Artillery in the Philippines.[19]

Subsequently, the military services in the United States struggled to maintain their peacetime strength in the face of continued cutbacks and reshufflings mandated by Congress and the administration in Washington. In order to furnish men for a fifth increment of the Air Corps, then being expanded, the War Department mandated a reduction in strength of specified infantry regiments by 208 men, placing one rifle company per battalion on the inactive list effective on September 1, 1931. The companies selected in the 15th were G (called by its members the "Go Get 'Em G" outfit) and L. Though steadily reduced in size and importance, the unit still remained, as one member of the 15th poetically stated it, "the Sons of the Free / The Sentinels of Liberty / Six hundred Loyal Soldiers / Of the Fifteenth Infantry," and they continued proudly "Marching on — Marching on — / Marching on, for Home and Country."[20]

These developments marked the last significant organizational modifications while in China, and it only remained for the most important change of all to ensue regarding the regiment: its withdrawal on March 2, 1938.

CHAPTER IV

Leadership

> Personally, there are many things about China that I don't like and there are other things that I do. In fairness, we must admit that this statement can be applied to most any place, for one has yet to find an earthly heaven and even the exact site of the Garden of Eden is in doubt.
>
> — Colonel William K. Naylor[1]

The question naturally arises as to what manner of men commanded the 15th Infantry Regiment in its China years. Brief profiles of selected colonels and the two brigadier generals who commanded the U.S. Army's forces in China give some insight into this matter. As to the quality of leadership, Lieutenant Colonel George C. Marshall, who served in China in the mid–1920s, once pointed out regarding the officers of the regiment — which certainly pertained to its commanding officers — they "had been selected for duty in China strictly on their merits. Competition for assignment to the regiment was the keenest imaginable. The character of service expected from this group of officers was well above the average." Furthermore, "owing to the peculiar situation of the American Forces in China and the contact they have with the troops and civilians of other nations here, high professional ability was not the only necessary requirement for the successful officer in China. With professional ability it was necessary to combine good sportsmanship and the ability to mingle with the nationals of other countries and to successfully perform the duties as a representative of his country."[2]

Colonel William F. Martin arrived in Tientsin on September 26, 1921, and departed the regiment in November of 1922. One of the oldest colonels to command the 15th, Martin was born on July 19, 1863, in Ripley, Ohio. Graduated from West Point on June 14, 1885, he was initially assigned to the 25th Infantry at Fort Snelling, Minnesota, and participated in the Wounded Knee Campaign. Routine garrison tours followed for the

"Old Indian Fighter," and in February 1899 he was sent to Santiago, Cuba, for occupation duty. Missing the Boxer Uprising, in August 1900 Martin sailed for the Philippines and engaged in action against the Filipino "Insurrectos" with the Fifth Regiment. He later attended the Army War College and from 1914 to 1917, he was on various General Staff assignments. Promoted to brigadier general on August 5, 1917, Martin assumed command of the 174th Infantry Brigade, 87th Division, which was assigned to the Services of Supply (SOS) in France. Martin accordingly saw no combat and was only present as an observer in the Meuse-Argonne campaign, though he commanded the 87th for a time after the armistice. Following the war, he received school and other assignments before being ordered to China. There his command was unspectacular, *The Sentinel* concluding that "with a quiet, sympathetic yet decided administration every man has felt that there was one who was doing all possible to train in efficiency and at whose hands all received justice and a square deal."[3]

Martin's successor was Colonel Campbell King, who arrived in Tientsin on April 12, 1923. A much more able man than Martin, King was one of the more successful commanders of the 15th. *The Sentinel* observed that his 15-month stint was indeed noteworthy and besides, as was often noted, he distinctly looked the part of a dashing military commander. From a distinguished family, King was born in North Carolina on August 30, 1871. After a brief stint at Charleston College, he enlisted in Troop K of the Fifth Cavalry on July 31, 1897. Soon promoted to corporal, on July 9, 1898, he was commissioned a second lieutenant in the First Infantry. He then served in Cuba, the Philippines and Hawaii, and was with Pershing on the Mexican border in 1916. In due course, he was a distinguished graduate of some of the Army's major schools including the Infantry and Cavalry School, the Army War College, and the General Staff College. During the Great War, he was chief of staff of the First Division, and, promoted to brigadier general, became chief of staff of the Seventh Army Corps and then the Third Army Corps, serving in such major campaigns as St. Mihiel and the Meuse-Argonne. Losing his temporary wartime general's rank — as was common at that time — he became a permanent colonel on July 1, 1920, and in the same year, was awarded a master of arts degree by Harvard.

Ordered to China with the 15th, as *The Sentinel* later noted, "when he arrived the morale of the regiment was low. We had been defeated in all branches of athletics for over a period of two years. The demoralizing effect of this was apparent." Accordingly, one of his first priorities was "to put athletics on a sound and secure basis." He did this by requiring everyone in the command to engage in some form of athletics during the

IV. Leadership

afternoons. As a result, new sports stars were discovered, and the colonel did everything possible "to foster clean and successful sports." The result was a "higher appreciation of the word sportsmanship" that then characterized the athletic contests of that era. "The resultant high morale from this one phase of activity [alone] [was] surprising," the paper declared. King did not neglect work, however, and during his regime, work and play were well-balanced. Consequently, the regiment's military professionalism was considerably enhanced.[4]

On November 22, 1924, Colonel William K. Naylor arrived in Tientsin to take command of the regiment. This was his second experience in the Orient. In 1899, he was involved in the campaign against the Philippine insurrectionists, and in 1900 was ordered to China during the Boxer Uprising, taking part in the Battle of Tientsin and the advance on Peking as a first lieutenant in command of Company F of the Ninth Infantry Regiment. A native of Illinois, Naylor, a graduate of the Michigan Military Academy and the University of Minnesota, was commissioned in the Army from civilian life on May 8, 1898. He became a graduate of the Infantry and Cavalry School, the General Staff College and the War College. Before the Great War, in addition to his involvement in the Philippines and in China. He lectured on strategy, military history, and the principles of war at the Army Service School at Fort Leavenworth and the Army War College, being reassigned to those duties at the war's completion.[5]

During the Great War, he participated in the Somme offensive with the Australian Corps of the Fourth British Army and in the Meuse-Argonne offensive with the American Third Army Corps and the 17th French Corps. He then became chief of staff of the American 33rd Division and, following his promotion to brigadier general, after the armistice he was made chief of staff of the American Ninth Army Corps. Just prior to his going to China in 1924, Naylor completed a tour on the War Department General Staff as assistant chief of staff, director of military intelligence. The colonel was also known for his scholarly attainments, authoring *The Principles of War*, *The Principles of Strategy*, and *The Marne Miracle*. His *Principles of Strategy* was translated into Japanese and used in their army instructional schools.

Precipitously ordered to the Philippines in January of 1926, Naylor departed his post as commander of the 15th under a cloud. It was alleged that he had been derelict in his duty, with suspicions of alcohol abuse. Later inquiries cleared him, with no damage to his subsequent career. It is certain that the men at the China station regretted Naylor's hasty departure. Those of the regiment's Service Company recorded in *The Sentinel* that "in losing Colonel Naylor we lose the most popular Commanding

Officer the 15th has possessed in years. It is seldom that an entire command will join in unqualified approval of a single officer but we are sure that the whole Regiment will join us in voting Colonel Naylor a 'square shooter.'" Another article asserted that the colonel's exodus "came as a great surprise to the entire command.... The Regiment has especially profitted thru Col. Naylor's ability as an instructor in military history. He has given us the advantage of his knowledge thru an extensive course of lectures on the World War."[6]

Naylor's successor was Colonel Isaac Newell of the Army's General Staff Corps, who formally took command on March 8, 1926. A native of Georgia, he was graduated from the Academy in 1896, being assigned to the 22nd Infantry. He was in Cuba in 1898 participating in the "Spanish-American Wrangle," that "little unpleasantness on an island, today famous for cigars and things that are prohibited by law in the United States." He then fought in the Philippines until 1902, and from 1903 to 1905, was engaged in the Moro Expedition in Mindinao. From 1908 to 1912, he was tactical officer at the U.S. Military Academy and from 1914 to 1917 was military attaché at Peking, service which undoubtedly "gave him an understanding of things Chinese which will be of great benefit to this Command."[7]

During the Great War he commanded the 51st Infantry of the Sixth Division in France. In 1920, he graduated from the Army School of the Line at Fort Leavenworth and the following year, on completing the course at the General Staff School, was selected for duty as an instructor in the school's tactical department. From Leavenworth, he was ordered to the Army War College in 1922 and on graduation was assigned to Headquarters, Second Corps Area, at Governor's Island in New York harbor. He arrived in China on March 6, 1926, taking command of the 15th Infantry on March 8.

Newell was interested in the general welfare of the men under his command and worked hard to improve their conditions of service, efforts which paid off. Accentuating the positive, he once editorialized in *The Sentinel* with a touch of hyperbole that the 15th Infantry was in excellent condition. The quality of officers and men was unexcelled, he declared, noting further that morale was high and the state of discipline was "most gratifying. ... We are fortunate to be members of this command," he went on, asserting that "service in China holds out more of professional interest than elsewhere in our army today. We have permanent barracks instead of dismal cantonments. Local prices and the rate of exchange has made it possible to provide generously of the best food. Recreation facilities in the way of athletics, skating and motion pictures are close at hand. The

Chaplain and the services in the Post Chapel are an inspiration for clean living to those who attend." At the same time, he announced that he had to depart Tientsin rather hastily because of a close relative's illness in the States.[8]

Newell's replacement was Colonel James D. Taylor who arrived in Tientsin on April 15, 1929, for a three-year tour. Born on February 3, 1877, in Florida, he graduated from Virginia Military Institute (VMI) in 1898. Entering the army as a second lieutenant on July 9, 1898, during the war with Spain, he took an active part in the Philippine "pacification," being acclaimed as "the officer who secured the information on which General Funston effected the capture of Emilio Aguinaldo," the famous Filipino insurrectionist. In the Great War, he commanded an infantry regiment "with great distinction," and graduated from the Army's staff schools and the War College after the War.[9]

Arriving in China just when the USATC was created, as the colonel commanding the 15th Regiment, Taylor was simultaneously head of U.S. Army Troops in China. Appearing at a time of relative peace in China, little challenged him militarily, and he had to be content with shaping up the regiment in smaller matters and in developing regimental tradition, at least in his own little corner of the Army's world. Encouraging an intense competition between the battalions, he focused on "spit and polish" with a vengeance, seeking many ways to "spruce up the troops and barracks." It was in his regime that the coolie work force was put in uniform; he was the colonel especially insisting upon spick and span barracks and in perfection on inspections and on the parade field. A lengthy article in *The Sentinel* at about mid-course in Taylor's regime noted that buildings and facilities on the post were for once in top shape, the mess halls, for instance, being "as inviting as any gleaming Child's Restaurant on a cold night." Dances were a regular feature at Recreation Hall and on these occasions, the orchestra was outfitted with tuxedos. Volleyball was introduced as a competitive game with its own trophy. Not the least, perhaps, "talkies" were introduced at the movies. More importantly, he zealously addressed the problem of venereal disease, a topic discussed later in this study.

A new pass system was instituted for his troops, conferring a wide range of privileges on good conduct men with "necessary restrictions" upon those not up to the mark. Taylor insisted upon stricter standards for recruits brought into the regiment, each individual having to pass a test given by the commanding officer in person before he was permitted to go on duty with his company. In other words, "he MUST QUALIFY to become a member." White gloves were issued to the troops so that small errors in the Manual of Arms were "readily noticeable and corrective training started promptly." Regular weekly talks on conditions in China kept the officers posted on the political and military situation in China, and an officers' military library was established to cultivate professionalism.[10]

Regimental pride was also addressed in various ways. In one instance, Taylor created the Regimental Commander's Color Bearers and Color Guards, composed of men recognized by their leaders for their outstanding military attributes and personal demeanor and conduct.[11]

In addition, a number of new trophies that organizations could win were instituted. One was the Taylor Military Proficiency Trophy, also called the Chickamauga Guidon, in remembrance of the regiment's Civil War exploits. To be competed for annually, it was awarded to the organization attaining the highest standard of proficiency in each training year's cycle. The newly-created Dinsmore Trophy was presented annually to the company with the best disciplinary record.[12]

One of the most intriguing of Taylor's innovations was the publication of a curious booklet, *Customs of the 15th Infantry*. Issued to new officers joining the regiment, who were ordered to carefully read and digest it, it informed them as to what was expected "in maintaining the best traditions of the regiment." Taylor may well have had in mind the involved, elaborate traditions of European — especially British — regiments, suggesting that their American counterparts might emulate them to advantage. It contained details as to social obligations, for instance, such as when flowers should be sent and to whom, and how often members of organizations should be visited in the hospital. When a child was born "to a married soldier of this regiment," the publication stipulated that it "will be presented with a silver napkin ring of standard design bearing the coat of arms of the regiment and a presentation inscription." Details of the holidays recognized by the regiment were set forth, as, for instance, the commanding officer's birthday, at which time the "regimental band [was to] serenade him, at his quarters, playing the regimental march and music appropriate to the season starting and concluding the ceremony with the 'three cheers.'" Charles G. Finney, an enlisted veteran of the 15th in the late 1920s, described this "strange little booklet" in his memoir, *The Old China Hands*, observing that "for some reason, it reminds one faintly of the *Spiritual Exercises* of Ignatius of Loyola. It is stark, dogmatic ... and has no nonsense about it."[13]

When Taylor departed China in late June of 1932, his troops were concerned that because of his recent serious illness, he had to be carried on a stretcher aboard a lighter anchored in the Hai Ho River. This vessel was to take the former commander and the departing troops from Tientsin to Taku at the mouth of the river, where they were to board the United

States Army Transport (USAT) *Republic* for their passage home.¹⁴ Never recovering — despite his having been given a replica of the god of longevity by the Chinese — he did not last out the year. Taylor died on Thanksgiving Day, 1932, at the Army's Walter Reed General Hospital in Washington, D.C. In his three-year regime, an obituary writer in *The Sentinel* recalled, Taylor "raised the standards of discipline and training, improved the marksmanship of his command, and by drastic measures greatly reduced the rate of [venereal] disease." Another writer observed that "possessing a forceful and decisive character, he was so insistent upon punctuality and all matters of discipline as to be regarded by some people as a martinet." Yet, like all such men, "there was a softer, and finer side to his character." In a revealing statement, the writer concluded that "perhaps few commanders have felt more pride in their men, and probably, also, few have known so little how to show it."¹⁵

Taylor's successor was Colonel Reynolds J. Burt. He was born at Fort Omaha, Nebraska, on August 2, 1874, into an Army family. Growing up on several Western frontier forts, he graduated from the Military Academy in June 1892. Unlike many career officers during this period, he served neither in Cuba nor the Philippines, his tours of duty being in the United States. As was the case with Naylor and Newell, however, he had previously been in China, specifically assigned to the 15th Infantry. As a captain, in the summer and autumn of 1915, he had served as commanding officer of Company C then at Tangshan as well as being in charge of the Hanku-Leichuang District along the Peking-Mukden railway. On November 11, 1915, Burt was detailed to the Quartermaster Corps, serving elsewhere in China at Chinwangtao, Shanghai, Hongkong and then in the Philippines. On July 1, 1916, he was ordered to Charleston, South Carolina, spending the remaining years of the Great War in the United States engaged in various duties, no doubt chafing at not being able to serve in France. In 1918 he was promoted to brigadier general and sent to Camp Meade, Maryland, in command of 22nd Infantry Brigade, 11th Division. In 1919, he reverted to his permanent grade of major, but was soon promoted to lieutenant colonel and a few weeks later, on July 1, 1920, became a bird colonel. Following War College attendance and service at various camps and cantonments, December 1, 1925, found Burt at Fort Screven, Georgia, in command of the Eighth Infantry, "the shootingest outfit of the Southeast." In July of 1928, he was sent to Washington for duty in the Militia Bureau where he remained until ordered to China.¹⁶

Burt had previously gained a bit of fame as a result of an announcement in 1926 in *The Infantry Journal*, the organ of the United States Infantry Association. This had identified the need for an official "rousing infantry song" and offered a princely prize of $350 for the winning submission. What was not wanted, the *Journal*'s proposal explained, was a hymn such as the Marine Corps boasted, but rather a march "that any man can sing or shout." This was desired, the prestigious publication asserted, "for the camp fire, for the barrack room, and for all occasions where Infantrymen are assembled." It was to be "a rattling good song, catchy and full of pep ... one with a swing and a lilt that will express the fighting spirit of the Infantry."[17]

The prize-winning piece, for which Burt wrote the words and a band leader, Warrant Officer S.A. Dapp, composed the music, was duly adopted by the Infantry Association. Entitled "Kings of the Highway," it was "a very pleasing melody [with] a light marching power," as one commentator described it. So proud was he of his creation that when he arrived in China, Burt ordered the band to play the composition "at all reviews, parades, and ceremonies for troops of this command passing in review." Captain Charles Lawrence Bolte, who served as the regiment's operations officer in the 1930s, and destined to be a four-star general and the Army's vice chief of staff, recalled that the band dutifully played the piece "one last time as Burt's ship sailed away—then as a man, the musicians threw all copies of the music into Chinwangtao Harbor."[18]

According to Bolte, Burt "wanted nothing to do with tactical training or the Chinese." He was mainly interested in music and in the theater, views which had considerable impact on the regiment's activities during his tenure as will be treated in chapter IX. Yet he continued to take an interest in the regiment's activities at the shooting ranges and in bivouac or in the field. For instance, in April 1933, he ordered the "dust-disturbing, mud-splashing 'Kings of the Highway,'" as the men sometimes referred to themselves in deference to Burt, to undertake a five-day, 20-mile operation in windy, muddy, bitter wintry weather to test their mettle.[19]

Burt's successor was Colonel George Arthur Lynch, called by one scholar "one of the army's rising stars after World War I." One of the more accomplished of the regiment's commanders, he did not possess much of Burt's thespian bent. Lynch was born at Blairston, Iowa, on March 12, 1880. Appointed to West Point following graduation in 1903 as an infantryman, he was assigned to the 17th Infantry then engaged in service against the Moros in the Philippines. After the Philippines were "pacified," Lynch became district engineer of the District of Jolo, constructing several bridges in the area. He returned to the United States in 1905 as instructor of modern languages at West Point, and then served with the 29th Infantry at Governor's Island, New York. From 1913 to 1917, Lynch was assistant to the chief of the Militia Bureau in Washington. He was then made editor of

The Infantry Journal and when the Army went to France in 1917, Lynch went with it. Serving on the General Staff of GHQ, he drafted the important *Infantry Drill and Combat Regulations* for the American Expeditionary Forces (AEF). Following the war, Lynch served in various capacities on the War Department's General Staff, and in August 1922 helped formulate the Army's *Field Service Regulations* of 1923. He graduated from the Army War College in 1930, and was ordered to the Philippines as executive officer of the 31st Infantry Regiment — the "Polar Bears" — and served with them when they were ordered to Shanghai in 1932. Back in Washington, in 1934, Lynch was named principal assistant to the New Deal's National Recovery Administration's (NRA) chief, General Hugh S. Johnson, and was acting administrator of the organization from April to November 1934. Then becoming assistant chief of staff, G-2, Second Corps Area, he was ordered to China, relieving Burt in 1935.[20]

Lynch, in all of his addresses to the regiment — and these were frequent — is revealed as an organization man with a sense of order and a "by the book" approach. He had a strong appreciation of the soldierly virtues, once observing that "next to the bond of religious faith and closely allied to it, the military tie which bound them together was the strongest that unites the minds and actions of masses of men." Indeed, it was this "which most distinguishes a military unit from any merely assembled group."[21]

It followed that Lynch had distinctive attitudes regarding the service of the 15th in China. In addressing new men arriving on the November 1935 transport, Lynch observed that "here in Tientsin as elsewhere on foreign service, there is a strong downward pull on human ambition." The men in China were living "in the land of the poppy and [the] lotus," and "with the abundance of servants to wait upon our every need," must continually be on guard against "breathing [in] too much lotus dust with the dust of the Gobi desert." Extolling the regiment, which had "a fine reputation in this community" and likewise with the armed forces of the other nations present, he emphasized the need for "good bearing and neatness." The men must also "refrain from any remarks critical of foreign troops or of any particular foreign nation.... In tense situations there is no way we can serve our country better than by the maintenance of a calm, impartial attitude. It isn't the soldier's business to start the trouble." Be fair to the Chinese, he also counseled, and "don't kick a poor coolie around just because you can or with the idea that you're going to build up face that way." (Yet, Lynch noted, "I needn't warn you that the Chinese merchants will try to play you for a sucker, but that's a part of the Oriental system of bargaining.") Reminding the men that the regiment had in times past "played an important part in protecting Tientsin from being over-run by fragments of defeated Chinese armies," they might at any time "again be called upon to stem an ebb-tide of battlefield fugitives." Accordingly, Lynch advised them to let their motto, in addition to "Can Do," be "Excelsior."[22]

In May 1937, FDR, going over the heads of several officers, appointed Lynch chief of infantry, returning him to Washington as a major general. He was formally relieved in Tientsin on May 14, 1937, by the man who was to bring the 15th home from China the following year: Colonel Joseph A. McAndrew who, from June 1936 to March 1937, had been the deputy commandant of the Army Command and General Staff College at Fort Leavenworth, Kansas.[23]

The personalities and actions of the two brigadier generals who were in command of the United States Army Forces in China during the 1920s also had considerable impact on the regiment in often sharply contrasting ways. On November 10, 1922, Brigadier General William Durward Connor was ordered to take command in China, arriving at his post on April 12, 1923. He was born on February 22, 1874, in Wisconsin. Graduated from the Military Academy June 11, 1897, he was assigned to the Corps of Engineers and served in it until his appointment as brigadier general on June 26, 1918. The Spanish-American War found Connor in the Philippines where he participated in the capture of Manila, later serving in the campaign against the Philippine insurrectionists.

During the Great War he was successively the assistant chief of staff, G-4, GHQ, AEF; chief of staff of the 32nd Division; commanding general of Base Section No. 2, AEF; and then chief of staff of the SOS (Services of Supply). Finally, on September 1, 1919, Conner assumed command of the American Forces in France, the liquidating agency for the AEF, withdrawing from France on January 1, 1920. Following the Great War, he had been in turn commandant of the Engineer School, director of the Inland and Coastwise Waterways Service, and assistant chief of staff, G-4, in the War Department. Promotion to major general on September 1, 1925, necessitated his withdrawal from China, and he sailed for the U.S. to take command of the Second Division at Fort Sam Houston, Texas. Connor, a popular commander with his troops, had also endeared himself to the Chinese, his diplomatic approach resulting in considerable good will on all sides. He was responsible for the introduction of the enforced study of the Chinese language for personnel of the 15th.[24]

In sharp contrast to Connor was his successor, Brigadier General Joseph C. Castner, who arrived in May of 1926. He had entered the Army as a second lieutenant of infantry in 1891 following his graduation from

Rutgers. In 1898, he was promoted to first lieutenant and served in the Santiago Campaign in Cuba. This was followed by arduous field service in the Philippine Insurrection, during the latter part of which he gained distinction as the commander of a squadron of Philippine cavalry. Just prior to the American entry into the Great War, he graduated from the Army War College. In France, Castner commanded the Ninth Infantry Brigade of the Fifth Division, participating in the St. Mihiel and Meuse-Argonne operations. He remained with the Fifth in Luxembourg until its return home in the late spring of 1919. In 1920, Castner graduated from the General Staff School at Leavenworth and a second time from the War College in 1921. The same year he was appointed a brigadier general in the Regular Army, assigned to command a brigade in the First Cavalry Division, and for a time, commanded the division itself. Headquartered at Fort Bliss, Texas, the First Cavalry was the largest mounted organization then in the U.S. Army.[25]

Castner was a bluff, no nonsense, hard-driving infantryman, temporarily — for four years — turned cavalryman, "of that irritating breed of military men who pride themselves on being simple, rough, and blunt soldiers." He immediately made a distinct impression on the 15th. Finney, in *The Old China Hands*, described Castner as "an enormous man, big of bone and big of belly. He looked like a fat but very muscular giant." He was also sloppy in his dress, often appearing in "an unpressed O.D. shirt, khaki breeches faded almost white, spiral puttees, and enlisted men's shoes." Indeed, Finney went on, "it was only by the silver stars on his shirt collar that one could tell he was a general." A stickler for physical fitness, he was "convinced that the way to turn out a well-disciplined, rugged command was by hard drill and long hikes, the latter led by himself at a pace that forced the men at the end of the column to run most of the time." *The Sentinel* once wanted to know, "how did an Officer with so much Cavalry service ever gain such undoubted efficiency in walking as demonstrated to the Infantry in China?" When on the occasion of Castner's birthday on November 18, 1927, Colonel Newell greeted him with the remark, "General, we all hope that when we become your age we can walk as far and as fast as you can," Castner wryly smiled and replied, "You shall have practice."[26]

The result of his views was that for some time during his tenure in Tientsin he endured a feud in which many of the 15th's officers — comparing Castner unfavorably to the popular, capable, much more cerebral Connor — tried to force his removal "on charges of mental incompetence." But Brigadier General Smedley — "Old Gimlet Eye" — Butler, who commanded the Marine Third Brigade in Tientsin for 18 months in the late

1920s, recognized a kindred spirit, regarding him as "a fine old type of Army officer [who] has been through all their schools and colleges but remains unspoiled." In other words, someone much like himself.[27]

In the months following Castner's appointment, *The Sentinel* was filled with details of his pain-inducing excursions. From his own vantage point, Castner was simply preparing the 15th to aid any evacuation of Peking or its relief by a forced march if needed, as had been the case in 1900 during the Boxer Uprising, which to most observers was by that time only a remote possibility. In any case, on October 28, 1927, Castner ordered the entire regiment on a 21-mile hike, which it made in five hours and 20 minutes, an average of 3.94 miles an hour. In a humorous column, "The Hike," in *The Sentinel*, "I. Emma Walker" suggested that "personally the only part of the hike that I didn't really relish was the last nineteen miles. There's nothing I like better than a good brisk walk in the early morning — a good, snappy hike of a few blocks. It adds zest to one's day. But blocks lead to miles and miles lead to townships and townships to counties and counties to provinces and Chihli Province, as the guide books tell us, is a flat alluvial plain stretching —." A poet in the outfit perhaps said it best, ending his poem with the observation that:

> If a man says that miles never tire,
> That hikes are his heart's great desire,
> That he loves on his back,
> The feel of his pack,
> He's more than a man — he's a liar.[28]

Encouraged by the regiment's showing in November, in the following month *The Sentinel* reported that in compliance with Castner's orders, there would be a run and walk by each company of not less than five miles on the morning of December 10, 1927, "and thereafter on the first Saturday morning of each month, personally conducted by all company officers under the supervision of the Regimental and Battalion commanders." Making it a regular competition, these hikes, "looked forward to by everybody and dreaded by many," were elaborately staged, with a large board with a map in place at the finish line so that each outfit's progress could be followed, with every milepost being equipped with a field telephone to transmit their progress.[29]

But Castner eventually went too far. He lay plans to march his men 100 miles in three days. On the first day, November 12, 1928, the regiment made over 30 miles, but was so exhausted the men could not go on. An Army inspector general, Colonel Louis I. Van Schaick, who had arrived for a survey of the command after a tour of inspection in the Philippines,

IV. Leadership

"The Foot Hussar." Cover of *The Sentinel*, April 8, 1927, by an unknown artist.

witnessed the day's exertions. Seeing the shape the regiment was in, he ordered Castner not to complete the march. Though outranked by the general, Van Schaick was armed with the authority of the Inspector General's Office in Washington, "and further told him he would cable Washington, if necessary, to forestall him. Castner bowed angrily to the edict and further hiking was called off for the nonce." Writing in 1960, Finney recalled that "even after thirty-two years, the memory of that hike still burns in the minds of the men who made it." In any case, because of Castner's hike and the presence of the inspector general on that occasion, Finney noted that the U.S. Army reexamined "the whole business of extended marches and modifying orders were issued." Henceforth, the most challenging march for the 15th was an annual five-mile combined hike and run which tested the men's athletic and soldierly prowess.[30]

Castner was similarly a bear regarding athletics, and he desired that all concerned cooperate to get the participation of as many men as possible not only for their own good, but also to "reflect credit on the command." He hoped to raise morale by bolstering athletics, which in his view had grown noticeably lax. He accordingly authorized the use of one half-hour in the morning training period for mass games, setting up exercises or other strictly athletic training for all individuals. In addition, status as "special duty men" was to be accorded candidates for the major team sports.[31]

The soldiers of the 15th were undoubtedly pleased to read in the February 2, 1929, issue of *The Sentinel* that General Joseph C. Castner, as a result of the decision to end the post of a general officer in China, had received orders for duty at Fort Lewis, Washington. The regiment was thereupon once more placed under the Philippine Department. Castner had no replacement in Tientsin.[32]

Some of the 15th's commanders continued their careers after China in impressive ways. In the late 1920s and into the early 1930s, General William D. Connor was commandant of the Army War College and from 1932 to 1938, commandant of West Point, where his fine mind and experiences could be put to good use. Promoted to brigadier general in July of 1924, in his later career Campbell King was assistant chief of staff in Washington, and then for four years from June 30, 1929, was commandant of the famed Infantry School at Fort Benning, Georgia, rallying around him several notable former Can-Doers. He retired as a major general on July 1, 1933. Lynch, as chief of infantry in the late 1930s, continued to have a hand in important developments of the infantry, seeking to modernize that arm as World War II approached, though for various reasons, the results remained limited.[33]

IV. Leadership

The top commanders of the regiment in China ranged from Indian fighters to those who later had the fate of the nation and even the civilized world in their hands in World War II. They carried the regiment, and by extension, assisted in projecting the U.S. Army from the era of the doughboy to that of the GI and beyond.

CHAPTER V

The Officer Corps and the Rank and File

Prayer of Company "H"
God grant that on the next boat, will arrive,
A captain, a company commander, to be our guide;
And may he be big and strong and brave,
And not be cock-eyed and puny with one foot in the grave.[1]

Especially in the mid–1920s, the 15th Infantry Regiment possessed an unusually large number of first-rate officers and enlisted men, many destined for future greatness. Indeed, it was at the levels below those of the top command that some of the most important leaders for the years ahead were to be found. The West Point class of 1915 has often been called "the class the stars fell on" because it included such future luminaries as Generals of the Army Dwight David Eisenhower and Omar Nelson Bradley. Similarly, it could be said that the 15th U.S. Infantry Regiment was "the regiment the stars fell on" because an amazingly large number of generals-to-be — running into several dozen — cycled through its ranks while it was on the China station.[2]

In various ways, these helped propel the regiment — and by extension the entire Army — from the "Old Army" mode and stance toward the eventual direction of the "New"; from the doughboy to the GI. In some respects, the 15th developed simply as a typical garrison outfit, though it was set in the complex venue that was China between World Wars I and II with its unique problems and demands.[3] At the head of any listing of these exceptionally competent and well-qualified officers would be Lieutenant Colonel George Catlett Marshall, Jr. Born in Uniontown, Pennsylvania, on December 31, 1880, he graduated from VMI in 1901. Commissioned a second lieutenant of infantry on February 2, 1902, his first tour of duty was

V. The Officer Corps and the Rank and File

in the Philippines. He returned to the United States in November, 1903. He later was an honor graduate of the Infantry and Cavalry School and the Army Staff College. Before the Great War he was an instructor at the Army School of the Line and the Staff College, and successively aide-de-camp to Major Generals Hunter Liggett in the Philippines and J. Franklin Bell in the United States. After America's declaration of war in 1917, Marshall sailed for France with the First Division as its assistant chief of staff. He was then with the Operations Section of the General Staff at General Headquarters, AEF, later becoming assistant chief of operations of the First American Army, then chief of staff of the Eighth Army Corps. In the spring of 1919, he was appointed aide-de-camp to General Pershing and served in that capacity until assigned to the 15th Infantry on July 8, 1924. Following his arrival in early September, he immediately assumed command of the regiment and the post.[4]

When the Chinese civil war poured over into the Tientsin-Peking area in 1924, Marshall found himself in charge. One of his major concerns was to establish an outpost in the American sector of Tientsin to prevent the defeated forces of warlord Wu Pei-fu from entering the foreign concessions. Acquitting himself well in this tense situation, Marshall was relieved on November 23, 1924, by the regiment's new commander, Colonel William K. Naylor, who had arrived the day before. Marshall then became the regiment's executive officer. A year later, on December 23, 1925, with the dismissal of Naylor, Marshall again assumed command. He once more faced a tense situation resulting from the occupation of Tientsin by the Kuominchun forces of warlord Feng Yu-shiang, which called for firm decisions and tactful handling. In his address on Organization Day, May 4, 1927, he recalled those stirring events: "Christmas dinner was interrupted by the attempted penetrations of our area from both the east and west, and finally, call to arms was sounded when a single squad was deployed before the advance guard of what proved to be a division of 5,000 troops crossing Race Course Road at the Dike. For a moment the resort to fire action seemed inevitable, but cool heads and good judgment avoided the fatal issue, while successfully diverting the division to the south. Critical situations continued for several days, each fraught with dangerous possibilities, but in each instance trouble was averted and our mission accomplished without provoking the fatal first shot." He continued in command until March 6, 1926, when Colonel Isaac Newell arrived to take over the regiment, Marshall once more becoming its executive officer. Marshall had therefore commanded the 15th during two of the most crucial periods of its history in China.[5]

Throughout, Marshall was favorably impressed with the 15th and his service in China in general. Soon after his arrival he wrote to Major General John L. Hines, who had become the Army chief of staff following Pershing's tenure in that office, that "I am delighted with the regiment." Writing to Brigadier General William H. Cocke, the newly appointed superintendent of VMI, he elaborated, noting that "my service in China has been delightful, interesting and several times, exciting. Politically it is the most interesting problem in the world today, and the most dangerous. From a military point of view, the service here has been more instructive than any where else in the army these days." Nor did time dim his earlier impressions as he wrote to Pershing: "I grow more and more satisfied with service in China. The officers of the regiment rate unusually high — as do their wives— and the training and school work is very interesting. They do a tremendous amount of athletics— soccer, rugby and American foot ball, basket and base ball, ice hockey, field sports, boxing and wrestling, &c." Most of the officers excelled in one or more sports and several are outstanding stars, he went on. "Just now we get a great deal of exercise and amusement out of our ice rink. They had not taken up skating for several years, so I got a big covered rink built, electric lights installed, warmed dressing rooms and a band room included, and we have fine sport. Three evenings a week we have music for the skating. Occasionally we have ice carnivals or ice athletic sports."[6]

Especially interesting to Marshall were the contacts "with the Chinese troops, some of them fraught with frightful possibilities, but so far we have been able to carry out our mission without provoking the fatal first shot. I think that the ability of every officer to speak Chinese, has saved us. This feature of training out here has grown so important since the rapid change in Chinese feeling regarding foreigners and their governments, that last winter I started classes in Chinese for the men, and we now have a list of about thirty who can talk the language sufficiently to carry on a negotiation regarding their military duties, with the Chinese officers they may happen to come in contact with." As to his own abilities, he declared, "I can speak far more of this language than I could French at the end of two years in France," though some of his contemporaries in China, including Chaplain Luther D. Miller and Captain Frank B. Hayne, remembered certain lapses in his linguistic skills. The chaplain also recalled that Marshall "loved the Chinese," and together with Stilwell, was one of the best loved of the American officers by the Chinese.[7]

It may well have been the case that Marshall was as happy in China as at any time in his long career, not least because he had commanded troops, something he had coveted and which would never be fully satisfied later in his career. Accordingly, when he left the regiment he noted that he regretted it, "for after all one's most pleasant moments are spent with the troops. There one comes to understand and know the greatest asset of all, Human Nature." His first wife, Elizabeth (Lily), née Coles, was also with him in China, to his joy. As was the case with the families of the regiment in general, the Marshalls greatly enjoyed the summer encampment at Nan Ta Ssu, where the firing range was located; Marshall noted that the "bathing here is fine, and the riding in the picturesque country nearby, is delightful." Marshall certainly enjoyed the "great deal of riding" done in the regiment, he himself owning two Mongolian ponies.[8]

Various sources, including *The Sentinel* on several occasions, give insight into Marshall's China experiences, in some cases affording new glimpses into his career and personality. The period at Nan Ta Ssu was a time when the officers and men of the regiment relaxed — when not on the firing range. In the summer of 1926, for instance, *The Sentinel* recorded that amid the "sand gnats, sand fleas and mosquitoes," high jinks were sometimes the order of the day. These were frequent at "Denny's Dump," the officers' club under the stewardship of Major Dennis E. McCunniff, which once staged a boisterous farewell banquet for two of the regiment's most popular officers: Lieutenants Philip E. Gallagher and Harvey J. Golightly, who were departing for the States. Even Colonel Marshall was drawn into the vortex of revelry, being prevailed upon to sing "Hai Ho! The Rolling River" (which flowed through Tientsin) "in a rich ginger ale tenor that was favorably commented upon by the leader of the [Chinese] Fisherman Choir who was listening to the concert from the vantage point of the beach."[9]

Other dimensions of Marshall's attitudes rather at variance with the usual views of him surfaced when he delivered the regiment's Organization Day speech on May 4, 1927. As *The Sentinel* recorded regarding the usually dour Marshall, "he spoke with deep emotion of the many interesting phases of the regiment's history," observing that a study and knowledge of the past was an important aid "in establishing and maintaining esprit de corps and morale, which in a large measure ... depend[ed] on tradition."[10]

Major General H.B. Lewis, then a captain, and a contemporary of Marshall's with the 15th, noted that his own contacts were "almost entirely social," and "because of the close tie which binds those who are together far from home, the social events were frequent and extensive." Explaining that his remarks were made "without intention of detracting from the magnificent accomplishments of later years," he desired to present them "with the idea of showing a side of a great man, not known to many." On the social scene, Lewis observed that Marshall habitually was most genial and hospitable, with a knack for organizing unique and interesting get-togethers with some form of entertainment to which he and others contributed. He often paraphrased the lyrics of then popular songs with application to the locale and persons present. He also upon occasion was a poet, as evidenced by the epilogue to *Lays of the Mei-Kuo Ying-P'an*, a collection of paraphrases of Kipling and others, written by Major Edwin Forrest Harding, the commander of the Second Battalion.[11]

Among the entertainments that Marshall was responsible for was a "Chinese Opera," entitled *At the Customs*, presented as a one-act play. The text of the playbill noted that the "Book Written [was] by Ma Tuan Fu, [the] Lyrics composed by Ma Tuan Fu, [and the] Music 'snitched' by Ma Tuan Fu," i.e., Marshall, whose name in Chinese was Ma Tuan Fu. This was presented on May 4, 1927, at the quarters of Colonel Newell, renamed for the occasion the "Newell Auditorium." In introducing the play, Marshall noted humorously that "Once upon a time an Army transport named the 'Thomas' sailed from Chinwangtao and landed at San Francisco. On board there were army officers and army wives, especially army wives. These wives were typical of any army transport, sweet, — beautiful, — precious, — but nevertheless wives under the skin."[12]

That Marshall greatly valued Army theatricals was made clear by an address that he delivered at a banquet honoring those responsible for a regimental show, *Goofus Feathers III*: "There are many capacities in which the American soldier is called upon to perform, among which, and not the least in importance, is that of theatrical performer. It is highly important, in that it contributes toward the contentment, pleasure and general welfare of the command." Praising the way that "the theatrical side of army life [had] been gradually developed in the Fifteenth," he wryly noted that "throughout rehearsals and performances there was a perfect Volstead regime," revealing a "fine spirit and a splendid self-control."[13]

Other dimensions of Marshall's personae while in China were recalled by the popular chaplain Luther D. Miller. He remembered that Marshall would sometimes sentence men of the regiment "to a month or six weeks in Church" for minor infractions of rules. Marshall played squash tennis and rode frequently, especially at the English country club, and when new officers—"Griffins"—arrived for service in the Regiment, Marshall took them on long horseback rides around Tientsin, which caused speculation around the Compound as to why he did so.[14]

In contrast to the positive views of Marshall were the observations of one knowledgeable, articulate enlisted man, Charles G. Finney: "As I recall, General Marshall (Lt. Col. in those days) had turned over the command of the 15th Infantry in Tientsin to Col. Newell by the time I joined the regiment in the spring of 1927, and, because I never saw him, he has always been to me a shadowy figure at best. I was only a raw recruit at any rate, and the gulf which separated commissioned officers and enlisted men in those days was, I believe, much wider than it is now. Marshall was mentioned from time to time among the men in the usual critical tone enlisted men employ when discussing their superiors. The men in the ranks had a certain affection for Col. Newell, which they did not evince for Lt. Col. Marshall. That, of course, was more than thirty years ago, and one's memory becomes blurry."[15]

In any case, when Marshall departed on the May 1927 boat, *The Sentinel* reviewed some of his accomplishments with warm praise. The regiment's Mounted Detachment owed its existence to him. He also conceived and developed the distinctive "Saturday Morning" review formation. The enlisted men's Chinese School was his creation. Well aware of the importance of morale, in numerous ways he sought to make life easier for all concerned. His efforts included the construction of brick walks at Nan Ta Ssu and the refurbishing of the bare and forbidding officers' assembly room at headquarters into the luxuriously furnished Blue Room. The staging of amateur-night entertainments was another of his innovations, and "those who have worked with him in any capacity have found him ever ready to listen to their own constructive ideas and generally a couple of jumps ahead of them in his conception of their pet project." Indeed, as *The Sentinel* explained at the time of Marshall's departure, he had been closely involved "in every phase of the life of the American Army Garrison. He has been not only of us and for us, but with us," and it had been a pleasure to serve with a man of his high professional attainments.[16]

More significantly, Marshall viewed firsthand the strengths and weaknesses of professional training in the U.S. Army. Thus the training agenda of the 15th had some consequences for the U.S. Army's future development well before World War II. In a letter to General Pershing he once confided that "with only five months of experience [in China] to judge from, I am more and more firmly of the opinion I held in the War Department, that our equipment, administrative procedure and training requirements are all too complicated for anything but a purely professional army. I find the officers are highly developed in the technical handling or functioning of weapons, in target practice, in bayonet combat and in the special and intricate details of paper work or administration generally, *but* that when it comes to simple tactical problems, the actual details of troop leading, they all fall far below the standards they set in other matters." In a few years, Marshall, as assistant commandant at the Infantry School at Fort Benning in the early 1930s, would be a key figure in American infantry reform. The

China station therefore contributed to that important revolution in U.S. infantry training.[17]

In another facet of Marshall's later career, he may well have anticipated some aspects of his later Marshall Plan if only in embryo. In a speech that he delivered on Organization Day on May 4, 1927, he referred to the marble gateway, presented to the regiment by the Chinese in 1925, that stood near where he spoke (and which now stands at Fort Benning), asserting that it represented "something quite unique in the eyes of this World, — soldiers on foreign soil receiving the heartfelt thanks of the inhabitants for protection against the ravages of the warfare waged by their own people." Indeed, "that little monument there testifies to the character of the duty performed by the 15th Infantry in China. It should inspire an apology from those of our citizens who in condemning war, characterize the Regular Army as a brutal and ruthless instrument of destruction." On the contrary, he went on, history proved it to be quite the opposite, and the U.S. Army had often appeared as "an instrument of peace, for the security of life and property and for the development of good citizenship." When American forces later played a major role in restoring peace following World War II, the Marshall Plan was implemented. Marshall's remarks delivered to the 15th in May of 1927 hint at his views as to how armed force could in fact have a positive dimension, on occasion at least, helping to rid the world of tyranny and preparing the soil for a resurrection of something positive and beneficial.[18]

In regard to future importance, Major Joseph Warren Stilwell was second in significance to Marshall among those who served in the 15th. He arrived in Tientsin in September of 1926, from the General Staff School at Fort Leavenworth, Kansas. His first duty was to replace Major Dennis E. McCunniff as commander of the Provisional Battalion consisting of Headquarters and Service Companies.[19]

Stilwell had already established himself in the Army before arriving in Tientsin. A graduate of West Point in 1904, his first service was in the Philippines with the 12th Infantry. In 1906, he was recalled to West Point as instructor of modern languages, remaining there until 1911, when he once more sailed for the Philippines. From the Philippines the Stilwells toured Japan for an extended period, Stilwell beginning the study of the difficult language. Sending his wife home to await their first child, Stilwell in 1911 visited China on the eve of its revolution, which came on February 12, 1912, when the empress regent abdicated. In January 1912, Stilwell served on garrison duty at the Presidio of Monterey in California. His first son, Joseph Warren, Jr., was born in Syracuse, New York, in March; a daughter followed in June of 1914. Meanwhile, in August 1913, West Point summoned him as instructor in the department of English and history. When America entered the Great War, Stilwell, in August 1917, became brigade adjutant of the Eightieth Division at Camp Lee, Virginia. In December of that year he went to France as a staff officer at Headquarters, AEF, then was made chief intelligence officer for IV Corps, serving with it to the end of the war and going with it on occupation duty in Germany following the armistice. Returning home in July 1919, on August 6 of that year Stilwell was appointed the Army's first language officer for China. Studying first at the University of California at Berkeley, Stilwell and his family sailed for China on August 5, 1920, returning to the United States in 1923 when his language studies were completed.

Stilwell's impact on the 15th was manifested at several levels. He served as chairman of the outfit's athletic committee and became infamous for the rigor of his weight reduction programs, such as his "advanced school of 'Esthetic Dancing,'" conducted for men and women alike.[20]

Stilwell, well known throughout his military career for his propensities to travel, took full advantage of the encouragement of the 15th's high command in this regard. Going beyond the usual provisions for leave, he often wangled periods of detached service of various lengths for trips to Manchuria, Korea, Japan and throughout China. Regarding the latter, it was commonly recognized in the regiment that Stilwell spoke the vernacular fluently and was "extremely well versed in Chinese affairs." For the entertainment of the 15th on one occasion, Stilwell discussed Japan ostensibly as seen through the eyes of a young son, Benny Watson Stilwell, II — a "Private" of Company L, 15th Infantry by adoption — born in Tientsin on July 11, 1927. In three issues, *The Sentinel* published Benny's lengthy, humorous "unexpurgated diary," being an account of the one year old's first trip to Japan with his parents.[21]

Indeed, it was Stilwell's knowledge of China and its language that enabled him to make his most important contributions to the regiment and the U.S. Army in general. Brigadier General Frederick M. Harris, who as a lieutenant served in China with Stilwell in the 15th, later recalled that when Chiang's forces were pushing north in the great Northern Expedition, which engulfed Tientsin and the 15th, Stilwell, then chief of staff of the U.S. Army Forces in North China "and who probably knew more about what was in the making than anyone else in North China" was "the driving force" behind the preparations of the Americans in meeting the onslaught coming up from the south. Harris noted that "he spoke fluent Chinese, and when he donned his Chinese clothing and applied a judicious amount of yellow makeup, he easily passed for a native. At least, he was never caught at it." Thus disguised, and in response to orders to carry out intensive patrolling to the south for "the purpose of contacting advance elements of Chiang's forces and determining their intentions," Stilwell "would disappear for weeks at a time and he always came back with his head and plenty of useful information in it."[22]

The high command was not the only beneficiary of Stilwell's knowledge and insights into contemporary Chinese developments. In November 1927, he began publishing a months-long series of articles in *The Sentinel*, whose readers were soon obtaining on almost a weekly basis detailed reports of the pattern emerging in China in the last throes of the long-lasting warlord conflicts and the coming of some semblance of a unity under Chiang Kai-shek. *The Sentinel*'s editor explained that "to most of us the political and military situation in China is little better than a hopeless puzzle," and "to those back in the States it is even more hopeless." But "fortunately for us, Major Stilwell does know or knows how to find out. For years he has kept abreast of the situation in China. He knows many of the leaders personally, and he has spent weeks in the field with some of the contending armies. There are few indeed of the special correspondents for the great news services that have a better grounding in the Chinese situation than Major Stilwell."[23]

In January of 1928, Stilwell began a parallel series on "Who's Who in the Chinese Situation," with an article on Chang Tso-lin, the articles gaining a considerable readership throughout the Army when many of them were subsequently reprinted in the prestigious *Infantry Journal*. Some of the most important were on such characters as the "Christian General" Feng Yu-shiang; Stilwell emphasized that Feng was untrustworthy, which was "a pity, for he has many excellent qualities, never allows his troops to abuse the people, is a real fighter, and tries to develop whatever section of the country he controls." As to the role of Christianity in Feng's forces — which Stilwell seems to have exaggerated — he stated that "none of his men were allowed to drink or smoke, loose conduct of any kind was frowned upon, every man carried a bible in his pocket, and no one could become a non-commissioned officer without passing an examination on the scriptures." Stilwell was impressed that Feng set up workshops for the troops to manufacture their own shoes, clothing, caps, soap, towels, buttons and leather equipment. Stilwell cynically noted that Americans, especially the "idealists and sentimentalists" were far too willing to see a new era emerging in China with Chiang's proclamation of a Chinese Republic. Ignorant of the "history of this land and the character of its people," they fondly imagined that "by calling black white, the color would change." But hopefully, he went on, the eyes of Americans would be opened to the facts that "China is a child playing with a razor, and unless some one takes it away from her quickly, the results will be simply appalling." There was not on the scene "the traditional man of destiny, who is supposedly always produced by national emergency." The Chinese had only a mere "paper republic," but they were aware of it, "for you cannot fool the Chinese much — they are as well aware as we of the universal corruption and venality of their leaders, and the general rottenness of the republican regime." They would hail "with joy the establishment of any system of government that would insure law and order, and would cheerfully barter all the trappings, ideals, slogans and maxims of democracy for a chance to earn a living in peace."[24]

Stilwell's later attitudes regarding China, often characterized by cynicism and disdain—"Vinegar Joe" in embryo—surfaced in his article on Chiang Kai-shek, in which he called him the "so-called generalissimo of the nationalists," who was being "advertised as a combination George Washington, Napoleon Bonaparte, and Julius Caesar." Yet, despite failures, "the man must be admired for his determination and energy in the face of the many disadvantages under which he is laboring, and if he wins out it will be largely on account of the resources he can find within himself. In such a case, the devil must be given his due and we shall be forced to the conclusion that China may still be able to produce men of sufficient ability to solve her problems and put her house in order." He saw that with the apparent victory of the Chinese Nationalists that "now the opportunity is here for the establishment of a real government of all China, if only the several leaders could sink their individual ambitions and work together for the common good." But unfortunately, "the mere fact of victory is not going to change the nature of the typical Chinese Militarist, and the substitution of the Nationalist flag and the arm-band for the five color flag and the Fengtien colors is not going to make patriots out of bandits." Still, Stilwell did not mourn those defeated by Chiang's forces: "Let them rest in peace; their successors can hardly be worse and may be better."[25]

By the summer of 1928 with China more or less pacified under the Nationalists, the restless Stilwell began to look elsewhere for subjects of interest, and his articles were lacking in a sense of immediacy. The editor rather regretted this, because the feature was "one of the most widely read in the magazine and always furnishes interesting reading for our subscribers." Later articles would only be printed if the situation in China seemed to warrant them. Subsequently, only occasionally before Stilwell's departure for the United States in April 1929 did he inform *Sentinel* readers of his continued doubts regarding Chinese affairs. Chiang's Kuomintang "is now on trial," he declared, and things generally were on hold; the jury still out. With the coming of spring and a new campaigning season, China might revert to its usual adventures in warlordism.[26]

In any event, Stilwell would not be around to see developments in China at first hand until later, from June 1935 to May 1939, when he was stationed at Peiping as the American military attaché. Meanwhile, he and his family returned to the United States in April of 1929. There in July, Stilwell took up his post as head of the Tactical Section of the Infantry School at Fort Benning. Serving under Lieutenant Colonel George C. Marshall, the school's assistant commandant, Stilwell's long experience in education and training stood him in good stead as he played his role in the emerging Benning Revolution in educational methods being developed under Marshall's leadership. Stilwell had also been promoted while with the 15th, *The Sentinel* being pleased to record on the occasion the elevation of "one of the most popular officers of the command" to lieutenant colonel. In addition, he was acknowledged as the unofficial "dean" of the regiment's Chinese Language College, and perhaps not inconsequently, he carried with him "the handball championship of the Orient."[27]

As Marshall had once pointed out regarding the 15th, "this particular regiment has the most remarkably efficient personnel I have ever seen gathered in one group. The officers have all been selected for the detail and the ranks are filled with fine old soldiers."[28]

Among the "remarkably efficient personnel" Marshall alluded to and a member of the "Damned China Crowd" in good standing was Captain — later Colonel — David D. Barrett, an old China hand of considerable attainments. He was born in Central City, Colorado, in 1892. A graduate of the University of Colorado in 1915, he taught high school English in Silverton, Colorado, for two years. He entered the United States Army as a second lieutenant of infantry in 1917, though he served in Utah rather than overseas in the years of the Great War. Following the end of hostilities, he elected to remain in the Regular Army, becoming "a member of the select minority of non–West Point graduates who served on active duty in the officer corps between the two world wars." His first duty after the war was four years as a junior infantry officer in the Philippines. The year 1924 found Barrett in Peking, assigned to the American legation as an assistant military attaché for language study. This set him apart from career-minded officers who considered attaché and language study duties as superfluous to true soldierly military experience, though two important exceptions who played a role in Barrett's later career, Marshall and Stilwell, thought otherwise. Barrett also now encountered the pure crystalline Pekingese language, the study of which he regarded "as a joy," and the Chinese people and their history and culture. He developed formidable language skills, savoring each nuance and inflection of the language's complex forms and tones, and acquired an affinity with China that never left him. Though there were attributes of the Chinese that Barrett did not admire, such as their insatiable curiosity and pervasive nosiness, he once wrote that "I frankly admit to being a pushover for the Chinese people. In general I find them the smartest (by far), the most charming, in many ways the most civilized, and for sure the best looking people in the world." Remaining at his studies until 1928, while in China Barrett also encountered Marshall and Stilwell, and developed contacts with them that were renewed when Barrett attended the advanced course at the Infantry School, Fort Benning, Georgia, in 1928. Following this course, Barrett was assistant professor of military science and tactics at the College of the City of New York, serving the ROTC program.[29]

Following his three-year tour of duty in the United States, Barrett was assigned to the 15th, arriving in October 1931 as regimental S-2 — intelligence staff officer. He also continued his language studies and ran the 15th's Chinese language program. He used *The Sentinel* as an avenue for his instruction, in February 1933 launching in its pages a systematic course, "Writing Chinese," which sought to assist the soldiers in attaining a "workable goal," the mastering of 1,000 Chinese characters. Indeed, Barrett propelled regimental Chinese studies to new heights during his tenure.[30]

When Barrett had initially begun his language studies his first choice had been Japanese, but because there were no vacancies he had to opt for Chinese, a choice thrust upon him which he never regretted. (Stilwell had had a similar experience.) Nonetheless, he visited Japan on several occasions and was impressed, as were many of his contemporaries, with the beauty of Japan, for example the breathtaking Inland Sea, though he never developed any pro–Japanese sentiment. Despite Japan's beauty and cleanliness, as he expressed it following one of his Japanese trips from Tientsin, he was thrilled to return "to the City of the Heavenly Ford and the Can Do Regiment." While "China may not be very pretty, and is certainly dirty," it was the home that he loved and was comfortable in.[31]

Barrett left Tientsin in 1934, and two years later was the assistant military attaché in Peiping serving under Stilwell. As war came in the Far East, for a time he was in the temporary Chinese capital at Hankow; early in 1939, he migrated to Chungking where Chiang Kai-shek established his wartime government. In 1944, on the orders of the U.S. Army high command, Barrett was in Yenan establishing contacts with the Chinese Communists, an event with deleterious consequences for his career. Following the fall of mainland China to the Communists in 1949, he proceeded to Taiwan still functioning as military attaché accredited to the Republic of China. There he remained until his retirement from the Army two years later. During the war years, Barrett served with men he had known at Tientsin, especially Stilwell and General Albert Coady Wedemeyer. He was also involved in Marshall's postwar diplomatic trip to China in 1945 during which Marshall sought — unsuccessfully — to end China's civil war; it ended in 1949 with the victory of the Chinese Communists. Following his retirement, Barrett was embroiled in the American domestic political scene and the searing debates of the McCarthy era, especially those concerned with the dubious subject of America's "loss of China" to the Communists after the war. He died in 1977 at age 84.[32]

Another outstanding officer to serve in the 15th was Major Edwin Forrest Harding. Joining the regiment on September 30, 1923, Harding commanded the Second Battalion for most of his career in China, though he also was interim commander of the regiment from July 24 to September 8, 1924. In January 1927, he relinquished command of the Second Battalion to Stilwell, assuming command of the Provisional Battalion, composed of the Service and Headquarters Companies. He remained there until being relieved on May 1, 1927, to return to the States. During the latter period, Harding was also post recreation officer on the staff of the commanding general, American Forces in China.

Within and beyond the garrison, in addition to his position as commander of the Second Battalion, Harding was known as an entertainer. For example, he appeared in a key role in a local production of *The Best People*, a play produced by a cast composed almost exclusively of officers and wives of the AFC.[33]

In China, Harding was perhaps best remembered, however, as the "Poet Laureate of the AFC." *The Sentinel* was a common venue for his Kiplingesque offerings, such as his poem "The Foot Hussars," dedicated to the 15th's mounted detachment. Harding was often called upon to recite it on regimental festive occasions. The first verse sets the mood and tone:

> . . . .
> I used to belong to the doughboys once,
> Hiked in the mud with full pack once,
> Learned how to shoot with a rifle once,
> But now I'm a Foot Hussar.[34]

Equally acclaimed was the poem "Tuttulius at the Dike," which recounted in poetic detail the exploits of Captain William B. "Wild Bill" Tuttle on Christmas Day, 1925, when the regiment narrowly avoided an armed clash with the Kuominchun, the army of Feng Yu-shiang then menacingly deployed before Tientsin. Tuttle, like most of the 15th's officers at the time, could converse in Chinese. His ability figured in the ensuing events when, reasoning with Feng's leaders in their native tongue, he persuaded them to withdraw:

> . . . .
> 'Twas then that Bill Tuttulius
> Made the play that won the war
> For on the Sullen Kuominchun
> He loosed his Chungua hus [hua]-erh.
> His tones were well nigh perfect
> and filled them with chagrin:
> The Army in awed silence stood
> While from Bill's lips poured forth a flood
> Of purest Mandarin.

In the upshot, Tuttle returned to the compound a hero, "To hear his praises sung / For oft we tell how his Chinese / Turned back the host of Feng."[35]

Tuttle, who had gained fame for his use of the Chinese language as a weapon of war, was by all accounts one of the most popular officers ever to serve in the 15th. A Texas cowboy — the "pride of Eagle Pass" — his personality was most congenial to many of the officer corps as well as the rank and file. One commentator from the regiment's Service Company, which Tuttle commanded, observed that regarding their chief, "sufficient it is to say that our Old Man didn't get his name ... for nothing — and the wilder they come the better we like 'em. If we'd wanted a spiritual mentor we'd have joined the Y.M.C.A.; if we had desired a slave driver we would have tried a hitch in the Foreign Legion. As it happens we hit the Service Company," and "if [our commander] suits us why the Hell should we worry as to what the rest of the world thinks about it?"

Certainly, Tuttle believed in "originality, whether it happens to be the best method for making you regret your indiscretions or making the arrangements for a damp party," all of which added "much to the gayety of life for those under his charge." A poem written by an anonymous member of the Company, entitled "Wild-Eyed Dementia," explained:

> . . . .
> We're wild, we're wild, I'll say we're wild!
> We're the wildest bunch in town,
> From Wild Bill at the blinkin' Helm
> And the Top Kick straight on down.
> We don't know the feel of a bit or curb,
> We're muddy and full of fleas,
> We don't give a damn for beast or man
> And we do as we damned well please![36]

Tuttle was best known for activities involving horses. When the regiment staged its first horse show in the autumn of 1925 — which was a marked success—"Wild Bill," a favorite of the spectators because of his "'Wild West,' daring style of riding," carried off individual honors.[37]

The Texas captain was especially prominent in polo circles. In 1925, when the city of Tientsin won the Forbes Inter-Port Polo Trophy for first time since 1914, Captain Tuttle and another of the 15th's stalwart polo players, Major Dennis E. McCunniff, were the heroes.[38]

In the following year, however, the Shanghai American polo team soundly trounced the Tientsin American Army polo team consisting of second lieutenants Edgar H. Snodgrass and James R. Pierce, First Lieutenant Donald W. Brann and Captain Tuttle. The Shanghai contingent, who "surpassed all expectations in the speed and endurance of their mounts and the excellence of their play," won handily, providing Harding with another subject for a poem, "The Four Horsemen." Presented from the vantage point of Tientsin Army wives, this concluded:

> . . . .
> The gong has sounded, the game is done
> With Shanghai leading by nine to one
> But it's no disgrace to suffer eclipse
> By the Horsemen of the Apocalypse
> We're proud of our husbands just the same
> "Honey, you played a wonderful game."[39]

The Tuttles also planned and staged paper hunts featured as major social events involving the regiment's "horsey set," and which perhaps foreshadowed a day "when standard uniform and equipment for drill will be pink coats and riding crops." One such event, at which both the band and the orchestra performed, also featured a verse composition contest in which Colonel Marshall's committee, "using modern quantity production methods," triumphed over Major Harding's.[40]

Another sterling performer who was closely engaged in the unsettled times in the Chinese ongoing civil war in 1924 was Captain Henry Harold Dabney, promoted to major in September of the following year. When in command of Company K, on duty at Tangshan, Colonel Naylor warmly commended Dabney and his company for "the admirable way in which you handled the recent strained situation at and in the vicinity of Tangshan. A situation that was fraught with the greatest possibilities of complications was handled by you with honor, with good judgment, and with efficiency and yet at the same time with an avoidance of friction." When Dabney was promoted to major he had to give up command of his company, which he had headed for two years, and took charge of the Provisional Battalion. This was a reward for the excellent record Company K had turned in under his leadership in various areas, especially in sports. He himself was a major player on the 15th's polo team. Unfortunately, in the morning of January 4, 1926, Dabney died of pneumonia.[41]

In the summer of 1927, a new rifle range and camp near the port city of Chinwangtao was named Camp Dabney in the late major's honor. This name persisted until it was renamed Camp Burrowes in memory of First Lieutenant Robert M. Burrowes, who died in Tientsin on February 14, 1928, also of pneumonia.[42]

The almost unending procession of young officers destined for greater things continued for as long as the 15th was in China. By the end of the 1920s, it was clear that service in China was greatly preferred over other overseas assignments. The prestigious *Army and Navy Journal* recorded that as of May 1, 1929, of the listing of 349 infantry officers wanting to serve overseas, 163 preferred China while 129 wanted to be ordered to the Philippines. Only 14 chose Hawaii and 19 Panama.[43]

The Sentinel routinely recorded the comings and goings of many of these of later fame, providing information sometimes difficult to obtain elsewhere. The issue of February 8, 1930, for example, noted the arrival in Tientsin of First Lieutenant Albert Coady Wedemeyer and his wife and two sons from Washington, D.C., where the lieutenant had been aide-de-camp to Brigadier General H.O. Williams. Tall and striking, even aristocratic in demeanor and appearance, his reputation as an up and coming soldier had preceded him to China, and he soon made an impression on the regiment for his military bearing and his skill on the rifle range. It was also rumored that he was a baseball pitcher, which would certainly have been a point in his favor in the sports-minded 15th. Indeed, the rumors were true: Wedemeyer himself noted that as a young man "I had a really passionate interest in baseball and pitched for the Army team." As to China, he later recalled that his duty in Tientsin "was particularly educational," specifically with reference to language study: "We sweated for six days each week until we could pass a satisfactory test." All in all, his time in China and the Philippines gave him "insight into the ferment that was just about to shake the Orient," and helped prepare him for his own substantial, often highly controversial involvement in World War II and beyond.[44]

Much less imposing in physical appearance was Major Walton Harris Walker who arrived in October of 1930 from Fort Monroe, Virginia, where he was instructor of artillery at the Coast Artillery School. Assuming command of the Second Battalion, he served competently and the battalion did well under his leadership. Born in Texas, he graduated from West Point in 1907. During the Great War he rose to the rank of lieutenant colonel of infantry and attended the usual service schools in the 1920s. Well beyond World War II, Walton was killed in December 1950 in an accident during the Korean War, where he commanded the United Nations forces.[45]

Walker's successor in Korea was to be another 15th alumnus, General — then Captain — Matthew Bunker Ridgway who remained less than a year with the regiment in command of Headquarters Company. He arrived in July 1925 and departed in May 1926.[46]

Yet another Can-Doer of later high achievement was Captain Richard Karens Sutherland, who commanded a unit of the 15th from 1937 to early 1938. Then transferred to Manila, he would later emerge as General Douglas MacArthur's highly controversial wartime chief of staff, attaining the rank of lieutenant general.[47]

Many of the officers in the 15th were aware of the good qualities of the enlisted men assigned to Tientsin. Writing to Brigadier General William H. Cocke, the superintendent at VMI, Marshall noted that "frequently we find privates who have been regimental sergeants major, and first sergeants who were captains and even major during the war." These facts led to some blurring of lines between the officers and enlisted men within the regiment. Having served as officers in the Great War, many had accepted enlisted status with the coming of peace, some maintaining ranks in the Army's Organized Reserve Corps (ORC). Several of these in the 15th spent their annual two weeks' service requirement as officers in the regiment, reverting to their enlisted rates thereafter. For example, in the spring of 1923, Corporal David C. Robertson, of Company H, was ordered to the regiment for 15 days as a first lieutenant. Another was Major Norman Braxton Howes, who normally served as first sergeant of Company E. "This bucko," *The Sentinel* reported, surely would "make a crack-a-jack wartime officer. He was with the 2nd Division overseas during the Big War, and held commissions from 2nd Looie to Major. Incidentally, he was recommended three times for the D.S.C."[48]

Some general observations, also applicable to the men of the 15th, were made by one regular soldier in the 1930s. For the most part, he noted, "the regular army enlisted man of the pre–World War II days was reliable, cheerful, willing, respectful, physically tough, proud of his outfit, and above all, patriotic. If there were horseplay and mischief at times, it was because he was young and led an active life. He considered his profession an honorable one and service to his country serious business."[49]

Can-Doers sometimes recognized the quality and attainments of their peers. One soldier writing in *The Sentinel* on the occasion of the departure

V. The Officer Corps and the Rank and File 93

of many of his buddies to the States was moved to explain: "We shall not catalogue either your names or your virtues — you are too well known to us to require any such refurbishing of past accomplishments. In truth, we dwell but fleetingly at this time on your past deeds, good or bad. Sufficient it is to know that all of you were good sports, good soldiers and good comrades. We know you to be, not, perhaps, what would constitute a Methodist Minister's idea of a good Christian, but nevertheless men upon whom we would sooner depend in our hour of trial than upon all the Saints in the calendar." Indeed, "in our particular corner of the Army, the Service Company, we have found you worthy of being judged, not by [any] ethereal and bloodless standards, but by the fact that you were men who would divvy your last dollar and your last cigarette with a buddy, men who were faithful to your comrades and to your organization, and, above all, men with nerve enough to look the rest of the world in the eye and tell it, individually and collectively, to 'Go to Hell!'"[50]

In his memoirs, Charles Finney has asserted that "although the old China hands were anything but Boy Scouts, I have thought it best not to stress at all their venery. If I set my mind to it, I could do it, of course. I could shovel out filth and profanity by the truckload. But everybody nowadays knows how babies are made and has a fair knowledge — even though not necessarily a working knowledge — of the Left Bank mechanics of the act of love." He did not wish to "clutter up our pages with dirty memories. Let us, instead, as does the fastidious sun dial, only mark the shining hours." But of course the serious student must give some space to the "dirty memories," with the full knowledge that, as Kipling has observed, troops were not the most exemplary of men and rarely turn into "plaster saints." Some aspects of the negative side are discussed elsewhere in this study.[51]

The regiment's high command often gave recognition to the rank and file for their various accomplishments. With little possibility of awarding medals, headquarters had recourse to issuing letters of commendation to men who served conspicuously, when the regiment confronted the warlord forces, for instance. The occasion of the departure of men for home provided other opportunities for commanding officers formally and publicly to praise selected soldiers for meritorious service and conduct. In addition, *The Sentinel* was filled with accounts of exceptional enlisted men of the regiment in its long-running feature, "Outstanding Men of the Regiment."[52]

Similarly, when certain soldiers made their way back to the regiment, sometimes with difficulty, *The Sentinel* proudly recorded the circumstances. In an article, "An Old Timer Returns," it detailed the odyssey of Raymond

R. Reeves, who had served with the Service Company from 1924 to 1927. Returning to the States to join the Seventh Infantry at Vancouver Barracks, he felt the call to return to China. He purchased his discharge and then started the long journey at his own expense back to China. He appeared at the adjutant's office stating that he wanted to enlist in the 15th. The adjutant found that the "recruit" was a likely candidate indeed. He was promptly enrolled, being first attached to Company L before joining his old outfit the Service Company. When asked why he came back to the regiment, he simply gave "the best reason in the world, he likes the regiment, enjoys service in China, and is back among friends." *The Sentinel* observed that "this attitude toward service with the regiment, will always be an asset to the organization."[53]

A representative listing of other outstanding men of the 15th would include those of varying attainments. One of the most impressive was Charles Grandison Finney. Born in Sedalia, Missouri, in 1905, he spent a year at the University of Arizona before joining the U.S. Army, applying for duty with the 15th Infantry in Tientsin. There as a private first class he served in Company E, where he "toted an automatic rifle," and was also a member of a regimental rifle team. Departing China in October 1929 after his Army service, in 1930, he joined the staff of the *Arizona Daily Star* in Tucson, remaining there until the mid–1960s. He died in 1984. He was the author of the widely read — and often-quoted — memoir of his China service: *The Old China Hands*. In 1935, he published his first work in the fantasy fiction field: the short novel, *The Circus of Dr. Lao*. This was followed by another short novel, *The Unholy City* (1937); another work, *Past the End of the Pavement* (1939); a collection of short stories, *The Ghosts of Manacle* (1964); and a final novella in 1968, *The Magician Out of Manchuria*, which clearly reveals his China experiences. Among other themes, in this story Finney bitterly deplored those in China responsible for the fact that "a way of life is passing, and all that once was mysterious, poetic and beautiful is being transformed — at the point of the bayonet — into crass materialism." This was all done "according to the restrictive precepts of a foreign polemicist-agitator [Marx], a man we never knew." Especially singled out were those Communist officials responsible for the "Great Leap Forward," which had bound the nation in chains. Perhaps only magicians could save China from its horrific condition. His short stories, non-fiction and fiction, appeared in *The New Yorker*, *Harper's*, *Paris Review*, and *Fantasy and Science*.[54]

Various other men became prominent in the regiment as correspondents or staffers on *The Sentinel*. One was Private Otto Beinke, of Company K. Arriving in China in 1924, he made an impression in the paper with several poems and a five-part diary delineating the trip to China from the United States on a troop transport, following up with a series of letters describing the life of a soldier in Tientsin. But the paper published several items noting that Beinke was suffering either from tonsillitis or "boozitis," and being absent and in the hands of the medical authorities, informed his buddies that the surgeon was undecided "whether to operate or pour him back in the bottle. He [was] on a liquid diet: Oxy-GIN, Hydro-GIN, Nitro-GIN, and Gordon's Dry GIN." Though the record is not clear, he may well have been sent home as an alcoholic, apparently departing China ahead of schedule in July 1925. In any case, his various writings provide graphic insight into life and service in the 15th Infantry in the mid–1920s.[55]

Another colorful character about the compound was Corporal John Henry "Major" Bowles, the scribe of Company E and also author of sports articles and other material for *The Sentinel*. Called "Major" after the radio personality in the States, he was also a quartermaster lieutenant in the Organized Reserve Corps. He had earlier served in the 15th from 1913 to 1916, was with Pershing in Mexico in 1916, and was a veteran of the Great War. Leaving China, he was attached to the Quartermaster Detachment — which he styled the "Jewish Infantry" and which had the advantage of riding in trucks rather than the "Hob Nailed Express" and toting a rifle — at Fort Bragg, North Carolina. There, building on the journalism experience he gained on the staff of *The Sentinel*, he launched a base newspaper, *The Quartermaster Gadget*.[56]

Private First Class John T. Fox of the Service Company also contributed numerous insightful, well-written features for the paper, including "A Trip to Peking," described by the editor as "not only ... a thrilling account of the sightseeing in the ex-Capital but an excellent description of China and its people." Other articles from his pen were "The Lure of the East," "Eating in the Orient," "The Money God," "The Company Pest," and "In Praise of the Native Mount."[57]

At an interval in history between the defenders of the Boxer protocol and those encountering insurgent Japanese, whatever else the 15th accomplished, it remains one of the most impressive of the U.S. Army's "nurseries of generals" and other officers and men of singular attainment.

CHAPTER VI

The Sentinel

> The *Sentinel* covers quite a field,
> Anything that you may choose
> Look in every week's edition
> For the best and latest news.[1]

Barbara Tuchman, in her solid study *Stilwell and the American Experience in China, 1911–45*, noted that *The Sentinel* "could have appeared without change at any regimental post in America."[2] To a far greater degree than she has suggested, however, the paper significantly reflected its time and locale and the conditions under which it was published. What the publication did in fact was to monitor the 15th's existence, reflecting its way of life, describing its service environment, and documenting the hopes, fears, anxieties and concerns of the little "Army family," stationed half a world away from its homeland, that it served. Editors at various times indicated the paper's purposes. One of these, First Lieutenant Howard W. Lehr, who took over the paper in the spring of 1925, asserted that its aims were "to serve the needs of the United States Army Forces in China, by fostering and promoting educational and recreational activities and athletics within the regiment and among the civic and educational bodies in North China, as well as the United States Marines stationed at Peking, China." A later editor, Major Frank U. McCoskrie, drawing from his "previous rich experience in the newspaper game," made *The Sentinel* a soldier's paper "as such a paper ought to be. It told the soldier things about the China which surrounded him, but it also told him things about himself, [and] about the buddies around him."[3]

By the early 1920s, the paper appeared each Friday — later on Saturday — published by the Tientsin Press, publishers of *The Peking and Tientsin Times*, a local English-language Chinese newspaper. Averaging about 28 pages, the price of a single copy was five cents U.S. currency; per month the cost was 20 cents; a one-year subscription cost $2. Its circulation was about 1,450 copies a week, 500 of which were mailed to the States, "there to act very much as a letter to home folks and others interested in any of us in far away 'heathen' China."[4]

Unlike many troop newspapers of the U.S. Army, such as the famous *Stars and Stripes*, *The Sentinel* was largely in the hands of officers. In early 1921, the editor in chief was Captain R.D. Bell, who headed up a staff of six officers and only three enlisted men. In addition, there were reporters, all enlisted men, for companies A through M — there was no J Company in the regiment — and also one for Headquarters Company, the Machine Gun Company, the Supply Company, Quartermaster Department, the Medical Company and the Signal Corps. The paper's official photographer for a number of years was a local Chinese, Ta Fang, replaced in 1926 by Chen Hua. By the spring of 1928, the paper boasted a regular photographic supplement.[5]

The Sentinel also sometimes published annual issues complete with detailed information about the regiment and illustrated with extensive photography. The annuals for 1924 and 1925 were especially noteworthy. Later, the paper compiled collections of photos that had appeared in its regular photographic section. Entitled *The Sentinel, Snapshots of China*, Nos. 1 and 2, these were promoted as attractive gifts to send home.[6]

Among other innovations of *The Sentinel* was a daily publication, *The Radionews*, which was posted around the compound. Appearing first in early 1929, it was made possible by the radio operators of Headquarters Company who obtained news by wireless from Cavite in the Philippines and San Francisco. *The Sentinel* also eventually undertook job printing and engraving.[7]

The paper, measuring about nine by 12 inches, resembled a magazine, but its makeup and editing were like a newspaper and the pages were regular newsprint. It had semi-slick stapled-on covers, many of which featured photographs but often employed cartoons or drawings. In the late 1920s, the covers often featured the artistic efforts of Private First Class L.M. Healy of Company L. Admitting that he had never formally studied art, and that his talent was on the whole, "natural," his covers "aroused [much] wide and favorable comment, due to their remarkably real and pleasing portrayal of [the] Chinese atmosphere." Stewart G. Davis of Headquarters Company also did occasional artistic covers, though his were not up to the level of Healy's.[8]

The origins and early days of *The Sentinel* are obscure. An old timer, Staff Sergeant James H. Beardsley, informed the paper's readers that in 1902, when the regiment was stationed at Monterey, California, and before it departed for service in the Philippines, it published a regimental paper called *The Army News*. According to Beardsley (then a private with Company E), having served as a printer in civil life, he was called upon to find suitable men and equipment and start a regimental paper. From this beginning, the paper grew to be an eight-page, five-column news sheet. The weekly persisted for several years in Monterey. Earlier, at Fort Omaha and Fort Leavenworth, another publication existed, though under what name is not clear. When the regiment was stationed at Fort Meade in North Dakota, however, Beardsley recalled that a paper appeared under the name *The Sentinel*. In any event, by 1935 the paper was proclaiming from its masthead that it was the "Oldest Army Organizational Periodical in the Service," having been published continuously in China from 1919 to that date.[9]

Drawing revenues from subscriptions as well as advertising, the paper was sufficiently profitable to underwrite free showing of movies in the compound's Recreation Hall on Sunday nights. The paper also paid for magazines and periodicals for the post library and the hospital, provided trophies and awards for competitions at the firing range, and for some years, constructed and maintained an ice skating rink for regimental personnel as well as civilians in the community.[10]

Central to the paper's efforts were the weekly columns from reporters representing the individual companies and detachments. The second platoon of Company L once advertised for a scribe who was "able to 'Spiel a wicked line' and [knew] how to handle slander." Editors, often disappointed in both the quality and quantity (not to mention the absence of material) from the rank and file, frequently goaded reporters, asking for improvement in their material. Agreeing that "literary ability isn't necessary," they did ask "that the notes have at least some connection with the men in the company and that they don't savour too strongly of casualties incurred on the field of amour." The latter was a consideration because *The Sentinel* was often sent home and, accordingly, there should be no alluring, compromising data about the "romantic battlefields of China." Then too, reporters were to "send in more than a couple [of] 'measly' paragraphs. It's no compliment to your outfit to admit, even by implication, that it's so dead that you can only dig up enough material for half a column." In order to encourage fuller participation by the reporters, the paper had recourse to various expedients. In the mid–1920s, cash prizes were offered for the best columns submitted, while on other occasions the paper printed black-edged "R.I.P." columns with notations that certain companies and detachments were obviously dead since they had not turned in any recent company notes. In short, if the enlisted men were not represented, it was their own fault.[11]

With the May 20, 1921, issue, by order of the commanding officer the paper was placed in the hands of a new editor and business manager, Chaplain Orville E. Fisher, who emerged as one of the paper's more enterprising chiefs. If Fisher sometimes argued that the paper was not the chaplain's publication though he was its editor, *The Sentinel* under his editorship nonetheless sought a high moral plane. Still, he faithfully carried out an editor's manifold duties through the issue of December 28, 1923, following which he was transferred to Camp Meade, Maryland. Fisher's predecessor, Captain R.D. Bell, while believing that the paper was "one of the best soldier papers in the Army," had been obviously relieved to give up the burden of editorship, acknowledging that "it has been very hard to fill its covers with readable matter."[12]

Taking cognizance of Captain Bell's often expressed complaints about difficulties in filling the paper's pages, Fisher, to assist would-be contributors in determining what might be acceptable, rather elaborately — and a bit factitiously — suggested that "If Any One Has —

> Killed a pig,
> Shot his wife,
> Got married,
> Borrowed a stamp,
> Made a speech,
> Joined the army,
> Robbed a bank,
> Bought a Ford
> Sold a dog,
> Lost his wallet,
> Gone fishing,
> Broke his neck,
> Bought a farm,"
> . . . .

or perpetrated other equally "noteworthy deeds," then "It's news — Send it to the Editor."[13]

The chaplain also desired more local material from his contributors, and "less resort to the scissors." For those finding writing a difficult task, he described how "Richard Washburn Child, the new Ambassador to Italy" accomplished the task. Well known as the author of several volumes of short stories, when asked how he wrote, Child replied, "I do it like this: I go into a room. I sit down at a desk. In front of me I put a pile of perfectly good, blank, clean paper. Then I say to myself, 'write, damn you, write!' And I stay there till I've written something. That's the secret."[14]

As is always the case with military publications, as Fisher acknowledged, censorship had to be considered, and while the paper was restricted more informally than officially, still all company notes had to be OK'd by company commanders. He admitted that there had been some few jokes submitted that could not be printed and "sometimes reference made to the character or reputation of others which would condemn not only *The Sentinel* but also the writer in the eyes of the readers." In addition, some anonymous writings were routinely rejected, as one from a soldier in connection with the pass system. Had this been printed it would have landed the writer — and it would not be hard to find the author's real name — in the jug for slanderous statements, falsehoods, and malicious references to the commanding officer. "If he had been sober when he wrote it, he wouldn't. So for his protection the Editor has [had] to censor it." Also, Fisher went on, the paper was read "by many others than of this command and we do not want to publish anything that will harm the reputation of any or cause anxiety on part of home folks." Contributors should realize, he explained, "there isn't a publisher in any land that published everything," and "many of the greatest literary and other writers have suffered many refusals for their products." Yet, "anyone with a real argument and willing to sign their name would find the columns of the paper always open to them."[15]

Later in the paper's career when tensions grew between the Chinese and Japanese and various foreigners, the editor was repeatedly asked why there was no coverage of these matters. The editor lamely observed that *The Sentinel* was "not that kind of a paper. Our purpose is primarily to record the doings of the regiment, and partly to inform the regiment of interesting 'things Chinese.'" Anything that might be said editorially, or that might be printed, could be mistaken for an expression of American Army opinion. All must be avoided which might even indirectly involve the United States government in any way. Therefore, readers must go elsewhere for traditional news reports and pictures of current disputed events in China that did not directly concern this regiment. "A commanding officer of American troops on foreign soil has difficulties enough without an editor creating additional complications for him," Fisher observed. Nevertheless, despite such limitations, much can be gleaned from the paper's content as well as inferred between the lines.[16]

To some readers there were other limitations to the paper's usefulness: its editorials. Far from being provocative and analytical, these were preachy to a fault, especially when Fisher was editor. Placed on the defensive, Fisher argued that they were included because "all up-to-date papers and magazines" had them; but in the case of *The Sentinel*, the topics covered, such as soldierly conduct and bearing; military courtesy, loyalty, and esprit de corps; drinking, the need to save one's money, and the like, were selected "with a view of improving conditions or bringing certain facts to the attention of our readers," all "with the vain hope that some would see the situation and do their part toward improving it."[17]

In addition to the editorials the surprisingly large numbers of poems written by the regiment's soldier-poets were another of the paper's staples. These were normally encouraged, "barring stuff that's *too* raw." But no doubt tiring of the reams of doggerel that he received, the editor plainly hoped for more solid original poetry from the readers, stating his case in his own poetic contribution:

> Poets and poems flock around us,
> As they never flocked before,
> But why do they constantly hound us
> With "The face upon the barroom floor?"
> "Dangerous Dan McGrew" took second place,
>   Been repeated its thousandth time;
> Oh why don't someone introduce
>   Another line of rhyme?[18]

Thus challenged, the readers responded, though their work perhaps inevitably mimicked the poems of Robert Service, Edgar Guest, James Whitcomb Riley, Walt Mason and, more frequently, Rudyard Kipling, who more clearly than anyone else influenced the poetic efforts of the local troops. Consequently, many soldiers felt the need to offer their apologies to the British bard when their own offerings hewed rather too closely to his venerable lines. Editors contributed to this trend by publishing numerous examples of the works of these poets. For a time, in the mid–1920s, there were "By Request" and "By Anonymous Request" columns in which poems of some interest or repute were reprinted when requested by individual soldiers of the regiment. In one issue, "The Shooting of Dangerous Dan McGrew" by Robert Service appeared; in another, "The Hoboes Convention"; in yet another, Service's "The Cremation of Sam McGee."[19]

Meanwhile, *The Sentinel* matured as the voice of the regiment and grew in scope and complexity. For one thing, its advertising steadily increased. Even as early as 1921 there was a considerable spread of ads often conjuring up hints of the "lure of the East" and illustrating the state of the art of business and commerce in Tientsin. See, for instance, the issue of July 1, 1921: There was an ad for the Chinese American Provision Company, a meat refrigerator installation at Victoria Road No. 25, in the British area of the city. There were ads for Perrin Cooper and Company, selling Butmer's Champagne Cider. At Aux Nouveautes on 40 Rue de

France, French perfumes were suggested as presents for home and at half the cost of the same products in America. The latest fashions could be had in Tientsin's many upscale shops such as that of J. Naftaly Company, which once featured "New silk materials of the latest 'JAZZ' designs." By May of 1928, the paper also included a classified section.[20]

Reflecting in precise ways the reason many of the troops were in China in the first place, the paper naturally included advertising for drinks of all sorts, such as the large variety of Japanese beers available, and for the innumerable clubs and bars such as the Nights of Cairo restaurant and cabaret. Featuring an orchestra playing the "latest musical hits," its clientele was welcome to "drop in [to] dance and be merry. [There were] pretty girls to drive your blues away." "Roaming Round the Town," a column in the paper by "Hiker," noted in 1931 that a new place, the Coffee Inn at 284 Taku Road in the British concession, had appeared in town. Operated by an American woman, it had a strong appeal for many of her countrymen famished for food from home. The only trouble "Hiker" noted was that when one saw such selections as "real" Mexican Chile Con Carne, Denver sandwiches, T-bone steaks and hot cakes on the bill of fare, "you're liable to break down and weep from sheer joy of meeting long lost friends at a strange and unexpected place."

Tobacco ads proliferated in those years of numerous heavy smokers; those for Piedmont, Chesterfield, Old Dominion and Capstan cigarettes were prominent, while Marlboros were "introduced to the smoking public of America during 1925," producing their first Marlboro Man in the process. The Ligget and Meyers Tobacco Company, makers of Chesterfields, consolidated their ties with the soldiers by annually presenting the Chesterfield Basketball Cup to winning regimental teams. Similarly, beginning in 1925, a Mr. Gunn of Whiteway, Laidlaw and Company, a clothing and footwear firm, presented the Gunn Cup to the company with the highest average in the Regimental Strength Test. Hirsbrunner and Company, of Tientsin and Peking, a tailor shop, made a specialty of military work. The men of the regiment, in view of their preoccupation with smart uniforms, no doubt patronized them in considerable numbers. Another frequent advertiser was the Robinson Piano Company, Ltd., not to mention the American Express Company at 27 Victoria Road. A half-page ad for Kaiping Coal, with its head offices in Tientsin and branches in Peking, Shanghai, Hongkong, and Manila, became a regular feature in the paper for some years. The firm also encouraged the regiment by annually presenting a cup for the highest scores fired on the range by a winning company. Such support, as well as their paid advertising, caused editors frequently to remind readers to "patronize those who patronize us." This

VI. The Sentinel

Captain "Wild Bill" Tuttle, of the 15th Infantry, as perhaps the first "Marlboro Man." Cartoon ad by an unknown artist in *The Sentinel*, May 21, 1926.

became even more pressing when the government cut off funding for servicemen's athletics, forcing military organizations to seek other means of financial support.[21]

But the War Department at length intervened, putting an end to substantial advertising revenues. Effective as of November 1, 1932, it decreed that no service paper could henceforth accept advertising from firms doing business with the government, i.e., "involving the expenditure of funds appropriated by Congress." This was in response to certain stipulations in the War Department Appropriation Act of 1932. Having carried ads for more than 13 years, the editor regretted that the paper could no longer accommodate many of its patrons. The sad tale was related in a black-edged box in the November 5, 1932, issue: "In Memoriam. Our advertisements passed away last week and it is with the deepest regret that we have to discontinue the practice of accepting advertisements in *The Sentinel*." The paper thereupon printed up certificates stating that any enterprise placing ads in the paper certified that the firm was "not engaged in transacting business with the Government of the United States, not with its departments, bureaus or branches involving the expenditure of funds appropriated by Congress." Thereafter, copies of the paper were vetted for violations by the staff judge advocate of headquarters, U.S. Army Troops in China. Shorn of much of its advertising revenue, the paper was immediately reduced to an average of 18 pages instead of the usual 28 to 32, and soon it was more often than not a 12-pager. The paper henceforth became steadily duller in appearance and content: a mere shadow of its former self, certainly when compared with its apogee in the mid-to-late 1920s.[22]

Earlier, in 1922, the War Department had issued other directives regarding soldiers' publications, requiring that no officers' names would appear as having connection with the publication and that it was to be stated that the publication was "in no wise the official organ of the Army and in no wise published at the expense of the government." *The Sentinel* complied, noting further that the paper was also not an official publication of the China Expedition. It was not until the issue of October 23, 1925, that the names of the paper's staff were once more included on the editorial page with an easing of some of these restrictions.[23]

Later, in 1931, another blow to military newspapers was mandated by an Act of Congress prohibiting the publication of military papers "where the personnel of the Army are employed," an action responsible for the suspension of several prominent Army papers, including the *San Antonio Military Review*, the substantial paper of Fort Sam Houston. Also lost were the *Infantry School Journal* and *The Soldier*, though *The Sentinel*, perhaps bending the rules somewhat, was spared because no Army personnel were engaged solely in getting the paper out.[24]

Meanwhile, *The Sentinel* continued to refine its areas of content. One of the paper's more prolific and articulate writers was Roger Jones—rank unknown—of Headquarters Company who contributed a regular column, "At Random," and also wrote short stories, such as "You Can Hang It on a Hook." In the February 13, 1925, issue he began a novella, *In Worldly Clutches*, which was published in ten installments, ending in the April 17, 1925, issue. Reminding the reader of Sinclair Lewis' *Main Street*, though with a male protagonist, it followed the career of an American soldier in China with useful commentary on the Chinese scene through the course of a rather mediocre but interesting plot. Other writers of note whose work appeared in the paper include a Private Haydock of Company K, the author of a graphic short story of contacts and conflicts between East and West, "His Belle of the Orient," which first appeared in *The Sentinel* in 1920 and was reprinted in the October 7, 1927, issue. Others with some writing skills included a Private Gardiner of Company G who wrote a detailed, amusing account of his company's activities at the rifle range and their visit to the Great Wall where it comes down to the sea at Shankaikwan, where they saw something of "Old China." Another was Private George R. "China" Becker, a popular reporter from Company H, who wrote many articles on China in his regular "Ramblings" column.[25]

Indeed, throughout *The Sentinel*'s career, a variety of features, columns and articles appeared as though in a kaleidoscope. These ranged from the long-running feature "In the Realm of Philatelists" to a bon mot column, "Chit on a Chingle," and the "Currycomb Column," concerned with the events surrounding the regiment's Mounted Platoon. There were also the provocative "Sayings of Mrs. Solomon," which appeared in the mid–1920s for several issues. The first topic, "Know Thy Man," was an amusing account of what men are really like for the benefit of *The Sentinel*'s female readers, with some insight that might be of use to the male contingent. The writer began: "I charge thee, my daughter, KNOW THY MAN: For, the world is full of woman-charmers and the flatterers are full of beautiful 'stunts.' Lo of men there are three varieties. Those who may be driven with a whip and spur. Those who must be coaxed with sugar and apples. And those who must be BACKED into the Garden of Love Like unto a mule!"[26]

Humor often appeared. Some ethnic jokes were included, especially featuring blacks, in columns borrowing from "My Favorite Stories" by Irvin S. Cobb (published in large numbers of newspapers in the States early in the 1920s). One of these was "'So you is a soldier, Sam?' 'Yessah.

I's one of dem famous blackguards'" (*The Sentinel*, April 4, 1931). Rather more sedate was another: "A Swede came down from the woods and, entering a saloon, asked for a drink of good old squirrel whisky. The bartender said: 'We have some good Old Crow.' 'Oh, Yudas Priest!' said the Swede. 'I don't vant to fly; I just vant to hop around a little'" (Reprinted from *Doings in Grain* in *The Sentinel*, October 9, 1925). Anti-Semitism was not absent: "Fitzpatrick says the Service Company Mess would be all right if they would only serve some Blintzes once in a while. Ov! Maype he vants to be Rejewvenated" (*The Sentinel*, March 26, 1926).

There was humorous commentary on love: "[Raymond] Stakelbeck was heard wooing his light of love with the pathetic ballad — 'Take back your heart, I ordered liver' the other evening and now we know why [he] is still single." On regimental affairs: "Payday has come and gone, the mourners are Sgts. Raymer, Sharp and Neilsen, also Pvts. Razee [and] Costilow." On world "events": "Corporal Travers claims that they used to make roads in France out of Gaul stones" (*The Sentinel*, March 10, 1922; March 19, 1926; March 25, 1927).

Other examples of humor were in such columns as "See If You Can Laugh": "Pardon me, Mrs. Astor, but that never would have happened if you hadn't stepped between me and the spittoon." And: "I guess I'm everybody's fuel," sighed Joan of Arc" (*The Sentinel*, May 21, 1932).

There was the mildly scatalogical: "Cook Campbell to Pvt. Mills, 'do you want some nice fresh beef's tongue?' Pvt. Mills, 'I wouldn't eat nothing that comes out of an animal's mouth.' Cook Campbell, 'Well how about a couple of nice fresh eggs?'" (*The Sentinel*, July 5, 1930).

Among the features most useful to the historian of the 15th was the column titled "A Letter." Addressed to "Dear Folks," and "Dear Buddy," and written by a soldier signing himself "Can Do" and later "Can Do, Jr.," these lively missives were in fact extended reports on the daily life and events in the career of the regiment in the late 1920s and early 1930s.

Movies were routinely reviewed in such columns as "By the Movie Editor," and "Movie Chats." Among other things, these columns trace the emergence of talkies during this era and occasionally presented solid analyses of films.[27]

The Sentinel reflected items of interest as well as fads and crazes that characterized the Roaring Twenties and the Jazz Age at home, and those on the local Chinese scene. In the early 1920s for a time the paper engaged in the relatively short-lived, lively form of humor called "You Tell 'Ems," including: "You tell 'em, cotton, I forgot my yarn"; "You tell 'em, corset, You've been around the ladies"; "You tell 'em, dollar, money talks"; "You tell 'em, fish, I am sure to flounder"; "You tell 'em, gravel, you got the grit"; and many more.[28]

What might be called "jazz talk"—as distinct from "jive talk," which came later—appeared in *The Sentinel* as "Americanisms": "Oh, dear, last night I met the most divine egg I have ever witnessed. He is the porcupine's quills, all of them. He has the biggest shoulders, they're too cute for words, and his nose and eyes are gorgeous, just gorgeous. Does he dance well? A regular St. Vitus, I mean to tell you. And not only that, my dear, he plays the saxophone like an angel out of heaven. He's the oil works, all right."[29]

A longer-lasting preoccupation, Mah Jongg, was parodied in *The Sentinel* in a regular column, "Pa Johng [sic] Says" which featured bon mots, many mildly antifeminist.[30]

With the coming of the crossword craze, a phenomenon that lasted for many years, the paper often printed puzzles with local content, many of them devised by the regiment's companies. A new pastime introduced in *The Sentinel* in the early 1930s, which also reflected interests in America, were cryptograms. This preoccupation sprang from the publication of the book *The American Black Chamber*, by Herbert O. Yardley, involving codes and international spying activities.[31]

Contests and debates were used from time to time to generate interest in the paper. In 1923, for instance, one encouraged readers to send in entries on the topic, "Resolved: 'That K.P. [the "Knights of the Pan"] is [a] more important branch of the service than M.P.'" Another, launched in the autumn of 1924, asked for manuscripts of 250 words or less devoted to the provocative question: "If I Could Vote," thereby perhaps assuaging some of the discontent sometimes surfacing on this issue, because soldiers stationed overseas were denied the ballot. One entry advanced the name of Henry Ford because he possessed all of the attributes of a leader: he was wealthy, he had untiring zeal and was a hard driver, he was powerful, and he had strong independent views. Another focused on the process of selection, declaring that he would employ the Pinkerton Detective Agency to scour the world seeking the right man. In the event, the ten-dollar prize went to the soldier who advanced the name of the cartoon character Andy Gump as his choice. He too possessed laudable attributes: "He's a family man [and] drives his own flivver like you or me." In another instance, *The Sentinel* awarded $5 local currency for the best article on the theme of "Why I Like Military Service in China."[32]

Informal debates sometimes broke out among the readership. On one occasion, the editor delightedly printed letters from two anonymous enlisted men who hotly discussed how Mother's Day should be celebrated. Their missives were prompted by a memorandum from Washington dated

March 12, 1924, which read in part: "You are directed to bring to the attention of every officer and enlisted man in your command, the desire of the Secretary of War that every officer and enlisted man write to his home on Mother's Day, the second Sunday in May, May 11, 1924, as an expression of the love and reverence we owe to the mothers of our country."[33]

Throughout its career, much of the paper's space was devoted to local sports coverage, though some attention was given to the national sports scene in such columns as those highlighting baseball news from the U.S., "Scribbled by Scribes" and "Caught on the Fly." Boxing matches and other sporting events, both local and on the American scene, were analyzed in a long-running column, the "Hot Stove League."[34]

The paper also served those among its readers interested in keeping tabs on developments in the Regular Army — who was promoted, transferred and the like — in columns such as "Army News" and in special features.

One of the most important contributions of the paper to its readership consisted of considerable ongoing information regarding China and the Orient. For instance, there was a general news summary featuring Far Eastern affairs written by Lieutenant G.S. Eyster, an intelligence officer in the regiment. A regular front page feature for some years was the "Pass in Review" column, and in 1924, when China was once more in major upheaval, it was supplemented by the column "Current Political Happenings in China." The much more substantial writings of Stilwell have been noted in chapter V.[35]

It should be noted that *The Sentinel* was not the only service paper being published during the 1920s; there were interesting contemporaries, some of which were on the paper's exchange list and from which the paper often reprinted material. As *The Sentinel*'s editor once observed, service papers were "always full of original dope," and appearing from "all over the various services are getting to be real news sheets and provide good reading material for the soldier, sailor and marine. Our only hope is that we can keep up with the rest of them." These publications included the *Legation Guard News*, "a clever sheet ... full of interesting reading," which was launched by the marines in Peking in 1922. Appearing twice monthly in the early 1930s, its name was changed to *The American Embassy Guard News*. In 1931, it produced a 96-page annual, which featured some illustrations by Captain John W. Thomason, Jr. (apparently then with the Legation Guard). Therefore, in troop paper publication, as in much else, there was incessant competition between the 15th Infantry and the marines.[36]

Other troop papers that were often exchanged with *The Sentinel* included *The Typhoon*, a publication of the destroyer squadron of the U.S. Asiatic Fleet, and another Navy sheet launched in mid–1925, *The Huron*

Flashlight, produced by the USS *Huron*, a cruiser then on the China station. Another shipboard paper was *The Asheville Skyline* published by one of the Navy's gunboats that frequented Tientsin and other Chinese riverine ports. Among Army sheets there was *The Standard*, published at Fort Riley, Kansas; *The Bullet*, the 25th Infantry's paper; and *Rock of the Marne*, the Third Division paper published at Fort Lewis, Washington. Also appearing outside of the continental United States were such publications as *The 14th Infantry Dragon*, out of Fort Davis in the Canal Zone. Another service publication that arrived in Tientsin as an exchange sheet was *The Fifteenth Tank Battalion Weekly*, the eight-page mimeographed paper of a unit stationed at Fort Benning, Georgia. One of its contributors wrote under the name of "Chin a Loo." He was in fact Private John Lomasney, who had served with the 15th in China, where he had written for *The Sentinel* using the same byline.[37]

One paper that titillated *The Sentinel* appeared closer to home. A Captain Kearney of the regiment, in early 1926, began putting out a weekly magazine called *The Tattler*. The scribe of Company I noted its arrival: "Well, boys there is another paper in circulation in Tientsin that has some snappy reading in it. The *Tattler* calls a spade a spade and you sure can wise up a little by reading it." But, perhaps it was too outspoken, and soon *The Sentinel* changed its tone, the correspondent for Company F declaring that *The Tattler* certainly lived up the meaning of the word, it being "an idle talker; one who tells tales...." Soon, Company H's column reported that after earlier success, Captain Kearney's *Tattler* was losing out and there were wide-spread hopes that "this anti everything and anything will [soon] die a natural death." This was unfortunate, as it might well have developed as a beneficial alternative, even oppositional sheet, to *The Sentinel*.[38]

More venerable publications in the United States that were often featured in the pages of *The Sentinel* included the perky and provocative *Fort Benning News*, from Fort Benning, Georgia; *The Infantry Journal*; *The U.S. Army Recruiting News*; and *The American Legion Weekly*.

Among the papers published by the other international forces in Tientsin was *The Thistle*, a quarterly journal of the Royal Scots published in Scotland and sent out to the men in the field. Formed in 1633, the Royal Scots was the oldest regiment in the British Army and its soldiers enjoyed a close relationship with troops of the 15th. While no doubt generating only a small following — if any — among the men of the 15th Regiment, the Japanese War Office announced in 1925 that it would henceforth publish an army newspaper "devoted to the ideals of the service." Called *Kokki* or "Glory of Empire," it was edited by a Colonel Sakurai, author of a book called *Human Bullets*.[39]

The *Sentinel* did not go unnoticed in the larger world of journalism. For instance, the editor of the popular magazine *Lloyd's Weekly* commended the regiment's paper in a warm letter in 1923. He received *The Sentinel* as an exchange, and was no doubt gratified that that paper often reprinted material from his own publication.[40]

Similarly, *The Sentinel* frequently received official recognition and kudos. In a letter dated July 30, 1921, Major General Charles S. Farnsworth, chief of infantry, stated that he read the paper with interest and especially noted the "avoidance of vulgarity and of suggestive immorality." He wished it continued success "in contributing information and news [and] in building regimental spirit and character." *The Sentinel* obliged, revealing much rich detail about the day-to-day activities of soldiers in China, in some ways differing little from their peers elsewhere. It expressed concern about events within the Army establishment and sought to develop pride within the regiment and in the Army in general. It was also a means of following American cultural, social and political developments: what women were doing, what the fads were, how Americans entertained themselves and what the latest news from home was.[41]

But while *The Sentinel* in some respects was similar to its contemporaries published by other American military units and at various installations, it differed greatly in its substantive presentations regarding the Orient. Readers could glean much insight about foreign service, the international scene and, specifically, much about China to which scholars can still profitably turn. There was always the possibility of armed clashes. When troops deployed in the field, they might be engaged merely in routine exercises but on occasion they had to be prepared for action. The firing ranges were not simply targets in the peaceful confines of Fort Benning, say, or Fort Lewis, but in northern China, sometimes exposed to threats from Chinese and later Japanese troops. Consequently, training reflected a harder edge lacking on more peaceful posts. All of this was grist for the editors' mills. Beyond this, because it enjoyed considerable circulation in the States, especially in military circles, and since some of the paper's key articles about China were republished in the United States, it informed a wider, often influential audience about matters of considerable import. While hardly the only source to which scholars should turn to study the deployment of the 15th to China, for many years *The Sentinel* produced a respectable, continuous collective memoir of the regiment's operations there, and as its name implies, within certain parameters, limitations and controls—which must always be taken into account regarding military papers—discharged its duties as watchman of the passing scene.

CHAPTER VII

Roundelay: Attitudes, Morale and the Daily Round

"Isn't there an Article of War that hands out the death penalty to any soldier found with money in his possession? Most of us believe there is and we're taking no chances."[1]

"We can beat our swords into plowshares, but what in the world can we do with the Sam Browne belts?"[2]

As one observer explained, "among Army officers, China duty was considered the cream of foreign service; young officers with only the finest records joined the 15th. The enlisted men were all volunteers, and they liked the life in China. For many, the prospect of early return to the United States was a punishment; some never left China, even after their discharge." Also, the officers could participate in an elegant social life. "The regiment enjoyed informal as well as official contacts with allied officers and their families, particularly with the British. Domestic help was inexpensive and plentiful, with six to eight servants the normal complement, allowing for a rather lavish round of dinner parties at little cost except loss of sleep." In addition, officers were free to travel extensively throughout China, Japan and Hong Kong, as in the phraseology of the Post Regulations, on detached service for "the purpose of visiting localities of military importance." One of the 15th Regiment's soldiers recognized that service in the East almost invariably created a new life that frequently was "much more indulgent and far less interested in hard work." Indeed there were dangers: some who had "missed too many boats" were never again fit for life in the United States, being "out of step forever with their own Country.... Most of them face[ed] a future that is far from enviable." Others, however, were not crushed by the East Asian influence, and some "young men with brains who stay out a year or two and get back as soon as they can," found that their experiences were broadening and helpful. In short, "at the right time and in the right place, soldiering can be a satisfying profession.... [In China] 'soldiering was interesting and pleasant and not drudgery, even prideful.'" As an American sailor noted regarding his own venue, "duty in China was like living in a mild version of the Arabian Nights—something enjoyable, mysterious, and not requiring a great deal of money."[3]

An "I" Company scribe writing in *The Sentinel* once outlined the 15th Regiment's daily round: A 5:45 reveille and assembly was followed by 6:30 breakfast call—"with eggs any style and a spicy meatball." Morning fatigue with coolies doing the work commenced at 7:00, followed by the first session of drill, combat problems and skirmish runs at 7:30. Sick call was set for 9:45 and 15 minutes later recess time with scheduled sports began. Recall came at 11:45 when all fatigue activities were suspended until the early afternoon.

Following the noonday meal and the first call for guard mount, fatigue call resounded once more at 1:30, but this was "just another dry run ... that doesn't bother us at all." Athletics then prevailed until 4:50 retreat and the evening meal with its "pass the chicken and pickled beets." Then, "After supper we take in a cabaret / Who originated that 'all work and no play'?" Lights were out at 9:00, and at 10:30, all troops, except those with passes enabling them to stay out later, were to be in the barracks. Taps, that "sad, sweet call," was blown at 11:00, ending the soldier's day.[4]

Relaxed duty routines prevailed in the regiment in times when no Chinese incursions intervened. A lieutenant in a rifle company, James E. Moore—later a general—recalled that the main problem in China was to keep the men busy "without boring them to death."[5]

A holiday routine was normally in force over Christmas and New Years'. Typically, as in 1932, this extended from December 23 to January 4, and "all duties except the necessary guard, fatigue and administrative [functions would] be suspended." Also a series of company entertainments for benefit of the regiment—by then numbering 600 men and about 50 officers—was staged.[6]

One became a member of this "easy living" outfit by signing up for an overseas hitch of three years and arriving by several routes such as by transfer from other units in the U.S. Army. It was also possible in those years for men to volunteer for a specific organization from civilian life. Such recruits were not sent to a recruit training facility but directly to the units for which they volunteered. With the arrival of each troop transport in China, for instance, the various organizations of the regiment took the new men in hand and drilled and instructed them in the rudiments of soldiering. On some occasions in the 1920s, the 15th's recruits were sent to the regiment's First Battalion in Manila for initial orientation. Between the world wars, career soldiers could also change organizations by purchasing a discharge, or when receiving a discharge at the end of their enlistment, could "re-up" for a specific outfit. Some joined from other branches of military service, a common experience being for a man to enlist in the Marine Corps, the Navy and the Army in turn. If the strength table permitted it, the new man might be enrolled in a former rank or grade or even promoted. More often, though, the enrollee became a private, in keeping with the system of "disratings" then common. Corporals and privates first class, for example, were usually reduced to private when being returned to the States for reassignment or discharge. Most men holding specialty ratings routinely lost these as well. The troops patiently waiting in China to fill these vacancies could then sew on their new stripes — appropriately "wetted down" at the nearest bar.[7]

Wherever they came from, new arrivals to the 15th were traditionally welcomed with a standard greeting issued orally and in the columns of *The Sentinel*. "Welcome Griffins," one such peroration began. (The term was applied both to a Mongol pony which had not run its first race as well as to the newly-arrived trooper.) In the first place, the spiel continued, "you won't like this country ... it is not a white man's country." It went on, "But don't lose your grip; [you will soon] get not to mind it." Indeed, "there are honors before you if you walk straight, keep away from the rotten women, and touch not the more rotten booze." But for lack of entertainment, "you will probably tumble like the rest." The men were advised that "if you have got to be a fool get over it quickly." As time went on, recruits were subjected to increasingly thorough indoctrinations lasting several days, ensuring that "everything has been done to safeguard the morals and military career of these just beginning." In any case, there was "no more reason why a man should go wrong here in China than in any other place. It's up to the man himself."[8]

Having been admitted to the regiment's ranks, new personnel normally undertook regular garrison duties, though the usual fatigue and menial chores, such as laundry, daily shaves, haircuts, and shoe shining, were done by Chinese coolies who were paid a nominal sum — typically four dollars in gold a month. This lack of K.P. and other onerous chores was reflected on poetically, if not sensitively, by one grateful soldier:

> The soldiers didn't really do it.
>   They knew of something finer.
> They sat and thanked their lucky stars,
>   That they were here in China.

> Where doughboys never mop the floor,
> Or scour out the sink.
> The buck is passed right on again,
> To the nearest little Chink.[9]

Exceptions came on the Chinese New Year when the coolies were given time off. The men then found themselves engaged in unfamiliar scullery and cooking tasks and having to man the brooms and mops on cleaning details.

Certainly, cheap and readily available servants were one of the "Lure[s] of the East." What the men could not normally avoid, however, was the care and cleaning of their weapons—though one suspects that some of this was done by the coolies as well—and one of the problems with keeping firearms clean was alluded to by another soldier-poet: "Tell me not in mournful whispers / That my rifle isn't clean / For I clean it every eve for Vespers / And sometimes in between."[10]

Ubiquitous guard duty was another unavoidable, wearisome part of garrison life. As one of the outfit's numerous poets lamented, "My name's on the list each time — / My life's a walking pantomine."[11]

Still, if not in much danger of collapsing under the strain of guard duty, service in China nonetheless threatened the men's health and general well-being. All-too-common features of *The Sentinel* were the black-edged death notices of regimental casualties. For instance, in March 1923, within two days of each other, Private Charles W. Houck of Company F died of an apparent heart attack, and Private Ralph F. Morton, Company G, succumbed to smallpox. In August of that year, two more men of the regiment died one day apart, one of unknown causes while at the rifle range, the other of spinal meningitis. To counter such threats, shots, such as for cholera and typhoid, were given when the "Medics [held] bayonet drill." Even more commonly prescribed for ailments were those famous "C.C. Pills" routinely dispensed to the men apparently for almost any conceivable illness. Perhaps salutary for minor ailments, these might even pull one through the more serious indispositions as one soldier suggested: "Army men need army treatment for / those good old army ills / Nothing else will ever cure them but / those famous C.C. PILLS."[12]

When the more dangerous diseases such as smallpox, spinal meningitis or typhus claimed victims, the medical department ordered quarantines for the affected companies or sometimes for the entire regiment. *The Sentinel*, in its January 7, 1921, issue, recorded that Company E had led off "with a measles quarantine," then "G" Company "not to be outdone tries one, too, and gets out only on Christmas Day." After getting a good taste of holidays, "A" Company developed a quarantine for scarlet fever "and [was] locked up over New Year." Nevertheless, the paper declared, "there is nothing in this sickness to be alarmed over. We get them all the time." Still, every man should watch his step, listen to the surgeon, heed the safety precautions issued by the commanding officer, and use common sense, or else "some little Bug is going to get you some day."[13]

Making for more dismal reading was an account in *The Sentinel* listing the names of one master sergeant, one corporal, one private first class and seven privates who had died in China in the past few months. Their bodies were sent back to the United States on the regular return voyage of the U.S. Army Transport *Thomas*. Unlike the men who returned from the battlefields of Europe with fulsome praise and triumphant parades, they would be brought home with only "a rendering of quiet homage tinged with sorrow." Still, they had proved themselves "ready to serve their beloved land at an instant's call," than which there was no greater honor, "and in serving they died."[14] These hard realities disheartened many of the men, some of whom came to detest China. Others, however, were equally emphatic that the Orient was a good place in which to soldier.

The Sentinel often received letters from former members of the regiment who had returned to the States and who were free with their advice to their buddies remaining in China. Robert La Prode, from Morristown, Tennessee, soon to be discharged, confessed to finding things difficult in the United States. He found Prohibition deplorable, the work hard, the wages low. Were he to remain in the Army, "I certainly would be right back to the land of slant eyes and small feet." Robert E. Quinn, late of Company K then stationed at Ft. McDowell in California, asserted emphatically that "from what I have seen I do not care to soldier in the States." Agreeing with a bon mot making the rounds, "Columbus was right. He sighted dry land," Quinn had other advice: "Tell Peek and all others who like [to] drink once in a while to stay in China." Certainly, soldiering in an area which knew not the Volstead Act made China a highly desirable venue for some, reveling "in the words of Pussyfoot Johnson: 'Slip me something east of Suez,'" perhaps a bottle of a local popular tipple, Five-Star Lager Beer, or maybe another favorite imported from Japan, Asahi Beer.[15]

To underscore the point about Prohibition America, the regiment's band playing at portside often gleefully sent off the soldiers returning to the States with a lively rendition of "How Dry I Am," a custom similarly followed for men departing the American zone of occupation in Germany. Not coincidentally, many who had served in Germany arranged transfers to China as soon as they could. Indeed, soldiers in the 15th often gloried in the fact that "the only thing prohibited in China [was] prohibition."[16]

"New Arrivals from Over the Bounding Foam." Cover of *The Sentinel*, October 1, 1927, by an unknown cartoonist.

VII. Roundelay: Attitudes, Morale and the Daily Round 117

The regiment's high command was perennially up against two hard facts of Army life in China: their soldiers' propensity to excessive drinking and their cohabiting with the natives. There was some concern with drug abuse — addicts were known as "snow birds"— but despite readily available sources, it never became a major problem. Rather, the argot of the day reflected a preoccupation with drink. "Up the Pole" referred to being "on the wagon," but the adoption of the motto "When intoxication is a bliss 'tis a folly to be sober" seemed more common. Certainly, there were countless opportunities for drinking, and accordingly, the compound's stockade was almost never vacant. The incarcerated troopers, commonly called the "Knights of Retreat" or the "Water Tower Gang"— the stockade was near the compound's water tower — whiled away their time in durance vile, "lookin' on the outside, waitin' for the evenin' chow." A usual sentence for alcohol abuse was a month's hard labor and its "inevitable concomitant — two-thirds [loss of pay]." There could also be other consequences of alcohol abuse. As Colonel Newell once stated, "You have come to a country where the 18th Amendment is not known and where the temptation to lead a sordid life is in every corner. A man can ruin himself physically in a few weeks.... [But] this regiment is not an old soldier's home. We will not tolerate a man who cannot control himself and is constantly getting drunk.... He will go home on the next boat."[17]

The other plague of the Regiment was the battle of the "rate," that struggle graphically revealed in the sinuous curve of the VD chart. The 15th was widely recognized as having infection levels that at times soared to at least three times the Army's average. Indeed, among the most voluminous caches of documents among the 15th's official papers concerned the problem of venereal disease and schemes to curtail it.[18] Some of the reasons for the "rate" were well stated by Colonel George A. Lynch in his traditional greeting to replacements arriving on the November 1935 transport. One important fact, he began, was that "these people have absolutely no standards of personal cleanliness. They live in the midst of the most revolting filth. The stench that arises around their dwellings defies description." In addition, venereal disease was "accepted with indifference," and "one would think," he went on, that "the sight of these revolting conditions would be sufficient to deter any white man reared to standards of cleanliness and decency from cohabiting with these people." But, unfortunately, "here some soldiers become beach combers and seem to lose all idea of the white man's standards. They take a Chinese concubine and go out and live in midst of Chinese filth." Some soldiers argued that their arrangements with concubines, sometimes called "sleeping phrase books," enabled them more easily to learn the language, thereby enhancing the military efficiency of the regiment.[19]

In addition, there was a complete lack of cooperation on the part of the Chinese authorities in containing prostitution. They regarded the situation "with more or less indifference as certain low ways of earning a living." The problem was further compounded by certain inconsistencies in official regimental policy that sometimes surfaced. In one instance, a certain Mrs. Brun living near the compound desired to open a "house of tolerance" fully equipped with elegant "household furnitures" and ten young European girls all of whom had been "registered by flattering Phisical [sic] Inspector." She formally petitioned Colonel James D. Taylor, "with great prayer," to have her establishment inspected by the compound's medical authorities and other involved personnel. Accordingly, the regiment's adjutant, provost marshal and chief surgeon visited the establishment. Reassured by Mrs. Brun's custom of weekly medical examination of the "inmates," the surgeon, while he recognized that "no approval can be officially given," concluded "that admission to this house should be sanctioned for the reason that it is more desirable than other places in this locality which are now patronized by certain members of this command." The provost marshal concurred, recommending "that this house be placed on limits for American soldiers."[20]

Many men of the regiment frequented the haunts of prostitutes wherever found. Tientsin was a ready source of women of all nationalities. Numerous brothels, for instance, specialized in White Russian women who had escaped the Soviet Union, making their way into Manchuria and on to Peking, Tientsin and Shanghai. Many prostitutes were to be found in the legendary street called Mukloo—sometimes spelled "Mucklu"—in the Chinese section of Tientsin, not too far from the American Compound. Private Otto Beinke, in a letter home which was reproduced in *The Sentinel*, revealed details of the area in a rather discreet way. Mukloo "resembles the Bowery a good deal (only dirtier)," he noted.[21]

If *The Sentinel* was reticent regarding details of the Mukloo district, certainly some of the better-known prostitutes and madams were discussed in its pages. Among these were "Lizzie," "Peepsight," and "Dutch Annie." The latter, a saloon owner as well as a madam, was an especial favorite, and a reporter for the Service Company who wrote under the pen name of "Beejo"—the Mandarin word for beer—commemorated her in his "Ode to Dutch Annie," praising "her rosy arms / Her round perfections and her secret charms."[22]

That there were dangers as well as attractions in Dutch Annie's establishment was a well-known fact, as one anonymous poet recorded in a paraphrase of Kipling's "The Young British Soldier":

> And when you're "knocked out"
>   In Dutch Annie's saloon
> And you act like a sap, or at times a baboon
> Take interval, distance or if you like, take sea-room
> And go to your bunk like a soldier,
>   Soldier, soldier, etc., etc.[23]

When the average soldier came up against both alluring women, from whatever venue, and liquor, he often did not have much of a chance of keeping on a even keel. An unknown Service Company poet reflected on the long odds, when "Cupid came against me in his might," especially "when he has Dan Bacchus on his side." The results seemed a foregone conclusion: "Against two gods how can one man abide?"[24]

The U.S. Army had previously mounted a vigorous campaign to control venereal diseases, especially during the Great War, and in the postwar years, in the occupied zone in Germany, China and elsewhere, continued its vigilance. Numerous expedients were employed to keep the rate down including exhortations in *The Sentinel*, official communications, and many others. One of the standing bulwarks in the defense against social diseases was the welcoming address of the regiment's high command. Pulling no punches, the new arrivals were strongly admonished about the VD threat. In addition, the Chinese part of Chinwangtao was usually declared off limits, though such restrictions did not unduly cramp the style of the veterans of the regiment well versed in the intricacies of sexual supply and demand. In 1924, General William D. Connor, commanding the American Forces in China, accentuating a positive approach, issued a letter of commendation to the commanding officers of three companies expressing his gratification that in a three-month period none of their soldiers had a single case of venereal infection.[25]

Other means utilized, enlisting every agency at the commanding officers' disposal, included the limiting of pass privileges to men of excellent character, the locating and removing of sources of infection, and lectures to enlisted men by medical officers. It was also hoped that the adjutant general's new policy (1923) of sending specially recruited men to China as replacements would have a salutary effect in the years to come. There was also the maintenance of organization dayrooms, and various clubs, such as the Service Club. Hours at the post library were extended and facilities of the YMCA and chaplain's office were fully utilized. Various forms of competitive athletics were organized and mandated for all of the men. Coupling this with the drill schedule, the command hoped "to have the men 'comfortably tired' when evening came." All known prostitution resorts and districts were put off limits and patrolled by a provost guard. The aid of Chinese officials and those of the French Municipal Council, where a more lenient policy was normally manifested, was solicited — usually with little result — in attempts to keep diseased women from plying their trade. Infected houses and districts were restricted. The pride of organization was appealed to, and men were encouraged to return members of their unit to the compound "when [they were] found drunk or about to become so." In this way, it was hoped "that the chances of [their] becoming infected with venereal disease [might be] materially lessened."[26]

Eventually, more drastic measures were necessary. Tiring of the continued poor showing in the VD rate, in November 1923 Brigadier General William Connor sought legal opinions from the adjutant general in Washington to support more strenuous action: "Diseased condition among Chinese so general that sexual intercourse with them after repeated instructions and warning is practically willfully contracting venereal disease and resulting disability practically self-inflicted incapacitation for duty," he declared. Under these conditions, might not the men who had been forbidden to have intercourse with such women be considered to have committed a military offense which could be punished under the 96th Article of War? The adjutant general's office replied that such action could indeed be tried by military courts; the surgeon general concurred. Accordingly, the adjutant general advised Connor that the essence of this offense "lies in the soldier's wilful impairment of his capacity to perform his military duties," and his failure to take a prescribed prophylaxis. Common punishments were being reduced to the ranks or disrated, in the case of rated specialists, as well as forfeiture of pay. In addition, the lost days of service resulting from the disability had to be made up. Finally, a stay in the hospital — in the infamous "corner pocket" — to effect a cure was required. Eventually, frequent physicals, the notorious "short arm inspections," were mandated.[27]

The court-martial dockets were soon filled with cases. One concerned a certain Company Sergeant Steely who was reduced to a private because, as his charge read, he failed to detect in the course of a daily inspection "of the private parts of Private Lee F. Minchk, of Company 'K,'" obvious manifestations of infection thereby revealing that his examination "was perfunctory and conducted with gross carelessness." In any event, perhaps no regiment's officers and men were better known to their buddies, whose "private parts" became all too familiar in the inspections that all personnel, in the wording of one directive, "were expected to attend." The ribaldry on such occasions can only be imagined.[28]

The troops themselves frequently complained about the incessant inspections and widely regarded the punishments as too severe. These had adverse effects, they argued, and consequently guilty parties tried to hide instead of coming in for treatment, or they were driven to quacks or sought to heal themselves, none of which was in the Army's best interests. Were the men only to lose their pass privileges or be fined nominally instead of being reduced to the ranks or confined to the stockade or the hospital, perhaps they would more readily accept the consequences of their lapses. The fact remains that only when the men were closely examined and held firmly accountable — officers and NCOs alike — was there improvement in the regiment's "rate."

One of the most active of the regiment's commanders in battling the problem was Colonel James D. Taylor, in command from 1929 to 1932. A survey of his campaign reveals much about the problem of VD in the 15th and how it was combated. He strongly attacked the stigma that "hung like a pall of black smoke over the regiment over a period of many years," and as a result of all concerned working together, by early April 1931 not one soldier remained in the "corner pocket" for the first time in the history of the regiment's service in China. The elated colonel announced liberal pass privileges and special holidays for the regiment.[29]

There were lapses later in the spring, however, "when a young man's fancy" turned in the usual direction. *The Sentinel* in its April 18, 1931, issue reported that one man had fallen by the wayside, and the "corner pocket" had a new arrival. In May, the deplorable curve once more asserted itself and rose alarmingly when the regiment went to the firing range in the summer, a common occurrence. This was true, the paper's editor declared, because the winsome "Miss Chinwangtao [always] anxiously awaiting [the soldiers'] arrival," proved a formidable opponent to the forces of decency. Later, in the autumn, when the troops returned from the firing range, there was improvement again.[30]

Captain William Howard Arnold remembered that Colonel Reynolds J. Burt also took a firm stance in the matter. On one occasion, standing before the colonel in his room at headquarters (known as the Blue Room because of the blue carpet on his floor), he was advised that "if you get more than two VD cases in a company in a month you've had it." Arnold and his fellow officers were accordingly compelled to act forcefully: "So we embarked on a program which was fantastic," he recalled. "We were in league with the doctors, and we did every thing we possibly could. For example, every time a soldier came in the compound after five o'clock in the afternoon, he was taken, whether he wanted to or not, and given a prophylactic."[31]

Burt's successor, Colonel George Arthur Lynch, did not let up in the efforts to combat the "rate." Speaking to his troops, Lynch stated candidly that "it is a matter of relative indifference to me whether you take a Chinese mistress or not. But if you elect to go out and live among these people — if you 'shack up' as the expression goes here — you need expect no consideration from me." In addition to the inevitable court-martial, he warned, "no man who has contracted venereal disease here will ever be given a rating nor will his tour of duty with this regiment be extended." Nevertheless, despite improvements from time to time in the "rate" curve, the problem of VD plagued the regiment to the end of its stay in China.[32]

The twin problems of drink and VD were the main causes of discipline problems and the reasons for the majority of stockade time and courts-martial. Article of War 104 gave commanding officers discretion in minor disciplinary matters without courts-martial being held. As to more serious punishment, which courts-martial could impose, common were dishonorable discharges, confinement in a stockade, usually at hard labor, and forfeiture of pay and allowances— usually the loss of two-thirds of the soldier's pay for a specified period of time.[33]

To be sure, there were other breaches of discipline with dire consequences. As was the case throughout the Army, dishonorable discharges were the result of conviction by a general court-martial for a serious offense such as murder, robbery, larceny, or desertion. The most common of these was desertion, but this was not normally pursued in the United States. As Victor Vogel has noted in his useful memoir describing soldiering between the world wars, "the culprits were seldom apprehended and the army made no attempt to find them. If a man was absent without leave for more than ninety days he was dropped from the rolls and forgotten." Not so in China, however. When two men of Company G deserted to northern China to join Nationalist Chinese forces in action there, they were brought back to Tientsin under an MP "escort of honor." They had become bored with the "piddling routine of garrison duty," and sought some excitement.[34]

In response to both moral and morale challenges faced by the troops, a full panoply of activities was in force, many of which will be considered in greater detail in chapter IX. In some measure, regimental commanders had guidance from the War Department's Circular No. 225 issued in 1920, addressing these matters. Accordingly, a memorandum from the China Expedition headquarters dated September 1, 1921, provided for the establishment of an Army Service Club dedicated to recreation such as staging dances as well as maintaining a restaurant. The club gained even more popularity when a woman hostess was employed.[35]

The Sentinel supported the club's activities by publishing a weekly column devoted to its activities as well as the bill of fare of films screened in Recreational Hall. Sometimes the movies were supplemented by amateur talent nights, with companies pitted against each other. The column also commented on the vocational courses offered by the command, but regrettably, only a few men of the regiment took advantage of courses such as shorthand and typewriting.[36]

In late 1923, the club movement gained new impetus when the Enlisted Men's Club and the Sergeants' Club were organized. The Enlisted Men's Club was named McNally's Emporium for the local Red Cross representative, Thomas J. McNally, who managed it. It was later called the Liscum Club, in honor of Colonel Emerson H. Liscum, commander of the U.S. Ninth Infantry Regiment, who was killed in Tientsin on July 13, 1900, during the Boxer Uprising. It featured the usual amenities including Mah Jongg and card tables and three bowling alleys. The Sergeants' Club was equally well-appointed and furnished.[37]

Changes in the club situation came from time to time as when in October 1929, in response to Colonel James D. Taylor's ongoing concern with morale of the rank and file, a Privates' Club was organized.[38]

The officers' need for clubs was met by impressive establishments in the Tientsin area and it was recognized that social life for the officers and their families "was perhaps even more gracious than in the Philippines," where the standards were particularly high.[39]

One popular spot was the Tientsin Race Club, which George C. Marshall described as "a really magnificent establishment, the most pretentious, except Long Champs[sic, i.e., Longchamps, near Paris] I have seen." It was owned by the British, which was understandable, as one American officer explained, because "as you know, when two Britishers get together they have a club, and if there are three of them they have a race course." Located on the outskirts of the city, in exchange for yearly dues of $30 local currency, members could participate in the regularly scheduled spring and fall race meets that were among the great social and sporting events of the year in Tientsin. Betting was a popular adjunct and even involved Chinese of means, who were great gamblers and enthusiastic supporters of the race courses, of which there were several in the area.[40]

Adjacent to the Race Club was the Tientsin Country Club, also a British institution. Both civilian and military personnel, who also had to be members of the Race Club, could become members. They paid five dollars — eight dollars for couples — for their membership, though there were additional charges for tennis and swimming privileges. The usual amenities were available, with dances, teas, games, and all of the rest. One American officer remembered that it was "one of the nicest country clubs I've ever been in. The dance floor was large and hung on springs, so it was easy on your dancing."⁴¹

The Tientsin Golf Club was also popular, with initiation fees of $50 and a $25 annual dues charge. The club boasted an 18-hole course "on the flat where Chinese graves constitute most of the hazards. Only a real enthusiast can obtain much of a thrill from the rather uninteresting course, but the fact that the luxury of two caddies may be enjoyed for the small sum of 40 cents Mex for 17 [18?] holes is a compensating feature." In addition, the existence of a nineteenth hole was an added attraction "for the unregenerated American exile." There was, in addition, an American Tennis Club with facilities for use at a small cost.⁴²

The American Army Polo Club was also a center of horsey and social events. Officers' wives were engaged in riding, having their own equitation classes, especially during the later 1920s. The Polo Club was a major venue on the Tientsin social scene and featured "tiffins" (luncheons) and other activities and events. With the ladies, the officers often staged paper hunts and sometimes hunted "Wanx"—or "Wonks"—wild dogs, usually of the chow variety. These animals, roaming the countryside in packs, were regarded as threats to humans and hence were fair game.⁴³

There were other institutions that helped in matters of regimental morals and morale. There was an active post exchange and commissary. There was, of course, also a base library; *The Sentinel* once recorded that in May of 1924, 845 books had been checked out, with mysteries and lighter reading by such authors as Zane Grey, Rex Beach, and Mary R. Rinehart, ranking among the most popular. The library also regularly subscribed to a considerable number of periodicals.⁴⁴

The YMCA, established in Tientsin in 1919, was in the forefront of helping the men to find wholesome ways to relax. Especially in the winter months, a program of "YMCA Sunday Afternoons" was inaugurated, featuring song services and Bible classes with the promise that if a soldier missed chow, "we will give you a fairly good substitute and it isn't beans." The YMCA was also the original site of Chinese language classes. Frequent dances and various tournaments were scheduled, such as pinochle, bridge and cribbage, among others. On occasions, "old fashioned parties" were held, featuring "taffy-pulls, the popping of popcorn, and the making of fudge." One officer was sufficiently impressed by all of these activities to declare "that the 'Y' was the only decent place in Tientsin where a soldier can go."⁴⁵

The "Y" greatly increased its role in 1925 when a large, spacious building on Race Course Road was taken over by the organization. Formally opened in late September, the building housed reading rooms, a pool room, a reception room, game rooms for Mah Jongg and cards, and a soda fountain "from which flows the best line of ice creams and soda to be found in China." Several spacious porches were in place, "where ... pleasant evenings can be spent." On the second floor, there were bedrooms transients could rent.[46]

On January 15, 1931, the Triangle Service League established the Tientsin Golden Dragon Chapter. Some years previously, the TSL was established by the Headquarters Office of the Army and Navy, and the Navy Department of the YMCA, as a service organization. Establishing chapters near many posts and stations of the nation's armed services, it sought to inculcate within its members the fourfold ideals of the "Y": to build up all servicemen physically, mentally, socially, and spiritually. Subsequently, the new creation enjoyed a measure of success in its Tientsin setting.[47]

Not to be outdone by the "Y," the American Red Cross had a substantial presence in Tientsin. The Knights of Columbus also boasted a cafeteria near the compound specializing in evening meals.[48]

In late 1927, another military, religious, and social society — or lodge — was founded at Tientsin: the "Can Do" Fortress No. 5, Century of Cornelius. The Century was a military and naval order that served U.S. forces both at home and abroad. The Tientsin body was established at the base chapel with the chaplain, Luther D. Miller, as its "Tribune." Other officers included those in the ranks of Centurian, Arareous, Outer Sentry, and at the highest level, Soldier. Subsequently, both officers and enlisted men and their wives and guests participated in various social activities, including formal dances and debates. On one occasion, the subject on the floor was: "Resolved: that there is more pleasure in bachelor life than there is in married life."[49]

The more familiar lodges, such as the Masons and Shriners, were active in Tientsin as well, as was the local Rotary Club, which took a special interest in the soldiers stationed in the city. Also boasting a considerable membership were the William Fitzgerald Camp No. 2 of the Spanish War Veterans and the Edward Sigerfoos Post No. 4 of the American Legion, named for Colonel Edward F. Sigerfoos, who commanded the regiment in 1917.

In addition, members of the 15th frequently performed service activities, especially on holidays, to benefit the youth of the American Army community. In the early 1930s, for instance, soldiers organized a Boy Scout troop.[50]

Chaplains certainly were of the opinion that they had something to do with the regiment's morals and morale, though over the years they varied in their interest and effectiveness. On the whole, they were a remarkable lot. One of the more active and energetic was Orville E. Fisher, who served the regiment in the early 1920s. Not apologizing for the role of religion in the Army setting, he argued that "religion is a necessity, not a luxury. Religion and patriotism are inseparable," he went on, declaring that "the idle worshipper becomes the worshipper of idols." In another of his regular columns in *The Sentinel*, he reminded the men that "you feed your body 21 times a week, whether it is hungry or not. Then why not throw your soul a bone once a week at least, even if it doesn't seem to be hungry. The poor thing may be too weak from starvation to make its wants known." As many chaplains had done over the years, he reminded his charges of the famous General Orders of May 2, 1778, issued at Valley Forge by General George Washington, directing that divine services be performed every Sunday at 11 o'clock in each brigade having chaplains; those without were to attend the places of worship nearest to them and officers were to set examples for their men by their own attendance. When, on the orders of the regiment's commanding officer, Fisher assumed the editorship of *The Sentinel* with the issue of May 20, 1921— extending to the December 28, 1923, issue — he had another platform for further exhortations and lectures, often in the form of editorials.[51]

The chaplain who most greatly influenced the regiment's life was undoubtedly Luther D. Miller. An Episcopal priest, he was one of the Army's outstanding chaplains. He was with the regiment from May 1925 until May 1928. An Army chaplain from August 1918, Miller had attended Thiel College and then the Chicago Theological Seminary, graduating in 1917. In Tientsin, he took in hand a long-felt need for a post chapel. For many years, Sunday services were held in the inadequate, unsightly Recreation Hall — the old "barn." With much volunteer help from troops and civilian friends, a large, bare room over General Headquarters was transformed into a chapel. Dedicated in the autumn of 1925, it boasted a vested choir, one of the few in the entire Army. One of Miller's innovations was to have each service sponsored by individual companies and organizations, thereby enhancing attendance, and his nonsectarian services appealed to all denominations.[52]

During his tenure in China, *The Sentinel* did not fail to note Miller's influence, once asserting that "this regiment is indeed fortunate in the type of Chaplain assigned to it. He is a man [who] enjoys every sport, indulging [in] many himself, [and] he conducts himself toward enlisted men and officers as one of them and has worked hard and faithfully to build up a spirit among the men that will lead in living a clean and comfortable life while on duty in China." On Miller's departure from the regiment an unusually warm note in *The Sentinel* recorded that his soldier-parishioners hated to see him go "because he is a 'man's man' and brings religion to us in a straight-forward way," and "because he was 'one of us.'" These attitudes forecast his future success, which was considerable.[53]

After China, Miller went to Fort Leavenworth, remaining from 1928 to 1937. Eventually, on July 14, 1945, as a major general, he became the Army's chief of chaplains, serving until his retirement in November 1949. Subsequently, he became canon precentor at Washington Cathedral, holding the post until 1961. Later, as a part-time canon, he often officiated at funerals in Arlington National Cemetery.[54]

Another man of the cloth of note to serve the 15th was Chaplain William L. Fisher, who came to the regiment in July of 1932. As was true of most of the chaplains to serve in China, he was well educated. He held the A.B. and A.M. degrees from Bethany College and a B.D. from Yale. He had also studied abroad at Oxford and in Germany, Switzerland, and Italy. A linguist, he possessed considerable knowledge of the Hebrew, Sanskrit and classic Greek languages. Fisher took full advantage of the opportunity to travel accorded his Army position and suspended all Protestant services in the base chapel for the entire month of February 1933, for instance, while he trekked across the vast expanses of the Gobi Desert.[55]

Regarding such excursions, the more enterprising and energetic chaplains often planned tours for the men of the regiment, enhancing their opportunities to travel. One of the most active was Chaplain Ora J. Cohee, with the regiment in the late 1920s. He was best known for his sightseeing trips to the Great Wall and other sites, including tours in and around Tienstin.[56]

Indeed, *The Sentinel* often encouraged the men to "see China while you are here." To these ends, by War Department order, every officer was allowed one month's detached service during his tour for travel in northern China, north of the Yangtze but including Shanghai, the "Paris of the East," a particularly attractive destination. Enlisted men traveled under separate leave arrangements.[57]

Some lengthy hunting, fishing and sightseeing trips ranged as far as Mongolia. In a typical excursion in October 1926, Lieutenants Cookson, Eugene W. Ridings and Thomas S. Timberman traveled to Korea and Manchuria, one of the highlights being the Diamond Mountains (Kongo-San) in the Chosun area of Korea.[58]

On many occasions, officers and enlisted men formed joint hunting parties, temporarily laying rank differentials aside. In the autumn of 1923, for instance, three privates, three sergeants and two officers—one being Lieutenant Colonel Albert Brevard Sloan, who for a time was the regiment's acting commanding officer — accompanied by two Chinese servants, scheduled a hunting trip to Shansi Province. The account of the expedition published in *The Sentinel* by the other officer present, Captain Jesse D. Cope, one of the most active of the regiment's huntsmen, extolled the "harmony and cheerful sportsmanship which prevailed during the time this party was together in camp and on the trail." "There was at all times," he went on, "a spirit of consideration, companionship, and gentlemanly treatment prevailing," and the trip had been both pleasant and profitable.[59]

Other men contented themselves with photography safaris, as one undertaken by Vance Lyndale and three companions. Riding donkeys out beyond Chinwangtao into the hills and mountains near the Great Wall, there they imbibed with pleasure the "bracing atmosphere away from civilization and society."[60]

Closer to home, provisions were made to accommodate the "epidemic of duck hunting going on amongst the foolish members of the Regiment." For example, Lieutenant John E. McCammon, of Headquarters Company, with Max Lorenzen, a civilian at Tientsin, staged a hunting trip to lakes in the vicinity of Taku frequented in huge numbers by migrating ducks. The venture was made by motor boat to Tangku and from there by Chinese houseboat.[61]

To facilitate this interest, for some years in the mid–1920s a duck hunting camp was maintained for officers and men who were sometimes deprived of more extended ventures because of the unrest that periodically plunged China into chaos. Underwritten by a substantial contribution from *The Sentinel*, this was another example of the paper's contributions to regimental recreational programs. The camp, located about five miles from the Hai Ho River on Lake Kuan Chiang near Taku, included the necessary amenities: comfortable sleeping quarters, messing facilities, sampans, boatmen and decoys. Transportation from Tientsin was furnished by Chinese river boats and sampans. Routinely, those interested in hunting were granted a four-day leave.[62]

In addition, for some years, hunting camps were maintained near the permanent facilities at the firing range, a destination especially favored by the regiment's enlisted men. The camp's proximity to the amenities of Chinwangtao was not merely incidental.[63]

Travel involved transportation and regarding China, there was the getting there in the first place. The U.S. Army Transports were the essential links tying the soldiers of the 15th to the States. These vessels usually sailed every two or three months from American West Coast ports and normally docked at Chinwangtao, the troops traveling to and from Tientsin on the Peking-Mukden railroad. On rare occasions, when the rail line was cut resulting from the incessant conflicts in the region, the transports would anchor at Taku Bar, southeast of Tientsin. In these instances, the troops would make the journey to the coast and back on the railway or on lighters towed by tugs on the Hai Ho River. In some cases, a Chinese coastal steamer would take the troops between Chinwangtao and Taku.[64]

Among the ships employed in serving the men in China was the USS *West Newark* which changed its name to the *Meigs* in honor of Major General Montgomery C. Meigs, quartermaster general during the Civil War. The vessel was an oil burner of 10,000 gross tons and was to be a freight and animal carrier replacing the transport *Dix*. Other vessels used included the U.S. Army Transports *Warren*, the *U.S. Grant*, and *Logan*. The *Grant* had been built in Germany in 1907, and was christened the *Koenig Wilhelm II*. During the Great War it was interned in the United States, and was taken over by the United States Navy, renamed the *Madawaska* and used for a troop transport. After the War, she was turned over to the U.S. Army and renamed the *Grant*. From April 1925 to 1928, she was rebuilt. This vessel replaced the old-time favorite, the USAT *Thomas*, the "Doughboy Special." For 29 years the *Thomas* had plied the oceans, logging 105 trips to the Far East, transporting about 40,664 officers and 170,000 men, never losing a passenger or crew member by accident. It had weathered numerous typhoons, one of which was named the Thomas Typhoon. She had been caught in that storm out of Manila but survived to reach port, "a badly battered ship."[65]

The *Grant* was much better appointed and more comfortable than the *Thomas*. In early 1932, though the *Grant* remained in service, this ship was in turn supplemented by an even more impressive ship, the USAT *Republic*, then the largest and most luxurious Army transport in use. It grossed 17,910 tons compared with the *Grant*'s 9,410. Another ship contemporary with the *Republic* which also made voyages to the Far East, was the *Liberty*.[66]

The comings and goings of the Army transports always aroused considerable interest. This was manifested in *The Sentinel*, which frequently published special editions— such as one styled the "Next Boat Edition"— which discussed the men departing and arriving in considerable detail. When ships were leaving or arriving, normal activities around and about the compound were suspended, including Sunday chapel services. For a number of years, a Chinese "Boat Bazaar" was held in the compound's Recreation Hall. Here numerous Chinese vendors and merchants provided visitors from the transports as well as departing personnel with a final opportunity to purchase Chinese wares.[67]

No matter how the men felt about service in China, they found irresistible the compelling cry, "There's a Transport in the Harbor / And I'm Ordered Home Today," or as a poem by Private Otto Beinke of Company K expressed it:

> There's a transport in the harbor,
> Which has a ruddy light,
> This transport in the harbor,
> Is leaving us to-night.
> With Tom, and John, and Harry,
> With Dick, and Mike, and Joe,
> And all that she can carry,
> To Frisco!—From Ching-Wang-Tao [sic].[68]

Certainly, orders for home were gratifying to many of the men, yet one writing under the pen name of "Beejo" admitted that "In my dreams I'll oft remember / How I trod your Foochow Road / How I groaned, and groaning staggered / 'Neath my weighty, liquid load!" Hoping that China would never know "the heel of a Volstead or a Bryan," he took the precaution of smuggling out "a Quart beneath my coat."[69]

Private George R. "China" Becker, a popular reporter from Company H, addressed other matters pertaining to sailing home in the last of his regular "Ramblings" columns in *The Sentinel*: "Two more days until we say goodbye, mayhap forever, to Tientsin and its sweetly scented environs, filthy grog shops, beautiful public parks, enchanting temples and last but not least the highly touted moon maidens that we heard so much about before we came over here." He especially hated to leave "H" Company, he admitted, "because there are plenty of good fellows in it and duty in a machine gun company in China is as light as it is anywhere in the Army in any outfit." He also liked the clean, orderly barracks, the excellent chow, the "Y" and the Privates' Club.[70]

Still, on balance, those going home knew what they were doing and had few doubts, recognizing what they were leaving behind and hardly regretting it. As one soldier-poet described it: "I am sick of the mongrel in China / I am sick of the Jap and the Chink / And faraway spots on the charts are / No place for yours truly, I think." He was weary to death of "curry and rice and all," as well as "bathing with Lysol, and washing with carbolic soap." He longed for "a wind with a tingle," and especially wanted to mingle, "With crowds that are white folks / and clean." He therefore cordially hated "damned lying poets" who sang "of the East as enthralling," sentiments which had started him to roam, but now "I hear the Occident calling / Oh Lord but I want to go home."[71]

On the date of departure, outside of the gates there came the rattle and bang of hundreds of firecrackers, the send-off of Chinese friends of

"There's a Transport in the Harbor." Troops departing from Chinwangtao, China, on the USAT *Grant*. Cover of *The Sentinel*, October 12, 1929, by Private First Class L.M. Healy of the 15th Infantry.

the soldiers from hundreds of little local shops. And then, their luggage accompanying them on motor trucks, the men marched to the station behind the band playing such selections as "Auld Lang Syne." One Company K man once described the station scene: "At first [I] thought it was Reno on a busy morning," he began, "so many separations, but finally decided that were it Reno there would be no tears." Tongue in cheek, he continued: "But really it was very sad and I think of the fatherless homes tonight in Tientsin and my heart goes out to the poor war widows with deepest sympathy in their great loss. Have often heard of the horrors of war but Monday [May 9th] was the first time I had actually seen any of them."[72]

Soon, the long special train carrying the passengers to Chinwangtao to board the homebound ship slowly got under way. Departing soldiers leaned from the windows waving last goodbyes and comrades with sad faces waved back. Indeed, of the number many obviously regretted their decision to return to the States and "decided, when it was too late to get the 'extension,' that China is a pretty good place after all." Many men "broke down at the last moment and cried like little children, their arms twined around the shoulders of the comrades they were leaving behind. The general idea is that the American soldier is not emotional but the last ten minutes on that station platform yesterday dissipates that impression," one account of the event noted. "The American soldier kisses the girl he leaves behind him and smiles but the American soldier says goodbye to the pals in khaki with misty eyes, with a terrific gulping down of that strange lump in the throat." These festivities caused one participant to reflect that "Army life, it seems, is just a long series of 'hello' and goodbye.'"[73]

The casual detachments were usually accompanied by those returning under guard, perhaps bound for the U.S. Penitentiary on McNeil Island or the U.S. Disciplinary Barracks at Alcatraz. Others were sent home for alcoholism or for other personal difficulties and deficiencies. On some occasions, the bodies of men of the regiment who had died in the past few months also made their last journey home on the same transport. There was an occasional suicide among the dead.

Others left behind, however, having had to put up with the exuberance of those departing for many days before the event, entertained less charitable thoughts and feelings: "All you hear now is 'steen days and a breakfast,'" (until the ship departs), or "thirty-eight days and a hot cake." Certainly, "we hate to see 'em leave, but all the same, we'll be glad when they're gone."[74]

The ship having at last sailed homeward, the regiment turned to absorbing the new arrivals. Some, including T.J. McCafferty, were stirred to regretful remembrance: "Oh, the time is getting shorter / And it surely makes me pine / That *Grant* transport is breaking up / That Old Gang of Mine," while "Rex," in his "So Long Gang," bid those departing a fond farewell and wished, "When China has become a memory / Back in that land where skies are blue / Have a thought for the Pals behind you / In the gallant old 'Can Do.'"[75]

Welcoming incoming 15th personnel at Tientsin's East Station. Cover of *The Sentinel*, June 29, 1929, by Private First Class L.M. Healy of the 15th Infantry.

Within China, forms of transportation varied from modern railway accommodations down to wheelbarrows and sedan chairs carried by coolies. Most of the railways in northern China were government-owned and travel was possible over all the lines in times of peace. There were first, second and third class passengers but ordinarily officers traveled only in first class. The Blue Express, running between Peking-Tientsin-Pukow over the Tientsin-Pukow line and making connections for Shanghai, was "the best train in North China," and the accommodations aboard the train surpassed many in the United States. The Peking-Mukden Railway permitted officers of the international military contingents in Tientsin, or their dependents, to travel on inexpensive Leave Warrants. Foreign hotel accommodations, all on the "American Plan," were available for rail travelers in most of the large cities in northern China.

Some of the regiment's personnel owned autos, though there were few usable roads and maintenance was uncertain and expensive. Because there were thousands of rickshaws available for hire at a nominal sum, the absence of a motor car was not a hardship. In cold or wet weather, however, the ride in a rickshaw was not comfortable.[76]

Throughout the history of the 15th various expedients were employed to enhance morale. One was the perennial subject of chow, always a matter of prime concern among soldiers. The regiment's leadership exerted considerable effort in feeding the men. The editor of *The Sentinel* once stated that "the old war cry in France — 'When do we eat?' — has practically no echo here in China," because the 15th was "the best fed regiment in the Army!"[77]

Traditional occasions such as July 4 were opportunities for elaborate feasts and picnics. In 1926, for instance, the 4th was celebrated over a three-day weekend, featuring baseball games, band serenades and other activities. The festivities ended with the serving of a huge meal, partially underwritten by the American community in Tientsin, which was enjoyed by soldiers and civilians alike.[78]

Christmas was, of course, not neglected and in 1925, one account recorded that the day was "chuck full of excitement and many pleasures" including dancing and singing following the excellent Christmas dinner. So important was the annual Christmas dinner that in 1931, Colonel James D. Taylor — who always had an eye out for troop morale — ordered a "Christmas Clemency," authorizing company commanders to invite members of their commands undergoing punishment for minor offenses to eat the "Big Feed" with their units.[79]

Other measures to enhance morale followed myriad paths. For instance, there was the awarding every three months of the Regimental Cup for Soldierly Conduct for the company excelling in several specified areas.[80]

Also important was the listing in *The Sentinel* of selected individuals who had been designated as the commanding officer's orderlies. These immaculate, model soldiers, either a private or private first class, were named at guard mount, adding some interest to that otherwise boring, familiar routine. Selectees received a special 24 hour pass.[81]

Added to the spirited competition between companies was the awarding of the Banner Blue on the second and fourth Saturday of each month — later once a month — to the company whose barracks and personnel, equipment and supplies within the barracks presented the most satisfactory appearance. *The Sentinel* explained the reasons behind the competition: "Our appropriations for rations and repairs are very limited, the buildings are in poor repair, and conditions outside the Compound are a constant menace to the health and efficiency of the command. It is therefore highly important that these be offset by the maintenance of excellent messes and comfortable and cheerful barracks." Multiple winners of the Banner Blue were presented with a miniature banner, which became a permanent trophy of the organization.[82]

One measure of how the commanders regarded the men of the 15th and of their levels of trust in them involved the pass system, often a subject of controversy and bitter debate. On one occasion a letter from "An Illiterate Private," writing to the editor of the *Infantry Journal* (May 1921 issue), which was reprinted in *The Sentinel*, assailed the too severe control exercised over the men throughout the Army who were kept "in camp like so many sheep." When they did get to town, he further complained, they were far too closely controlled by MPs. "Why is it that we are shut down on so tightly?" he wanted to know. "Is it because our superiors have no confidence in us, or is it because they think that a man that will voluntarily come into the Army is a fool and needs a wet nurse?" Indeed, these policies had "taken all the pride, ambition, and self-respect" out of the troops.[83]

The private's remarks might well have been aimed specifically at the rigid control experienced in the 15th during the early 1920s in the regime of Colonel William M. Morrow, widely perceived as a martinet. When he departed in the summer of 1921, it seemed a good opportunity to introduce a new system. The interim commander was Lieutenant Colonel Albert Brevard Sloan, who was warmly welcomed, and certainly, "the gray, quiet, considerate old gentleman who relieved Colonel Morrow ... has a different view of the [pass] situation. He knows he is in command of a regiment of soldiers composed of real men, and he intends to treat them as such."[84]

Accordingly, in early June of 1921, Regimental Headquarters instituted a liberal pass system closely tied to conduct.[85]

But after a few months it was clear that it had failed largely because of abuses when "liberty was mistaken for license." Pass restrictions were reinstituted and when Sloan's interim command ended with the arrival of Colonel William F. Martin in the autumn of 1921, the troops could only mourn his departure with tinges of regret and reflections on their own shortcomings, failures and missed opportunities.[86]

Throughout the history of the 15th in China, sticks as well as carrots were employed to influence the attitudes and conduct of the soldiers. *The Sentinel* often served as a sounding board and avenue for lecturing and advising the troops as to their proper conduct. Many topics seemed fit subjects for consideration: there was some concern about swearing and the paper printed a letter from Lord Chesterfield to his son advising him to abjure vulgar language. Even slang seemed suspect, one soldier deploring it as "an enemy of sincerity."[87]

Gambling was excoriated and the men were enjoined to avoid the hazards of the "speckled hand grenades." Another perennial subject was the need for enlisted men to salute their officers—and those of the foreign nations as well.[88]

A frequent exhortation in *The Sentinel* read: "When Did You Write Home Last? Do It Now." Colonel James D. Taylor was sufficiently concerned about his men's writing home to relatives and friends that he made it a matter of a standing order, which stated in part: "In order that the families of enlisted men may know about them and not be subjected to unnecessary worry every man will be required to write a letter to some one in his home at least once a month." Organization and detachment commanders on the last day of every month "would submit with the Morning Report a report to the commanding officer, stating that every man in his organization has written a letter home or stating the names of the men who have failed to write with reasons therefore, if any."[89]

There were also frequent warnings to the men that they must curb their tendencies to run up too much "jawbone," that is, credit. Especially repudiated was a prevailing notion that "the gang plank will pay all debts." Many stores in Tientsin, such as Whiteaway's, a popular clothing emporium, categorically stipulated: "Terms Cash.—NO CREDIT." Other businesses offered a ten percent discount for cash. Nonetheless, it was far too easy to run up a bill, and regimental punishment could result if a soldier ran up large debts.[90]

There was another side to this coin, however. It was also recognized that the Chinese often took advantage of unwary and gullible soldiers, and the 15th's high command refused to act on behalf of merchants seeking to collect bad debts, observing that "The Government is not a collecting agency nor is it in any way responsible for the debts contracted by enlisted men or their families unless agreed to by commanding officer of the man."[91]

CHAPTER VIII

The Training Cycle

Heard in the day room: "The Chinese sure ought to be the best shots in the world, as the squeeze system comes natural to them."[1]

> So polish up your Springfield,
> And perfect your Eagle Eye,
> For it'll be "God Help the Man
> Who doesn't Qualify!"[2]

In December of 1927, *The Sentinel* published details of the regiment's training program for 1928. The training year was to run from December 1, 1927 to November 30, 1928. There were two general periods, the first consisting of garrison training, extending from December 1, 1927, to March 15, 1928, the second for the remainder of the year. Ordinarily the daily round of training was to run for four hours, ending at 12 o'clock noon. The afternoon was to be devoted to schools, administration, athletics and recreation. Integral to the training cycle, competitions were held, such as an annual Drill Competition, Horse and Transportation Show, which would be scheduled in April, followed by a regimental Athletic Meet and Strength Test, in May, concluding with the Gallery Practice Competition, or smallbore firing, on an indoor range. In the summer, the men would be at the firing range at varying locations near the port city of Chinwangtao, where combat problems were also staged. This round was followed by the bayonet course. In some instances, field exercises near Tientsin and hikes and marches in the Chinese countryside were interspersed with the other activities. With variations, this pattern, barring interruptions by actions of various Chinese warlords, was followed by the regiment for years.[3]

Of these events, the annual firing for qualification was undoubtedly the most important. The troops were constantly reminded that they were Regular infantry soldiers of the U.S. Army, an important distinction. After all, the badge signifying their military specialty was the crossed muskets, symbol of the traditions of the infantry as "Queen of Battles"; as the "Flower of the Army." As Colonel William K. Naylor, the regiment's commanding officer in the mid-1920s, put it, "There is no part of a soldier's training, particularly the regular soldier who is apt to be the first line of defense in an emergency, that is more important than the handling of the rifle." This stance was in keeping with official U.S. Army doctrine which, despite the advances in armaments so prominently displayed in the Great War, still determinedly emphasized the role of the infantryman armed principally with rifle and bayonet.[4]

There were more substantial incentives beyond exhortations. Those who reached expert level received five dollars "drinking and tobacco money" per month in extra pay, while sharpshooters received three; those attaining only marksman level, though qualifying, received no extra money. These inducements were all the more welcomed because the War Department, struggling with budget constraints, repeatedly raised the scores required for qualification with the rifle and the machine gun, thereby saving on "shooting pay."[5] In addition, the commanding general of the American Forces in China, as well as the regimental and battalion commanders, usually offered cash incentives as high as $20 for the individuals posting the highest scores. The Kailan Mining Administration, a British-Belgian-Chinese mining company, "in appreciation of the services rendered by the regiment during the recent Civil War in North China" (1922), thereafter presented a silver loving cup to the organization making the highest individual average percentage in annual target practice with rifle or machine gun. Other shooting prizes were offered by most of the rifle companies and certain individuals. One of the latter was Ralph Freeman, owner of the Stag Cafe in Tientsin — and a former member of the regiment — who had a branch establishment at the range. He offered five-dollar cash prizes to enlisted personnel for the highest score with rifle, the Browning automatic rifle (commonly called the B.A.R.), the .45 caliber pistol, the 37 mm one-pounder gun, the Stokes trench mortar and the machine gun. A consolation prize of 12 bottles of beer went to the highest-scoring man in each category who did not qualify, easing the pain of the losers. Finally, *The Sentinel* sometimes awarded silver medals to the enlisted men who made the highest scores with rifle, machine gun and pistol.[6]

On the other side of the coin, failing to qualify labeled one a "bolo man," the butt of sarcastic comment and innumerable gibes, and gave one the knowledge that he joined the 10 percent of those in the U.S. Army's infantry outfits who had not qualified with the rifle. The term "bolo" stemmed from Philippine service at the turn of the century when these long, heavy machetes were used by the Moros as weapons. Thus, if a man could not shoot well, he could conceivably use a bolo, but was thenceforth considered a disgrace by his peers, though in jest. Fear of this failure was once captured poetically:

> . . . .
> I must go to the range again, for fate of a bolo shot,
> Is a hard fate, and as sad a fate as falls to a doughboy's lot.
> But all I ask is a steady breeze, and a little help from the pit.
> With slack, hold, squeeze, and wobbly knees,
> And the Captain throwing a fit.[7]

The excuses of those failing to qualify were legion, one man blaming his rifle: "For Sale. One U.S. Army rifle, model 1918, calibre 30 complete with all accessories and one slightly used score book. This rifle is a product of the Flinching and Blinking Manufacturing Company and is guaranteed to furnish plenty of alibis on any range.... Reason for selling—owner has been issued a bolo and has no further use for [a] rifle." Another with a low score also had recourse to an ad: "Lost—one bullet—Reward. Staff Sgt. Hakala Hqrs. Co. Apparently strayed on the way to the target."[8]

One soldier had trouble with the Browning automatic rifle. "They're heavier than a railroad gun," he complained, and further lamented:

> You set them "Semi-Auto'"
> And the damned things fire a burst!
> They handle like a remount mule,
> And jam like things accursed!
> Why, a doggone issue pillow
> Is a better weapon far
> Than the **)&+%***@ B.A.R.
> . . . .[9]

In the last analysis, each soldier perhaps had only himself to blame for any failures, though his buddies in the pits behind the targets, who were pasting up holes and marking the scores, might be suspect: "Santa Claus ain't putting out boys— / You get just what you hit / I think the whole damn pit-detail / Is rotten and half of them are lit."[10]

Perennially, *The Sentinel* was a convenient venue used to encourage and admonish the men regarding their activities at the range. A certain Lieutenant Passailaigue, author of the article "For All Who Would Make Expert Shots," advised the men by means of key dos and don'ts: shooters should not disobey camp orders by "slipping out at night or sitting up

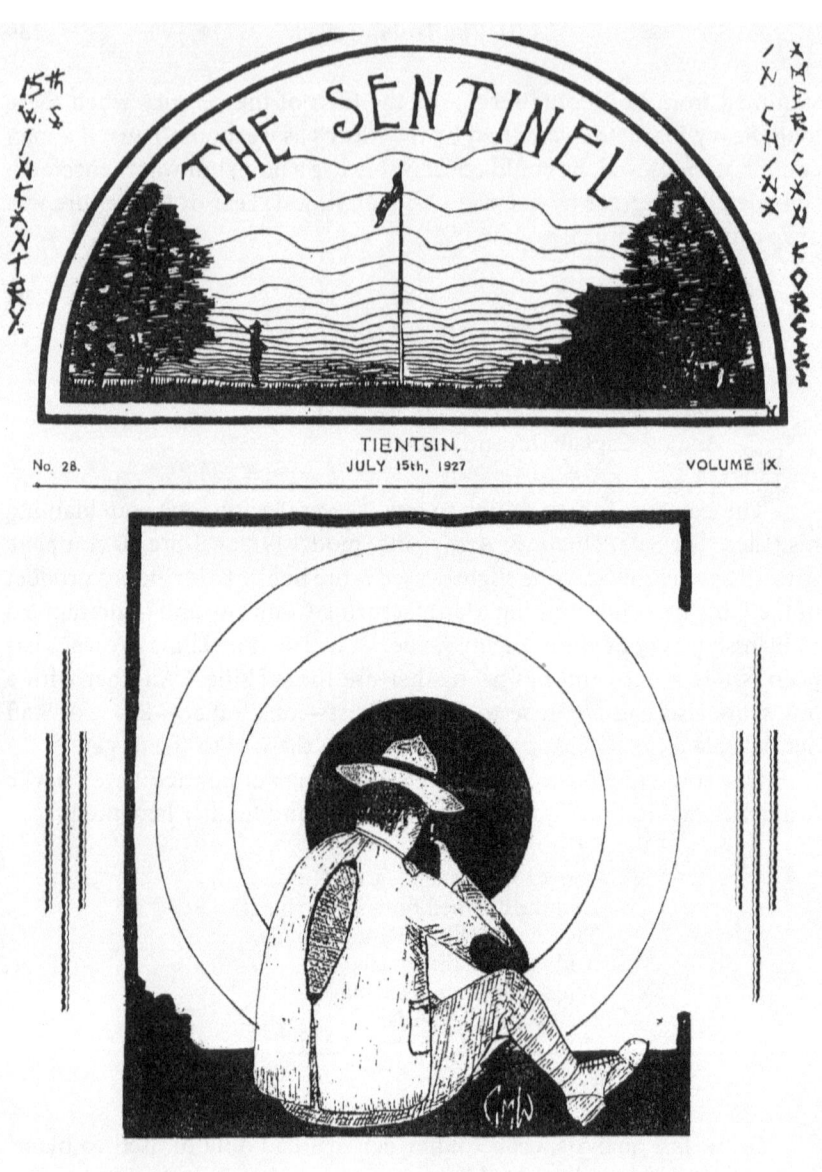

"Fanciful Target." Cover of *The Sentinel*, July 15, 1927.

after taps," he warned. Neither were the men to "smoke excessively, or drink at all during the time of firing preliminary and record." Positively, all were urged to "do your thinking, eating, sleeping, talking, all about the old rifle." Finally, for those who wished to "see the old white disc" they must recognize that as one wag put it, "just [as for] the girls," the shooter should "hold 'em and squeeze 'em," and if one holds and squeezes enough, "in either case he will be successful."[11]

Further advice was offered pistol shooters. Lieutenant Louis J. Harant of the 23rd Infantry, in an article, "Pistol Shots, Like Other Shots, Are Made — Not Born," published in that unit's paper, *The Trail*, emphasized special muscular development, noting that the pistol-shooting aspirant must "be in a higher developed state of physique than required of his brother rifle shot." Form was important, and could be practiced before a mirror in the bedroom, "for this is the place to correct [mistakes] without colliding with embarrassment." Harant also suggested dietary modifications because a "light stomach" aids in breath control, he declared, while hard-to-digest food increased the pulse, hindering a good performance. In addition, a "clogging" of abdominal organs must be avoided, and fruit should be eaten to help prevent it. Pistol shooters should drink only water, avoid tea and coffee, and "keep away from 'bright' lights, retire early and arise 'at first sign of dawn', and salute the new day by 'dry' shooting at some target."[12]

Unfortunately, such exhortations were not always effective, at least in the periodic competitions with the marines, though the regiment normally fared better against other competitors such as sailors from the U.S. Navy's gunboats on duty in Tientsin, or British soldiers from their detachment there. The marines were usually those from the Legation Guard in Peking, and though numbering fewer than the regiment, more often than not bested the infantry. The soldiers complained that the marines brought in "ringers" when shooting in competition, thereby restoring the balance resulting from drawing from a smaller force. There were exceptions to the usual course of events: "It's been a long time since we've cleaned up on the Marines," one writer in *The Sentinel* exulted, "but boys, she has been did!" he noted in the late summer of 1923.[13]

One of the banes of the training program was the plethora of training manuals that the men were expected to master, or as one expressed it, "A loaf of bread, a jug of wine / And thou Oh! Training Guide." The bored soldiers poked fun at the publications, the *Manual of Courts-Martial* being described as "the usual detective and crook story [which] tries to show that Lincoln's remark about Liberty and Justice for all applies to the Army. Everybody knows it does not but the author seems to think so as he uses 806 pages to tell the story. Snappy in parts but too long between those parts. Would be better if illustrated." The *Manual of Interior Guard Duty* was described as a "little book of blank verse, [which was] rather sentimental, especially about prisoners. Sometimes the verses are difficult of interpretation, [however], as the one entitled 'The Officer of the Day.'"[14]

The months of June, July and August were designated for summer training and target practice. The two battalions alternately proceeded to camp for a period of several weeks each. The time of departure at the East Train Station of the battalions for camp were festive occasions. One soldier, writing in *The Sentinel*, recorded that there were "plenty of folks to see the soldats start for camp.... The usual following of girls were there to see their soldier friends get away. Funny but you never can move soldiers without seeing a lot of dames at the train to bid the boys goodbye."[15]

When the Peking-Mukden railway was unserviceable because of civil wars, it was necessary for the men to be shipped to camp by boat, departing from Tangku for Chinwangtao. In 1928, for example, the Navy's USS *Pecos* and other vessels transported the soldiers to the rifle range. These sea voyages were invariably criticized as being markedly inferior to the usual rail transport, and dirty boats, crowding and inadequate food were often complained of.[16]

For some years, the rifle range was located at Leichuang, "one of the filthiest little villages to be found in a country where filth is the password," as one account noted. It was located on the Peking-Mukden railway about 105 miles northeast of Tientsin, "in a little pocket between absolutely barren rocky hills [and] sand every place," with "not a river not a tree." There in their tent city the men endured many plagues, including "sweltering in ... Hades" and clouds of mosquitoes; all too frequently, their tents were inundated by flood waters. They used donkeys to ride to and from the range.[17] But there was a positive side to the Leichuang range. After their strenuous work on the target range, until 1921 when civil unrest in China and a late summer flood put an end to it, the men went to a summer tent camp on the beach near Chinwangtao for combined recreation and maneuvers. There, they could swim, rides horses, fish, hike or stroll along the beach. Baseball games and endless rounds of bridge were played, and movies were screened. The more venturesome took donkey trips into the hills behind Chinwangtao.[18]

For various reasons, especially because of its filthy surroundings, its being subject to flooding, and its offering no range for field firing nor opportunities for diversion for the men, the installation at Leichuang was abandoned, and in 1923 a new place was chosen at Nan Ta Ssu, on the Gulf of Chihli. Between 1923 and 1927, the 15th leased this site from the Kailan Mining Administration. It was situated on a ten-mile stretch of beautiful crescent beach between the Chinese resort city of Peitaiho (Beidaihe) and the port of Chinwangtao—about six miles south of the latter, with its docks, ships and visiting fleets. The view was exceptional, and in the distant background were the mountains around the city of Shankaikwan, 12 miles to the north. Soon affectionately known as "Nanty Zoo," it was more grandly referred to as "Nan Ta Ssu by the Sea." There, residents had the opportunity of watching "the cute little gnats gnating, and the flying fish flying and the sand fleas fleaing." But despite its drawbacks, the men eagerly looked forward to being on the beach, a haven from the torrid heat and enervating humidity of Tientsin.[19]

Certainly, Nan Ta Ssu was an altogether much more satisfactory location than was the earlier one. "The Country Place," as Chaplain Orville Fisher styled it, was in no danger of flooding. The bathing beach was ideal, access to which greatly relieved the tedium of the target range routine. The water supply was abundant, and there was train service within half a mile. The men's health seemed to be greatly improved and morale was excellent, he reported.[20]

There were three separate installations at the new location. One, the rest camp, was initially called Camp Spoerry. Housing officers and their families, it was named for Lieutenant Gottfried W. Spoerry, who built it and was initially in charge. There was also the enlisted men's camp and finally, the target range lying between the railroad and the sea with the targets and butts on the edge of the beach. The officers and their families eagerly availed themselves of the amenities of the rest camp, which glaringly accentuated the clear distinctions between the commissioned and enlisted ranks. In 1926, "Officers' Row" along "Gold Fish Boulevard" was about 300 yards from the main soldiers' camp and a minute's walk from an excellent bathing beach. The rifle range was about a five minute walk. Tentage was provided as shelter. The tent floors were bricked and covered with Chinese matting, making quite comfortable living quarters, and the cost of meals and incidental expenses were minimal. Tea was served daily in quarters at a small extra charge, and a special kitchen was provided for mothers who desired to prepare their children's food. The adults' usual sport consisted of riding, swimming and hiking. For the children, members in good standing of "The Sand Dune Club," there was playground equipment including swings, seesaws and merry-go-rounds. Basketball and baseball games and swimming events were among the other activities pursued.[21]

Reflecting the spirit of "the season," in 1923, *The Sentinel* boasted a society column, the "Nan Ta Ssu Zephyrs," written by Barbara Spoerry, the wife of the builder of the officers' camp, in which she detailed all of the doings of the regiment's social set. Various tents at the camp taken over by various families had been named. These included the "Haven of Rest," "Dew Drop Inn," "Seldom Inn," and others of similar tenor. General and Mrs. Connor visited the tent camp the previous Saturday, she reported.

As guests of Colonel and Mrs. King, they remained for dinner before returning to the city of Peitaiho, where the general had taken a cottage for the summer. Other distinguished guests included the U.S. minister to China, Dr. Jacob Gould Schurman, accompanied by Colonel R.H. Dunlap, the commanding officer of the Marine Legation Guard at Peking. In other activity, officers of the USS *Tracy*, a destroyer anchored at Chinwangtao, came to the beach in motor boats, transporting a party to their ship for dinner. Visiting firemen were frequent, as, for example, General Takada, in command of Imperial Japanese Forces in North China, who dropped in with his staff.[22]

One excursion that officers and their families took advantage of at the range was to ride the supply train from Nan Ta Ssu station to Shankaikwan, where the Great Wall drops down to the sea.[23]

By the summer of 1926, Nan Ta Ssu no longer had the appearance of a "temporary camp in the midst of a desert," but had assumed the aspect of a permanent garrison post. Its regime included a 4:30 A.M. rising which reminded a former farmboy in "K" Company "of sneaking up on [the] wild oats down on the farm."[24]

Lieutenant Colonel George Marshall was in charge of the improvements at camp, and perhaps only a lack of time prevented him from introducing "all the features of Atlantic City," including a "Million Dollar Amusement Pier and a Bathing Beauty Contest," one wag observed. In place of sand, brick walkways were in place. Street lamps had been added and a radio station permitting communication with Tientsin was set up. Though the camp was still under canvas, there were welcomed additions. For those all-important drinks, there was the Stag Cafe, the Sergeants' Club, across the tracks, as well as Jim Crow's Place, and the Union Club. More sobersided was the roomy, comfortable YMCA building made of straw matting, with its many amenities.[25]

There were water sports, bathing beauties and general high jinks. Swimming lessons were provided for all the troops stationed at Nan Ta Ssu, though there was at least one drowning reported in 1926, that of Private Alfred H. Pickard, of Company F. This did not deter the campers from swim meets and umbrella races, the object of the latter being to swim with an open umbrella, never letting it touch the water.[26]

Many of the bathing beauties were drawn from the ranks of the families of both officers and enlisted men. To accommodate and help entertain the women present, in 1926. Lieutenant Helmer W. Lystad conducted a ladies' physical culture class which met daily on the beach at 11:30. He had much previous experience along this line under the tutelage of Flo Ziegfeld of "Follies" fame.[27]

The Sentinel regularly reported on such leisure-time activities as the "Funny Fancies at Camp," such as dressing up in tacky clothes and dancing to while away a rainy day. This all manifested a Chinese version of America's Jazz Age as interpreted by the unusually high-spirited collection of younger officers—and the not so young—who populated the regiment. Even Marshall revealed a more relaxed aspect, at variance with his usual restrained demeanor.[28]

Other star attractions at the beach were the Chinese fishermen engaged in surf fishing. The manner in which they conducted their business captured fascinated onlookers who eagerly examined the catches, noting details of the activities of the buyers and sellers who animatedly and vociferously debated the monetary worth of each net haul. One *Sentinel* columnist describing these sights noted that the scene was especially interesting at night, "when the plaintive wail of the fisherman's chant wafts into camp on the ocean breezes."[29]

The main business of Nan Ta Ssu remained the range firing and other training exercises. As a supplement to firing at static bull's-eyes, small boats were launched to provide at least a modicum of experience in firing at moving objects. In addition, giant Chinese kites and moving targets carried on cables were used for makeshift anti-aircraft practice.[30]

Among the activities carried out at the range was the selection of the Chief of Infantry's Combat Squad of the 15th Regiment. This was initiated in 1924, when the War Department ordered that an honor combat team be selected annually from all infantry regiments. The members of the squad were those judged to be the most proficient in the infantry exercises described in *Training Regulations 145–6, Musketry*.[31]

An innovation much discussed in the paper and about the compound added another dimension to the training program. In 1924, men of the Third Battalion, following their stint at the firing range at Nan Ta Ssu, were ordered to break their return rail journey to Tientsin at Tangshan, about 85 miles to the east of the compound. From there, they hiked home with full combat packs, demonstrating their ability to take to the field if required. The outfit averaged 21 miles per day, a good clip considering that "the entire route was over uncharted roads and in places no roads at all and the best of them of Chinese manufacture and that the weather was intensely hot."[32]

After the field problems were completed, the remaining residents of Nan Ta Ssu departed, and, as one described it, "like the Arabs of old we will silently fold our tents and steal our way back to Tientsin to remain thruout [sic] the long dreary Winter until the call of the wild overcomes us once more."[33]

Indeed, especially for the brass and their families, these summer experiences remained a high point of the regimental year. But of whatever rank, undoubtedly Nan Ta Ssu was one of the more desirable and memorable venues for members of the regiment.

Despite the success of the range at Nan Ta Ssu, in 1927 a new site was sought for the summer camp. The one selected was about six miles east of the old camp and one mile south of the train station at Chinwangtao, and about 400 yards from the beach which, though satisfactory, was not quite up to the standards of Nan Ta Ssu. Everything else was a vast improvement: there were more targets — 25 instead of about a third of that number — speeding up the firing process. In addition, a better machine gun range was set up and supplies did not have to be hauled as far. Also, electrical current was available from Chinwangtao, making possible lighting and the operation of motion picture projectors and other equipment. A branch post exchange also operated. As to other amenities, dues of ten dollars per month entitled one to all the privileges of the Chinwangtao Club, which boasted excellent tennis courts and a fine golf course. The main attraction, however, remained ocean bathing and swimming. The atmosphere was relaxed, one soldier noting that "the work was not the most strenuous we have ever encountered." It was also now possible for all of the regiment to be at the range simultaneously, a situation long desired by General Castner. A permanent detachment, composed of an officer and 21 men, was thenceforth stationed at CWT (Chinwangtao) — as the post was called for short. The men would serve as caretakers and continue construction work.[34]

The new installation was initially named Camp Dabney in honor of the late, lamented Major Henry Harold Dabney. After Camp Dabney's first year, it was renamed Camp Burrowes, to commemorate First Lieutenant Robert M. Burrowes of Company E, a Phi Beta Kappa graduate of Yale and a veteran of the Great War, who died in China in 1928.[35]

Infantrymen were also required to qualify annually with the bayonet, the next item on the regimental training agenda. The bayonet course normally initiated the regiment's autumn activities. The 15th's for some time was located at Tientsin, but at other times at Tangshan. In any case, the "fighting spirit which the bayonet exemplifies" was stressed. A favorite Civil War story that made the rounds seemed to capture the proper tone. This concerned the secretary of war in 1865, who once observed that no one could "do anything with Southern Troops who when they get whipped they'll retreat to them Southern swamps and bayous. You haven't got the fish nets made that'll catch them," he declared. "Oh yes, we have," remarked an unnamed general. "We've got just the nets for traitors, in the bayous or anywhere." "Hey? What nets?" "Bayou-nets!" and "he pointed his joke with his fork, spearing a fish ball savagely."[36]

That spirit was perhaps even better captured by an anonymous poet in his "Freedom's Blade": "I AM THE BAYONET," it proudly proclaimed. "I am the wrath of Jehovah"; "I glitter in the sun like the soul of man unloosed." And, "I am valor's comrade and the poltroons nemesis / I am courage incarnate." The cold steel was also "the avenger of murdered babes and ravaged women," and "the hope of civilization, the doom of tyrants"; in short, it was "the fear of God."[37]

This part of the training cycle became immeasurably easier in 1932 with the introduction of a new, less challenging, bayonet course enabling a 100-percent qualification as experts of all the rifle companies. *The Sentinel* explained: "The elimination of the shell holes removed much of the former danger, and many men with weak knees and bad legs who were formerly excused had no difficulty in qualifying."[38]

After the return of the regiment from the range and the completion of the bayonet qualifications, the autumn activities—and also those in the spring—normally involved maneuvers and field problems, conducted to the extent possible within the limited training facilities and terrain in and around Tientsin. The troops drilled on vacant lots near the compound and the fields to the south, though this area was "much cut up by irrigation ditches, truck gardens and brick kilns, and from July to September is usually under water or boggy." Further out, there was an open plain, "without gardens and with but few ditches, which extends four or five miles to the south." One officer, Captain Charles L. Bolte, who served as regimental operations officer under Colonel Burt, deplored the conditions, stating that about all that could be done "were some elementary and largely unrealistic attempts to teach the squad in the attack and defense." Occasionally the regiment "deployed to its emergency defense position as part of the inter-allied plan to defend Tientsin. This was a half-hearted and uncoordinated effort," and he recalled "no exchange of views on tactical planning with the legation, the allies, or even within the 15th Infantry."[39]

But this view was too pessimistic. Despite the limited circumstances, over the years the 15th maintained familiarity with possible defense dispositions in their local area and prepared for possible hostilities, in this way distinguishing the 15th from the usual training pattern for U.S. Army rifle regiments operating within more peaceful surroundings. An editorial in *The Sentinel* explained: "Tuesday was maneuver day. It usually seems to the man in the ranks as just one more day for a hike over dusty roads, wandering through the ditches and beside the ancient graves and marches through the ungodly smells of dirty villages. But it all is planned for a purpose and those who try to put themselves in the way of learning the why of the thing will find that it is shaping this outfit up to the high requirement of a fighting unit in readiness for any demands."⁴⁰

One account described the sights common on these occasions: "The long column will soon be seen swinging to the music of our splendid Band, through the Compound gate in the early morning, winding its way on the dusty Roads and through the filthy villages toward the Ex-German Target Range to engage in the usual battle problems, full field inspections [and] individual cooking.... With all the Machine Gun organizations, the Howitzer and Stokes Mortars, our little regiment will appear like an Army on the move to the front. The Mess Sergeants and Cooks with their Rolling Kitchens will also play a very active and important part in the fall operations of this command."⁴¹

The success of the maneuvers and the reaching of objectives, in the words of one commentator, were made possible by soldiers first wading "through a hundred training guides," and then "storm[ing] every potential Chinese stronghold in the American sector." To these ends, the troops were provided with copies of maps of the American Defense and Maneuver Area in and around Tientsin featuring the key villages and locales.⁴²

In various exercises, the regiment had occupied the important positions so many times "the Spring, Summer and Autumn smells of each subsector are so familiar that a ... ground scout can locate himself instantly even in the dark of the moon." Among the important locations was the "maneuver-torn village" of Hei-Niu-Cheng which the regiment had "taken and retaken so often that the natives of that strategic village deem themselves to have lost face if a month passes without at least one savage attack upon their otherwise peaceful habitation." In fact, when the natives of the village saw an advance guard moving against them toward the end of a hard winter, "they hail[ed] it as a sure harbinger of spring." It was undoubtedly "the favorite objective of savage attacks by the Second and Third Battalions for the good military reason that the assault can be delivered against it in time to allow the victorious shock troops to return to the compound in time for dinner."

Another village which saw considerable "action" was Tu-Cheng, a "teeming metropolis ... situated on Taku Road, ... the Via Appia of Tientsin." It had also figured in actual military operations on occasion. When Chinese civil war operations converged upon the "Capital of Chihli"—Tientsin—"(as it always does), Taku Road becomes a source of concern to the U.S. Army Forces in China. Frequent patrols traverse its dirty course and, when things become critical (as they always do) an outguard is established at Tu-Cheng. Members of the 15th Infantry who have

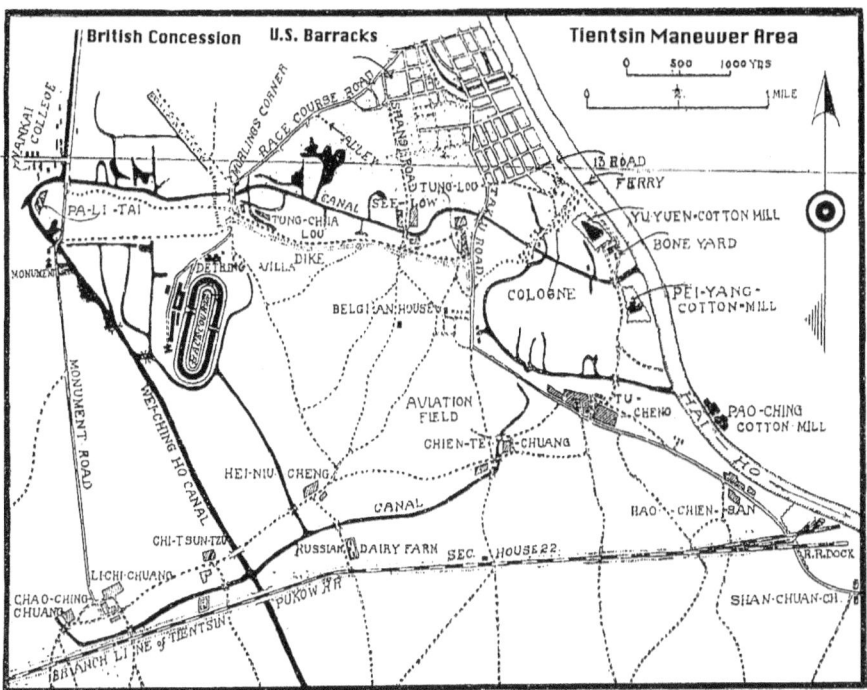

Tientsin Maneuver Area. Modification by the author of a map from *The Sentinel*, April 23, 1926.

not performed at least one twenty-four-hour tour of outpost duty at Tu-Cheng may well feel slighted."

There were other well-known landmarks on the map. One was "The Belgian House." Though the origin of its name was lost to history, "its chief function in these days is to give a machine gunner occupying the famous dike line something to estimate distance to." Li-Chi-Chuang, a "fashionable suburb [of Tientsin] has been the scene of many a bloodless encounter between the 15th Infantry and the imaginary enemy that habitually marches eastward along the Tientsin-Pukow Railway." Then there was Section House 22, "a famous reference point on the Tientsin-Pukow branch line which parallels our southern front. In our regimental tactical exercises the hostile Red Forces habitually detrain at this point prior to their inevitable defeat and destruction by the ever-victorious 15th Infantry." Therefore, to "our maneuver-scarred veterans, Section House 22 has an historical reputation which compares with that enjoyed by the Stone House at German Town, the Alamo and Blockhouse 14."[43]

Related to these exercises in the defense area were "Estimating

Distance Competitions," in which troops demonstrated their knowledge of the ground "we are in China to defend." The estimates were made from memory, "depending entirely on familiarity with every portion of the Defense Area and Outpost Zone."[44]

The fall maneuvers were often coupled with inspections by the ranking brass in China and visiting VIPs. In 1931, for example, the regiment operated in the field under the observant, critical eye of Major General John L. Hines, the Army's former chief of staff, who was then commander of the Philippine Department in Manila. The regiment greatly impressed the visiting general.[45]

Also in late autumn, trophies of various kinds were usually handed out, for example in the early 1930s, "The Taylor Military Proficiency Trophy," with its emblem, the Chickamauga Guidon, awarded to the company attaining the highest standard of proficiency in the regiment for the training year just completed.[46]

The training of the regiment was also related to ceremonial activities as, for example, on Memorial Day, Armistice Day, Organization Day, July 4th, and other occasions when formal parades were held.[47]

The arrival of cold weather dictated indoor training programs and exercises. Included were the annual officers' schools, which consisted of courses on such topics as mess management, horseshoeing, chemical warfare and the employment of artillery in attack and defense. These sometimes included lectures and practical work on map problems. One such exercise involved an imaginary participation of the 15th in a war of the "Reds" and "Blues" in the neighborhood of Gettysburg, Pennsylvania. Colonel Taylor and his staff, joined by the regiment's battalion commanders, were hypothetically headquartered at a point in the Cumberland Mountains, the 15th being ordered to move along the Chambersburg pike toward Gettysburg. The problem developed by the issuing of orders taking into account time and distance considerations, and concluded with extensive critiques.[48]

Meanwhile, some of the enlisted men pursued Army correspondence courses, usually to attain promotions or commissions in the Officers' Reserve Corps.[49]

The Sentinel was also frequently involved in instruction by publishing articles devoted to specialized, often technical, subjects. There was some interest in the regiment in foreign military doctrine, even that of such nations as Switzerland. In the spring of 1933, the paper published a series of articles by General Emile Sonderegger, former chief of the Swiss Army. Widely recognized as one of the leading military thinkers of Europe, he wrote on the subject of the infantry in attack.[50]

VIII. The Training Cycle   151

But the regiment's activities involved much more than book work. Military tournaments were scheduled for the winter months as well, the one for 1926 featuring 23 separate mounted and dismounted events, all calculated to "develop a friendly rivalry between organizations and a system of training which will benefit the greatest number of officers and men; and also to present for comparison methods which are most instructive to the command at large. The ultimate object [was] to inculcate in everyone a desire to attain the highest state of military activity and efficiency."[51]

It became the custom for the garrison phase of the training round to terminate with an endurance marching test. For instance, on Saturday morning, March 5, 1927, 405 men of the regiment began the trek, set at a distance of 8.558 miles. Company G, the winner, made the round in one hour and 29.5 minutes, for an average of 5.73 miles per hour. Colonel Newell was highly pleased with the regiment's performance, noting that only six men fell out of the grueling event. He awarded a special holiday to the regiment "as a special mark of [his] appreciation."[52]

The men's attention was then directed to activities related to the ushering in of the more active phase of the training year. The athletes of the regiment — and there were usually many — always rose to the occasion of another form of competition with military aims and utility: the annual strength contests. These sought to identify the fittest individual and collectively the most fit company. Typically, five events were held: the 100-yard dash, running broad jump, running high jump, shot put, and grenade throw, though one wag wanted to know, "why not have 'fence climbing' in the strength contest? We have a couple of good men we could enter."[53]

Athletics then gave way once more to more martial activities, especially small-bore shooting calculated to help the men prepare for the more serious activities on the firing range. This indoor firing was made the more pressing "in view of recent reduction in ammunition allowances," making it "imperative that a great amount of instruction with U.S. Magazine, Caliber .22 Rifles be inaugurated." The practice normally concluded with inter-service small-bore competitions.[54]

Part of the regiment's training responsibilities involved officers of the Officers' Reserve Corps (ORC). Usually in late spring, they were ordered to active duty for 15 days of training. Some of these were enlisted men in the 15th. Others ordered up included civilians in China, many on the faculties of Chinese universities or with businesses in the East.[55]

More generally, as Victor Vogel has observed in his memoir, between the two world wars "the old army had completed its mission of training leaders and furnishing cadres for wartime divisions in the best tradition of the United States, and the time had come for the new army to take over that responsibility." The 15th assisted this development with an Asian orientation that enhanced the Army's store of knowledge and experience. By inculcating this within many officers destined for high rank, this aspect of its training cycle paid dividends during World War II and beyond.[56]

CHAPTER IX

Athletes, Thespians and Musicians

"And you say the musician killed her with his instrument?" "Yes, yes, with the trombone of an ass."[1]

"No, Ruben, there are no saxophones in heaven."[2]

"We have met the enemy and they are curs!" proclaimed an article in *The Sentinel* recounting a basketball victory of the 15th. In view of the fact that the "enemy" was the U.S. Marines—the "Devildogs"—from the Legation Guard in Peking, the sally seemed appropriate. But the marines took offense, and their commandant, in a spirited rejoinder, demanded—and got—an apology. Lamely alleging a typographical error—what was intended was obviously "ours" instead of "curs"—the paper's editor backpedaled smoothing over the ruffled feelings. Nonetheless, the incident indicates how seriously Americans in China, whether marine, doughboy or sailor, took athletics. Certainly, "the playing fields of Tientsin" often rang with the traditional noises of athletic contests and such events were "a most important feature of the amusement program," one writer declared. Indeed: "In the spring a young man's fancy lightly turns to thoughts of not necessarily love, but very often to [the] big outdoors."[3]

Building upon past athletic developments, especially during the Great War, the War Department from time to time reviewed athletic programs in the Army and what it expected regarding them.[4] For example, in a directive in October 1924, one reads that "it is the desire of the War Department to foster and encourage athletics of all kinds in the Army in every legitimate way practicable and to render all possible assistance to athletic officers in carrying out their duties." So as to "democratize" athletics, it was further stipulated that "beginning January 1, 1925, all football, baseball, basketball, and soccer teams organized in the Army will normally be composed of enlisted men. Not more than one officer will be permitted on any team at any time in any game." This was to support "the ideal to be striven for" of having "the greatest practicable number of enlisted men participate in all sports." Nonetheless, all commissioned officers "should strive to develop any athletic ability or talent [they] may possess." This was to enable them "better [to] fulfil their obligations to the Government and ... more efficiently perform their duties with respect to the Army itself." As a result, those in command scheduled considerable time for athletics.[5]

The 15th persisted in its athletic agendas until its withdrawal from China. As Colonel George Arthur Lynch made clear to new arrivals in November 1935, it was necessary that the men constantly be kept in a state of physical fitness. To this end, he noted, "when you are sent to duty with an organization here, you will be assigned to a sport in which you will regularly participate." Each company was to maintain the usual sports teams and each also "will have a boxing squad."[6]

The normal daily routine of the regiment allowed much time for athletics. In addition, holiday routines commonly provided for a regime of games and sports, as well as the traditional feasts and social rounds. For instance, July the Fourth normally featured a baseball game and Thanksgiving Day celebrations usually scheduled a football contest.[7]

Yet, in times when sports were stressed to a great degree, as when Colonel King was the regiment's commander, unrest surfaced in the ranks with complaints that too much was expected. Such attitudes provoked one education and recreation officer, Lieutenant Laurin L. Williams, then editor of *The Sentinel*, to mount an assault. In a pair of editorials, "Genus Crab" and "Sell Your Hammer and Buy a Horn," he insisted that there was too much grousing while far too few men participated in athletic events, either as participants or observers. Both Colonels King and Naylor had set the policy of emphasizing athletics, and Williams insisted that "when the Commanding Officer's decision or policy has been definitely announced it is time for everyone in the organization to lend their support and wholehearted co-operation."[8]

Whatever the prevailing attitudes, the regiment's sports calendar followed that traditionally found in the United States. Athletics were conducted at two levels: teams competed within the regiment and, in addition, there were competitions with organizations beyond the compound involving other national and intramural teams. The extent of the 15th's sports interests was reflected by the wide range of trophies that were annually contended for, both within the international community and in regimental contests. These included, among many others, the French Tug-of-War Cup for international competition in this event; the *Sentinel* Track Team Cup, presented to the company winning the annual regimental track meet; the Chesterfield Basketball Cup, donated by Ligget and Meyers Tobacco Company, awarded to the company winning the annual regimental basketball series; and the Margetts Cup, donated by Lieutenant Colonel Nelson E. Margetts, the military attaché in Peking, to basketball winners competing in an annual tournament held by the marines in Peking. There was also the Dickinson Challenge Cup, awarded to the winner of the Golf Championship of North China. When Major Walter C. Gullion of the regiment won in 1926 — the first time it had been captured by an American Army officer — it was regarded as "another brilliant illustration of what the Army does besides fighting." Finally, as to awards, the regiment's Athletic Committee presented sweaters to lettered athletes.[9]

But the differences in emphasis of athletics in large part reflected the proclivities of various commanding officers as to whether sports or music and thespian productions would have pride of place, though usually a combination of various forms of entertainment prevailed. Education and Recreation officers also often played a major role in determining direction of the entertainment and athletic programs pursued by the regiment.[10]

A major event each spring was the regimental Organization Day Track Meet held on May 4. From the winners of this meet the 15th's entries were selected for the International Track and Field Meet held each year at the French Barracks, Tientsin. This included the immensely popular and hotly contested ten-man-team tug-of-war contests, the 15th and French squads often vying for the championship. Among the major participants in track and field events were the French, ever enthusiastic supporters of their hosted event, and contestants from the civilian Tientsin Junior Athletic Association, Tientsin's Nankai University, Tientsin Anglo-Chinese College, the British Regiment, and on occasion Chinese soldiers from some of the warlord armies.[11]

During the summers, there was an active North China Baseball League, composed of teams from the 15th Regiment, the Tientsin civilian and Japanese civilian aggregations, and the Peking marines. These might be joined by a few visiting Japanese university and college squads, one of the most popular being that from the University of Waseda, as well as contingents from various ships of the U.S. Navy. Boxing cards and basketball games were scheduled for the long, cold Tientsin winter afternoons and evenings. Those not otherwise occupied enjoyed the skating rink that the regiment constructed each year outside the compound.[12]

Occasionally, the British and Americans competed in the national sports of the other, one Briton observing regarding a gridiron contest that it was "as clipping a hog looked to the old Norseman who summed up the result of that process as 'a great cry but little wool.'" Apparently more successful were the contests that the 15th engaged in with the Tientsin Cricket Club's largely British membership.[13]

Certainly, there was much emphasis on what one editorial in *The Sentinel* rather playfully referred to as "physical straining," with emphasis on the need to properly train men using the latest techniques, regimes and programs developed by sports science. Even the distaff side should not have been exempt, in Williams' view, and *The Sentinel* under his editorship was the venue for a discussion of the need to involve some of the "prominent young social heavyweights of the weaker sex," who had found that living in China made it "difficult to keep a perfect thirty-six." Accordingly, he suggested a detailed exercise and dieting regime.[14]

If the men were not being hounded regarding their participation, they were perennially reminded about good sportsmanship. As *The Sentinel*'s editor once intoned, "we don't expect you to rush out and kiss the referee on the forehead but for the love o' Mike give him a chance." Furthermore, in the frequent encounters with the marines, the 15th's most persistent opponents on the firing range and on the playing fields, the editor urged that when they "make a good play, applaud. Show them we are sports! Looked kind of bad the other night, in the basketball game, when some of our men raised a big noise while the opponents were trying for a free basket. That isn't done."[15]

But in the summer of 1922, in a hotly contested baseball game, the marines quit the field after a dispute with the umpire, forfeiting to the 15th. *The Sentinel* rather piously deplored the action, concluding that "the brand of sportsmanship displayed Monday afternoon on the diamond when the pleasure of the whole afternoon as well as the good reputation of the teams was spoiled is unworthy of any branch of the U.S. Service." The marines clearly lacked a willingness to abide by the umpire's decisions and must learn that the umpire runs the game and not one or two "cantankerous players."[16]

Relations between the marines and the 15th were always a bit strained. To ease matters, a decade later when the Legation Guard won a basketball game in Tientsin, and with it the Margetts Cup, Colonel Taylor wrote a letter to Colonel J.C. Breckinridge, commandant of U.S. Marines in Peking, congratulating them on their victories. Breckinridge replied that the letter was "an example of sportsmanship to all of us," and though the 15th had lost, "we respect the 15th U.S. Infantry even more than we would have done had they won the games and thus deprived us of knowing what good and gentlemanly sportsmen they really are."[17]

Other difficulties involving sports emanated from the War Department, which in the mid–1920s, in a chronic funding crunch, cut off money for Army educational and recreational programs, thereby ending E. and R. departments. This placed the support of athletics on the shoulders of individual organizations, which, as was the case in the 15th, depended upon an athletic association — or committee — to regulate regimental athletics and to raise cash. The regiment responded by staging theater productions, by eliciting support from business firms in Tientsin, and tapping *The Sentinel*'s resources, including much of its advertising revenue.[18]

The Sentinel was a prime avenue for popularizing and publicizing regimental athletics. Though the paper's scope was much greater than athletic coverage, this was central to much of its effort and it seemed only appropriate, therefore, that the editor would often be the regiment's education and recreation officer. This was the case in the mid–1920s, when for several years the paper was edited first by Lieutenant Laurin L. Williams and then by Lieutenant Howard W. Lehr. For a number of years *The Sentinel* also supported regimental athletics by sponsoring a physical efficiency contest to determine the best all-round athlete in the regiment.[19]

Boxing was perennially a favorite sporting event and pugilistic carnivals and smokers were common, with the British and sometimes the Italians and French as participants, as were boxers and teams from various U.S. Navy ships that frequented the Tientsin area. One rollicking, distinctly Chinese feature of any boxing card was a "Battle Royal," always a crowd pleaser. This matched seven or eight "husky coolies from the various companies" who mixed it up in a no-holds-barred free-for-all which included kickboxing. The solitary coolie left standing was awarded a purse that might amount to as much as 1,800 coppers for his winning performance.[20]

Football, as was the case with some of the other sports, seemed ideal for soldiers to be engaged in. As *The Sentinel* once editorialized, "Can any other sport boast the heroes that the gridiron has borne? Will any other sport install in a man the 'never say die' spirit as will the game of football? There is but one other game that can even approximate it, the game of War itself." Football therefore fulfilled the purpose of an Army in times of peace, which was to "train its men for the duties imposed upon it in time of war," inculcating in the participants the "spirit of loyalty, [and] the heart of a fighter."[21]

Less martial was ice skating "under the roof of [a] bamboo-straw-covered hut," a popular addition to the regiment's outdoor activities helping the men to battle the monotony of the long winter months. Serenaded by the Regimental Band or music coming in by wire from Recreation Hall, large crowds enjoyed the locale. The rink, finally established permanently at "Can Do" athletic field, was financed by *The Sentinel* and on other occasions partially by the "Y," which made generous donations. It was further supported by membership fees, each officer and some civilians paying five dollars each. A coffee and hot dog stand raised additional revenue. The competitive spirit of the regiment poured out into this arena as well, and an annual ice meet featured the awarding of the "Skater's" or the "General Connor Cup," donated and presented by Brigadier General William Durward Connor.[22]

Golf in China was a bit unusual, to say the least, as Eileen O'Brien Leonard, wife of Major John William Leonard (in China in the mid–1930s), has explained in an amusing account. The course's 18 holes were located in the former Russian concession across the Hai Ho River from the American Compound. The links, she explained, looked "like a drab field," and "it was no uncommon sight for a Chinese funeral or a wedding to take [a] short cut across the 'fairway.'" In the autumn the grounds were raked clean by Chinese villagers, who used the dead grass, mixed with tar and coal dust, formed into hard balls, and baked in the hot summer sun, for their winter fuel. Captain James Edward Moore — later a four-star general — a contemporary of the Leonards in Tientsin, agreed that "it was interesting playing golf there. We would drive off the grave mounds. They had great big mounds of earth over the graves and put the tees up there. We had sand greens." The golfer needed two caddies, he further explained, one ranging out in front to watch for the ball "so he could prevent anyone from stealing it before it stopped, and one to help you with the bag."[23]

There was a lively thespian tradition in the U.S. Army in which 15th Regiment participated, and the compound was often enlivened by the staging of theater productions by various organizations. Some of these were ambitious. Early in 1924 for instance, under the general supervision of the Education and Recreation Officer Lieutenant Laurin L. Williams, an extended cast under the direction of Lieutenant Cliff H. Boyles put on a full-scale regimental musical variety show entitled *Goofus Feathers*. As *The Sentinel* explained, the name was derived from the story of the "Princess and the Pea," having to do with the selection of a princess to marry a certain prince. The father of the prince, the king, "always a practical joker," secreted a pea in the bed of the princess under 20 mattresses, the assumption being that only a genuine princess could detect such a slight irritant. The son, Prince Goofus, having determined that the princess was bona fide royalty, married her, and ordered a bed made of the softest feathers for his bride. Various materials were tried out, the final choice being made of the fuzzy down from peach skins, a material fancifully labeled as "Goofus Feathers."[24]

There were high hopes for the production from the outset: "We are already dreaming of the Empire Theater [in Tientsin], and even at times we can hear the plaudits of the Peking public. Join this show and your reputation is made," the editor of *The Sentinel* declared, a prophecy that was realized. There were indeed several performances: the grand opening was at Recreation Hall at the compound, followed by a matinee and two nights at the local Empire Theater, and one night at the Olympic Theater. In addition, the cast and support personnel of over 40 persons journeyed to Peking, playing one night at the Pavilion to a full, enthusiastic house. Among those in attendance was Colonel S.A. Cheney, the military attaché in the capital, who reported to Williams that, "I agreed with the Marine I overheard in the lobby of the theater during the intermission who said, [it was] 'The best show I've seen since I left New York.'"[25]

What the appreciative audiences saw was a lively musical production. "Easily the star of the evening" was Lieutenant Phil E. Gallagher, the popular adjutant of the Second Battalion, who played "Hiram" in a skit, "County Fair." Two of his numbers, "Oh Gee, Oh Gosh, Oh Golly, I'm in Love" and "Louisville Lou," for many a day thereafter could be heard being whistled and hummed in the American Compound. While "distinctly the best of the company, others who took leading parts did well — much better than ordinarily is the case in amateur performances," a critic writing in the *Peking Leader* declared. All in all, theater audiences witnessed "one of [the] best and amusing shows that has been here in years."[26]

When January 1925 rolled around, the memory of the former year's theatrical triumph suggested an encore. Again under the direction of Lieutenant Clifford H. Boyles, another cast was recruited, some having been members of the original troupe. Originally named "Can Do," borrowing the regiment's motto as its own, it was also "fitting [in that] it typifies the spirit of these who are putting the show over." But popular demand led to the adoption of the name *Goofus Feathers II*. Enjoying even more success than garnered the year before, the new show, after premiering at the compound's Recreation Hall, appeared at Tientsin's Empire Theater "before the most enthusiastic audience that ever witnessed a show in Tientsin."[27]

For several years, another regimental innovation was an amateur night schedule at Recreation Hall for the purpose of providing entertainment for the command during the Christmas holidays, and "to develop ability to stage attractive vaudeville skits." Each organization was limited to one performance not to exceed 20 minutes, "not including bona fide encores." In 1926, the talented Company H captured first prize with its *School Days*, "a scream from beginning to end [which] kept the audience in a continuous fit of laughter," and which was judged the best act shown in Recreation Hall since *Goofus Feathers II*. Even more ambitious was the creation of the 15th Infantry Stock Company, membership being open "to anyone with talent." Among other things, this group put on short sketches as prologues to selected feature films.[28]

As has been previously noted, the regiment's commanding officer who was perhaps most interested in music and theater was Colonel Reynolds J. Burt. After the heyday of Marshall and others in the 1920s, theatricals had been moribund for several years. Colonel Burt turned the regiment firmly toward stage productions as its major form of recreation, though apparently without seriously detracting from the usual preoccupation with sports. He ordered companies to provide the regiment with monthly entertainments—a demanding agenda that could not be maintained. Accordingly, the pages of *The Sentinel* were filled with details of stage productions, especially early in his tenure. One of his creations was the American Army Dramatic Club, called the Can Do Players, composed of officers and ladies of the regiment. With Burt as president and chief member of the casting committee, the club subsequently performed numerous entertainments for the 15th and members of the Tientsin community, its specialty being one-act plays.[29]

In the extended holiday season from December 23 to January 4, 1932/33, several shows were staged, including one by Company M—the "Men, Mules and Machine Gun" outfit. Called *The Machine Gunners' Burst*, it featured comedy sketches and musical numbers; one scene entitled "The Battle of Rollin' Bones" portrayed a bunch of "Cullud Folks" in the frontline trenches in France.[30]

In addition, minstrel shows were popular. One staged by Company F, entitled *Happy Days*, featured "Amos and Andy" with a rickshaw instead of their usual taxicab.[31]

Other avenues of considerable entertainment for men of the regiment, though civilians and members of other national contingents were also reached, were the 15th's excellent band and several musical combos. In existence since April of 1921, for most of that decade the band was led by Warrant Officer Francis E. Lee. In addition to its daily performances at guard mount, regimental parades, escorts of the colors, reviews, inspections, retreat, and guards of honor, during the summer season a series of outdoor concerts were given in Victoria Garden. As there were three foreign military bands stationed in Tientsin, each playing one public concert weekly, the rivalry was keen and the standards high.[32]

The 15th's musical groups also included a 24-piece symphony orchestra, and there were various salon ensembles for weddings, receptions, and

IX. Athletes, Thespians and Musicians   161

The 15th Infantry's regimental band on parade in the American Compound, 1927. Courtesy of the National Archives, Washington, D.C. (111-SC-106231).

dinners, even at private homes. A dance orchestra under the leadership of Sergeant Felipe Pascual was one of the most popular musical units in northern China. Early in its career the band's repertoire followed the views of John Philip Sousa encapsulated in his article "The Force of Music."[33]

But as was common on the American social scene during the Roaring Twenties—the Jazz Age—the band and orchestras had to pay increasing attention to jazz. To be sure, there were many jokes and incessant sniping—good natured and otherwise—at the ever-more-popular musical form, one wag promising that "some happy day we shall beat our swords into plowshares, and our jazz bands into unconsciousness," while another asked: "'Do you believe that jazz is dying?' 'I don't know, but it sounds as though it were suffering horribly.'"[34]

A poem also sought to define what some regarded as an obnoxious musical form:

> A tin dishpan and an auto horn,
> A squeaky fiddle and a rat eating corn,
> A baby's rattle and a puppy's whine
> A cowbell jangle and a rosined twine —
> That's jazz.
> . . . .[35]

As time went on, enthusiastic supporters of jazz came to greatly outnumber the detractors, and a letter from one soldier to the editor of *The Sentinel* regarding the band concerts frequently performed at Tientsin's Victoria Park asked that more jazz be played rather than the endless selections of classical music which were dull, putting many listeners to sleep.[36]

Various theatrical offerings were available for the men of the regiment. One account filled with advice to the men noted, however, that unless one were well educated about Chinese drama, "it is advisable to do your theatre going before leaving the United States." There was an annual engagement of an Italian grand opera and an occasional visit of "a second rate British vaudeville troupe." Better bets were the excellent Tientsin moving picture theaters. The 15th's time in China coincided with the rapid development of film as an entertainment medium. Like millions of others, Can-Doers saw *The Jazz Singer* with Al Jolson. Until the bugs were worked out and they became acceptable as a movie medium, "talkies" were rather derisively styled the "Squawkies," though the Olympic advertised itself as the theater "Where Sound Sounds Right." In various columns devoted to movie criticism, *The Sentinel* focused on major films of the time. *All Quiet on the Western Front*, it noted, was indeed "a giant looking down upon pygmies." Another film attracting considerable attention was *The Rough Riders*, viewed by many while at the rifle range, who called it one of the best war films ever screened. Its cast, headed by Noah Beery, was appreciated for creating a film with action and comedy as well as a love story. The local cinemas, the Empire Theater, the Empire Cinema (Kwang Ming), the Peking Pavilion, the Olympic and the Biograph in the ex–German concession, all did considerable business, both in stage shows and film presentations. There were various showings at the compound as well, especially those sponsored by *The Sentinel*, which used some of the proceeds from subscriptions to show films on a regular basis. The chaplain, the YMCA, and other agencies also screened movies.[37]

The state of the art in electronics extended to record players, especially those known as Orthophonic Victrolas. Individual organizations took pride in their own sets and often amassed large record collections. They were aided by a number of record stores in Tientsin which gladly provided records to the Regiment for the popular Sunday afternoon Orthophonic concerts scheduled in Recreation Hall during the winter months until the weather was too good for the men to remain inside. Certainly, the air around the American Compound perpetually vibrated to such tunes as "Mountains Ain't No Place for Bad Men," and many others.[38]

Another popular diversion that became a craze sweeping the Anglo-Saxon world in the 1920s was Mah Jongg, the Chinese tile game. The popular magazine *Lloyds* once asserted that women in particular seemed addicted to it, and "there ain't no Pasteur treatment yet discovered wot's capable o' counteractin' the effects." In an article, "The Evils of Mah Jongg," one imaginative writer humorously recounted how the Chinese, their own nation ruined by the plague of the game which had created a generation of idlers—indeed, "many a silk worm died from the negligence of its master in forgetting to feed it"—decided to ruin foreigners, so that when they were brought low, China could regain its ancient world prominence. Accordingly, "by soft language and mysterious names the game was cautiously introduced to a few carefully chosen foreigners." The ploy worked, and because there was nothing so contagious as idleness, "it was not long before this group of foreigners was so infatuated with the game that work ceased almost entirely." Certainly the game was all the rage for much of 1924 in the 15th Regiment, and *The Sentinel* was filled with accounts of the local society round which for some months often featured Mah Jongg parties, especially among the officers and their ladies.[39]

The game's effects were well described by a soldier-poet, G.S. Neighbors of Company G, in his "Mah Jongg: As It May Be Played in the 'Y' in Tientsin":

. . . .
Pedro and Euchre and Bridge, Wist and Rhum,
Cribbage and Hearts I will play as they come;
Any old game that you fancy I will try,
But love for the Chinaman's sport I'll deny.

Perhaps I'm too old or perhaps I'm too young,
But I can't sit all night waiting to "pung,"
And I haven't the patience of Minister Wu,
With that tedious wait for the seven bamboo.

But before too many months had elapsed, the Mah Jongg craze had given way to another: the crossword puzzle.[40]

World-renowned personalities also appeared in Tientsin for speaking engagements. One of the most popular was Dr. Roy Chapman Andrews, the famous Gobi explorer, who on several occasions spoke and showed slides and screened movies featuring his ventures and sensational archeological discoveries in Mongolia. A generous man and an enthusiastic polo player, he turned over some of the proceeds of his presentations to benefit the Tientsin Polo Association and also to help the compound's chapel to finance a new carpet.[41]

Will Rogers—the Bob Hope of his day—was another notable speaker. Seeking to entertain Rogers with various dinners and parties, the brass was informed that he would rather speak to the troops. As always, Rogers was well received, and to the delight of the men, frequently ordered the commanding officer about without fear of reprisal.[42]

Rogers had been traveling with another celebrity, the renowned war correspondent Floyd Gibbons. They were together in Manchuria to assess the situation there, Rogers humorously noting that without Floyd, "the war isn't official. It just has to be fought over again." A few days later, appearing in person, Gibbons—complete with his trademark eye patch—reported to the troops on his two-week stay in the field in Manchuria with the Japanese army. He was "much impressed with the fighting spirit and patriotism of the Japanese soldier and of his supreme confidence in the Emperor," he declared.[43]

There were ad hoc entertainments from time to time. In March of 1922, for instance, a 16-day cruise was arranged on the USAT *Merritt* so that officers and their families, joined by some enlisted men, could sail around Philippine waters on a combined pleasure and official trip, inspecting the abandoned military reservations in those islands and investigating the colorful details of native life. On another occasion, the American Legion, which was quite active in China, chartered a boat for a moonlight cruise. The regiment's saxophone band furnished dance music for this happy occasion.[44]

In addition to the usual holidays, another recognized time for regimental celebrations was Organization Day (May 4). For some years, a "Forty Niner" event, featuring pastimes of the 1849 era including poker, craps, roulette, keno, and many other forms of gambling "unknown to the editor," was scheduled. Each man received $10 in "Gambling Currency," which was worth "considerably less than its equivalent in cash." While the band and orchestra played, and participants feasted on coffee and peanuts, a gambling mania ensued. The occasion was often attended by men from U.S. Navy ships in the area, and by personnel from the resident British and French army regiments and the Italian Marines.[45]

Naturally, personnel could also entertain themselves, as *The Sentinel*, in parodies of traditional social columns in newspapers often amusingly suggested: "Mr. and Mrs. Joseph H. Barlow were hosts at a delightful dinner on the evening of the 15th. After a very progressive conversation several courses of watermelon seeds and chop suey were consumed"; "Mr. and Mrs. Will Black entertained last Friday at 'Black Jack.' After a delightful and profitable game, Sgt. Duke entertained by rendering 'Sandy Mac' in 'A' minor"; and "Luke J. Ratigan was entertained at a supper by Joseph W. Stout. The table was decorated with sardines and Five Star [beer]. Music was furnished by the diners."[46]

Other informal entertainment was far more common: the incessant drinking and the consorting with the fair damsels of the Mukloo district and elsewhere, such as along "Slam Door Alley." Far from being bored, the Can-Doers were ensured a variety of entertainment and recreational activities at many levels and venues, which contributed greatly to the appeal of service in China.

CHAPTER X

The Chinese Land, History and People

It may be all very well while in Rome to do as the Romans do, but in China few of us would survive if we did as the Chinese do!¹

China
Dear old China quaint, fantastic, like a bit of Dresden rare
Art and nature strangely blending, in your dark dust-laden air
And your brilliant bursts of sunshine, sunny skies of azure blue
Fretful, smiling, gay, beguiling, winsome, wayward, false and true.²

Though one commentator has noted that the 15th "was almost solipsistically inwardly focused," which was certainly partially true, still there is little doubt that soldiering in the Orient was an endlessly fascinating business transcending the metes and bounds of the American Compound in Tientsin as well as service in the U.S. Army elsewhere. Despite the hardships and the perpetual threat of military action, which added to the excitement, at all levels China kept the men of the 15th beguiled and on the qui vive.

To Americans stationed in China the land remained at once a mystery and a source of wonder mingled with amazement and puzzlement, often evoking irony and even revulsion and ridicule. With the inherent tension between repulsion and fascination in encountering China ever at hand, there was endless speculation about it. Perhaps the impression common among many Westerners of a prevailing kaleidoscopic Topsyturvy-dom in China might answer for what was not understood, or maybe the notion of an Alice-Through-the-Looking-Glass world in which things were done "in a way contradictory to our [own]" might explain things. Yet, Can-Doers were often reminded that in their own frames of reference many of the "curious" ways of the Chinese were as rational — perhaps even more so — than Western customs.

Part of the picture was the exposure to the impressive centuries-old Chinese cultural heritage and civilization, which several thousand Americans in the era between the world wars experienced. Some understood that superficial appearances could not mask the maturity and sophistication of Chinese culture. Thus, in the midst of filth, those obnoxious smells and incessant noise, there were lotus blossoms as well.

At another level, for military dependents there were all of those attentive servants and the wonderful shopping, those languid summers at rest camps such as at Nan Ta Ssu, which invariably evoked fond, nostalgic memories of service on the China station. For officers and their families especially there were the endless rounds of entertainments and social activities, such as golf, polo and riding events at a most stimulating level. In any case, contacts with the Chinese would reveal men of the Regiment, and other Americans then in China, at both their best and worst.[3]

Rudyard Kipling had once suggested to his readers something of the eternal face-offs between East and West in his line, "A Fool lies here who tried to hustle the East." One of the regiment's soldiers, styling himself "How Kee," seemed convinced that this was true, as his poem "With Apologies to Mark Anthony" illustrates:

> Friends, Soldiers, Countrymen,
> Come, lend me your ears,
> I'll tell you about the Chinese,
> The cunnin' little dears,
> In ancient days, long past,
> Their land was wonderous [sic] well,
> But now in nineteen twenty-one
> It has simply gone to ruin.
>
> It's graft for this, and squeeze for that.
> They steal, lie and cheat,
> And though you try your durndest,
> They simply can't be beat.
> The Chink he says with smiling face,
> SURE CAN DO,
> Of course the meaning is,
> Can do. YOU. And he does.[4]

The fascination with China cried out for ways and means of understanding it, if this were possible. One of the most important avenues leading to a knowledge of and interest in China within the 15th Regiment were the language programs pursued at varying degrees of depth and intensity. Another path was the long-running column in *The Sentinel*, "Things Chinese," frequently supplemented by experts writing in the paper or speaking to the men on lecture circuits. Of course, the broad as well as the personal intimate contact with the natives at various levels, not to mention the military involvement as crisis followed crisis, especially in the 1920s, remained important avenues of knowledge about China. Travel was another way of encountering the Chinese and their land. Finally, the rise of Japan in the Orient provoked much analysis about the future with considerable emphasis on comparisons of the Japanese and the Chinese.

As to the Chinese language ventures, *The Sentinel*, from time to time for many years, published lessons in Chinese. In addition, the YMCA held classes in the Chinese language on a volunteer basis in connection with the regimental education and recreation officer's office. A typical class numbered about 20 officers and men, and met five mornings per week for an hour with another scheduled in the evenings. Starting in February of 1924, officers were required to take the Spoken Chinese (Mandarin) Language course which was formally instituted and maintained in one of the garrison's post schools. It was conducted by an officer of the Chinese Language Detail from Peking — later by the post school officer — assisted by several Chinese instructors, "according to the methods of the North China Language School." The school, frequently revamped and refined, had rather modest goals. It was created "to teach the officers sufficient Chinese to carry out the missions of the command without the friction which arises from misunderstanding and being misunderstood, i.e., to be able to run an international train; to command an outpost detachment; to converse with villagers sufficiently to obtain information of the character usually required in campaign; and to be able to check approximately the work of a Chinese interpreter." Beyond this, it was to furnish the Army with a number of officers who understood the fundamentals of the Chinese spoken language and to afford them an opportunity to compete for the detail as language officer in Peking. General Connor was pleased with the program and in one of his annual reports noted that "The results have been generally very satisfactory, as the officers are interested.... After five months of instruction, several officers have demonstrated their ability to make themselves understood in Colloquial Chinese when on duty that carried them into the interior of the country."[5]

First, there was the basic course of 12 months' duration, with ten hours a week instruction being required for the first six weeks, followed by a reduced schedule of six hours a week until the course had been satisfactorily completed. After eight months, an officer could request to be examined to determine whether or not he had attained satisfactory proficiency to end the course. An advanced course was also instituted to help officers maintain proficiency as well as advance their knowledge.[6]

While officers had been expected for some time to study the language, a course for enlisted men was initiated only in January of 1926, "somewhat in the nature of an experiment," as a consequence of Chinese developments that had demonstrated the great importance "of our patrol and detachment commanders having some knowledge of the Chinese language." The course had initially been prepared so that only those words and sentences required in the performance of military duties on patrol or outpost were studied. But it was soon apparent that every noncommissioned officer on detached duty coming into contact with Chinese soldiers "should be able to make clear to them his orders and intentions, and to do this in both a tactful and definite manner." To these ends, a textbook was issued and the course broadened to encompass more general conversation. Initially, with about 28 men enrolled at Tientsin and another group of ten at Tangshan, the efficiency of the regiment had been enhanced by their knowledge and skill, and the names of those fluent in Chinese were routinely recorded at headquarters. These men were selected for details involving contact with the Chinese people and given preference in travel leaves and promotions. In places such as Tangshan, which was the site of many important bridges on the Peking-Mukden railroad, an enlisted man having a knowledge of Chinese was routinely assigned to each bridge guard and one noncommissioned officer was held in readiness to accompany an armored car in case it should be needed. The course was later standardized at 250 hours of instruction.[7]

The Sentinel often published articles describing how a workable knowledge of the Chinese language enhanced the regiment's fulfilling of its mission. In one instance, Staff Sergeant Henry H. Denning of the Post Veterinary Corps, during upheavals involving the regiment, frequently took long rides on horseback. These ventures often carried him many miles into the country south of Tientsin, "where he was able to observe and learn much concerning troop movements." His knowledge of the Chinese language was a "big asset" in obtaining information "which otherwise would have been impossible." By 1926, the high command of the regiment was of the opinion that with more than half of the officers having completed two years of study of Chinese, "thereafter, this command should be able to operate in North China, fairly independently of interpreters." While relatively few enlisted men gained competency in the language, the great majority of the officers did, a remarkable record setting the 15th apart from the U.S. Army's run-of-the-mill regiments.[8]

A regimental memo dated November 23, 1927, provided for formal recognition of officers and men attaining a recognized level of proficiency in the Chinese language. A cloth arm patch, called a "Chung"—for "Chinese"—was authorized, soon becoming a greatly-sought-after uniform accoutrement. It also became customary for officers and men who succeeded in attaining some level of proficiency in the language to be recognized in other ways, mainly by treating them to trips to Peking, Shanghai, or Kalgan—located north of Peking—and to other locales.[9]

Instruction in Chinese varied in focus and intensity according to the commanders involved. Brigadier General William D. Connor was the chief founder of systematic Chinese language study. Colonel Taylor also was interested in the study of the language as was Marshall. But Colonel Reynolds J. Burt, according to Captain Charles L. Bolte, who served as the regiment's operations officer under him, had little use for the language. Nevertheless, it was in Burt's tenure that Captain David D. Barrett, one of the 15th's most accomplished Chinese language instructors, appeared. He elevated language instruction to perhaps the highest level it attained while the regiment was in China.[10]

Chinese language studies engaged some of the regiment's best officers. For some time, Lieutenant Colonel George C. Marshall was the officer in charge of the Chinese course, and Stilwell was later recognized as a fine instructor as well as being the dean of the Chinese Language College. Another distinguished teacher of Chinese was Captain Woodrow W. Woodbridge, a field artillery officer who had been a language student in Peking and was author of Book No. 1 of the Officer's Chinese Class.[11]

The regiment's dedication to the study of Chinese usually impressed visiting inspecting officers. Major General Eli A. Helmick, inspector general of the Army, noted that the regiment's officers were "deserving of especial credit in my opinion for the interest they have taken in the study of the Chinese language.... It is an indication of the high character of the officers generally that they are willing to spend time outside their regular duties to study and make themselves familiar with [it]."[12]

The Sentinel was another major means of informing the 15th's community about China and the Chinese. Among outsiders drawn upon were authors of articles such as "Chinese Traits," drawn from the book *Through the Dragon's Eyes*, by Lewis Charles Arlington. George E. Sokolsky, an Asian correspondent for the *New York Times*, also contributed articles for *The Sentinel*. Another avowed expert on China—and especially Tientsin—was O.D. Rasmussen (on the staff of the influential newspaper, the *North China Star*), whose book, *Tientsin: An Illustrated Outline History*, was mined for material. Rasmussen's Tientsin writings were supplemented by presentations by Miss G.M. Rees, who wrote features on the history of Tientsin, together with detailed descriptions of prominent city buildings. Her offerings were subsequently bound and distributed as a pamphlet. Though *The Sentinel*'s staff could not guess at his future significance, some of the work of another rising journalist, Edgar Snow, was reprinted. Various Chinese publications such as the *China Review* were also sources for articles.[13]

Beyond this, the regiment produced a bevy of its own experts on China. Unquestionably, the most important of these was Major — later Lieutenant Colonel — Joseph Warren Stilwell, as has been discussed in chapter V.

Other articulate regimental observers of the Chinese scene contributed to the paper as well. An unnamed private of the Second Battalion, while on the target range near Chinwangtao in the summer of 1925, witnessed a horrifying occurrence. As he crossed the rail yards of that port city on his burro — a common means of transportation for men at the range — he noticed a gang of Chinamen grouped around an object on one of the tracks. Pushing his way through the crowd, he saw a Chinese boy who had just been run over by a train. He "was an awful mess, both of his legs were cut off close to his body and one of his arms cut off at his elbow," he related. He was "moaning and bleeding to death," he went on, and the Chinese present, including a policeman (shimbo), simply stood about gaping. The lad's father, who was "crying like a child," seemed as helpless as the others. The soldier bitterly swore at the men present for their inaction, to no avail, whereupon, deciding "that if anything was to be done I was the one that had to do it," he hopped on his burro and went to a drug store, only finding a can of ether that might be of any use. "Back I hastened with the can ... and placed my handkerchief on the boy's nose and dumped the contents on [it].... Presently he stopped moaning so I shoved off, leaving the ether-saturated handkerchief on [his] nose." When asked whether or not he feared that he might have killed the boy, he responded: "Oh, Hell, he would have died anyway, so I figured that I would make it as easy for him as I could."[14]

Private Willis E. Cunningham, an assistant editor of *The Sentinel*, similarly reflected with sensitivity on the death of a rickshaw coolie:

> The other morning I ambled down the road to a place where a dead ricksha coolie had been parked by the police and self-possessedly looked him over. It wasn't a very interesting survey due to the fact that they had placed him inside the ricksha and covered him up so that all that was visible was a pair of rather unedifying knees, whose bland countenance revealed nothing. As I have said, he was a particularly uninteresting specimen, so I soon quit elongating my neck and went back to the more prosaic but less easy

job of "push and pull." Later, however, the incident led me to reflect on the relative importance of human beings. Were you ever around soon after the Stewpan of Wuniung or some such notable had unconcernedly kicked the bucket? And did you witness the row all his friends, relatives, debtors, creditors and concubines proceeded to make over him? Palanquins, carriages, brass bands, papier-mâché figures, huge idols and a host of other thingumbobs [sic] accompany him to the place where they lay him on his back and shovel dirt in his face. Now turn back to Mr. Ricksha Coolie. As far as I know he is still reposing in the ricksha. Two or three shimbos [policemen] came around and propped up the front end of his vehicle so that he wouldn't fall out and obstruct the traffic, threw an old piece of sack over his head and let it go at that. Sometime, I suppose, after he is well cured, they will haul him away to the Municipal Garbage Dump and that will be the end of the matter. "Verily, nowhere in the world is there so much of a gap between the greatest and the least as there is in China!"[15]

In a more direct contact with the Chinese, the regiment employed numerous laborers at various levels. One was Li San, an employee of the Quartermasters. He had served the U.S. government since 1892 when he was first employed at the American Legation and Military attaché's Office in Peking. During the Boxer Uprising he performed hazardous duty as a runner carrying vital messages from Peking to Tientsin, also serving as a guide for the first troops to relieve the besieged legations in Peking. The report of his death in June of 1928, which appeared in a black-edged box in *The Sentinel*, was written with a measure of respect usually absent in connection with references to the Chinese. The troops were asked for financial assistance for his widow and two minor children, now "left in destitute circumstances." Perhaps some who reflected on Li San's death may have recalled the familiar Chinese proverb that "it is better to have one more good man on earth than an extra angel in heaven."[16]

American soldiers stationed in the Orient, many of them World War I veterans who had witnessed the horrors of that conflict, often found it difficult to reconcile themselves to the massive, pervasive suffering that they found in China. In a small way, some took steps to alleviate it. In one instance, men of the regiment's Howitzer Company came upon a small Chinese boy wandering the streets of Tangshan where they were temporarily stationed, "with nothing on but a smile and a coat of mud," they explained; "we liked the smile, but we didn't like his other garment." So, he was taken in hand, given numerous baths, crammed with food, and suitably clothed, eventually in a miniature uniform. Subsequently, having advertised his situation in the event someone might be seeking him, when no one claimed him he was adopted as the company's mascot. Nicknamed "Bill Howitzer," he was soon speaking fluent English, though he could also swear "better than any soldier and gamble[d] with the best of them as well." If not an altogether satisfactory outcome, in any case, his life was spared, with the possibility of better days to come.[17]

The example of "Bill Howitzer" revealed that the American presence in China had a strong positive side which *The Sentinel* reminded its readers of from time to time. Americans were spending 10 million a year in missionary, educational, medical and evangelical work in China, one report indicated. Nearly 3,000 Chinese were attending American colleges, 400 of whom were supported by returned Boxer Indemnity Funds. It was a measure of pride that after 1908, the American portion of Boxer Indemnity Funds, which the Chinese government had to pay to recompense foreigners for costs and damages sustained in the Boxer Uprising and its suppression, were designated for college scholarships. In the spring of 1924, President Calvin Coolidge earmarked the residue of these funds for transfer to Tsing Hua College, Peking.[18]

Much of the travel done by members of the 15th was for leisure purposes, but more serious journeys were undertaken in connection with relief programs. One example was a fact-finding trip by Major M.F. Waltz, who investigated the operations in the Red Cross Famine Area in northern China. More daring was a venture of an intrepid journalist, Ruby M. Sepulveda, wife of Lieutenant Sepulveda of the regiment. An experienced journalist who had previously covered various revolutions in Mexico, she then spent a year and a half in China with her husband. Becoming restless in Tientsin, when her husband "hied himself to the sand storms of the target range at Leichuang," she joined the Red Cross working in Shansi Province, one of the "most beautiful and picturesque parts of China." Traveling from Peking on the Peking-Hankow railway, after some mishaps she arrived at Ping Ting Chow. In Shansi, she observed Chinese workers building roads in exchange for meager food supplies and small sums of money. Sepulveda harshly criticized these activities, charging that missionaries rather than the suffering Chinese were the main beneficiaries. Even more damning, she observed considerable inefficiency on the part of missionaries and Red Cross officials, not to mention the venality of Chinese officials who systematically plundered the funds raised by the Red Cross for China relief.[19]

American sympathy, or at least some understanding of China's woes, stemmed from the endemic famines and recurrent floods. While the 15th was in China, rampaging waters repeatedly affected their compound and other sites connected with their activities. Foremost among the culprits was the Yellow River, "The River of Death"—"The Sorrow of China"— "the most destructive stream on the face of the earth."[20]

But the Yellow River was not alone; it shared its villain's mantle with the Yangtze, which in 1931 embarked on one of its own monumental rampages. In this instance, the Chinese were aided by the American aviation hero Charles Lindbergh and his wife, Anne Morrow Lindbergh. The pair flew extensively over the huge flooded areas on relief surveys, and also transported medicines and physicians to the hardest-hit areas. *The Sentinel* reproduced a Chinese map revealing the dimensions of the tragedy and included flood accounts by the American journalist Edgar Snow in its "Things Chinese" column. Snow estimated that 12 million homes and 55 million people were affected, one fifth of whom "are utterly destitute." Comparing the tragedy with floods in the USA of that era, he could only be saddened by the seemingly-unending afflictions that befell China. "I have been in China many months," he began, "and I have a love for it, yet a deep sorrow, too. I have seen so much pain and suffering here that much of it has entered my own blood. Perhaps because I am still young I have felt these things more than others; they distress and disconcert me. It seems to me that people with such fineness and robustness of character as you often find among Chinese peasants merit better treatment than they have received from the elements and from man. Americans should do everything possible to restore in them the desire to live," he concluded.[21]

Women associated with the regiment sometimes had a clearer insight into the real conditions in China, and particularly the often-objectionable attitudes of Westerners in general. A good example was the article, "'Boy'— The Call of the East," by Eleonore von Eltz, reprinted from *The Outlook*. In the early 1920s, Eltz had been a hostess in charge of the 15th's Service Club. "Boy! Bring me a whisky 'n' soda!' so says a newly arrived American in China or the Philippines. "That's the Call of the East for you," Von Eltz asserted, and strongly castigated such racism: "The American Army officer en route to drill his company raps out briskly, 'Boy! Gimme that Sam Browne, kwai-kwai!' (Chinese for 'Make it snappy!') Later, at the close of an arduous day in the field, he may be found in an attitude of pained reproach due to the discovery that his wrist watch has run down. And now the plaintive cry is, 'Boy, didn't I tell you to wind watch every day? One day, two day, *ting puhao* (very no good). *Must* wind every day.'" Then there might be a soldier hoping to impress a buddy new to the ways of Tientsin:

> The doughboy … will probably drop into the vernacular: "Hey! Shohysa! Jobee!" (Hey! Boy! Rickshaw!) Taking his pick of the dozen which rush to his command, this young lord of creation in khaki lolls back at ease, manifestly the monarch of all he surveys. Suddenly he spies a buddy, likewise lolling and bound for the same goal. Does he alight to run an honest race

on his own "pins," as he would term them? Not at all — let Boy do it! The only exertion he permits himself at this point is to lean forward, the light of conquest in his eye as he growls, "Boy! Kwai-kwai!" Boy, ever faithful, senses the situation instantly and the race is on, both coolies flinging taunts at each other, and, although they may be panting their poor lungs out, apparently enjoying the fracas as much as the soldiers. Arrived at the barracks, the winner — perhaps the loser too — will probably pay his Boy three times over — assuming, of course, that these events occur within three days after pay day.

"And now we come to the American Army wife," Eltz went on — calling her perhaps among the worst offenders in such matters — and "the meaning to her of this call of the East." Typically, a wife and her husband had but recently arrived in Tientsin "having perhaps spent a recent tour in a camp on the Mexican border where she has frequently scoured her own frying pans in the desert sands." The newly arrived couple immediately found the Chinese situation, with its plentiful supply of servants, "exhilarating." In short order, the American Army wife learned the call of the East, "and 'somewheres east of Suez,' she will never call in vain," von Eltz ruefully concluded.[22]

Also revealing was an article by a Chinese writer, Ku Hung-Ming, a reputable Chinese journalist. Writing in *The Peking and Tientsin Times*, he provided insight into the thinking and attitudes held by many well-to-do Chinese regarding foreigners. He related that a certain woman, whom he styled a "Treaty Port Lady," and her husband, an important adviser of a distinguished civil official during the Qing Dynasty, Li Hung-Chang (Li Hongzhang) and hence a "Treaty Port Gentleman," were by definition "Somebody in China." Returning home, "with the intention of passing the rest of their days in their own country," they came back to China after two years. When asked why, they replied that they were "Nobody" at home, "but here in China we are Somebody"— the "Lure of the East" with a vengeance. Ku Hung-Ming could only bitterly reflect, "My mind was occupied with the thought what a curious country China has become when in order to be 'somebody,' ... [and hence] entitled to travel in a first class railway car, one needs only to be able to speak a few words in English."[23]

Even more compelling and instructive is the poem "Brothers," by an anonymous soldier in the regiment's Service Company. Strongly reminiscent of Kipling's "Recessional," because of its clarity and comprehensiveness, it merits full quotation:

        The Missionary Speaks.
     "Brothers are we," the Preachers say
     From their pulpits 'neath the Cross,

> "Your skin is naught to the One above,
> To Him all flesh is dross.
> And when on the final day you come
> To His throne for your just deserts,
> He'll reck no more of your yellow skins
> Than he does of the White Men's shirts.
> But think you must as the White Men think
> And bow to the White Man's rule,
> For the only God is a White Man's God
> And He hateth the face of a Fool."
>
> The Merchant Speaks.
> "Brothers are we, the Bible says,
> And I am a Christian True.
> I pay the Clerics of every faith
> And send them along to you,
> To tell you the error of heathen ways
> To discourse of the horrors of hell,
> So list you close to these rev'rend men
> And learn how to buy and sell.
> For think you must as the White Men think,
> And bow to the White Man's rule,
> For the only God is a White Man's God
> And He hateth the face of a Fool."
>
> The Soldier Speaks.
> "Soldiers are we, our Masters say,
> And our Masters are Christians True,
> We carry the Flag of a Christian Race
> And our Rifles are Christian too.
> So look you well to our bayonets,
> For their points are the Christian Hell,
> They speak with a silent Voice to you
> — Pay heed and listen Well!
> For think you must as our Masters think
> And bow to our Masters' rule,
> For the only God is our Masters' God
> — And death is the end of a Fool!"[24]

That there were innumerable conflicts as well as strained relations, misunderstandings, and outright exploitation of the Chinese was much in evidence. The Chinese, by the late 1920s, were in a mood of open defiance of foreigners. Among the most radical in their antiforeign stance were Chinese students, some of whom had studied in Western colleges and universities. They took their views back to China and often agitated on campuses in China where communistic influence was likewise frequently in evidence. Unrest among students in Hunan Province, in institutions in Changsha, Yigang, Singtan, Liling and others, attracted some attention in the regiment. There the spirit that animated the Boxers a quarter of a century earlier was revived. Certain exhortations on a giant placard set the tone: "Arise! Perceive your enemy!!! Down with Christianity!! Foreigners come here from a sword, and you can see the blood but Christianity (Ki-tuh Kiao) kills you without your perceiving it!!" There were also dangerous organizations such as the YMCA: "Beware!! ... what kinds of places are these? They induce us to go out and frolic, to see free pictures, and to play at football." But these were in fact "just like the trap-birds of the Red Light district of Shanghai, who only lure you to your doom with fine appearances!!!"[25]

Also by way of protest, students and others annually commemorated 24 "Humiliation Days." These included "The Twenty-One Demands" of Japan during World War I, "Weihaiwei leased to Great Britain," the "Sino-British Opium War," and "The 1901 Boxer protocol with the Powers," among others equally hated.[26]

Discussions and lectures about Chinese Communism proved popular among men of the regiment. But if many Americans were greatly disturbed by it, one Chinese scholar, no doubt speaking for many in China, asserted that he had no fear of it because "China has tried it three times; once before the time of Confucius; once, some centuries after; and again, some five centuries ago." It had never worked, he declared. "It is contrary to the genius of the Chinese people; it will not work now."[27]

In addition to Communism, other organizations, some with religious affiliations and overtones, were of concern to Westerners and duly monitored by the 15th's commanders. Among these were the Big Swords, a group of bandits who embraced the quaint notion that they were invulnerable to bullets if they swallowed small strips of yellow paper upon which was written a magic yet illegible word. They then blew their breath, now infused with the magic, on their hands and rubbed all parts of their body. This produced a spell lasting for about two hours. Big Sword men normally armed themselves with swords, that is, ancient traditional weapons; those who used rifles—or modern weapons—were not invulnerable to gun shots. If a man were felled by a bullet, it was explained that not all parts of the body had been rubbed by the hands, and hence there were chinks in the body's armor.[28]

Sharing some of the same notions were the Red Spears, or the Buddhist Brotherhood of Sacred Soldiers of the Virtuous Way. A religious and military society, some members had a reputation as bandits, but in some parts of the country they were trained, disciplined rural troops employed as an unofficial police force to preserve law and order and protect their homes from brigands. They too professed to be "endowed with magical qualities which make them impervious to bullets," and also used only swords and spears, eschewing rifles as "foreign curses."[29]

Given such manifestations, Colonel Newell, in greeting new arrivals in May of 1927, advised them that they were "arriving in China at a period when conditions are even more upset than usual.... The attitude of the Chinese towards the foreigner has undergone a marked change. You will find the Chinese peace loving and quick to respond to a smile and considerate treatment. On the other hand, in these days of suppressed feeling they are equally quick to resent unfair treatment and abuse. A thoughtless act on the part of any of us may precipitate trouble."[30]

The Sentinel went to considerable lengths to inform its readers as to their China bailiwick. Of particular utility was the column "Things Chinese," which it regularly published for many years beginning in March of 1928. Derived from many sources, often from the important, informative book by James Dyer Ball, *Things Chinese*, this addition became a key focal point of the paper's instructional and information efforts. It also serves on occasion to indicate the limitations of Americans as observers of the Chinese scene.[31]

Annually, the colorful Chinese New Year celebrations which invariably attracted the attention of the soldiers were described, the accounts explaining the traditional use of gaudy colors and fireworks, the almost non-stop feasting, the need felt by all to visit members of their extended families, and the attempts to collect debts while adroitly seeking to avoid paying those that they owed to others. On this occasion the Chinese served tea, provided tobacco and plates of watermelon seeds for guests, though in the homes of the wealthy, seeds of the lotus flower were provided instead. Another favorite dish for the occasion was orange beef. Of interest—and controversy—was that the new Chinese government of Chiang Kai-shek, from its relocated capital in Nanking, had ordered the keeping of the foreigners' New Year's Day in 1931, but Chinese stubbornly clung to February 17, the traditional date.[32]

The intricacies of the Chinese calendar also came in for its share of attention. The birthday of Confucius (551–479 B.C.) was an occasion for *The Sentinel* to enlighten its readers on the significance of that sage, as well as highlight the lengthy history of China. In October of 1924, the men were reminded that the philosopher's 2,475th birthday was then being celebrated. Readers were also informed that Confucius had taught that filial piety was the greatest of Chinese virtues and disobedience the most heinous of crimes, which explained much about Chinese attitudes and behavior that otherwise seemed inexplicable.[33]

Chinese religions and the deities of China were other topics of some interest, addressed in such articles as "Number Beyond Reckoning." Colin K. Cameron, the British-born chaplain's assistant of the 15th who often wrote incisive articles for "Things Chinese," recognized that superstition was more important than religion to many Chinese, proclaiming "the Chinese ... the most superstitious people on earth." To be sure, in general, the Chinese feared evil spirits and their "wicked machinations," which pervaded the whole of their society.[34]

These superstitions closely involved the animal kingdom. Especially important were the fox, snake and badger, all alleged to reveal supernatural powers "if they [had] lived to a great age and have collected virtue," and especially if found in old temples or dilapidated buildings. If they were badly treated or disturbed, they were capable of making a great deal of trouble for people. Sometimes when trouble came, specialists were employed to find out what kind of animal was involved and devise remedies for their disturbances. This profession, called *Ch'ao Hsiang*, was, however, declared illegal by authorities because of frauds and malpractices. It persisted, though the practitioners were often forced to act in secret. When a 15th's nurse's lack of knowledge of Chinese customs led to an "ill-fated attempt to rid [a] pantry area of rats and mice," she selected the traditional "wedding day" of rodents for her foray and her Chinese friends direfully predicted lamentable consequences. Formidable rain gods or water spirits must also be respected, and the coming of precipitation often halted such activities as building construction. When Tientsin was flooded on one occasion, the Chinese held "five-legged Pete," a turtle with five legs, responsible for the violent wind and rain storm that had produced the deluge.[35]

As to animals, nothing was more pervasive in Chinese life than the dragon, hardly mythical to the Chinese, but considered to be as real as anything on the planet. The imperial dragon and the phoenix, a symbol of the empress, were encountered everywhere. The Fifth Day of the Fifth Moon was traditionally the day of the Dragon Boat Festival at which time, as on the Chinese New Year's day, all debts were supposed to be settled, the failure to do so resulting in a loss of face. This festival and the New Year were the two most important of the Chinese holidays, though there were many more.[36]

The matter of face, one of the Oriental attributes better known in the West, had religious connotations. The British soldier-adventurer F.A. Sutton explained its concept at some length, seeing it as "a definite social problem, inexplicable, maddening. A word. A religion. A Philosophy. A national cowardice." He explained further: "Either you had face in which case you were solvent and respectable, or you hadn't it, and were mud. To lose face was to lose hope. A whole social system skated on this particular thin ice above the dark, deep waters of disgrace and defeat. You paid for face. You bribed face. You stole for it, murdered for it, pretended, aped, tipped, whispered, prevaricated. Face was God. Face was wrath. Face was Solvency. Or it was Power."[37]

Chinese preoccupation with *Feng-shui*, also known as geomancy, took on the attributes of religious belief. Among other things, this had to do with the physical placement of buildings, for example the location and direction which they faced. Concerns with these matters often led to a strenuous opposition to progress along Western lines, such as the construction of railways, telegraph lines and other foreign innovations. Governments desiring to implement technological advances often forcibly had to override widespread popular opposition.[38]

Noted for their pithy wisdom and deriving from the primacy of Confucius in the culture, Chinese proverbs abounded and obtained a following among the paper's readers, as: "True gold fears no fire," "A man's a man whether short or tall," "He who talks much must err; he excels who says nothing," and "Talent does not always accompany beauty." Learning was traditionally of great importance to the Chinese: "He who studies ten years in obscurity, will when once preferred, be known universally," and "The words vanish, the writing stays," as well as "Some study shows the need for more."[39]

The games the Chinese played came in for discussion, such as chess, that ancient game which some said originated in China about 1,120 B.C. Significantly, the Chinese always regarded it as "mimic warfare," which, because it involved the matching of wits, seemed an acceptable substitute to actual battle.[40]

Common utensils and practices generally well known in the West, as the ubiquitous chopsticks, the amazing bamboo plant and its countless uses, and the familiar silk culture, were described in turn. Chinese native or herbal doctors, who generally prescribed various diets, drugs, herbs, physical exercises and acupuncture, often referring to old books of prescriptions, potions and practices handed down through the family for generations, were discussed. The Chinese aided a suffering fellow citizen with some trepidation as a long-standing Chinese principle dictated that any aid given to an injured, ill or maimed person meant assuming responsibility for that individually subsequently, though doctors by necessity were exempted from these strictures.[41]

The lovely art and stimulating literature of China were featured in numerous columns, including discussions on Chinese painting and artists and how they worked as well as comparisons between Western and Chinese art and artists. Chinese fans were not ignored. Nor were figurine arrangements of the so-called Eight Immortals, or the *Pa Hsien*, Taoist representations of persons believed to have attained immortality, usually centering on the divine philosopher, Lao Tzu. Unusual wrought iron pictures, favored by the Manchus and popular among foreigners, were mentioned. Carved lacquer was also discussed, as were wood block printing methods. Other articles analyzed Chinese classical and romantic literature. For example, one piece on a fairy tale chosen from the *Liao Chia*, the Chinese Grimm's Fairy Tales equivalent, noted that "contrary to general opinion the Chinese are of a romantic nature." Other selections included a story having to do with the Japanese — "Wo tsz."[42]

Chinese opera, theater and music came in for attention, though as Elsie McCormick in her column "Shanghai Sayings" in *The Sentinel* once observed, rather maladroitly, "the only thing worse than a man trying to learn to play a cornet is a man learning to play a Chinese musical instrument. The trouble is you never can tell when they have learned."[43]

Some Westerners were fascinated by Chinese institutions. For instance, in China, the pawnshop, unlike in the West, largely functioned as a poor man's bank. Many were venerable joint stock companies highly prominent in local affairs, and pawn brokers held a high social position in China. The beggar fraternity, regarded as despicable in the West, also enjoyed esteem in China, despite the deplorable practices whereby some mothers deprived some of their children of sight so that they could make their living as blind beggars, who were especially regarded as worthy of respect. In other instances, Chinese resorted to self-mutilation to the same ends.[44]

The Chinese recognized a hierarchy of professions, traditionally holding scholars in the highest esteem, followed by farmers, artisans and then merchants and only last, soldiers. The relative importance of the farmer was exemplified by the prominence of the Temple of Agriculture in Peking. Traditionally, the emperor inaugurated the commencement of the farming season at each spring equinox by symbolically plowing there, following the plow on foot in person.[45]

But the average American soldier was little concerned with hierarchies, often meeting mostly street vendors, who hawked myriad products to meet the daily needs and desires of the populace, ranging from chow for rickshaw men to much else. These merchants employed a wide range of distinctive loud cries or shrill calls, each of which advertised their particular product or service, as well as the noises of gongs and drums, a great deal of it abounding in "simple, and often beautiful melody." Indeed, Chinese streets were characterized by noise, the people incessantly talking and shouting, their voices intermingled with clash of cymbals, the clang of gongs, drums, and harsh and shrill flutes, altogether with an "absence of *piano* effects." Then there were the firecrackers, including the two-chambered giant prohibited in most states of the U.S. because "of its almost lethal qualities." The noisy streets sometimes echoed to the sounds of arguments. Westerners were fascinated by the fact that in most instances, no blows were exchanged, the Chinese were of the opinion that such lapses meant that the loser had run out of ideas and the will to express them effectively.[46]

But perhaps the rickshaw (sometimes spelled "ricksha") boys or "jopeys," ("*chiao-p'i*" or "*lachudee*" in Chinese) were of greatest interest because the American soldiers met and used them daily. Numerous articles recounted details of the mechanics of rickshaw pulling and focused on the rickshaw pullers' hard life. Rickshawmen often acted as pimps as well as agents of restaurants and shops, getting kickbacks for bringing in customers.[47]

The soldiers often marveled at the rickshaw boys' stamina and abilities to sprint for long distances, a fact which often produced impromptu races through the streets of Tientsin as soldier passengers spurred on their drivers, sometimes with disastrous results. Rickshaw boys were not always victimized, though they certainly were on occasion. A rough and ready "union" or rickshaw brotherhood existed to aid their fellows, and Chinese bystanders sometimes intervened on their behalf when altercations arose, sending soldiers scurrying to safety.[48]

Similarly noteworthy was the concept of cumshaw, referring to a gift, a dole, or a fee. It meant charity as well as an earned commission on sales. Small, ragged tots, the countless beggars on the streets, often called out "cumshaw," expecting a handout. Not to be confused with "squeeze," which was graft, cumshaw was on the contrary regarded as "a gracious gift given out of graciousness." On New Year's Day, all employees expected cumshaw, with the understanding that it would equal a month's salary. In this way, they were paid for the thirteenth month when it came due as based on the lunar calendar.[49]

The personal characteristics and attitudes of the Chinese proved equally fascinating and often figured in the "Things Chinese" column. It seemed remarkable that the concept of time was virtually meaningless to the Chinese, which made for endless difficulties when East met West in any sort of contact or relationship.[50]

Throughout, the soldiers also marveled at the good humor and gaiety of the Chinese, who often "shrieked with laughter" at almost any occurrence. Indeed, "considering the conditions under which those wretches existed, their general good humor was a source of never-ending wonder." In addition, the Chinese loved amusements, processions and shows, into which they unfailing entered "with great gusto and zest."[51]

There was a darker side as well. The Chinese could be notoriously cruel, and *The Sentinel* noted such things as the widespread use of torture both by legally-constituted authorities and illegally carried out. Nor was slavery unknown. Executions were public occasions and there were numerous accounts of these that men of the regiment witnessed. The *Da Dao*, the fearsome yet fascinating beheading sword, became a collector's items for the American soldiers when one could be found and procured.[52]

The practice of beheading was banned — at least officially — when Chiang Kai-shek's government established some semblance of order in China in the late 1920s, and execution by firing squad was substituted. This was not proof against untoward incidents, however. On one occasion near Tangshan a firing squad bungled its duty, accidentally shooting an onlooker. As *The Sentinel* rather ruefully reported, "This caused great amusement among the spectators who clapped, laughed and considered the entire affair a huge joke. The idea of two men being killed with one shot was considered very clever and whereas this sad incident would have shocked the community at home [in the States] in this case it gave cause for considerable enjoyment and amusement."[53]

Themselves addicted to various vices, the men of the 15th noted that everyone of both sexes of China smoked incessantly, and had done so since the introduction of tobacco from Luzon in A.D. 1530 despite official prohibitions from Ming rulers and other officials, suggesting that the use of tobacco was not only a source of solace but perhaps a means of protest as well. As to the Chinese use of liquor — they often found their drinks in a pawnshop — one writer noted that the favorite drink of Tientsin, both among the Chinese and many men of the regiment, was cherry brandy.[54]

While the men's daily round was focused on Tientsin and other points along the Peking-Mukden railway, they also wandered farther afield, picking up new, often lasting, impressions as they went along. Peking, the destination of numerous sightseeing tours, was especially familiar to the men of the regiment. There the men were quartered and fed by the "Y," or on occasion by the marines of the Legation Guard.[55]

By the early 1930s, another dimension of China arose of paramount importance. This was the rapid emergence of Japan on the Chinese scene. The men of the 15th accordingly began to compare the two, sensing portents for the future. Much of the travel taken by officers now focused on Manchuria, Korea and Japan. Before 1931, most Americans were favorably impressed with the Japanese in Manchuria. They often praised the progressiveness and favorable appearance of these areas and the cities of Mukden and Port Arthur (Lushun). For some time to come, Japan never failed to impress visitors with its beauty, cleanliness and sense of order that prevailed.[56]

As the Manchurian conquest by Japan unfolded, *The Sentinel* published articles assessing it. Accounts of visiting firemen were common: Captain Dudley W. Knox of the U.S. Navy, an author of important works on naval history, put in an appearance. So did Lieutenant Colonel James G. McIlroy of the Army's General Staff Corps, who spoke to the officers of the regiment. McIlroy, who had completed language studies in Tokyo, was slated to take up duty as military attaché in the Japanese capital.[57]

In late 1931, clashes occurred between the Japanese in Tientsin and the Chinese, notably at the boundary between the Japanese concession and the Chinese native city. All of the foreign detachments were soon involved in defensive operations. The British, for instance, moved onto Race Course Road, and soon "tents sprang up, Lewis guns peeked over tufts of earth, and squads went into position." The Americans sent out observation units, including the mounted detachment, and dug gun positions along Woodrow Wilson Field. Colonel Taylor promptly placed both the native city and the Japanese concession off limits to all Americans at the same time, declaring that "Our mission is the protection of American lives and property. With other matters we are not concerned." All the troops were instructed to use caution in their actions and words; no opinions must be expressed; no one offended." Nonetheless, the Japanese were often viewed as the aggressors, which added to the debate and concern about the role of the Americans and other foreigners in China.[58]

Being fighting men, it was understandable that the relative merits of the Japanese and Chinese as soldiers began to be aired frequently and in depth in *The Sentinel* and among the men of the 15th. In a lengthy article, "Chinese Fighting Men," Major John Magruder, who had served two terms as military attaché in Peking, noted that on their social scale the Chinese ranked scholars, farmers, artisans and merchants above soldiers. This view was affirmed in such popular Chinese proverbs as: "Nails are not made from good iron; honest citizens never become soldiers." Magruder saw the Chinese as being, on the whole, "practical pacifists." They would fight if need be but much preferred indirect methods, which they employed with ceaseless persistence and infinite patience. "A favorable decision promptly and abruptly reached is less pleasing to the Chinese than a decision obtained after circumlocution," he declared. Chinese wars were characteristically defensive — even passively defensive — and intrigue and bribery were often the preferred weapons. Though the Chinese had "studied war" at the feet of the Japanese and also German military advisers in the modern era, they had an unshakable faith in their destiny and in the continuance of their race, which had, after all, persevered over the centuries no matter who had conquered them by military methods. Their patience and persistence was "expressed in a locust-like mass momentum and propagation." Accordingly, Magruder declared, "the Chinese have no military history worthy of scientific study." Whether or not they would evolve as a militaristic nation, Magruder concluded, depended upon whether they could be fundamentally altered as a people willing to accept force of arms as a means of pursuing national goals.[59]

Another expert with similar views was George E. Sokolsky, one of the correspondents of *The New York Times* in China. In his article "China Versus Japan: A Clash of Tempos," Sokolsky noted that the Manchurian conflict revealed the essential differences between the Chinese and the Japanese. The Chinese by temperament were a contemplative, philosophic and individualistic people. The Japanese were a people of action with a willingness to accept regimentation. In addition, the Japanese were a people of the present; "they take time by the forelock." The Chinese rather "look back into the dim past and wait for the long future to solve their problems." Chinese cities and villages were lazy places, the products of antiquity where life was slow, leisurely and scholarly. In China, "work, somewhere, somehow, [was] being done," but a leisurely pace was the norm. Chinese of means would "rise late, spend hours at a lunch which is not only a marvel of the gastronomic art but an occasion of brilliant talk, of matching puns and playing with double-edged words of keen analyses of the life and thought of a nation." Even coolies were adept at such an approach to life. In short, the Japanese were "eager, swift, hard," dependent upon driving action, while the Chinese were "patient, slow, [and] pliant," depending upon "the wearing-away influence of time" to remove all their obstacles. Thus, China did not need speed; it needed time. Such considerations seemed to suggest that Japan, not China, stood the best chance in winning any conflict between the two peoples.[60]

These conclusions seemed borne out when significant clashes came in Shanghai in 1932 between the Japanese and the Chinese. Western observers were sometimes impressed with Chinese military successes but were even more so by Japanese actions. In one skirmish, three soldiers of the Japanese Shimomoto Brigade had jumped into a Chinese position with explosives tied to their bodies. They ignited, blowing them to pieces but also destroying wire entanglements, thus opening a passage for their comrades to rush the stronghold and capture it. Their dramatic deaths produced a great sensation among the Japanese as well as Westerners. The military authorities in Tokyo conferred on them the highest order of merit, the Order of the Golden Kite, and reported their names to the Japanese Throne in recognition of their "matchless bravery." Yet many of the 15th's troops who visited with Chinese troops stationed around Tientsin, usually living in local temples, were impressed by their soldierly bearing and especially with their thoroughly clean automatic rifles, which they invariably noted were superior to their own weapons. It also became increasingly clear to the more knowledgeable of the 15th's officers that the Chinese had traveled a long way from the days of the Boxer Uprising.[61]

Another conception of China that surfaced among men of the 15th was "as a power as pervasive and as incontestable as the forces of Nature." Such forces present a continuity, and it was commonly said that "if the people of China were to file by, one by one, the procession would never end; for before the last man of this generation could pass, another generation would have come upon the scene." The Chinese were the only people to have lived under continuous organized institutions with an established culture present since when "Homer sang and when Moses wrote the laws on Sinai — and they are still living under substantially that same culture." The consciousness of belonging to a mighty group with this unending history produces "an imperturbability and often a self-satisfactory attitude that ... has been extremely disconcerting to foreigners."[62]

When the Chinese appeared most exasperating, slovenly, and slow to act, the soldiers were reminded that "this is China and over the last five thousand years no man has ever hurried a Chinaman. The impatience of the average foreigner means nothing to him. He calmly goes his own sweet aromatic way and does things about as he pleases. Bribes, threats, or force are of no avail, [and] he will do his job when he wants to and how he wants it." The wishes of any foreigner would be simply ignored and all wishing to deal with a Chinese must recognize that patience was his motto, which should be adopted as one's own, realizing that that which was desired would eventually, in good time, be forthcoming.[63]

Captain John C. Whitcomb, one of *The Sentinel* editors, elaborated on this when addressing his remarks to new arrivals:

> China is China. It is the oldest civilization on the face of the earth today. It has existed for more centuries than most of us have lived years. We can't change it to suit our fancies so we must take it as it is. A dozen times a day we find ourselves criticizing the way the Chinaman does this or that. We stand by with impatience or amused tolerance as we watch him live his own life. And yet his methods of living and doing have stood the test of more time than any other methods in human life. Let's give him credit for

that at least. China had a well developed system of living when Cheops started the pyramids of Egypt. China had a civilization two thousand years old when Rome was a group of huts on the banks of the Tiber.[64]

Of course, not all the American soldiers were favorably impressed with what the Chinese had accomplished over the ages. In an article that he had written for *The Sentinel*, one doughboy joyfully recorded that "I'm going home, back to the hum of the trolley, the song of the news boy. Away from the sordid, the dirt, the ignorance, the dross, the gross, the artificial." Indeed, it would be glorious, he concluded, to be "away from the 'Call of the East' whose only call is the 'Call of the Wild.'"[65]

CHAPTER XI

Les Femmes

There was a young girlie from Chih-li
Whose hair was straight, black and not curly.
To a young *Meigua-ping* she said: "Buy me a ring?"
He said: "Girlie, not me. It's too early."[1]

The eternal subject of the fairer sex naturally figured in the regiment's concerns. Officers, and a few higher ranking enlisted personnel, were able to bring their families to China where they were promptly spoiled by a house full of attentive servants. Other soldiers, warmly embracing ancient Chinese customs regarding concubines, made their own domestic arrangements.

Undoubtedly, the often beautiful Chinese women had a strong appeal. One commentary on the subject, "Just a Little Short Chinese," explained:

> There's a girl he met in Texas, and
> there's one in Alabam',
> Then there's one down in old Cincy,
> who liked to "rush the can."
> Next a girl he knew in London, just
> as blond as she could be,
> But the latest one he smiled at, is
> a little short Chinee.
>
> . . . .
>
> But there's a girl at home in Denver,
> whom he never more must see,
> 'Cause the latest one he smiled at
> was a little short Chinee.[2]

Certainly, to many troopers in China the Chinese women were more desirable than their American counterparts reveling in new freedoms, the consequence of the Great War and the newly-won right to vote. Their fashions, featuring short skirts, backless dresses, and other shocking trends, elicited endless comment, jokes, and, of course, poems. "It's a mighty little man who'll hide behind his wife's skirts," one wag noted, while another advised: "Be brief — look what a hit short skirts have made." But perhaps the females themselves were the ultimate victims, or so one poet thought: "Cold winter comes apace / When girls must face the breeze / With little on their backs / And nothing on their knees." Indeed, one practice which startled the men was the propensity of the girls to roll down their stockings, a daring, sensuous venture that was apparently an attempt "to help out the struggle of men to see the stocking top." Accordingly, the expression "rolling their own," usually referring to cigarettes, took on a distinctive new meaning, all of which was to help attain the ultimate: "To feel the coolest and look the hottest."[3]

At the center of the maelstrom about the modern woman was, of course, the flapper. The fascination with these wonders extended to China, and much talk and numerous poems were preoccupied with this manifestation of the Roaring Twenties. "And talk about flappers Oh Boys I know you are just dying to see them and I wouldn't try your nerve by telling you of them but honestly they are a sight for sore eyes," one soldier enthusiastically wrote from California to his buddy back in China. One of the 15th's ubiquitous poets thought that he knew how Kipling might regard the new phenomenon:

> . . . .
> Flappers flapping everywhere, on
>   corners and in nooks;
> Their thoughts, I fear, are on the
>   boys, on dancing and their looks,
> And if they have their powder
>   puffs, why, never mind their books,
> As they scandal off to High
>   School in the morning![4]

An unknown poet, in his offering, "The Flapper" — this time with apologies to John Greenleaf Whittier — had further comment:

> Blessings on thee, little dame.
>   Bare-backed girl with knees the same.
> With thy rolled down silken hose,
>   And thy short transparent clothes.
> With thy red lips reddened more,
>   Smeared with lip stick from the store.
> With a makeup on thy face,
>   And thy "Bobbed Hair's" jaunty grace,

> From my heart I give thee joy —
> Glad that I was born a "boy."⁵

But then perhaps flappers had been present throughout history. Eve, undoubtedly the first one, was described by one poet as that "wild and winsome coot" who made poor Adam "taste ... forbidden fruit," and "This Cleopatra maiden fair / For whom great Caesar tore his hair / Who was this vamp debonaire? / A Flapper."⁶

The question of women's rights arrived in due course in Tientsin as elsewhere, *The Sentinel* once announcing rather superciliously that "Miss Suzane Butterworth, who lives at Bald Knob, will lecture next Friday nite at Maledion Hall on 'Wimmins Rites.' Some say Suzane is a rite smart talker."⁷

More disturbing to many soldiers were fears that some women, in view of their growing success in the business and professional worlds, might next aspire to military careers. One apprehensive soldier-poet, writing in the publication *Here and There with the 31st Infantry*, in his "Why Can't Woman Be a Soldier?" hopefully suggested that perhaps the engineers would be closed to them, because "when it comes to cutting mountain roads and trails / There'd be no time for dressing or manicuring finger nails." As to the infantry, this might suit her, "providing they did not do more than a two-mile hike," but certainly, "The morning drills might not always pass without a fuss / And she couldn't stand the atmosphere, when the Top began to cuss." On the other hand, she might find the medical corps congenial and the exception, and she could issue Epsom salts and quinine with the best of them, and the soldiers would respond appreciatively when they learned "that a woman was prepared to care for the ill." Otherwise, the quartermaster corps was out, unless she would "lift a thousand pounds," and all that stooping, bending and other graceless arts, would "cause her lots of worry, working and mending," and, in any case, "they never could pitch a tent, in a Merry-Widow hat." Then, too, "Her discriminating taste for tender foods, and garden greens / Could never stand the test of Army Slum, [and] Hash, and Beans." Indeed, "Our Army and Navy is always rough and ready / That's the place for the men, [but] not for the Lady." The poet could only conclude that, though times might change, "I hope the day will never come / When women lay aside the broom, and hatpin for a Gun."⁸

What constituted the ideal army wife in the eyes of many in this era was revealed in a *Sentinel* article entitled "To Army Women." This stated in part that "In war, she is his bulwark and strength; in peace, his homemaker and consolation.... Onwards thru life she goes, spreading sunshine and contentment, lending the tenderness of a mother's love to the rigors of Army life. Dear Army women — we salute you."[9]

The Sentinel was a source for informing and educating American soldiers about the role of women in Chinese society and prevailing attitudes towards them, which caused negative comment in some quarters. Helen Ward Bromfield, in a column, "China Notes," drawing from the journal *Birth Control Review*, indicated that the Chinese regard birth as a boon only when it is of the masculine gender: "They do not, as a rule, love children, regardless of what may be cited in occasional instances—they love themselves—and acts of filial piety are not acts of affection but investments for future felicity," she declared. These views were clearly set forth in a well-known Chinese nursery rhyme that Bromfield quoted:

> We keep a dog to watch the house,
> A pig is useful, too;
> We keep a cat to catch a mouse,
> But what can we do
> With a girl like you?

The point was made even more graphically in a poem translated from the Chinese classics by James Dyer Ball, which began by noting the lot of male offspring: "Sons shall be his—on couches / lulled to rest," but the situation for female babies was quite different:

> . . . .
> And daughters also to him shall be born.
> They shall be placed upon the ground to sleep;
> Their playthings, tiles; their dress, the simplest worn;
> Their part alike from good and ill to keep,
> And ne'er their parents; hearts to cause to mourn;
> To cook the food, and spirit-malt to steep.[10]

The Sentinel also reported on the institution of concubinage in China, which was usually a debasement of the wife. One writer was fascinated by the fact that husbands sometimes obtained the consent of their wives to take on a concubine. The wives usually did so, however, only after gaining concessions of one sort or another.[11]

Generally, though, the lives of Chinese girls and women — and Buddhist priests—all being relegated to the category of "drones in the hive," were filled with hardships. At least priests could officiate at funerals, while the small girl "was merely tolerated in her helplessness to donate either material or spiritual increment to the family wealth. Of sentiment there is none." In the "families of the extremely poor she is fortunate if not sold into slavery, or handed over to a stranger with no consideration for the fate that may befall her. Higher up the social ladder her destiny may be that of a concubine or secondary wife, or one of many concubines—but always the daughter-in-law who submits to the will of her husband's parents and whose first duty in the morning is brewing the mother-in-law's tea, who must keep the incense burning, and obey the husband's family at all times." But there were winds of liberalizing change sweeping over ancient China regarding the role of women by the 1920s.[12]

Also regarding the ladies, *The Sentinel* was filled with features and comments about the White Russians, who one observer referred to as that "something new—more glamorous and exciting" which had appeared on the local scene in the early 1920s. "Love is grand, particularly the Russian variety," another account asserted, leading one soldier to bemoan that "those Russian Dames are bustin' up that old gang of our'n." One lass—among many others—who helped in "busting up the old gang" was Valentine N. Balandin, who married Corporal Paul Nickel of "I" Company. The wedding ceremonies were performed at both the garrison chapel and the Russian Church in Russian Park with large crowds from the compound and the Russian community in attendance. They may well have met while engaged in one of Tientsin's popular pastimes: promenading in Russian Park, where various regimental "sheiks" "strutted their stuff."[13]

There had been Russians in China for centuries, and Tientsin had a Russian concession established after the Boxer Uprising. But in 1920, China terminated the rights of the Russian Empire in China, and the Soviet Union formally relinquished any concession arrangements in 1924. Nonetheless, many Russians remained and their numbers were soon swelled by a new wave of White Russian immigration following the Japanese withdrawal from Siberia in the autumn of 1922. The withdrawal left thousands of White Russians stranded to face the sweeping Red Communist tide, which now consolidated the Soviets' grip on all of Siberia at the end of great civil war between the Red and White Russian forces. The fleeing White Russians were added to other former Russian subjects in Sinkiang, Mongolia and Manchuria, also victims of the Soviet onslaught, who now sought a new home. Pouring into China, the now-stateless, near-penniless but usually well-educated Russians found themselves in competition with hordes of coolies happy to work for a few coppers. The Russians set up a Russian Emigrants' Committee and a Council of the United Russian Public Organizations to assist in finding employment or relief and help regulate the lives of the new immigrants. Subsequently, Russian men worked as chauffeurs, mechanics, bus drivers, tram car inspectors, and bodyguards for rich Chinese, and served in the armies of the numerous Chinese warlords common at the time. Some aviators, for example, provided some of the warlords with a semblance of an air force. The women worked as teachers, nurses, and assistants, as dancing partners in bars and as prostitutes. In the major Chinese cities, such as Shanghai, enclaves of "Little Russia" were established, where the "strong odors of cabbage soup" blended in with signs in Cyrillic and the music of the balalaika and the accordion. In revivals of Russian officers' clubs, "old Czarist diehards drank gallons of tea and argued over past campaigns and future victories when they would supply the military push that would bring the ramshackle Soviet anathema down."[14]

The American women of the regiment brought in the customs and attitudes current in the States both in civilian society and characteristic of Army garrison life of that era. These were superimposed on their Chinese experiences.

The usual social arenas normally dominated by women at home also prevailed in Tientsin. *The Sentinel*'s "Social Notes" column often reported the details of the rounds of garrison entertainment featuring bridge games and tournaments and, in the mid–1920s, focused on the latest sensation, Mah Jongg. On one typical evening, the officers and ladies of the regiment enjoyed an elaborate Army dinner dance in February of 1927, the women fully engaged in planning and preparation, though Marshall was the major planner on the Army side, doing a commendable job. At about the same time, Colonel and Mrs. Newell sponsored a skating party at the regimental ice rink, the Colonel's wife doing the honors as hostess. Such activity was commonplace for a commanding officer's wife — she being generally referred to rather callously as the "COW" from the appropriate initials. Later, along the same lines, when Santa Claus visited the garrison kids at the compound's Recreation Hall on the afternoon before Christmas in 1930, Mrs. James D. Taylor, the commanding officer's wife, presided over the festivities which included a band concert, a children's choral performance, a "talkie" motion picture of *Felix the Cat*, and the anticipated visit of Saint Nick with the inevitable bag of toys. Easter egg hunts were planned and carried out by many of the regiment's women, as the one in 1933, conducted after the eggs had been examined by the compound's medical personnel. Benefited were the children of Army personnel as well as those of sailors of the USS *Sacramento*, the U.S. Navy's gunboat then stationed at Tientsin, though significantly no local Chinese children were invited.[15]

Other avenues of service included the Junior Department of the American Barracks Sunday School with about 35 children enrolled. Under the supervision of Mrs. Luther D. Miller, wife of the chaplain, other women were no doubt involved as well. The school later mounted a drive to collect toys which were sent to the "Cheap Dining Room," a local welfare institution maintained by the Tientsin Women's Club. There they were distributed to about 100 poor Russian children, though again no Chinese children were beneficiaries.[16]

Among the American women prominent in compound activities were the wives of YMCA personnel, especially of the directors, who conducted Bible classes, held dancing lessons, and in general worked in myriad ways to make military personnel feel at home in the local YMCA's facilities. The base's Army Service Club, at one time or another, attracted the services of other women who added to the popularity of the institution.[17]

The women of the regiment with a thespian bent (and there were usually several of these), fully participated in the theatrical productions that were staged in surprisingly large numbers with considerable variety during the tenure of the 15th in China. Some of these were joint efforts of the Western civilian community in Tientsin together with women — and men — of the regiment. For example, one of the major events of Christmas week of 1926 was a performance of the *Messiah* at Tientsin's Empire Theater on December 23. Sponsored by the Tientsin Rotary Club, it was directed by Mrs. Ruth Kingman of the city. Rather unusually, the chorus was made up of all nationals residing in Tientsin, including Chinese girls in silks, Japanese girls in vivid kimonos, blonde and brunette English and American girls, girls of France, and "stately and fair Russians," together with men of an equal number of nationalities, some in Army O.D. joined by their counterparts of Britain's East Yorkshire Regiment "in their bright dress uniforms."[18]

Naturally, marrying, begetting and dying occurred in China among the female residents of the American Army community as anywhere else. Regarding the nuptials parade, daughters of commanding officers were often the desired mates of ambitious officers of the regiment. One of these was Mary Winifred Martin, the daughter of Colonel and Mrs. William F. Martin, who became the wife of Captain Le Roy Welling Nichols, of the 15th. Similarly, Colonel Naylor's daughter, Margaret, married Lieutenant Dwight Lyman Adams of the regiment. Failing to land a commanding officer's daughter, another officer, Lieutenant Edgar T. Conley, decided that Cecile Olive Truesdell, the daughter of the regiment's executive officer, Lieutenant Colonel Karl Truesdell, might serve just as well.[19]

Major Jacob J. Gerhardt, commander of the Third Battalion, took as his wife Ruth McCann, an American girl living in Tientsin with her parents. She had taught in Tientsin's American School and joined her new husband at Fort Eustis, Virginia, to which he was transferred following his tour of duty in China.[20]

One wedding of an enlisted man caused some comment: that of Maybelle Holmes and Master Sergeant Samuel Guy Forrest. Maybelle was the daughter of Tech Sgt. Harry Holmes, and hence the son-in-law outranked his newly acquired father-in-law.[21]

As to births, after early 1932, birth certificates given to all children born into the regiment were adorned with an image of the famous Great Wall. Also, according to regimental custom, the newborn child of an officer was presented with a silver cup with the regimental coat of arms and "other suitable inscription engraved thereon," as well as a "personal letter of congratulations" written by the regimental commander. In addition, "in order that the child may be baptized and christened under the Regimental Colors of his father, the colors will be available for this ceremony upon request of the parents."[22]

One such happy event was the birth of "two daughters of the Regiment," Marilyn Pomerene to Lieutenant and Mrs. Joel De W. Pomerene, and Cornelia Miller, to Chaplain and Mrs. Luther D. Miller, on June 29 and July 4, 1927, respectively. Another announcement on September 6, 1927, heralded the birth of a "Son of a Gunn," Robert Murray Gunn, to Lieutenant and Mrs. Damon M. Gunn. Becoming almost a tradition, births of sons were greeted with announcements that a "new trooper" had been enrolled in the ranks of the regiment as a birthright. They were often adopted by a particular company.[23]

Children died in China too. One was Elizabeth Patricia Willingham, infant daughter of Captain and Mrs. C.M. Willingham, who succumbed at the station hospital on June 4, 1927.[24]

Adults expired there as well, including some women of the regiment. One particularly tragic instance was the demise of Mrs. Alf B. Larsen, who died in the compound hospital on June 1, 1923, of complications following an appendicitis operation. The wife of Staff Sgt. Alf B. Larsen of the medical corps, she left behind a baby girl in addition to her grieving husband.[25]

In sum, the troops, as was common with American males in the era, took a rather macho stance vis-à-vis womanhood. They assumed a bemused view of the flappers, and took advantage of the women of easy virtue in China, while those who could—some enlisted men and many of the officers—brought their families to China where they enjoyed a privileged existence, surrounded by platoons of servants and participating in endless shopping expeditions, though they also shared the dangers to life and limb that the soldiers faced. The officers' wives brought to Tientsin their familiar country club and social and church organizational activities. They participated in the social life of the Tientsin community, establishing contact with those like themselves, especially among the English residents. Only on occasion did they include their Chinese and Japanese counterparts in their programs. Conversely, women associated with the regiment sometimes evinced levels of insight and sensitivity regarding women in general and Chinese women in particular — as well as China itself as has been noted above — that few males approached. Their — and their children's — exposure to things Chinese certainly enhanced their larger world views.

CHAPTER XII

The Regulars, Horses and Other Matters

I guess I'm pretty ornery; and I here take off my hat
To all the clever lads that back me up
They're full of food and glory, education and all that
But the Infantry's the Army, For'war, HUP![1]

Tho' the Q.M. Gen'ral lauds you, Army Mule
He will never make me love you — I'm no fool
Tho the papers sing your praises, how I wish, O brute, to blazes
They would use your pesky hide and heels for fuel.[2]

While the theater of operations of the 15th was China, its personnel revealed prevailing attitudes of American Army men in general between the world wars regarding several matters: the status of the Regulars, the lure of the service, the sometimes pressing matter of reenlisting, the place of animals in the Army, and, finally, research and development programs as they pertained to China, as the Army absorbed — or neglected — the lessons of the Great War and looked to its future.

Building upon the accomplishments — real and imagined — of the U.S. military forces on the battlefields of Europe in the Great War, there emerged, especially for a couple of decades after 1918, a swelling pride in the role and status of the Regulars with particular reference to the infantry. Strongly remembered were such attitudes contemptuously expressed before the Great War regarding the Army by public signs such as "no dogs or soldiers allowed."[3]

One soldier-poet stationed China with the 15th Infantry left little doubt about how he and many of his buddies felt about wearing the uniform, at the same time revealing a Kiplingesque approach which was common among American soldiers in this era:

> We're not ashamed of the uniform,
>   And if you are a friend,
> You will never say against it, any
>   Word that will offend.
>
> It has covered honored bodies, and
>   By heroes has been worn,
> Since the days of the Republic, when
>   The Stars and Stripes were born.
> . . . .

The poet asked that civilians might "Grant us ... your kind forbearance / We'll appreciate it more / Than a lot of noise and cheering / When we're going off to war."⁴

His views were seconded by another who observed that "most folks" were of the opinion that soldiers were nobodies who were "outcasts of the world / And are always in the way." Indeed, the poet observed that the hardest battle of the soldier was in the time of peace, "When you laugh at him and scorn him / And treat him like a beast." But though often roundly condemned, the soldier should instead be clasped by the hand, "For the uniform he's wearing / Means protection of our land," and he hoped that a soldier might simply be treated "as a friend."⁵

But there had been many soldiers in the Great War who were not Regulars, all the more reason why the latter perhaps should, in an era of peace, be advanced front and center. Poetry was once more the venue of choice for asserting the importance of such matters. A typical example that appeared in numerous American Army publications following the end of the Great War was entitled the "Reg'lar Army Man," by Joseph Crosby Lincoln, a popular late nineteenth century American rhymester and novelist who had earlier addressed the subject:

> He ain't no gold-lace Belvedere, ter sparkle in the sun;
> He don't parade in gay cockade, and posies in his gun;
> He ain't no "pretty soldier boy," so lovely, spick and span, —
> He wears a crust of tan and dust, the Reg'lar Army man;
> The marchin, parchin', pipe-clay starchin',
> Reg'lar Army man.
>
> . . . .
>
> He makes no fuss about the job, he do'n't talk big or brave, —
> He knows he's in ter fight and win, or help fill up a grave;
> He ain't no "Mama's darlin'," but he does the best he can,
> And he's the chap that wins the scrap, the Reg'lar Army man.
> The dandy, handy, cool and sandy
> Reg'lar Army man.

Indeed, there were many positive things to be said for "The r'arin', tearin', sometimes swearin', ... [and] ... "The rattlin', battlin', Colt or Gatlin' / Reg'lar Army man."⁶

Yet, there was foundation for some of the criticism of the Army. One man admitted that there was controversy, "From Seattle to New Jersey," as to whether or not a soldier could be truly be a gentleman. He pulled no punches and asked: "Is any man a gentleman when he's beastly drunk?" Now, to be sure, "There are gentlemen that's born thus / Others made by act of congrus [sic] / But it ain't a case of chevrons or a case o'shoulder straps." What was needed was for all — officers and enlisted men alike — to "solve the riddle with a bit of common sense," and act as they should, and then all those in uniform might indeed be gentlemen "who fight in Right's defense."⁷

In this discordant atmosphere, to many soldiers what seemed to be needed was to assume the offensive, asserting with vigor the importance of the Regular Army. This pride seemed especially pronounced in the infantry, the "Queen of Battles." Some troopers thought that a focus on the term "infantry," together with something of its origins, might contribute to these ends. The expression "Mon Captain, mes enfants," as employed in the French Army, denoted a close relationship between officers and their men, one *Sentinel* editor declared. He was convinced that "Mes infants" was therefore the origin of the term "infantry"; and the U.S. Army had not only adopted the French name, it had "also incorporated the French spirit of the love of officer for his men. The Army is, then, a team, bound together by ties much stronger than any that money can buy."⁸

An explanation of the origins and meaning of term "doughboy" also seemed appropriate: "Who, what, and why, is a 'doughboy'? Well he is an American *Infantryman*, of course, as distinguished from all other wearers of Uncle Sam's uniform, and about the best two-fisted and two-legged fighting man of which there is any record anywhere." The title "doughboy," of whatever origin and use, was in fact "infantry property and belongs [by] right to no other branch, all of which have their own popular nicknames. We are proud of it and justly resent its misuse," an editorial in the paper declared. As to its meaning, one observer, mixing metaphors, noted that the "Infantry was the 'flower' of the Army," and was hence always "kneaded." To make the distinctions even clearer, some infantrymen derisively referred to coast and field artillerymen as cosmolines, while the quartermasters were sometimes labeled "the Jewish Infantry."⁹

A consideration of the essential nature of the doughboy might further enlighten the scornful. A typical effusion came from the pen of Senator Francis E. Warren, of Wyoming, the father-in-law of General John

Joseph "Black Jack" Pershing, commander of the American Expeditionary Forces during the Great War: "In my opinion, the heart and core of the Army is its Infantry force, no matter how ably supplemented and assisted by other forces of water, land, and air," he declared. "So it has been in the past, and so it will be in the future, no matter what implements of warfare and methods of fighting may be devised." Along the same lines, a Captain Gerald Egan declared that it was only necessary to give the infantryman "his Springfield, his bayonet, his rounds of ammunition, his canteen and his rations, and he will stride on [ever] confident of victory."[10]

Perhaps a formal creed might even better state the case, and one was available: "I am an Infantryman. Being an Infantryman I realize the value of team work. I am a prospective team member.... I will not hold to myself but will pass on to others that the team may benefit. Being an Infantryman my aim is to make the Infantry first and I realize that only by a conscientious effort on my part, on the part of every individual, can the desired result be attained.... [Finally], I will comply cheerfully with all regulations and make the best of existing conditions."[11]

If there was a creed, why not also ten commandments? In China, Private William A. O'Connor of the 15th's Headquarters Company devised such a list advancing high ideals of soldierly conduct. In the first instance, the soldier was advised, "Keep your eyes and ears ready, and your tongue in the safety notch. For it is your soldierly duty to see and hear clearly. But as a rule you should be heard mainly in the sentry challenges or the charging cheer." One, naturally, must "obey orders first and if still alive kick afterward if you have been wronged." A good soldier would keep his arms and equipment clean and in good order and treat machinery "as though it belonged to you," as well as treat animals "kindly and fairly." In addition, this paragon would always "tell the truth, squarely face the music and take your punishment like a man, for a good soldier won't lie, he doesn't sulk and is no squealer." He would also bear in mind "that the enemy is your enemy and the enemy of humanity until he is killed or captured, then he is your dead brother, or your fellow soldier, beaten or ashamed whom you should no further humiliate." Soldiers should "be merciful to the women of your foe and shame them not for you are a man. Pity and shield the children in your captured territory for you were once a helpless child." Then, among other things, and finally, the soldier, would "dread defeat but not wounds, fear dishonor but not death, and die game."[12]

Other matters warmly discussed within the Army in these years—likewise echoed in China — were the appeal of the service and the related matter of reenlisting. There was no denying the attraction that the military had for some and soldiers were often clear on the main reasons for their career choices:

> Give me to live and love in the old bold fashion;
>   A soldier's billet at night and a soldier's ration;
> A heart that leaps to the fight with soldier's passion;
> For I hold as a simple faith there's no denying;
> The trade of a soldier's the only trade worth plying;
> The death of the soldier's the only death worth dying.[13]

For one columnist in *The Sentinel*, there was indeed a "peculiar lure to the Army which can be matched nowhere else in this materialistic age." In the first place, there were the stirring notes of the bugle sounding "First Call," "Mess Call," and all the others culminating in the "sweet, sad strains of 'Taps.'" Adding to the attraction which "brings old soldiers back" was "the crunch, crunch, crunch of marching feet; the sharp blast of a sergeant's whistle; the creak and rattle of a mounted outfit swinging into the saddle; in the whinnying, squealing animals on the picket line." Finally, "there is a distinct fascination in living with men who are men, who like the things you like, and share your sports, your joys, your sorrows, and who will take the very shirt off their back for a 'buddy.'"[14]

Related to the desire to serve was the matter of reenlisting. Many, after being discharged, regretted it and longed to return to the colors. One of those was Joseph Andrew Galahad, who in his poem "Soldier Heart" reflected:

> Oh once I was a soldier man
>   A soldier man
>   A soldier man
> And if Uncle Sammy says I can
> I'll be one all my days!
>
> . . . .
>
> My discharge was a lovely thing
> Till it was in my hand:
> 'Twas then the most unwanted thing
> In all my native land!

Identifying the positive, enduring things that he remembered about his former status and the men he soldiered with, he especially noted that the very things that civilians might "cuss 'em for / Is things that makes 'em men," and for his part, he concluded: "I hanker for their company," and if "Uncle Sammy" would allow it, "I'm goin' back again!"[15]

The author of the poem "'Hamlet's Soliloquy,' 1925" stated the dilemma in classic terms: "To reenlist, or not to reenlist — / That's the question — ." Was it indeed better "to rub up against / A cold, unfriendly and forgetful public," in search of largely nonexistent jobs or don the uniform once more? In these dire conditions Old Glory looked good to him, and he hastened to reenlist.[16]

Another man resolved his doubts and reenlisted also. Borrowing substantially from Kipling's "The Vampire" (1897), which he recognized with apologies to the poet, he set forth the reasons in his "A Fool There Was":

> A fool there was and he made a vow,
>   Even as you and I,
> That he'd feed no more on Government chow.
> But he's back again in the Army now,
> For he tried to work, and didn't know how —
>   Even as you and I.
> . . . .

He manfully sought to make it on the "outside," "Till he passed, one day a flag-draped door / Where he held up his hand and solemnly swore / That he'd try it again for three years more, — / Even as you and I."[17]

To be sure, if attempts to become a civilian failed the soldiers could take some comfort that "When the seat of your pants gets thin, boys / In your belt you're taking up slack / The grand old flag flies everywhere / And you're always welcome back."[18] But many discharged soldiers found to their dismay that they were not "always welcome[d] back." Recruiting offices, unlike almost everything else, were not affected — except positively — by the Depression ushering in the 1930s, a time when "lots of people who used to live on Easy Street have moved around the corner." This state of affairs resolved the issue for many who might have otherwise been tempted to live in the civilian world. John T. Fox, a former member of the Service Company of the 15th, wrote *The Sentinel*'s editor that "It takes my breath away when I think of the foolish act I committed when I stepped out of the Army in the venture of self-support in such dark days." As another soldier explained, many who often averred "never again" reenlisted on the day after their discharge because they decided "that the army is not such a bad place after all, and that all you have to do is 'soldier,' and everything will be right with the world."[19]

The coming of the Great Depression also persuaded many men safely enrolled in the service to "re-up," i.e., to take on "another stack." Honorable military service with pension at end of road made the soldier's life definitely "do-able," and the hard times could be weathered. One of those convinced was Staff Sergeant Leslie H. Austin of the 15th's Medical Department, who decided to stay in the Army until he found out just why "the old grey mare ain't what she used to be."[20]

In China, decisions regarding reenlisting involved the desirability of requesting continuances with the 15th. To some of the men, service in the Orient was too onerous to be seriously considered. Others, including Private Harry P. Gibson of "K" Company, were of a differing view. In a prizewinning essay, "Why I Like Service in China," published in *The Sentinel*, he explained. He emphasized a love of adventure, a taste for the bizarre which China certainly supplied, the knowledge that he was getting a practical education, and a recognition that his pay "reaches farther than it would anywhere else in Uncle Sam's Army." When many of the states began paying wartime bonuses many soldiers were tempted to buy their discharges—which was still possible in the regular Army in the 1920s and 1930s—hoping to make it "on the outside." *The Sentinel* repeatedly warned men of the regiment of the folly of this decision, citing the difficult times at home: "It's going to be a long pull back to normal in the States [during the Depression] and there is plenty of time for you to get going after you serve this enlistment." Reenlistment was becoming difficult as well, and only men with excellent characters could apply. As the paper had earlier editorialized, many officers and soldiers "who could not stand the gaff and quit to become 'millionaires' have found out what we already knew, that 'three squares a day beat a bob-tail flush.'"[21]

Numerous veterans decided the issue about returning to the States by opting to remain in the Orient following their discharges. *The Sentinel* was filled with accounts of these men. One was Sergeant Joseph C. Wise, of Company M, who after 23 years of active service—14 of which had been spent outside of the USA, including the Philippines, Alaska, and Germany—was remaining in Tientsin as a civilian. Similarly, after seven years of service in the U.S. Army as a veterinarian, Lieutenant J.D. Moore departed the Army to take up a civilian practice in his profession in Tientsin. The decision to remain in China came easy for Private First Class Harry Jushner, who left the regiment and entered the Tientsin tailoring firm of Krugliak and Co.; Krugliak was his father-in-law. Frank McKenzie Henry, a former 15th Infantry Battalion Sergeant Major who had retired in China in 1917, remained with Standard Oil Company until 1931, becoming a respected citizen in Tientsin. Many of these men also went beyond the casual encounters of the brothel or informal concubinage and established families on a common-law basis, planning to live out their lives in China. Subsequently, the typhoon of World War II swept away many of these "Old China Hands," who were never to be heard from again.[22]

Related to manifestations of pride and the lure of the service were the continuing pressures of Congress and the President on military budgets. If pacifists and isolationists and just plain fiscal conservatives succeeded in their agendas, perhaps there would be no Army to serve in. One anonymous poet addressed his lively concerns and fears in his clever offering, which can resonate even today:

> As I was walking through the land, as I have often done,
> I saw a lonely soldier man a cleanin' of his gun;
> And as I touched him for a chaw I says, "who might you be?"
> "Why, brother," says the soldier man, "I am the Infantry."
> The Cavalry's at the corral, massaging of his steed,
> Which has to live on crop reports since Congress stopped his feed.
> The Field Artillery's asleep — his given name is Jawn —
> But the bloody Corps of Engineers, I don't know where he's gone.
> The Infantry laid down his gun and matched me for the beers,
> And then we both went out to hunt the Corps of Engineers.
> (He and the Quartermaster Corps are both delightful chaps)
> And the Army played three-handed bridge until they sounded taps.[23]

An encomium in *The Sentinel* further made the case for the desirability — even necessity — of the continuation of a standing Army: "I am a soldier. Than my profession there is none older.... Ever have I been the most honored of men when they need me; after peace for a little time comes I am despised by the self-seeking politician and his prey, his fellowmen." Nevertheless, "between mankind and its folly have I stood always," and when the nation waxed fat, "and fathers teach their sons all day to bargain and store up wealth which soon conquers them, and our women want yet more jades, and corruption comes in high places, and God is no longer in my countrymen's hearts, and then when the enemy comes to take our riches and lands, and when my comrades call on me to lead them, they follow me out to their new salvation and I bring them back, lean and sleek of body and with purified souls, knowing that to die is not so bad, realizing why it is better to live and for what, having resuscitated the God in them." Finally, "when our politicians have all spoken, and fair words have failed, and minds will not bend their wills to give up their ideals, when the very last word has been said, and when body must complement mind and soul, then in my humble wisdom, having read aright the progress of mankind, written as it is in its own blood, and being fit of body to do, of mind, clear in purpose, with the pure fire of patriotism in my soul, and with a spirit convinced of its unconquerableness answer the call of my kind to lead to new sacrifice. I am a soldier!"[24]

The men of the 15th also joined in the debates throughout the U.S. Army in the post–Great War era regarding the use and retention of horses and mules, though with particular reference to Chinese conditions. In addition, they conducted research and development programs with a similar orientation. The pages of *The Sentinel* were venues for such matters. At one level, it was polo which was attractive to many, both as a means of recreation and to build upon the strengths of the Old Army, which was literally based on horsepower. One of the many proponents of the continuation of the mounted arm was cavalryman Captain Fenton S. Jacobs, who maintained that "there will always be opportunities for horsemen, well led, to get in on their enemy with sword and pistol, as in the beginning of the World War." Obviously therefore, cavalry would "always endure." Conversely, others just as emphatically deplored that in the modern age "that is motor driven and steam and electrically powered," that the "army sticks to the horse and the tradition of the army mule." To one man's way of thinking, the "weight of the horse's inertia is an overwhelming burden upon the professional soldier."[25]

In whatever light the horse was considered, by the mid–1920s polo had gained considerable impetus among the officers in China. This was no doubt partially because the sport was not as expensive there as elsewhere on U.S. Army posts, a consequence of the regiment's decision to replace their American animals with native Chinese — or Mongolian — ponies and native mules. From that time on, no more horses would be supplied from the States. Officers not on mounted status could use government horses if they chose not to purchase their own. There was but one playing field at or near Tienstin: the Tientsin Race Club. Polo equipment, except helmets and mallets, were furnished from regimental equipment, and the mallets and helmets could be purchased in Tientsin for about one-half their cost in the States.

Thenceforth, the 15th would deal with native dealers who journeyed to Mongolia in search of suitable mounts both for the regiment and for individuals desiring to purchase their own. This marked yet another way in which the China regiment differed from its stateside counterparts, and was another area of contact with Chinese. The untried racing animals were called griffins. The regiment eventually maintained three polo teams, the Reds, Blues, and Whites, and all were soon quite well mounted. Nevertheless, the horses were distinctive: initially, their coats were long and shaggy, their legs stiff and they appeared awkward, with hoofs frequently worn down after the long journey across the Mongolian plain. Those not suited for the track were sold at reduced prices for polo mounts or hacks.[26]

In any case, the Chinese pony appealed to many and articles in *The Sentinel* discussed this animal at great length. In addition, features were published on the subject of training the polo pony, whether Chinese or not.[27]

In the course of the years, especially in the 1920s, regimental teams had considerable success playing international and other American opponents. In 1925, for the first time since 1914, Tientsin won the Forbes Trophy at Peking in an inter-port international polo match. In another match, U.S. Army officers defeated the Peking American polo team.[28]

The following year, however, in a match between the Shanghai Americans and the Tienstin American Army Polo team, the Shanghai Americans, who "surpassed all expectations in the speed and endurance of their mounts and the excellence of their play," won handily. Their mounts were considerably larger than those ridden by the locals and in speed there was no comparison. The local team held their own during the first four chuckers, but then their ponies could not maintain the pace.[29]

Bolstering the distaff end of horsey activities with varying degrees of success were several ladies' equitation classes. One of these was conducted in the autumn of 1928 by Mrs. Cummins, the wife of Lieutenant Colonel Joseph M. Cummins, the 15th's executive officer. With the women involved, riders of both sexes participated in various riding events, such as jumping and racing, paper chases, and "wonk" hunts; that is, the cross-country pursuit of vicious wild dogs of the chow strain.[30]

While polo was the privilege of the officers, certain enlisted men, drawn from various organizations of the regiment, were occupied with horses in an unusual way. For many years the 15th boasted its own mounted section, being therefore one of the few regiments in the Army having a cavalry troop composed of doughboys. Normally made up of 28 riders, the troop was under the command of an officer, usually with cavalry experience. The detachment had been formed on orders from Lieutenant Colonel Marshall in December 1925. Its orders stipulated that its members, functioning as the "'Eyes' of the U.S. Army Forces in China," were to be deployed as scouts and gatherers of intelligence. Indeed, "their use and mission here in China is such that they can replace many times their number of foot troops and execute their mission with greater dispatch." Marshall was pleased with his creation, calling it a "sporty-looking cavalry troop."[31]

In addition to their more martial duties, the detachment fitted in well with the garrison's considerable ceremonial requirements, and gained a reputation for spit and polish. Thus, though useful in several respects, they sought renown as that "Terrible Mounted Section," or the "Reckless Riders" of "the Chinese-mounted Infantry." Though desiring to participate "in one mad moment of a dashing cavalry charge," the only semblance of any harrowing escapade they experienced was "when they [were] polished for inspection and pass in parade."[32]

There were other sorts of quadrupeds in the 15th, the mules and burros, which also commanded much space in *The Sentinel*. At the same time that horses were replaced by Mongolian mounts, mules from the States were supplanted by local Chinese animals. Unlike the horses, however, Mongolian mules were not available because, while they were worth more than ponies, they were not bred by the Mongols, who utterly despised them. Hence the Chinese had to breed them themselves. To these ends, they often used mares from Mongolian herds to cross with donkeys, producing the valuable animals.[33]

They were indeed useful to some outfits of the 15th, notably "H" Company — the "Mules, Machine Guns and Men Company." The Service Company also stabled mules and horses, a matter of some pride to at least one of its soldiers: "I hail from the Service Outfit — / Hurrah for the sad-eyed mules — / I come from the Service Company / We're the pushin'-pullin' fools."[34]

The mule, then, the creature that was neither horse nor ass, "without pride of ancestry or hope of posterity," and "unloved and unsung," came in for considerable attention. Some affection for these animals was manifested by their being considered as more than mere beasts of burden. One hinny was named Alice, a "lady of quality and mascot extraordinary" of the Service Company. This outfit also boasted the presence — and enjoyed the antics — of Jerry, her donkey stablemate.[35]

Time also took its toll of these animals and from time to time those obviously too decrepit to continue in service were shot, on one occasion seven Chinese and eight American corral occupants becoming carcasses auctioned off to Chinese butchers. One was old Ben, a saddle horse who had come to China in 1912 with the regiment. Three mules, who had arrived at the same time, were similarly dispatched, one being "stiff old 'Blue,'" who had "been on the water wagon for a long time." Thus their foreign service tours ended, and "it is hoped they make good chewing," one "mourner" noted. Stable fires accounted for others.[36]

More cheerful was the first "15th Infantry Gymkhana and Horse Show," held on October 30, 1925. The event was preceded by much practice, even the chaplain becoming involved, proving that the "Church can stay in the saddle as well as can the congregation." It was a gala affair to which the foreign community of Tientsin was invited; the families of the regiment attended in great numbers as well.

The major events included a potato race, rickshaw polo, mounted wrestling, a cigarette race, polo pony class entries, jumping events, a competition for the best appearing gun squads, and a "machine gun-in-and-out-of-action race." The potato race involved the transferring of potatoes from one bucket to another, and created much mirth because the mules naturally often refused to cooperate. The cigarette race included both officers and their chosen ladies. The officers at the start of the event were dismounted. At the signal to mount, the officers rode to the opposite end of the compound and handed their ladies a box of matches and one cigarette. The lady had to light the cigarette and return it to the officer, who then returned to the starting point. The first over the line with the cigarette still lighted won.

The concluding event of the afternoon was a rickshaw polo game between coolies of the Second and Third Battalions. While exciting for the spectators, this was hardly the case from the rickshaw coolie's viewpoint, "as he was kept busy jumping and dodging the polo sticks as they were being wildly swung at the ball, for very often the ball would be missed and the blow land on the coolie's shins."[37]

Subsequent shows proved as interesting and eventful. That of 1927 included children's riding events, ladies' trot, walk and canter contests, and mixed pair riding performances. The 1930 gala, styled by then the "Horse and Transportation Show," was also a big success, featuring wrestling matches by men mounted on native mules and a tug of war on native mules, and ending with an exhibition by the mounted platoon, which would have been "the envy of any cavalry outfit."[38]

The focus on riding also provided considerable humorous copy for *The Sentinel*, specifically with reference to the frequent unseating of riders by their steeds, and numerous accounts appeared on the topic of "dry diving," i.e., those engaged in "flying off" of their saddles. This led the paper, in the 1930s, informally to award the "*Sentinel* Dry Diving Trophy" for those making the most spectacular descents from horses—and mules. Sparing no one, men, women and even the chaplain were sooner or later victims of unruly, recalcitrant mounts.[39]

In a time when the Army was moving toward modernization, especially regarding tanks and aircraft, and often fiercely debating these matters, the 15th was engaged in research and development at an entirely different level, much of it involving animals. To some members of the high command in the regiment, "one of the greatest problems that has faced the American Forces in China has been the question of transportation. The standard Army mule and escort wagon is in no wise suited to conditions here," one report observed. In the first place, "the wagons are too heavy and too wide to travel on the native roads and then they must be pulled by imported animals that cannot exist on the forage produced in this country." Therefore, "all forage must be imported and the problem of feed in case we should ever have to take the field is one that cannot be overlooked." In order to meet this difficulty, the War Department granted authority to experiment with native animals and to devise some type of wagon that would be suitable to local road conditions. At length a useable vehicle was adopted.[40]

In addition, new machine gun and ammunition carts were developed using Chinese mules as draft animals. The carts proving satisfactory, their drivers also liked the native animals, widely regarded as superior to their larger American cousins, which would be phased out as fast as they became casualties or superannuated.[41]

Other areas of development concerned forage, the Army running tests on a compressed horse feed which proved promising. In addition, the crude Aparejo and the equally unsatisfactory English pack saddles were replaced, after many experiments, with the Phillips saddle. Designed by Lieutenant Colonel Albert E. Phillips of the cavalry, it had been adopted in the States on July 26, 1924, but was only introduced to China in 1931. Weighing only 50 pounds, it proved especially useful in transporting machine guns, eliminating the need for the cumbersome machine gun cart.[42]

Because of the specific needs of service in China, the 15th perforce was involved in the employment of animals. These last vestiges of Old Army traditions, as the regiment's involvement in China itself, would rapidly recede into history. The outfit, moving from the Old Army to the New, would take its place in the mainstream of U.S. infantry development following its return to the United States in 1938.

CHAPTER XIII

Withdrawal of the 15th from China

So Farewell China Farewell,
There's not much I can say,
I've had my fun, and I'm glad I came,
But I'm going home to stay.[1]

While the warlords engendered much of Chinese strife in the 1920s, in the next decade Japan would be the principal instigator of events. In 1931, the Japanese began the occupation of Manchuria, culminating in the creation of the state of Manchukuo. The Japanese established a protectorate over the new puppet state and installed the former Chinese emperor Henry P'u-i as regent, promoting him to emperor in 1934. Also in 1931, riots in Tientsin, undoubtedly fomented by the Japanese, occurred at the boundary between the Japanese concession and the Chinese city. All of the Allied contingents manned outposts and defensive positions. Colonel Taylor declared that the American mission only involved "the protection of American lives and property. With other matters we are not concerned." He ordered all personnel to use caution in their words and deeds so as to avoid offense in any quarter.[2]

In 1932, the focus was on Shanghai where large-scale operations began between Chinese and Japanese forces when the Japanese attacked Shanghai, compelling the foreign powers to bolster the defense of their concessions and businesses. The 15th was especially interested in the dispatching of the 31st Regiment — called the Polar Bears because of its involvement in Siberia after the Great War — from Manila to Shanghai on February 5, 1932, it being the only American Army unit ever to be stationed in that city. There it joined troops of the Fourth Marines and other allied contingents, establishing especially close ties with the British forces before being withdrawn on June 30, 1932.[3]

In 1933, Japanese troops moved south of the Great Wall, and in the same year, forced Chinese troops to evacuate the Tientsin area.

Six days after the departure of General Castner on March 10, 1929, and the formal termination of his headquarters and role in the Far East, the 15th's commanding colonels once more assumed the burden of U.S. military power in China. The continued presence of the regiment in China was now more intently, and almost continually, reassessed. By the early 1930s, it appeared to Lieutenant Colonel Karl Truesdell, the outfit's executive officer, that there were even more pressing reasons than before for the withdrawal of the USATC. He explained these in a secret memorandum to Colonel Walter S. Drysdale, the American military attaché in Peiping. In the circumstances, he asserted, the 15th's personnel could be used to better advantage in the United States in connection with FDR's New Deal measures, such as the Civilian Conservation Corps. In addition, a substantial savings would accrue if the 15th were based at home. More importantly, the 15th obviously was "too small to accomplish its mission."

It was widely acknowledged among the occupying powers still in China that even "the combined forces present could not accomplish their original mission in the face of changed conditions in China's military forces." Accordingly, the "United States mission has in effect been amended so as to limit it essentially to the protection of American lives and property." Because this was "the usual Navy mission," that branch of the service "could accomplish as much, if not more, than the present army contingent in Tientsin." Even more daunting was the bare fact, often remarked upon, that the United States had no concession to defend, and consequently was "in the paradoxical position of acting under extraterritorial rights with no appropriate territory." In the event of hostilities involving a combined defense of Tientsin, if the other contingents withdrew into their concessions, permitting access by hostile forces to the Chinese areas originally contained within their defense lines, the United States would be in an untenable position and would only have recourse to pleading the "inherent right of a force to protect itself." Furthermore, maintaining national prestige by a display of military force was not an acceptable stance and "has been decried by the United States Government." Beyond this, he declared, the troops were always a potential source of danger and certain State Department officials alleged — at variance with official policy — that their presence made "the task of the diplomat the more onerous." In addition, considering the specter of a "remotely possible war with Japan," the presence of the United States Army Troops in China "would not only be of no value, but might even precipitate the crisis or aggravate a grave situation." This aspect came increasingly to the fore in the months following. American troops had originally been brought in to "assist in preventing a possible recurrence of the Boxer uprising," but this no longer applied, because "the possibility of [this] ... is exceedingly remote under the changed conditions in China." Finally, from the standpoint of the welfare of the military establishment, "the location of troops in Tientsin is bad. The men are unduly exposed to diseases of the Orient; they are deprived of the refining and restraining influences of the contacts with their own kind, and they are subject to temptations to a greater degree than elsewhere."

Truesdell was well aware that there were objections to the regiment's withdrawal. This act, he said, "would probably reopen the questions of extraterritoriality, [and] of termination of the Tientsin military occupation," and alter relations with China and other countries, "especially Japan." Tientsin, as a useful base for any future needs of Americans in the Orient, would be forfeited. Naval forces could not be counted on in an emergency to meet American requirements there. Withdrawal would have a deleterious effect upon the viability and safety of American commercial interests in the Orient. In addition, the 15th Regiment afforded a training ground, "one of the few we have, for our forces in stations other than on the continent at home. It is a station for training in Oriental contacts, and for education in Oriental language and characteristics." Finally, "the mere presence of United States troops in Tientsin serves to accomplish, in a measure, the mission for which they were sent here, i.e. the prevention of anti-foreign action."[4]

All things considered, from a purely military standpoint, the maintenance of such a small force in China was unsound. Therefore, the regiment's continuance had to do with the foreign policy of the United States, and not military considerations. Accordingly, it was "to the Department of State that the military must turn for justification of its mission." It was clear that the American garrison could mainly rely only "upon persuasion and diplomatic representation," and the War Department and State Department would only with difficulty formulate a common policy. For instance, would a threat be countered by military action or "persuasion, expostulation, and bluff?" In any case, assistance from other international forces was problematic. The 15th must recognize that in fact it was "on outpost duty"; its supporting forces were weak, it was separated from the United States by an ocean, and without a local base or a suitable nearby harbor, its isolation was complete. The only thing that it could reasonably do in the circumstances, short of outright withdrawal, was to maintain itself "at a maximum state of tactical efficiency."[5]

With variations, the 15th sought to do just that. Contingency plans were frequently revised in the light of changing conditions. In addition, regimental preparedness was fostered by a "friendly spirit of competition" encouraged between the units of the command through competitions and athletic events such as were discussed in chapter IX. In the officers' schools, the history and politics of China were studied, the courses of the civil wars were scrutinized, and the politics and movements of the other foreign garrisons in northern China were monitored.

This passive, hunkered-down stance also seemed indicated by the realization in Tientsin that Washington was increasingly preoccupied with the Depression and much else that it had to consider during those years. As the historian Akira Iriye has noted, "numerous official memoranda written at this time [by various American officials] on the East Asian question were rationalizations for the basic lack of policy and of interest in East Asia. Moral globalism and political parochialism could only be reconciled by tortured argument, and the officials were engaged in countless experiments in such argument after 1933." Involved were debates as to what America's interests in Asia truly were. Were they fundamentally economic? Should missionaries be strongly supported? What of the growing stridency of Japan? Should not America avoid provoking the Japanese Empire? There was the role of the Chinese Communist Party to consider. Was its example a threat to Depression-plagued America? Should not China solve its own problems without American intervention? Isolationism and pacificism also became stronger on the American domestic scene as the 1930s unfolded, with increasing demands that American forces in Asia be completely withdrawn. Consequently, the 15th's continuation in China seemed increasingly problematic.[6]

Meanwhile, incidents involving the Japanese and the 15th multiplied. On one occasion, Japanese troops began maneuvering in a menacing manner on the borders of the summer camp at Chinwangtao when women and children were present, causing considerable concern. On another, when American troops on their train at the rifle range allegedly photographed a nearby Japanese troop train, an armed clash was narrowly averted.[7]

The 15th's situation worsened considerably following the events of July 7, 1937, when, near Peiping, Japan began military operations against China, effectively launching the Far Eastern theater of operations and initiating World War II. Peiping was seized on July 28 and Tientsin the following day. From August 8 to November 8, 1937, the Shanghai campaign resulted in the fall of the city to the Japanese. This was followed by their energetic drive up the Yangtze River. These Japanese successes forced the Chinese on November 20 to move their capital from Nanking to Chungking, a timely move. Nanking fell to the Japanese on December 13 after bitter fighting. "These hostile actions, which the United States protested but did not contest, eliminated the Army mission to protect the Tientsin-Peking railroad."[8]

It is clear, though, that even before the outbreak of fighting in July of 1937 the State Department was developing plans for the 15th's withdrawal. In February 1938, U.S. Secretary of State Cordell Hull informed the Chinese ambassador in Washington to this effect, noting that the War Department also wanted the regiment returned, a course that many in the Army had long maintained, arguing that "it was not considered a wholesome policy to keep these troops in one place and away from this country for an indefinite period of time." Hull concluded that the conditions then existing in China further indicated that "they are no longer of any great use where they are now located."[9]

Variously interpreted, this stance clearly marked a change in U.S. policy, though this was denied in official circles. On the ground in China, many observers saw this as indicative of U.S. disapproval of Japanese action in China in the undeclared war between the two countries. On this point, Hull stated officially in early January 1938 that the withdrawal of American troops then being contemplated was for the preservation and encouragement of peace in the Far East, which was the main American policy in the Orient. The troops were in China for "the protection of Americans primarily against mobs and other uncontrollable elements," he stated. But all along, the secretary disingenuously asserted, "it has been the desire and the intention of the Government to remove our armed forces from China when the performance of their function of protection is no longer called for." Those conditions were obviously now met, and the time for evacuation had plainly arrived, marking at last the end of American adherence to the Boxer Protocol of 1901.[10]

Though plans to withdraw were laid earlier, it may well have been the *Panay* incident that was the major factor in the decision as to when to return the regiment to the United States. This refers to the sinking of the U.S. Navy gunboat *Panay* in the Yangtze near Nanking on December 12, 1937, by Japanese aircraft. The Japanese apologized and paid an indemnity but isolationist Americans, by then a powerful force in U.S. domestic politics, raised an even greater cry for U.S. withdrawal from China. As a result of the invidious position that various aspects of the Chinese situation put Washington in, the Roosevelt administration adopted "what was eventually a compromise plan. United States policy would henceforth be directed towards the maintenance of American rights and interests in China by means of diplomatic protests." At the same time, the government would urge its nationals to evacuate the area of hostilities as quickly as possible.[11]

Though neither the provenance nor the exact occasion for issuing the final order to leave China has been ascertained, on February 4, 1938, the State Department announced in Washington that "with Japan now dominating the entire territory, standing by to keep the railway open had become a diplomatic fiction." Accordingly, the department "had decided to reduce the number of the American armed forces in North China by withdrawing the Fifteenth Infantry ... and transferring to Tientsin two companies of the United States Marine Guard stationed at Peiping." Simultaneously, the commanding officer of the 15th Regiment, Colonel Joseph A. McAndrew, received a confidential radiogram from the War Department directing him to evacuate the regiment—at the time consisting of 677 enlisted men and 31 officers—from China to its new station at Fort Lewis, Tacoma, Washington, on board the USAT *U.S. Grant*.[12]

On February 23, the regiment passed in review in the main compound of the American Barracks for a double ceremony. One commemorated the retirement of Master Sergeant William A. Willoughby, of the Service Company, 31st Infantry Regiment, attached to the 15th at the time of his retirement. At the second, the American community in Tientsin presented the regiment with a silver tripod "as a token of appreciation of the cooperation and goodwill shown by the Regiment to the American Community." On the same date, a detachment of the regiment participated in an International Guard of Honor ceremony given as a farewell courtesy in a park in front of the French Municipal Building in the French concession. On the 27th, Company K proceeded to Camp Burrowes, Chinwangtao, as a guard for the Regiment's freight and supplies to be loaded on the *Grant*.

On February 28, the British community of Tientsin entertained the regiment's commander, Colonel Joseph A. McAndrew, and his officers at the Tientsin Club, presenting them with a silver salver inscribed with the motto of the British Municipal Council: *Comitas inter Gentes*, "Courtesy among Nations."[13]

March 2, 1938, marked the last date that the 15th was on active service in China. Early that morning, there had been a changing of the guard, the U.S. Marines formally taking charge of the compound. Soon after, the 15th marched through the streets of Tientsin, lined with troops of the European garrisons, notably the British, French and Italians, and with bands of these three forces playing, proceeded to Tientsin's East Station and the train that would take them home. At 9:30 A.M., the entire body of troops, with some unassigned personnel temporarily attached to the regiment for transportation to the States, departed the city. After the 167-mile rail trip to Chinwangtao, they boarded the *Grant* by 6:30 P.M., the ship sailing a few minutes later, bound for Honolulu and Tacoma, Washington, where it arrived on March 24.[14]

An American Army officer, Frank Dorn — later a brigadier general — who witnessed the regiment's exodus from China, wryly — and on the whole, accurately — observed that the "American 15th Infantry, having long enjoyed the good life at Tientsin, was ordered to depart its cushy post for reassignment in the United States." After its 26 years of service in China, he wrote, "the tasks of packing up and of breaking off relations with their Chinese and White Russian women were enormous; but eventually the sad-eyed men of the regiment marched through the streets of the city, flags flying and bands playing, and boarded the trains that would take them to Chinwangtao and a transport [the USAT *Grant*] waiting to return them to the rigors of a discipline and training they had not known for years."[15]

On March 1, the two companies of U.S. Marines, totaling about 200 officers and men, had arrived from Peiping where they had been members of the Embassy Guard. They were determined to "Show the Flag" and "demonstrate the United States' determination to support China." Officially, as the State Department noted, even though Japan now dominated the region, the presence of the marines in Tientsin meant that "technically the United States [was] yielding none of its rights." Subsequently, these became victims to the nation's clinging to its rights in this fashion. Many of the marines then arriving in Tientsin were destined, on the eve of their own ordered departure for Manila in December 1941 after Pearl Harbor, to become prisoners-of-war of the Japanese. Their ordeal has been recounted in a book by one of their number.[16]

In any case, the 15th could now turn its undivided attention to realizing what Vogel has suggested that the Old Army perhaps did best: to prepare the New Army for its far more demanding missions. Though the 15th was not to serve in the Far East during World War II, some of its veterans including Stilwell, Barrett and Wedemeyer kept its ghostly presence there alive. Later in the Korean War, Walker and Ridgway, former Can-Doers, were in charge of operations on the ground. All in all, the years 1912 to 1938 had been fateful ones for many Americans associated with one of the U.S. Army's crack regiments. For good or ill, these had experienced the vicissitudes of East meeting West in a momentous time: the years of the emergence and evolvement of modern China.[17]

CHAPTER XIV

The Regiment's Chinese Legacy

But it shall be remembered, in all days beyond all wars,
In all lands where, gray embered, dead camp-fires face the stars, —
Your labors and your leavings, your searchings and believings,
Your wanderings and grievings, by the red light of Mars.[1]

Any assessment of the 15th Regiment and its China deployment encompasses a wide variety of scenarios and events and much opinion regarding them. At one level, the men of the 15th might perhaps be referred to as the Great Observers and the outfit styled the Reluctant Dragon Regiment rather than viewed as an active, meaningful participant in Chinese affairs. Indeed, the regiment being more interested in place (exotic China) than people (the Chinese in particular), they may well have missed opportunities to ascertain more of the significance of Asia, a consequence of being often myopic and self-centered, a tendency which became more pronounced in the 1930s in the face of the growing Japanese threat. As First Lieutenant William H. Arnold, who was the regiment's plans and training officer in the mid–1930s — he was later a lieutenant general — candidly admitted regarding contact with the Chinese, there were "practically no contacts at all. You only had contacts with your servants." Though Chinese officials had to be met with from time to time, few of the regiment's officers had significant contacts with Chinese civilians.[2] One consequence was a failure to comprehend fully the complexities of the Chinese world, though Brigadier General William D. Connor, Lieutenant Colonel Joseph W. Stilwell, Captain David D. Barrett and others were notable exceptions. The study of the language and other exposures to the mysteries of China notwithstanding, this stance was much in evidence, and beyond this era, has often afflicted — and continues to adversely affect — much of the American presence throughout the globe.

Nor did the 15th engage in any major conflict. Yet, in the words of a secret memorandum generated at its headquarters, its being on duty and "showing the flag," and "the mere presence of United States troops in Tientsin serve[d] to accomplish, in a measure, the mission for which they were sent here, i.e. the prevention of anti-foreign action."³

There is one tangible memorial of the positive effects that the 15th could have on the Chinese when it did become involved. Observant visitors to Fort Benning, Georgia, might notice a stone gateway of white Chinese marble situated on a grassy plot at the fort's Main Post on

Chinese marble gate, Fort Benning, Georgia. Drawing from the 15th Infantry Regiment. *Customs of the 15th U.S. Infantry.* Tientsin, China: Peiyang Press (c. 1930).

XIV. The Regiment's Chinese Legacy

Morrison Road near the officers' club. While it is rather unprepossessing and a bit out of the way, its presence and symbolism stand for something noteworthy in the history of the U.S. 15th Infantry Regiment in particular, the U.S. Infantry in general and certain dimensions of U.S. policy in China at a time of monumental change in the Orient. It had originally stood near the barracks of the regiment's Headquarters Company in the American compound and was often the focal point of regimental assemblies such as Armistice Day and Organization Day ceremonies. In March of 1938 when the regiment reported to Fort Lewis, near Tacoma, Washington, its commander, Colonel Joseph A. McAndrew, presented the gateway to the Infantry School and had it shipped to Georgia. An engraved inscription on the monument, in both English and Chinese, noted that it was intended as "A Remembrance of the Golden Deeds done by Officers and men of the United States Army Forces in China During the Civil Strife, 1924." It had been "respectfully presented with pleasure" to the regiment in April of 1925, by citizens of some 30 Chinese villages in the vicinity of the American base. The Americans were recognized for maintaining law and order in Tientsin and surrounding towns and villages when the tides of Chinese civil war surged across the area in 1924. The text ended with a poem etched in Chinese characters together with an English translation which stated in part: "The sons of Uncle Sam so gallant in their deed/Day and night so strict defense took greatest heed/And through their strenuous effort and suffering/Peace among us all was kept and maintained," and the villagers wished to accord "Honor to those to whom honor is due."[4]

The commander of the United States Army Forces in China, Brigadier General William D. Connor, graciously accepted the memorial in an address in fluent Chinese "which was understood and deeply appreciated by all." It was "perhaps the first time that an American Army Officer ever addressed a representation of Chinese people at a military function in their own language," an account of the event declared, and would no doubt "go far in maintaining the friendly and cordial relations which exist between China and America." Connor hoped that "long after this stone has decayed the friendship between our two countries may exist, and that as long as this stone endures it will be a memento to all the world of the friendship that grew up between us during the troubled days when China was awakening."[5]

The selection of the final site for the monument and its transporting to Fort Benning was something of a minor odyssey. When Colonel McAndrew presented the gateway to the Infantry School, the War Department and the chief of infantry, Major General George Arthur Lynch, who had earlier commanded the 15th in China, were of the opinion that the gateway was the property of the regiment and that McAndrew had no authorization to present it to the Infantry School. The colonel argued that it belonged to the United States and was only in the custody and care of the regiment while in China. He cited his orders regarding the withdrawal of the 15th, which gave him the authority to dispose of the regiment's property as he saw fit. This carried the day, and the War Department allowed the monument to proceed to Fort Benning, perhaps appropriate after all because so many of the "China Hands" were closely involved there, especially in the 1930s. Subsequently, it was formally unveiled on October 13, 1939, with Captain Philip E. Gallagher — who as a first lieutenant had been adjutant of the 15th's Second Battalion when the gate had been presented by the Chinese — delivering the main address. Gallagher concluded: "I know of no other case in history where the common people of a country in which a foreign army was stationed ever presented such a memento of their gratitude to that foreign army for protecting them against forces of their own country engaged in civil war."[6]

The Fort Benning memorial gateway is a positive affirmation of the regiment's activities in China, which were otherwise often unclear, uncertain or viewed negatively. Thus America's presence was perceived as being of some value to the Chinese at least on some occasions, if in a minor way.

Beyond this, was not the deployment of the regiment of greater import for both good and ill? It has been argued that "what is most striking is how long the American military stayed in China — and how successfully." Reference has been made to the fact that "the U.S. armed forces in China were never adequate to deal with a determined foe. They could perform only a policing role, and that mainly through bluff and swagger," strategies which "worked almost until the very end." Still, the premises for the regiment's being in China in the first place must be called into question. It has been maintained that the influx of Westerners in the form of missionaries and businessmen provided real benefits to the people and politically schooled Chinese in Western methods of governance, most of which were fundamentally altered or swept away by the triumph of Chinese communism. It has been further asserted that "Western imperialism could be seen as neither a blind alley nor a crippling burden but as a promise delayed, an opportunity deferred." Or as the Harvard Sinologist John King Fairbank has expressed it, "imperialism might be truly exploitative in some situations but in others more like a crude form of development. Sometimes it was even materially good for you," i.e., "imperialism was like a medicine that builds you up as it tears you down."[7]

It is certainly the case that elements of capitalism and democracy embraced by China in the twenty-first century owe something to foundations earlier laid, often by force, by Westerners in China. But it remains arguable whether the positive influences of such actions outweigh the negative. As Fairbank has also admitted, "the real bite of imperialism was psychological. It was most of all humiliating and therefore a political evil to any proud people." Indeed, foreign encroachment in the form of unilateral imperialism, however styled or labeled, remains a highly questionable exercise of national power whether in China or elsewhere on the globe.

Thus, there were two sides to the involvement of the 15th in China. In the main, few Chinese saw foreigners in their midst, including Americans, during these decades in a positive light. General Connor perceived that though the Chinese apparently liked Americans better than other foreigners, they were, still, foreigners and should not therefore expect any special treatment.[8]

Therefore, the 15th's negative legacy: it was in China, and it was foreign, and if not fundamentally imperialistic in the classic sense, it nonetheless experienced the wrath of the Chinese because of bitterness at their treatment at foreign hands which, becoming intolerable, periodically flared up. The laudable, then, was inexorably overshadowed by the despicable and the gross violation of human rights by the incursion of foreigners in their land. Kipling had earlier warned that in the end the "captains and kings" would depart and that the peoples of India — and of course China — would be in command of their own fortunes and future. The 15th's involvement faded away like all of the concessionary powers and its incursions in China remain ephemeral. Chinwangtao was hardly another Plymouth Rock. The Chinese proceeded along their own path, increasingly intent upon their own devices to attempt to solve the country's massive problems. It was at length recognized that no outside power, not even Japan at the height of its imperial might, could dominate China. Many American soldiers understood this. One of these, Brigadier General Conner, expressed sympathy for the Chinese efforts of self-government and urged standing up for treaty rights— though these were themselves invasive —"in a way that would least offend the Chinese or injure their sensibilities."[9]

When the marines arrived in substantial numbers in Tientsin in 1927, their commander, Brigadier General Butler, similarly supported Chinese self-government but with the qualification "that while they are doing it, they must not molest our citizens. I think that is enough of a policy for Marines."[10]

Still, there were important dimensions quite apart from what had been anticipated when the 15th was deployed to China. To some members of the 15th, such as Captain Charles L. Bolte, "soldiering in China was artificial, and the 15th Infantry was just a little isolated garrison, unconcerned about what was going on in the rest of the world." Roy Flint, a scholar and Army veteran, concluded that "Bolte's assessment is probably accurate, for no one saw the 15th Infantry in China as other than a liability in war," and its training would have been, in the last analysis, worthless.[11]

Yet the careful student of the 15th must quarrel with such assertions. The fact remains: Regardless of the reasons for the regiment's presence, there were significant consequences and attainments. In the last analysis, the 15th's involvement in China had more to do with American than Chinese history. Service in China was not always simply carousing with the "Dutch Annies," the imbibing of Asahi and Five Star Lager Beer, polo and shopping. Regarding China and the rise of Imperial Japan to the forefront of world affairs, the exposure of the men of the 15th in China as a captive audience witnessing the development of fateful world events, was of use to the United States in the years to come.

It was in the area of training that the 15th also made some major contributions because it was training on a particular stage — that of China — that was of value. This being the case, there was a point to the exercises and the constant preparation, as one soldier recognized: "That's one thing about duty in China, there is always the possibility of seeing some real action and that means a lot, it makes the training we go through seem as though it were for a definite purpose and not in the distant future." Lieutenant Colonel Karl Truesdell, executive officer of the regiment in the 1930s, identified other larger dimensions in this context, once observing that the 15th afforded a training ground, "one of the few we have, for our forces in stations other than on the continent at home. It is a station for training in Oriental contacts, and for education in Oriental language and characteristics. If the detail of language officers in Tokyo and Peiping is sound, then the use of the United States Army Troops in China for similar purposes is also sound." He might well have added that the many contacts and confrontations with the Japanese were also significant, not to mention the camaraderie of those who served there — the learning from and about their comrades — and the greatly instructive travels routinely taken by the 15th's officers throughout the Orient.[12]

Perhaps by chance, service in the 15th selected out an impressive company, known in some circles as "that Damned China Crowd"—the "D.C.C."—members of which for a time were especially "thick on the ground" at Fort Benning and its Infantry School.[13] Accordingly, the regiment was the avenue of formative hands-on experiences for a significant number of pivotal leaders in the U.S. Army, especially for the years of

World War II but beyond into the Korean War era as well. Though China hardly provided all of their tutelage, it was clearly a stepping stone for many career officers. By the 1930s, as one who was in China candidly remarked: "I don't know of a single officer who served at the time I was with the 15th Infantry that didn't become a General." (No doubt this is overstated — not all officers who served in China at any given time obtained their star.) That service in the crack 15th was regarded as important and highly desirable was attested to by the scramble of Regulars for assignments to China, both for themselves and their sons. These offspring included George Van Horn Moseley, Jr., son of the commanding general of the Fourth Corps Area in the United States, Major General George Van Horn Moseley. Another was Stilwell's eldest son, Joseph Warren Stilwell, Jr., who as a lieutenant served with the regiment while his father was the American military attaché in Peiping. There was also Lieutenant Homer P. Ford, the son of Brigadier General Stanley H. Ford of the Philippine Department who himself, as a captain from January 5, 1915, to August 15, 1917, commanded the regiment's Company M before serving as regimental adjutant. His son was in Tientsin from 1929 to 1932. Also enjoying this legacy was Lieutenant Stephen Ogden Fuqua, Jr., the heir of the chief of infantry in the early 1930s, Major General Stephen Ogden Fuqua. Lieutenant Lawrence Castner, son of Brigadier General Joseph C. Castner, was also in China for a time before having to return to the United States because of illness.[14]

Certainly the generals-to-be who rotated through the ranks of the storied 15th, while learning differing lessons in China with widely different applications of them, found their instruction to be of considerable value. They shared many things in common. In the first place, simply put, they had served in China. Because China, that nation of 450 million souls, was to be an important player on its particular stage during World War II— referred to as the China-Burma-India Theater — the impressions and enlightenment that they gained had impact on the course of the war and much else in the postwar period. They also obtained some understanding as to how World War II should be fought, assessing the relative importance of China and Japan in the total scope of the conflict. In this regard, Marshall did not allow his China exposure to deter him from a "Europe First" stance, which was undoubtedly the correct one when assessments of relative dangers to the world were considered. Japan was a juggernaut but the Chinese were essentially correct in concluding that the Japanese would be to some extent absorbed by China's mass and depth. Marshall and others had seen China, and undoubtedly appreciated its capacity to contain much of Japan's thrust and power, though at frightful cost to the

Chinese — there were at least 15 million Chinese killed in the struggle. The generals' vision of the possibilities in the Orient, and by extension elsewhere in the world at the time, owed something to their common experiences in the East. They, and dozens of other general officers charged with waging World War II, were not operating without a measure of comprehension; they "had measured the ground" in China.

The service of these men in China had consequences for the U.S. Army's future development well before World War II. Marshall had commanded the regiment as interim commander during two of the most significant contacts that it made during the actions of the ongoing Chinese civil wars, specifically in 1924 and 1925. Here he experienced leadership of American troops in the field, which he loved and valued. Looking beyond the positive dimensions of the 15th's training programs, Marshall had also ascertained the need for a new infantry training regime in the U.S. Army. Soon, as assistant commandant at Fort Benning he would be in a position to remedy many of the shortcomings that he had perceived in China, with far-reaching consequences.[15]

In addition, Marshall gained knowledge of the men in China from whose ranks, when he was chief of staff of the Army, he would select some of the commanders to lead American forces in World War II. While one did not learn much about soldiering from the saddle of a Mongolian pony, one could certainly assess something of the mettle of those one rode alongside of or served with in other ways. Such insights, when put into practice, would later serve the nation well.

Less clear were the parameters and content of larger policy pertaining to China in Marshall's mind, representing perhaps what he also failed to learn. "How the Powers should deal with China is a question almost impossible to answer," Marshall once declared in a letter to Pershing. "There has been so much of wrong doing on both sides, so much of shady transaction between a single power and a single party; there is so much of bitter hatred in the hearts of these people and so much of important business interests involved, that a normal solution can never be found." And "there would be absolute justice in these demands of the Chinese [for the foreigners to depart] if they had any form of stable government to guarantee the fulfillment of their obligations under more normal treaty relations," he wrote to Major General John L. Hines. "But, unfortunately, there is neither a central nor a stable government; there are merely strong men, or clever men, temporarily acting virtually as dictators. If there was a single outstanding individual who was, throughout China, accepted or feared as a dictator, the situation would be vastly improved." What Marshall and many others consistently missed was that what was central to the "hatred in the hearts of these people" emanated from the original involvement of foreign powers. Because of foreign intervention, there was no hope outside of full withdrawal that would have a chance.[16]

Yet Marshall may well have perceived in his China years some of the underpinnings for his policies following World War II, as has already been discussed in chapter V.[17]

Other generals-to-be prepared specifically for their wartime roles. Stilwell and Wedemeyer come to mind, though they hardly absorbed the same lessons regarding the Orient. Stilwell learned enough to direct soldiers of China in the field in World War II with some clear perceptions as to what the Chinese could and could not do, what their political proclivities were and perhaps most of all, the limitations of Chiang. After all, he had seen the generalissimo in action from the beginnings of his career "up close and personal." This preparation for wartime service in China undoubtedly—despite important differences with Chiang Kai-shek and others—assisted in the coming of the eventual victory over Japan. Wedemeyer, replacing Stilwell in 1944, brought these endeavors to a successful conclusion, though Wedemeyer imbibed other lessons, especially his strong opposition to the Chinese Communists. His hard line would be especially deleterious to the careers of members of another group, the Old China Hands, diplomats and Army officers, including Colonel David Barrett, who had also served in the regiment. Charged by McCarthyites and other "fellow travelers" of that baleful coterie with "losing China"—as though it were the West's to lose—Wedemeyer played his own nefarious role. Anti-Communism was not a concept foreign to men of the 15th. Colonel Isaac Newell, for another, had warned departing members of the regiment as they sailed for home in May of 1927 of the necessity to heed the potential threats here. He noted that they had "seen the devastating effects of communism," and that "the United States is not wholly free from communist agitation. I urge you men, who know now the perils of communism, to strike down every evidence you find of this devastating doctrine at home."[18]

Other prominent Can-Doers such as Sutherland, Walker and Ridgway, among dozens of others too numerous to name and discuss in this account, also prepared for their later roles in World War II and beyond in Korea.

Certainly, at the level of the rank and file, those old Regulars, many with command experience in the Great War, served the regiment well. One should not be disillusioned by the abuses of some—indeed, no doubt too many—over the years regarding excessive drinking and the "rate," their involvement with Asian women being a notable exception to the regiment's propensity in general to shun the Chinese. On occasion, they undoubtedly failed the 15th and tarnished their nation's honor. But there were enough solid soldierly citizens to keep the faith and maintain alive and well the best of the spirit of "Can Do." A correspondent for the Second Battalion writing in *The Sentinel* perceived something of this. Observing that "while the 2nd Battalion hasn't undergone a real trial by battle during recent years, it has a well-grounded notion that it will give a good account of itself if it is ever called out for the real business for which it exists." In fact, members of the Second Battalion — not to mention the other battalions in the regiment — later performed quite competently on the battlefields of Europe.[19]

The considerable pride that the 15th manifested in many ways has been noted in this study. This was contributory to and immeasurably enhanced by the outfit's subsequent history. Following the regiment's return from China, at Fort Lewis, on January 12, 1940, the regiment was assigned to the Third ("The Rock of the Marne") Infantry Division, joining the Seventh Regiment — the "Cottonbalers," and the 30th Regiment, "San Francisco's Own." The 15th's First Battalion, which had been deactivated in Manila in 1929, was also brought on board. In these pre–World War II years the Third Division was engaged in intensive training activities, especially involving amphibious operations.[20]

With the coming of America's involvement in World War II, the Third Division, including the 15th — regarded in many circles as conceivably the best regiment in the Army — landed in North Africa on November 8, 1942, when the Allies invaded, fighting its way from Morocco into Tunisia. Whether or not the best, the 15th was undoubtedly a major pillar of the Third Division, as its war record makes clear. Following the Axis defeat in Africa, the 15th prepared to participate in the invasion of Sicily, which began on July 10, 1943. At the end of this successful venture, the regiment crossed over to the Italian mainland, landing on September 18, 1943. There it fought on the Volturno River, participated in the Anzio landing, and was in on the capture of Rome in June 1944. On August 15, the 15th landed at St. Tropez, France, proceeded along the Rhone River Valley and crossed the Vosges Mountains. Reaching the Rhine on November 26, 1944, from December 1944 to February 1945 it helped reduce the heavily fortified Colmar Pocket. The regiment then advanced into Germany in March 1945, broke through the Siegfried Line and assisted in the capture Nuremberg in April 1945. Following VE Day, it remained on garrison duty in Austria until September 1946, returning to Fort Campbell, Kentucky, eventually being assigned to Fort Benning, Georgia.

Since World War II, the regiment, or units of it, have fought in Korea, participated in the occupation of Germany, and in Operations "Desert Shield" and "Desert Storm." Parts of the regiment were deployed to Somalia in 1993, and others were sent to Macedonia to deter Serb aggression. In February 1996, the First Battalion was returned to Fort Benning, Georgia, while the Third was ordered to Fort Stewart, Georgia, home of the U.S. Army's Third Infantry Division (Mechanized). These are the two active battalions currently with the 15th. At this writing in February 2004, the First and Third battalions have been involved in "Operation Iraqi Freedom" as part of the Third Infantry Division, suffering the loss of three soldiers killed in action. Both battalions have recently been rotated home and are currently at Fort Benning and Fort Stewart as noted above.

In the course of its history, the regiment's men were awarded 18 Congressional Medals of Honor: one in the Civil War, 15 in World War II — including the one to Lieutenant Audie Murphy — and two in the Korean War. The 15th continues to be the custodian of one of the most illustrious regimental histories of the U.S. Army. Significantly, it retains the "Can Do" motto and the coat of arms adopted in China in the early 1920s, though the dragon on the shield has assumed a more modern appearance.

In any final accounting, the 15th Regiment in China, at one level, served to delineate the parameters of how Americans chose to wield their power between the world wars. The regiment, by providing its men with exposure to combat, also acclimated its soldiers to service abroad, a perspective that proved no doubt of considerable use in the developing Army after its return from China. To be sure, the 15th was typical of many regiments in many ways, but its China deployment made it distinctive. No safe stateside berth for it! Even service in the Philippines, Hawaii and Panama was not the same thing. No wonder that up and coming officers and men wanted to serve in China: that was were the action was—to the extent that U.S. forces could be involved. In any event, the supplanting of the Old Army, sometimes alive and well in the 15th, by the New Army that emerged on the eve of World War II, was foreshadowed in China. This may be more succinctly indicated by noting that the 15th, as personified by some of its commanding officers, ran the gamut from such old Indian fighters as Colonel Martin, through the regime of Brigadier General Castner, that crusty old infantryman-cum-cavalryman, proceeding to Philippine veterans such as Colonel Taylor, who was determined to create an even deeper sense of regimental pride and tradition. This pattern continued to include the Great War leaders such as Lynch and Marshall, who perforce had to look to the future and prepare what would emerge as the New Army. Put another way, the 15th began its China venture looking back to the Boxer Uprising; it ended by being impelled toward World War II, provoked in part by the Japanese militancy so apparent to men of the regiment in the 1930s. Thus its course traced the arc from the doughboy to the GI that the U.S. Army in general traversed in the years between the world wars.

There is, then, an unbroken chain running from such men as Private Raymond R. Reeves, returning to China in the mid–1920s from the United States at his own considerable expense to rejoin the regiment that he loved, to those such as Audie Murphy, who served in the 15th so heroically in World War II. As *The Sentinel* observed on the occasion of Reeves' return: "This attitude toward service with the regiment, will always be an asset to the organization." Other assets would be the courage of men like Captain Jesse D. Cope and others meeting hostile Chinese forces while aboard an abortive international train run in late 1925, not to mention Captain "Wild Bill" Tuttle standing in the face of thousands of Chinese at the dike near the American compound, also holding firm. Despite Major Harding making poetic sport of both Cope and Tuttle on these occasions, there is no arguing the audacity and acumen displayed. To be sure, such armed encounters turned the hair of men at the War Department grayer by the minute, knowing the risks that were run. The man in command at the time of some of the more serious encounters, George C. Marshall, faced up to his duties as well, learning lessons of lasting import. The 15th clearly was more than a mere parade outfit or a "spit and polish" regiment. It was more, too, than a VD-ridden and alcohol-besotted assembly of "sad sacks." But in China, the regiment stored up experience and developed a determination to stick to duty, facing with resolve the dangers out front, that added to the regiment's collective, historic spirit that would be drawn upon almost daily in World War II and beyond. In indefinable though genuine ways, part of the solidity of the Third "Rock of the Marne" Infantry Division in the 1940s derived from the 15th's actions in and around Tientsin in 1925 and numerous other confrontations and alarms experienced in China, years before. Such military traditions and the pride instilled thereby are not, after all, mere fanciful inventions lacking substance.

In sum, in an ever-increasingly dangerous situation and confronted with what seemed to be perpetual "missions impossible," that "Damned China Crowd," both officers and rank and file, performed rather well in China. Accordingly, it seems a useful exercise to have encountered some dimensions of their involvement there while seeking some insight into aspects of American military history that remain relatively little known.

Chapter Notes

Preface

1. Charles G. Finney to Brigadier General Frederick Mixon Harris, February 13 and September 29, 1965, the Frederick Harris Collection, folder 1/4, George C. Marshall Library, Lexington, Virginia.
2. For this upheaval, see Diana Preston, *The Boxer Rebellion* (New York: Walker and Company, 2000); Joseph W. Esherick, *The Origins of the Boxer Uprising* (Berkeley: University of California Press, 1987); and Paul A. Cohen, *History in Three Keys* (New York: Columbia University Press, 1998).
3. In 1923, these troops were designated the American Forces in China. In 1924, they were renamed the United States Army Forces in China, and finally, in 1929, were styled the United States Army Troops in China.
4. See Richard McKenna, *The Sand Pebbles*, various editions; Kemp Tolley, *The Yangtze Patrol: The U.S. Navy in China* (Annapolis, Maryland: Naval Institute Press, 1971); and Dennis L. Noble, ed., *Gunboat on the Yangtze: The Diary of Captain Glenn F. Howell of the USS Palos, 1920–1921* (Jefferson, North Carolina: McFarland, 2002).
5. A magazine in overall appearance, the publication was edited and written as a newspaper. Though some issues are missing, *The Sentinel*, for the period January 1921 to December 1935, can be obtained on microfilm from the New York Public Library. Students of the 15th in China must also consider several especially useful books and articles including Charles Grandison Finney, *The Old China Hands* (New York: Doubleday, 1961); Barbara W. Tuchman, *Stilwell and the American Experience in China, 1911–45* (New York: The Macmillan Company, 1971); Dennis L. Noble, *The Eagle and the Dragon: The United States Military in China, 1901–1937* (Westport, Conn.: Greenwood Press, 1990); Edward M. Coffman, "The American 15th Infantry Regiment in China, 1912–1938: A Vignette in Social History," *The Journal of Military History*, vol. 58 (January 1994), 57–74; Louis Morton, "Army and Marines on the China Station," *Pacific Historical Review*, vol. 29, no. 1 (February 1960), 51–73; and Roy Kenneth Flint, "The United States Army on the Pacific Frontier, 1899–1939," *The American Military and the Far East: The Proceedings of the Ninth Military History Symposium, United States Air Force Academy, 1–3 October, 1980*, ed. Joe C. Dixon (Washington, D.C.: Government Printing Office, 1981).

Chapter I

1. The Chinese were sometimes called "the Celestials" (in reference to the notion of China as the "Celestial Kingdom" held by Chinese for centuries), "Yeller Kids," or "John Chinaman." This poem was by "V.L.," and was published in *The Sentinel*, January 14, 1921. Articles VII and IX of the Peace Protocol of September 7, 1901, detailed the provisions of foreign involvement in China following the Boxer Uprising, which included the stationing of garrisons along the Peking-Mukden railroad. See *The Sentinel*, March 31, 1922 and Preston, *The Boxer Rebellion*.
2. *The Sentinel*, September 23, 1927, anonymous.
3. Much of the following is derived from diary excerpts published in five installments in *The Sentinel*, March 20–April 17, 1925.
4. Something of the ambience of these voyages was captured by newspapers published on board the transports; these were usually

edited by the ship's chaplain. See, for example, *The Whisperin' Wave*, a mimeographed sheet published on board the U.S. Army Transport *U.S. Grant*, Saturday, May 20, 1933; copy in folder "Ship's Newspaper, 'The Whisperin' Wave,'" in the John William Leonard Papers, Archives, the U.S. Army Military History Institute, Carlisle Barracks, Pennsylvania. (Hereinafter as "The John William Leonard Papers," USAMHI.)

5. Sometimes even the Chinese were in awe of the Gobi sand; one observer recorded that "last Monday afternoon we had quite a peculiar atmospheric condition arise that had the Chinese population quite excited. About noon the sky became overcast with a haze about the color of the Gobi dust, as a matter of fact that's what it was, but there was no wind and it was not noticeable on the ground. The sky kept getting darker and darker and by five o'clock it was brick red and the electric lights had an uncanny white glow." It then began to rain and soon cleared the sky, but the rain appeared as drops of mud because of the heavy deposit of Gobi dust in the air (*The Sentinel*, April 27, 1929). For further discussions of the Gobi and its storms see ibid., March 11 and 25, 1921, and April 4, 1924.

6. See one description of the graves in *The Asheville Skyline*, paper of the U.S. Navy Gunboat *Asheville* (p. 21), quoted in *The Sentinel*, April 9, 1932.

7. *The Sentinel*, July 12, 1930.

8. Ibid., November 6, 1925; December 17, 1926.

9. Ibid., March 6, 1925.

10. "Ricksha Thrills," in ibid., September 9, 1927; and a novella, *In Worldly Clutches*, by Roger Jones (rank unknown) of Headquarters Company published in ibid., February 13–April 17, 1925, in ten installments. Sometimes spelled "rickshaw," this Japanese invention was readily embraced by the Chinese and their term, *jin-riki-sha* means "man-power carts."

11. Part 3 of a novella, *In Worldly Clutches*, by Roger Jones, ibid., February 27, 1925.

12. See "Conditions of Service in China" *The Infantry Journal*, vol. 29 (August 1926), 167–74; reprinted in *The Sentinel*, September 24, 1926, under the title "New Arrivals Furnished Information." There is a diagram of the compound as of July 1, 1930, in folder "353.5 Guard Duty," entry 5960: General Correspondence, 1925–38, Record Group 395: General Records, U.S. Army Overseas Operations and Commands, 1898–1942, U.S. Army Troops in China, 1912–38 (hereinafter as folder "353.5 Guard Duty," entry 5960, RG 395). Information regarding the Compound is located in *The Sentinel*, March 11, 1927, and December 1, 1928; in several folders, including "600 to 600.914 — Buildings and Grounds," and "600. 915 to 623 — Barracks and Quarters," and others, in entry 5960, RG 395; and in Annual Reports in folder "Countries— American Forces in China, 123.61 to 333.3," entry AGO 1917–25, Record Group 407: (The Adjutant General's Office) Central Decimal Files Project Files, 1917–1925. Countries. American Forces in China to Cuba 350.2 (hereinafter as folder "Countries— American Forces in China, 123.61 to 333.3," entry AGO 1917–25, RG 407).

13. *The Sentinel*, August 12, 1927.

14. Ibid., April 1, 1921. Other details are in the article "Conditions of Service in China," 169.

15. For discussions of Tientsin, see Gail Hershatter, *The Workers of Tianjin, 1900–1949* (Stanford: Stanford University Press, 1986), 9–24 and *passim*; O.D. Rasmussen, *Tientsin: An Illustrated Outline History* (Tientsin: The Tientsin Press, 1925); and Brian Power, *The Ford of Heaven* (New York: Michael Kesend Publishing, 1984). Power was an Englishman who grew up in Tientsin in the 1920s and 1930s. By the 1930s, the city was the largest center of industry in North China and second only to Shanghai in volume of foreign trade.

16. Rasmussen, *Tientsin: An Illustrated Outline History*, 13–31, 95, 231–37. For the importance of the Chinese salt industry in general see John King Fairbank, *The Great Chinese Revolution: 1800–1985* (New York: Harper and Row, 1986), 53, and Kwan Man Bun, *The Salt Merchants of Tianjin: State-Making and Civil Society in Late Imperial China* (Honolulu: University of Hawai'i Press, 2001).

17. *The Sentinel*, August 12, 1927; an account by Harry A. Ferguson of Company I in ibid., July 6, 1929; paper, "Great Decision," by Brigadier General Frederick M. Harris in the Frederick Harris Collection, folder 9, George C. Marshall Library, Lexington, Virginia; and Power, *The Ford of Heaven*, 15–25.

18. Paper, "Great Decision," by Brigadier General Frederick M. Harris in the Frederick Harris Collection.

19. *The Sentinel*, June 1, 1929.

20. "Conditions of Service in China," 169–70. There is a listing of officers' addresses and phone numbers in *The Sentinel*, March 1, 1930, and other issues.

21. Anonymous poem, "15th Infantry Prayer," in *The Sentinel*, August 15, 1924. For a compe-

tent discussion of Chinese money in the period between the world wars see Kemp Tolley, *Yangtze Patrol: The U.S. Navy in China* (Annapolis, Maryland: Naval Institute Press, 1971), 213–17.

22. Tolley, *Yangtze Patrol*, 215. See also *The Sentinel*, July 13, 1929, and October 4, 1930. The currency in common use consisted of so-called "big money," which was paper coupons or bills of less than a dollar in value in denominations of ten, 20 or 50 cents bought new in packs at banks and carried as easy dispensation for tips and ricksha fare. "Small money" was silver — dimes and 20-cent pieces, which varied daily as to real value. There was also the Chinese penny or "copper," not as handy because of its relatively large size and weight but nonetheless the heart of coolie finance. Paper money of larger denominations of a dollar and up was issued by many central and provincial banks and other agencies which usually had their currency printed abroad, "where too large a proportion would not stick to the machinery." There was a wide variation in the value of this from city to city and province to province — and even within cities. It was usually discounted if used outside of its immediate area of issue, and counterfeiting was common.

23. Paper, "Great Decision," by Brigadier General Frederick M. Harris, in the Frederick Harris Collection.

24. Ibid.

25. Poem by Major Edwin Forrest Harding, commander of the Second Battalion and sometime "poet laureate of the Regiment," in his *Lays of the Mei-Kuo Ying-P'an* (Lays of the American Compound) (Tientsin, China, privately printed, n.d.), 19–20. This publication was sold in the post exchange for one dollar (Mex.). There is a copy of the publication in folder 14, the Frederick Harris Collection. Lieutenant Colonel Richard H. Jordan was the regiment's quartermaster in the late 1920s. Yet, Harding and his family did not do half-bad in this regard. They returned with an elaborate doll and toy collection, impressive Chinese screens, a large array of swords and knives, and fine examples of Chinese "iron pictures," all now the pride of the Harding home and museum in Franklin, Ohio. See also the letter from Lieutenant Colonel George C. Marshall to Major General John L. Hines, December 23, 1925, in Larry I. Bland and Sharon R. Ritenour, eds., *The Papers of George Catlett Marshall*, vol. 1 (Baltimore: The Johns Hopkins University Press, 1981), 283. "My enjoyment of service out here grows with each month. The work is interesting, the conditions exciting and the time flies. Mrs. Coles [Marshall's mother-in-law] and Mrs. Marshall also like it, especially the shopping."

26. There were listings of commissary prices in *The Sentinel* in the issues of May 29, August 14, and November 6, 1925, and others.

27. Ibid., April 22, 1921.

Chapter II

1. Robert Hart, *"These from the Land of Sinim": Essays on the Chinese Question* (London: Chapman and Hall, 1901), 169.

2. See Headquarters, U.S. Army Troops in China, *Conference Troop School, Officers, 28 Nov. '33 — Mission and Objectives, U.S.A.T.C.* (Syllabus), Tientsin, 1933, and *Officers School Notes, U.S. Army Troops in China — School Years 1933–34, 1934–35* (Tientsin, 1935), as quoted in Charles W. Thomas III, "The United States Army Troops in China, 1912–1937," unpublished manuscript (Stanford University, June 1937), 23–24 and *passim*; copy in U.S. Army Military History Research Collection, USAMHI.

3. For the impact of the opium war see Raymond Chang and Margaret Scrogin Chang, *Speaking of Chinese: A Cultural History of the Chinese Language* (New York: W.W. Norton and Company, 1978, paperback edition, 1983), note, 50–51.

4. Discussion in James Dyer Ball, *Things Chinese*, 2nd revised edition (London: Sampson Low, 1893; 4th edition London: John Murray, 1904), 685–693.

5. Hart, "These from the Land of Sinim," 119, 130–31, 134–35, and 163.

6. Ibid., pp. 124, 143, 163, and 165–66. *The Sentinel*, in an editorial in the January 25, 1930, attempted to explain "extrality" to its readers.

7. Hart, "These from the Land of Sinim," 136 and 179.

8. Historical account of Company C, in *The Sentinel*, December 23, 1927.

9. Articles VII and IX of the Peace Protocol of September 7, 1901, set forth these provisions in detail. See *The Sentinel*, March 31, 1922. As part of these arrangements, American troops were stationed at Tientsin and other points on the railway, while, after 1905, American marines, relieving units of the Army's Ninth Infantry Regiment, guarded the American Legation in Peking.

10. Hart, 84, 111 and 118.

Notes — Chapter II

11. Ibid., 52–53, and 122.

12. Historical account in *The Sentinel*, January 25, 1930. See also historical data in the "Strength Returns of the Regiment" in Microcopy 665, returns from Regular Army Infantry Regiments, June 1821–December 1916, Roll 172: Fifteenth Infantry, January 1910–December 1916, National Archives, Washington, D.C.

13. See relevant documents dated January 4, 12, 16, and March 16, 27, 1912, in folder "370.091—Guarding of Railroads, China," Entry 5960, RG 395. The American commander was further reminded that "the guarding of the railroad is not hostile to China, but is by harmonious cooperation of the Powers concerned. You should therefore strive to maintain the most cordial relations with the military representatives of these powers, as well as to safeguard the susceptibilities of the Chinese."

14. Ibid.

15. *The Sentinel*, March 31, 1922; April 4, 1931.

16. See Roy Kenneth Flint, "The United States Army on the Pacific Frontier, 1899–1939," *The American Military and the Far East: The Proceedings of the Ninth Military History Symposium, United States Air Force Academy, 1–3 October, 1980*, ed. Joe C. Dixon (Washington, D.C.: Government Printing Office, 1981), 148. The 15th's commanding officer, Colonel Frank B. Jones, had been ill for some time at the Army hospital in Hot Springs, Arkansas. He arrived in China on April 25, 1912, taking charge of the regiment and the China Expedition. In China, most of the 15th's companies were based at Tientsin, though there were detachments located at sites along the railway: Leichuang, Tangshan, Kuyeh, Wali, Linsi and Kaiping. Of these, Tangshan, where major shops of the railway were located, was the most important and it became routine for one company to be based there for a six-month stint, and companies rotated between there and Tientsin. This arrangement continued until 1928, when Tangshan was deleted from the regiment's guard agenda. For some years Leichuang was also important, being the site of the regiment's firing range.

17. Andrews, *Under a Lucky Star*, 148. The situation in China was never as simplistic as Westerners then imagined. Modern scholarship has done much to shed light on the complexities of Chinese history in these years. See, for example, the substantial study by Arthur Waldron, *From War to Nationalism. China's Turning Point, 1924–1925* (New York: Cambridge University Press, 1995).

18. See Hanson's memo to John Van Antwerp MacMurray, the American Charge d'Affaires in Peking, September 11, 1914, and Memo No. 1278, John Van Antwerp MacMurray, then the secretary of the American Legation in Peking, to Colonel H.C. Hale, the commanding officer of the U.S. China Expedition, July 11, 1916, in folder "370.091—Guarding of Railroads, China," entry 5960, RG 395. Following the withdrawal of the German troops later in September 1914, the Americans did in fact take over the guarding of some points along the railway from the German troops, including Hanku.

19. Andrews, *Under a Lucky Star*, 148–49.

20. The May Fourth Movement marks a major turning point in Chinese history with the beginning of an intense nationalism and a growing cultural renaissance. There is a discussion in John King Fairbank, *The Great Chinese Revolution: 1800–1985* (New York: Harper and Row, 1986), 182–83 and *passim*. The Soviet Union formally surrendered extraterritoriality in 1924.

21. *The Sentinel*, March 31, 1922, and Dorothy Borg, *American Policy and the Chinese Revolution, 1925–1928* (New York: Octagon Books, 1968), 1–19. The conference did produce a Sino-Japanese Treaty (February 4, 1922) which forced Japanese troops to evacuate Shantung and restore to China all former German interests there.

22. For the development and details of warlordism see Waldron, *From War to Nationalism*; James E. Sheridan, *Chinese Warlord: The Career of Feng Yu-hsiang* (Stanford, California: Stanford University Press, 1966); and the same author's *China in Disintegration: The Republican Era in Chinese History, 1912–1949* (New York: The Free Press, 1975).

23. *The Sentinel*, January 14, 1921. It should be noted that the view of the Chinese civil wars as farce is a misperception, a consequence of Western ignorance and ethnocentrism. For a corrective, see Waldron, *From War to Nationalism*, 55 and *passim*.

24. *The Sentinel*, March 31, 1922.

25. Ibid., August 11 and October 13, 1922. The question as to why the 15th was in China was often discussed in *The Sentinel* and elsewhere. See, for example, the front-page article, "Legal Status of American Soldiers in China," by Captain John C. Newton, 15th Infantry, in ibid., October 27, 1922. See others in ibid., August 8, 1924; November 6, 1925;

Notes—Chapter II

December 28, 1929; July 19, 1930; and Captain Jesse D. Cope, "American Troops in China—Their Mission," *Infantry Journal*, vol. 38 (1931), 174–77. Foreigners other than personnel of the 15th were vitally interested in the issue as well. See "What We Owe to Extraterritoriality" in the *Peking and Tientsin Times*, October 16, 1924. This baldly admitted—with a strong dash of arrogance—that without extraterritoriality, the position of foreigners in China would be untenable. It was reprinted in *The Sentinel*, October 17, 1924. Despite much discussion, it was understood that to go into all the details "would require volumes." Accordingly, the men of the 15th, even the officers, reduced the issues down to a couple of essentials. See, for instance, the conclusions drawn by First Lieutenant—later Lieutenant General—William Howard Arnold, who served with the 15th under Colonel Burt: "The only mission we had as far as I know ... was to keep the railroad open and to get along with our allies." See in the William Howard Arnold Papers, USAMHI.

26. For involvement of the 15th at this time, see *The Sentinel*, June 2, 1922.

27. General Connor's Annual Report to the Adjutant General dated August 24, 1923, in folder "Countries—American Forces in China, 123.61 to 333.3," entry AGO 1917–25, RG 407; *The Sentinel*, April 13, 20, 27, and May 4, 1923. See General Order No. 44, October 24, 1922. The new entity became formally established on April 1, 1923. Connor assumed command on April 12, 1923. There were further refinements when the designation "American Forces in China" was changed as of July 1, 1924, to "United States Army Troops in China." See War Department, Washington, D.C., Section II, General Orders 16, as cited in Charles W. Thomas III, "The United States Army Troops in China, 1912–1937," 23–24. For the struggles in Washington regarding the role of the 15th in China and the designations of American forces there, see the discussions by Louis Morton in his article "Army and Marines on the China Station: A Study in Military and Political Rivalry," *Pacific Historical Review*, vol. 29, no. 1 (February 1960), 51–73.

28. Confidential letter, Charles Evans Hughes to John W. Weeks, Washington, November 8, 1922, folder "American Legation, Peking, China—Miscellaneous," entry 245, Records Relating to Marine Activities in China, 1927–1938, RG 127: Records of the United States Marine Corps (Hereinafter as: folder "American Legation, Peking, China—Miscellaneous," entry 245, RG 127); Connor's Annual Report, Tientsin, China, August 24, 1923, in folder "Countries—American Forces in China, 123.61 to 333.3," entry AGO 1917–25, RG 407.

29. See the series of agreements by the Allied commandants from December 14, 1923, to April 8, 1924, in folder "381—Defense of Tientsin, Document 5," entry 5960, RG 395. Among these were contingency plans for the creation of a general reserve of the Tientsin garrisons. These forces were to consist of about a sixth of the military strength of each contingent's Regular infantry units. It should be noted that the senior commandant present during these years was the Japanese commander. The Japanese saw to it that he outranked all of the others, even to the point of appointing a Lieutenant General to command only a few hundred troops stationed at Tientsin.

30. *The China Review* (New York), reprinted in *The Sentinel*, April 28, 1922.

31. Connor to Jacob Gould Schurman, Tientsin, August 20, 1924, in folder "091—Foreign Countries-China-Political," entry 5960, RG 395. Connor further noted that "the Chinese mind does not work according to the rules of occidental logic. Hence the results from the most logical reasoning of an American on certain causes and their probable effects may differ radically from the actual results produced on the Chinese." In short, they remained "inscrutable," a factor that had to be taken into account when dealing with them. See article and picture of Jacob Gould Schurman, the newly-arrived American minister to China in *The Sentinel*, September 2, 1921. A former president of Cornell University, he had previous experience in the Far East, having served as head of the First Philippine Commission in 1899. He had further diplomatic experience as the U.S. minister to Greece and Montenegro in 1912–13.

32. There is a detailed article on Chang in *The Sentinel*, September 19 and October 3, 1924, in which the author called the complex and contradictory character "the most colorful personality in China today."

33. Ibid., September 19, 1924; poem, "The Three Crows," in the October 3, 1924, issue; and cover of the issue of October 10, 1924. There is a much sounder discussion of the Second Chihli-Fengtien War's background, origins and a detailed delienation of operations, as well as an analysis of its importance, in Waldron, *From War to Nationalism*.

34. *The Sentinel*, October 31, 1924.

35. Ibid., September 26, 1924. Many of the

Russians became Chinese citizens following the war, having repudiated their former nationality when enlisting in Chang's army. Ibid., December 12, 1924. Many of Chang's Russian soldiers were women. The Russian aviators flew British Handley-Page and French Breguet aircraft of World War vintage.

36. Ibid., September 26; October 31; November 7, 14, 21; December 12, 1924. In a facetious poem, "Mother Goose up to Date," in the November 14, 1924, issue, *The Sentinel* traced the conflict's action, again revealing the superficial, supercilious view common among Americans regarding China's contemporary internal affairs. It concluded:

> Hey diddle diddle
> The cat and the fiddle,
> Wu jumped back to Tientsin,
> Chang Tso-lin laughed
> To see such sport,
> And Feng ran away with Peking.

37. Ibid., December 5, 1924.
38. Ibid., October 17 and November 14, 1924, for accounts and photographs of Allied trains successfully making the run from Tientsin to Shankaikwan.
39. See Connor's Annual Report of Fiscal Year 1925 (1924–1925), to the adjutant general in Washington, dated August 24, 1925, and his Annual Tactical Inspection Report of January 5, 1925, to the adjutant general in folder "Countries—American Forces in China, 123.61 to 333.3," entry AGO 1917–25, RG 407. During these trying months the morale of the command was excellent, and Connor rated the military efficiency of the regiment as "above average" and that of the officers as "well above average."
40. Annual Report of Fiscal Year 1925 (1924–1925), to the adjutant general in Washington, dated August 24, 1925, in folder "Countries—American Forces in China, 123.61 to 333.3," entry AGO 1917–25, RG 407.
41. For Feng, see Sheridan, *Chinese Warlord*, 74–90 and *passim* and *The Sentinel*, March 23, 1923.
42. See poem, "Casey Cope," about Cope, one of the regiment's noted nimrods, by Edwin Forrest Harding in his publication *Lays of the Mei-Kuo Ying-P'an*, 15–16. This concluded in a burst of unwarranted braggadocio: "Captain Cope wants to go hunting / Captain Cope wants a tiger skin / Captain Cope wants to shoot a tiger / Wants to shoot a tiger and Li Ching Lin." See also *The Sentinel*, December 18, 1925.
43. See *The Sentinel*, January 1 and 8, 1926, for accounts of the stirring events of December, 1925.
44. Ibid., January 8, 1926.
45. Ibid., January 1 and 8, 1926. For more details of military operations at that time, see letters, Captain Frank B. Hayne to Mrs. Anne Dulany Hayne, December 22 and 28, 1925, the Frank Hayne Collection, box 16, folder F-1, George C. Marshall Research Library, Lexington, Virginia.
46. Colonel William D. Naylor's annual report for the calendar year 1925, to the adjutant general, Washington, dated April 13, 1926, in folder "A.G. 314.73—15th Inf. (4-13-26)," entry AGO 1917–25, RG 407.
47. On April 9, 1925, John Van Antwerp MacMurray, an expert on Far Eastern affairs and former assistant secretary of state, became U.S. minister to China. He had served there for a number of years previously. Bland, *The Papers of George Catlett Marshall*, note 282–83.
48. Connor to MacMurray, January 25, 1926, in folder "370.22 — U.S. Army Troops in China," entry 5960, RG 395. Indeed, Connor concluded, "I do not believe that our government has ever reaped so great a return from so small an investment as it has from the $1500 spent annually on its Chinese instructors."
49. On November 3, 1926, the War Department instructed the American commander in China to this effect. See in Thomas, "The United States Army Troops in China," 32.
50. Andrews, *Under a Lucky Star*, 251.
51. *The Sentinel*, June 10, 1927.
52. Ibid., June 10, 1927; Hans Schmidt, *Maverick Marine: General Smedley D. Butler and the Contradictions of American Military History* (Lexington, Ky.: The University Press of Kentucky, 1987), 182 and 188; and folder "3rd Brigade, General Butler's Final Report," entry 245, RG 127; Smedley Darlington Butler, "American Marines in China," *Annals of the American Academy of Political Science* (July 1929), 128–34.
53. *The Sentinel*, June 17, 1927.
54. Schmidt, *Maverick Marine*, 173 and 186; *The Sentinel*, March 16, 1928; Chester M. Biggs, Jr., *The United States Marines in North China, 1894–1942* (Jefferson, North Carolina: McFarland & Company, 2003), 158. See also *The Sentinel*, December 9, 1927, which featured a cover photo of Butler and a lengthy article on his career.
55. Schmidt, *Maverick Marine*, 186.
56. Ibid., 186, 194–97, and *passim*.
57. Ibid., 173–75, 179, and 200.
58. Folder "3rd Brigade, General Butler's

Final Report," entry 245, RG 127. See also Anne Cipriano Venzon, ed., *General Smedley Darlington Butler, The Letters of a Leatherneck, 1998–1931* (Westport, Connecticut: Praeger Press, 1992), 265–94.

59. Schmidt, *Maverick Marine*, 176–77, 185–86.

60. Venzon, *General Smedley Darlington Butler*, p. 285; folder "3rd Brigade, General Butler's Final Report," entry 245, RG 127; the *Peking and Tientsin Times*, Tientsin, January 9, 1929; *The Sentinel*, November 24 and December 29, 1928 and January 19, 1929. At this time, the United States moved its embassy to Nanking but maintained a staff at Peking in the American Embassy compound which continued to be defended by the Marine Legation Guard.

61. Memorandum No. 4, Headquarters, U.S. Army Troops in China, Tientsin, China, March 24, 1930, in folder "041.2 — Bureaus of the Department of State," entry 5960, RG 395.

62. Communication, J.V.A. MacMurray, the American minister to China, to General Castner, Peking, June 2, 1928, in folder "381— Defense of Tientsin, Document No. 5," entry 5960, RG 395. The Allied commandants were advised that their diplomats in Peiping had decided that no international trains would be reinstituted as some of them had contemplated. Another consideration recognized at this time was that even under the Protocol of 1901 the regiment had no legal status in northern China because that document specified that the mission was the maintenance of open communication between the *capital* and the sea, and the official capital was then Nanking, not Peiping.

63. Schmidt, *Maverick Marine*, 186, 194–97, and *passim*; Andrews, *Under a Lucky Star*, 277.

Chapter III

1. Anonymous, writing in Company L column in *The Sentinel*, May 13, 1926.

2. See diary excerpts published in five installments in ibid., March 20–April 17, 1925, by Private Otto Beinke, and ibid., August 5, 1921. In athletic circles, the men were known as the "15th Infantry 'Chinks.'" Explaining "jawbone" to newcomers, Beinke noted that "every Chinese merchant is your creditor," and "every liquor dealer is looking for you as a prospect. If you draw $21.00 month [the base pay of a private at that time]—you have [an automatic] $42.00 credit." Every Chinaman knew his business and if he got half of his money before the enlistment of his prospect ran out—or if the soldier operated on the principle that the "gangplank [of the homebound ship] cancelled out all debts"—he still profited substantially from it.

3. See the regimental history compiled in 1920 by First Lieutenant Warren J. Clear. This was on sale in the Post Exchange for many years and was often excerpted in *The Sentinel*, as in the May 4, 1923, issue. See also an account by Captain H.R. Brinkerhoff, "The Fifteenth Regiment of Infantry," in *The Army of the United States: Historical Sketches of Staff and Line with Portraits of Generals-in-Chief*, ed. Theophilus Francis Rodenbough and William L. Haskin (New York: Maynard, Merrill and Company, 1896), 610–628. See also John K. Mahon and Romana Danysh, *U.S. Army Lineage Series, Infantry, Part I: Regular Army* (Washington: Center for Military History, 1972). The regiment's current status and aspects of its history can also be accessed online at a Web site maintained by the 15th Infantry Regiment Association.

4. The strength of the regiment was then about 1,325 officers and men. Much of the foregoing has been derived from data in the regiment's Strength Returns in Microcopy 665: Returns from Regular Army Infantry Regiments, June 1821–December 1916, roll 172: Fifteenth Infantry, January 1910–December 1916, National Archives, Washington, D.C.

5. See historical accounts in *The Sentinel*, August 25 and September 1, 1928, and January 25, 1930. See also a useful series of articles in ibid., March 1, 8, 15, and 22, 1930, by Sergeant Palmer A. Ferguson of the regiment's Service Company, who was a member of 15th from 1908 to 1932.

6. Historical account in ibid., March 2, 1928. The average rifle company consisted of 82 men and three officers. Company H, popularly called the Flying Aitches, emerged as one of the 15th's key organizations and for years demonstrated its prowess in the athletic arenas and on the firing line—particularly with the machine gun—and in other regimental endeavors.

7. See General Orders No. 1, Headquarters, Fifteenth Infantry, Tientsin, China, January 2, 1921, in compliance with paragraph 7, Circular No. 19, War Department, 1920, as quoted and discussed in ibid., February 11, 25 and August 19, 1921.

8. Ibid., March 11, 1921. See sketch on this issue's front cover. The words also appeared on the masthead of *The Sentinel*, beginning

with the February 11, 1921 issue. See also ibid., July 22, 1921; May 4, 1923.

9. See discussions in ibid., May 4 and June 8, 1923. The editor asserted that some might shudder at use of slang as a motto, but it was appropriate for the regiment when one considered its history. In any case, the men were enjoined to live up to the spirit of "Can Do" in the Wars of Nations, Sports or Life. The crest and shield was authorized by the Office of the Adjutant General on April 30, 1923, and amended to correct the wording on July 14, 1924. The insignia was approved by the Office of the Adjutant General on April 22, 1924. These details are in a letter to the commanding officer, 15th Infantry, from the Heraldic Services Division, Quartermaster Activities, Cameron Station, U.S. Army, Alexandria, Virginia, June 29, 1959. This division is now the Institute of Heraldry, Fort Belvoir, Virginia. See also *The Sentinel*, April 20, 1928.

In addition, several of the outfit's companies adapted their own mottoes, Company E designating itself the "Will Do" company while men of Company L facetiously called themselves the "Do Do's."

10. *The Sentinel*, September 18 and October 2, 1925, and August 12, 1927; Flint, "The United States Army on the Pacific Frontier," 149; Frederic E. Ray et al., "The United States 15th Infantry Regiment, 1925," *Military Collector and Historian* (spring 1965), 18–19.

11. *The Sentinel*, January 4, May 17 and July 19, 1930; April 4, 1931; April 9 and November 26, 1932.

12. This patch was circular, measuring two and one-fourth inches in diameter with a red outer circle one-fourth inch wide and an inner green field, with the Chinese character in red in the center. See discussion and description in ibid., December 2, 1927, and illustration. For the "wampus fish," see ibid., December 12, 1924; March 29, 1930; July 16, 1932.

13. Ibid., November 20, 1925.

14. Schmidt, *Maverick Marine*, 173–201.

15. Consider the struggle of the U.S. Air Service — later the Air Corps and the U.S. Army Air Force — to establish its own unique uniform, certainly one of the motives leading to the creation of a separate Air Force in 1947. Note also the strong desire of the U.S. Army's Green Berets to cling to their own headgear in the year 2002.

16. See poem, "Parade of the 15th U.S. Infantry," in *The Sentinel*, October 8, 1926.

17. Ibid., August 11 and October 13, 1922; May 13, 1927; May 4, 1929.

18. See War Department General Order 44, October 24, 1922. Details are in ibid., April 13, 20 and 27, 1923.

19. Ibid., March 16 and May 18, 1929. See General Order No. 13, Headquarters, Philippine Department, August 15, 1929, and discussion in ibid., February 23 and September 7, 1929.

20. Ibid., July 11, August 15 and 29, and September 5, 1931; poem, "Six Hundred Doughboys," by J.B. Houchin of Company E, in ibid., March 19, 1932.

Chapter IV

1. *The Sentinel*, November 20, 1925.

2. Marshall to Brigadier General William H. Cocke, superintendent of VMI, December 26, 1926, in Bland, *The Papers of George Catlett Marshall*, Vol. I, 298–300; *The Sentinel*, September 24, 1926. See also Lieutenant James E. Moore — later a general — who served in the regiment in the mid–1930s as assistant adjutant and provost marshal, who noted "the officers were hand picked. It was a prize station, and the officers on a whole did very well." He also observed that throughout the Army, "Everybody was looking for service in a foreign country," and hence China was a desired destination. Interview of Moore in the James E. Moore Papers, USAMHI.

3. *The Sentinel*, October 7, 1921; June 23 and November 10, 1922. While in China, Martin's daughter, Mary Winifred, was married to Captain Le Roy Welling Nichols of the regiment.

4. See King's career in ibid., April 20 and May 4, 1923; July 25 and August 15, 1924; March 30, 1928; March 9, 1929; July 22, 1933. See photos of King in ibid., May 4, 1923, and July 25, 1924.

5. For details on Naylor's career, see accounts in ibid., November 28, 1924, and January 15, 1926, and Colonel William K. Naylor, "Christmas in China During the Boxer Rebellion, 1900," a memoir note in *The Military Collector and Historian*, vol. 54, no. 4, ed. Alfred E. Cornebise, 169–73.

6. *The Sentinel*, July 24, 1925, and January 8 and 15, 1926. For a less favorable assessment of Naylor, see Forrest C. Pogue, *George C. Marshall: Education of a General, 1880–1939* (New York: Viking Press, 1963), 235, 237–38. From time to time, *The Sentinel* reported on Naylor's subsequent career, noting in its January 26, 1929, issue that the former commanding officer was on duty with the General Staff at Governors Island, New York City.

7. For Newell's career see *The Sentinel*, January 29, March 5, 12, and December 24, 1926; August 19, 1927.
8. Ibid., December 24, 1926. He was originally scheduled to depart in April 1929, but left in January instead. See ibid., June 30, 1928 and January 26, 1929.
9. Ibid., June 30, 1928.
10. Ibid., April 20, 1929; April 4 and September 19, 1931; June 25 and July 2, 1932; Flint, "The United States Army on the Pacific Frontier," 149.
11. These men obtained special privileges: they only stood one tour of guard duty per month, they were given a white pass card and were excused from all fatigue details, and they were authorized to wear a distinctive silver star on the left sleeve of their coats and overcoats. *The Sentinel*, September 20 and October 4, 1930.
12. Ibid., November 15, 1930; February 28, 1931.
13. Finney, *The Old China Hands*, 77. *Customs of the 15th Infantry* was initially published on Taylor's orders by the Peiyang Press of Tientsin-Peiping circa 1930. It was reprinted in facsimile in 1959 by C.E. Dornbusch, a military bibliographer on the staff of the New York Public Library, at the Hope Farm Press in Cornwallville, New York. Edward Sprague Jones, who wrote the introduction to the Dornbusch edition, observed that it "was a handbook of usage. It [was] neither recollection nor reconstruction, and is the only example of its kind about which we know." For a brief consideration of the regiment as a military entity, see Michael Huebner, "The Editor's Column," *Relevance*, vol. 12, no. 1 (winter 2003), 2.
14. This was an unusual departure procedure. Normally, the returning men boarded a train at Tientsin's East Station and were transported to Chinwangtao and there boarded their transport home.
15. *The Sentinel*, February 13, July 2 and December 3, 1932.
16. See ibid., June 4 and July 2, 1932; National Archives: Microcopy 665: Returns from Regular Army Infantry Regiments, June 1821–December 1916, Roll 172: Fifteenth Infantry, January 1910–December 1916; The Reynolds J. Burt Papers, USAMHI. Another source, Don G. Rickey, Jr., *Forty Miles a Day on Beans and Hay* (Norman: University of Oklahoma Press, 1963), contains scattered references to Burt's early years on the frontier with his father, Andrew S. Burt, and family. For a few months in the 1890s he served on his father's staff. Andrew S. Burt was eventually a major general; Reynolds J., a brigadier.
17. *The Sentinel*, April 9, 1926.
18. General Orders No. 2, Headquarters, Fifteenth Infantry, February 27, 1934, in folder "007 — Music and Songs," Entry 5960, RG 395; Flint, "The United States Army on the Pacific Frontier," 150; *The Sentinel*, December 26, 1931, and April 29, 1933. See words to Burt's song in ibid., September 5, 1931. Band leaders were more often than not warrant officers in those years. For U.S. Army bands in the era between the world wars see William Jay Smith, *Army Brat: A Memoir by William Jay Smith* (New York: Penguin Books, 1982). Smith, a noted poet, critic and translator, was the son of Corporal Jay Smith, a bandsman in the U.S. Army for many years.
19. *The Sentinel*, April 29, 1933; Flint, "The United States Army on the Pacific Frontier," 150.
20. See folder "Biographical Information, George A. Lynch," in the George A. Lynch Papers, USAMHI; C.D. Alcott, "A New Major-General," *The Yankee Clipper*, Shanghai, China (March 1937), n.p.; *Time* magazine, December 2, 1940; William O. Odom, *After the Trenches: The Transformation of U.S. Army Doctrine, 1918–1939* (College Station: Texas A&M University Press, 1999), 36.
21. "Address to the 15th U.S. Infantry, May 4, 1937," in folder "Address to the 15th Inf. Rgt., U.S. Troops in China," and address called "Efficiency Reports," delivered to the Conference — Officers School, 15th Infantry, April 16, 1936 in folder "Presentations, Lectures Given by Lynch," both in box "15th Infantry Regiment in China and National Recovery Administration, Chief of Infantry, 1930–1940," the George A. Lynch Papers, USAMHI.
22. "Address to Replacements Arriving on November 1935 Transport," by Colonel George A. Lynch, in folder "Speech to Replacements Arriving at Tientsin, China, No. 1935," box: "15th Infantry Regiment in China and National Recovery Administration, Chief of Infantry 1930–1940," the George A. Lynch Papers, USAMHI.
23. See General Order No. 7, May 14, 1937, folder "General Orders Nos. 2–15, 1937, H.Q.U.S.A.T.C., Tientsin, China," entry 5963, General Orders, 1914–29 and 1936–38, in RG 395.
24. *The Sentinel*, April 20, 1923; August 14 and September 4, 1925 (misdated as August 4, 1925); May 13, 1926.

25. Ibid., May 13, 1926; August 19, 1927.
26. Ibid., August 19 and November 25, 1927; Finney, *The Old China Hands,* 65.
27. Schmidt, *Maverick Marine,* 190–91; Tuchman, *Stilwell,* 147–48.
28. *The Sentinel,* November 4, 1927.
29. Ibid., December 16, 1927. See also ibid., March 16, 1928, for article and cover cartoon of a "Five Mile Hike," or the "15th Infantry Derby," as one wag of Company K called it. See also cartoon on cover of the April 8, 1927, issue of *The Sentinel* of "The Foot Hussar."
30. Finney, *The Old China Hands,* 76. He appropriately titled his chapter devoted to the march "The Foot Cavalry." See ibid., 57–76. Castner retired from the Army in 1933 and died in 1938. At the time of the 25 mile hike, he was 60 years old. Finney wanted to know "how could a man of his age walk the derrieres off 899 men all younger than he was?" The answer: hiking was his hobby. Apparently earlier in his life, Castner had hiked from Alaska to Seattle, and "conceivably, was the only white man ever to have done so." Finney also observed that "in Tientsin on Sunday mornings the officers and ladies of the regiment customarily would take a genteel horseback ride at the Race Course. Castner would be there, too, but he wouldn't be riding. He would be hiking, pacing, pacing, pacing that bulk of his around the track, toning his leg muscles and timing himself." Ibid., 75. Also for details of the hike, though with little criticism of Castner, see various features in *The Sentinel,* November 10, 17, and 24, 1928.
31. See *The Sentinel,* September 29, 1928, for details of Castner's Special Memorandum on the subject of athletics, dated September 26, 1928.
32. Ibid., February 2, 1929.
33. See discussion in Odom, *After the Trenches,* 140–42.

Chapter V

1. *The Sentinel,* July 7, 1922.
2. The William H. Arnold Papers, US-AMHI. Arnold, who served in the regiment in the 1930s as a first lieutenant under Colonel Burt, asserted, "I don't know of a single officer who served at the time I was with the 15th Infantry that didn't become General."
3. The higher quality of personnel sent out to the 15th was in part the result of the policy adopted by the adjutant general by the late 1920s that only the best available would be transferred to China. See discussion in *The Sentinel,* December 7, 1929.
4. He formally took command on September 8, 1924. For Marshall see Bland, *The Papers of George Catlett Marshall,* vol. I; Forrest C. Pogue, *George C. Marshall: Education of a General, 1880–1939* (New York: Viking Press, 1963).
5. *The Sentinel,* May 6, 1927.
6. There had been regimental ice rinks before Marshall's arrival. For instance, in January 1921, one had been constructed on Race Course Road near the compound. See in ibid., January 7, 1921.
7. Letters, Marshall to Major General John L. Hines, September 21, 1924, and December 23, 1925; to Pershing, January 30, 1925, and August 25, 1926; and to Brigadier General William H. Cocke, superintendent of VMI, December 26, 1926, in Bland, *The Papers of George Catlett Marshall,* vol. I, 266–67, 273–74, 283, 286, and 298–300; Chaplain Luther D. Miller — Marshall Bio, George C. Marshall Research Library Research File, folder "Tientsin, China, 1924–1927," George C. Marshall Library, Lexington, Virginia. The chaplain did recall that Marshall hired a Chinese teacher to spend an extra hour in the afternoon. For more on Marshall's failings as a Chinese linguist, see Captain Frank B. Hayne to Mrs. Anne Dulany Hayne, December 22 and 28, 1925, the Frank Hayne Collection, box 16, folder F-1, George C. Marshall Research Library, Lexington, Virginia; and an article by Caspar Nannes, "A Visit with Chaplain Luther D. Miller," *The Chaplain,* vol. 26, no. 2 (March–April 1969), 11.
8. *The Sentinel,* May 6 and October 14, 1927, with notice that the regiment was deeply saddened by notice of the death of Mrs. G.C. Marshall at Walter Reed Hospital. The regimental commander cabled a message of sympathy and condolence to Colonel Marshall. Letter, Marshall to Pershing, August 25, 1926, Bland, *The Papers of George Catlett Marshall,* vol. I, 293. After Marshall's departure from China, his main pony was raffled off, being won by Sergeant Alexander Dunbar of the Service Company. See in ibid., August 19, 1927.
9. Ibid., September 10, 1926. The Chinese fishermen at the beach at Nan Ta Ssu were noted for their singing, as were Chinese fisherfolk generally.
10. Ibid., May 13, 1927.
11. Major General H.B. Lewis to Forrest C. Pogue, October 10, 1960, George C. Marshall Research Library Research File, folder "Tient-

sin, China, 1924–1927," George C. Marshall Library, Lexington, Virginia. Marshall's poem referred to was entitled "Retaliation," and playfully excoriated Harding's poetic skills. It began:

> Night after night we sit abject,
> Our good wives sit adoring
> While Forrest, Poet Laureat[e],
> Another hit is scoring
> A little fun at our expense,
> With laughter as a recompense.

See also *The Sentinel*, February 18, 1927, for an account of a successful Army dinner dance for officers and ladies of the post held on February 11, 1927, with Marshall in charge.

12. See notes and copy of the program in the Frank Hayne Collection, box 3, folder F-2. There may well be a need for a scholarly study of the role of amateur dramatics in the history of the U.S. Army.

13. *The Sentinel*, April 29 and May 6, 1927.

14. Chaplain Luther D. Miller — Marshall Bio, George C. Marshall Research Library Research File, folder "Tientsin, China, 1924–1927."

15. Charles G. Finney to Forrest C. Pogue, December 22, 1959, George C. Marshall Research Library Research File, folder "Tientsin, China, 1924–1927."

16. For Marshall's departure see features in *The Sentinel*, May 6 and 13, 1927.

17. Letter, Marshall to Pershing, January 30, 1925, in Bland, *The Papers of George Catlett Marshall*, vol. I, 273–74. See also the useful discussion in Odom, *After the Trenches*, 87.

18. *The Sentinel*, May 13, 1927. In 1944, Marshall would be made a five-star general of the Army.

19. Ibid., September 24 and October 8, 1926; January 28, 1927, and the important study by Barbara Tuchman, *Stilwell and the American Experience in China, 1911–1945* (New York: The Macmillan Company, 1971).

20. Stilwell's weight-reduction program was commented on in *The Sentinel*, including a poem, "Ballade of Reduction," whose author lamented that despite all of his and Stilwell's efforts, "I am no thinner than before!" *The Sentinel*, March 4 and May 27, 1927.

21. Ibid., September 9, 1927; January 20 and May 25, October 20 and November 3 and 10, 1928; March 9, 1929. Stilwell had earlier exhibited an example of his humor, for which he was well known in these days. On Benny's birth, he sent a radiogram to the regiment's commanding officer: "One recruit joined 15th Inf. stop no descriptive list stop no clothes stop already kicking stop request assignment to Company L stop Stilwell." The answer read: "Have Private Ben Stilwell, serial number unknown, report Camp Dabney immediately. Plenty of time to complete preliminary and record [firing] in next two days. Company L welcomes live ones. Congratulations to mother and dad." Ibid., July 15, 1927. Stilwell's other son, Joseph Warren Stilwell, Jr., while in China was "adopted" by Company H, before his appointment to West Point. Ibid., February 16, 1929.

22. Paper, "Great Decision," by Brigadier General Frederick M. Harris in the Frederick Harris Collection.

23. See first article in the series complete with sketch map of "The Chinese War Situation," in the November 11, 1927, issue. See also ibid., November 18, 1927.

24. Ibid., January 27, February 3 and 10, 1928.

25. Ibid., April 6 and June 2, 16, and 23, 1928.

26. Ibid., August 18, September 1, 8, and December 22, 1928.

27. Ibid., May 25, 1928, and April 13, 1929. The paper also noted some years later that when Stilwell was once more back in China as the American military attaché at the embassy in Peiping, his son, Lieutenant Joseph W. Stilwell, Jr., recently graduated from the Military Academy, was serving with his father's old outfit, the 15th Infantry. Ibid., October 5, 1935. In 1944, Stilwell would earn four-star rank.

28. Marshall to Brigadier General William H. Cocke, Superintendent of VMI, December 26, 1926, in Bland, *The Papers of George Catlett Marshall*, vol. I, 298–300. *The Sentinel*, in its issue of September 24, 1926, discussed a number of these outstanding members of the Regiment.

29. John N. Hart, *The Making of an Army "Old China Hand": A Memoir of Colonel David D. Barrett* (Berkeley: Center for Chinese Studies, 1985), 1–18.

30. *The Sentinel*, February 18, 1933, and subsequent issues. Barrett also wrote feature articles in the paper further to instruct his students in Chinese culture. See, for example, his article "Chinese Restaurants," in the September 2, 1933, issue.

31. See his series "A Mei Kuo Wu Kuan Takes a Look at Japan" in *The Sentinel*, May 20 and 27, 1933.

32. Barrett's career can be followed in Hart, *The Making of an Army "Old China Hand,"* and in his own memoir of his contacts with

Notes — Chapter V

the Communists: *Dixie Mission: The United States Army Observer Group in Yenan, 1944* (Berkeley: Center for Chinese Studies, 1970). For the travail of many American officials and officers with Chinese ties and experience under fire in the McCarthy era, including Barrett, see E.J. Kahn, Jr., *The China Hands* (New York: Viking, 1975).

33. For Harding see *The Sentinel*, January 28, May 6 and 13, 1927; Leslie Anders, *Gentle Knight: The Life and Times of Major General Edwin Forrest Harding* (Kent, Ohio: Kent State University Press, 1985); and the General Forrest Harding Memorial Museum in Franklin, Ohio. Harding ended his military career as a major general

34. *The Sentinel*, November 19, 1926; and Harding's *Lays of the Mei-Kuo Ying-P'an*, 1–2.

35. *The Sentinel*, May 13, 1927; Harding's *Lays of the Mei-Kuo Ying-P'an*, 21–25. In 1925, Tuttle was in command of Company G — the "Go-Gettem" outfit. See Company G notes in *The Sentinel*, December 25, 1925. Harding's poetry collection was dedicated to "the congenial spirits of the Army Garrison who have been my inspiration, theme and audience."

36. *The Sentinel*, August 19, 1927, a special "Old Man" issue, and ibid., June 24, 1927.

37. Ibid., November 6, 1925. Mrs. Tuttle, an accomplished horsewoman in her own right, also acquitted herself well on this occasion. On the occasion of the Military Tournament and Horse Show, April 21–23, 1927, the mixed pair riding exhibition was won by Tuttle and his wife, while their daughter, Norma May, won second in the children's event. Ibid., April 29, 1927.

38. Ibid., October 16, 1925.

39. Ibid., October 1, 1926; Harding, *Lays of the Mei-Kuo Ying-P'an*, 29–30. The defeated riders were also chided by their wives: "They're off again, those Shanghai birds / But, Honey, you used some awful words."

40. As was common during those days, Major Harding closed the meeting by reciting the "Foot Hussars." *The Sentinel*, February 11, 1927; September 23, 1927. The Tuttles arrived in China January 16, 1924, and departed on the September boat in 1927. Also for Tuttle see the Marlboro ad in ibid., May 21, 1926, in which Captain Tuttle was depicted as apparently the first "Marlboro Man." Tuttle ended his military career as a colonel.

41. *The Sentinel*, December 26, 1924; September 25, 1925; January 8, 1926. See General Orders, No. 1, Headquarters Fifteenth Infantry, January 4, 1926, signed by Marshall as commanding officer, and a lengthy obituary column in ibid., January 9, 1926.

42. *The Sentinel*, February 17, 1928, and General Orders, No. 13, Headquarters, U.S. Army Forces in China, April 24, 1928, in ibid., April 27, 1928. Burrowes had graduated Phi Beta Kappa from Yale in 1914. A veteran of the World War, he was also the author of one of the best of the regiment's histories. Another prominent ivy leaguer in the regiment was Captain Elbridge Colby, commanding officer of Company E and later editor of *The Sentinel*. It was a matter of pride, at least to some in the 15th, that he possessed an A.B., A.M., and Ph.D. from Columbia University. Ibid., October 4, 1930.

43. As reported in ibid., July 6, 1929.

44. Ibid., March 29, 1930; March 21 and June 6, 1931. Wedemeyer only remained on duty in China for just over a year, departing for duty at Corrigidor. For his subsequent controversial career, see Albert Coady Wedemeyer, *Wedemeyer Reports!* (New York: Heny Holt and Company, 1958), 45–48; and Kahn, *The China Hands*. Wedemeyer replaced Stilwell in command of U.S. forces in China in October, 1944. After his retirement, he was promoted to four-star general in 1954 by act of Congress.

45. *The Sentinel*, October 25, 1930; November 14, 1931: March 5, 1932; February 4, 1933. Walker was made a lieutenant general in 1945. He was in command of the U.S. Eighth Army and the South Korean forces in the Korean War until his death in an automobile accident in December 1950. Walker was later honored by the naming of a light U.S. Army tank, the M41A3, as the Walker Bulldog. There is an example on display at the Infantry Museum, Fort Benning, Georgia.

46. *The Sentinel*, July 24, 1925; May 13, 1926. From China, Captain Matthew B. Ridgway was ordered to Ft. Jay, New York. He became commander of UN Troops in Korea in the Korean War, replacing the deceased General Walker; later, as a four-star general, he was the U.S. Army's chief of staff. See his *Memoirs* (New York: Harper and Brothers, 1956), and *The Korean War* (New York: Doubleday and Company, 1967).

47. For Sutherland, see Paul P. Rogers, *The Good Years: MacArthur and Sutherland* (Westport: Praeger, 1990) and *The Bitter Years: MacArthur and Sutherland* (Westport: Praeger, 1991).

48. Letter, Marshall to Cocke, in Bland, *The*

Papers of George Catlett Marshall, vol. I, 299; *The Sentinel*, May 11 and 18, 1923.
49. Vogel, *Soldiers of the Old Army*, 8.
50. *The Sentinel*, May 6, 1927.
51. Finney, *The Old China Hands*, 20–21.
52. *The Sentinel*, January 16 and 30, 1925; ibid., May 6, 1927. For the paper's coverage see, for example, ibid., January 10, 1931, which gives an account of the retirement review for Master Sergeant Samuel Stewart, who had been in the Army for 30 years.
53. *The Sentinel*, August 25, 1928. The October 20, 1928 *Sentinel* recorded that Reeves had made private first class; the issue of May 11, 1929, noted that he was promoted to corporal and named the regiment's "Outstanding Man of the Week." See also ibid., October 26, 1929, and June 27, 1931, for another odyssey, that of Private Leonard X. Shedlebower of Company I, who returned to the 15th seeking shelter from the Depression in America. Shedlebower reported that conditions were so bad at home that "there is hardly any such thing as a desertion any more for men are walking the streets [with everyone] out of work." The Depression was also the cause for numerous requests for extensions of service terms in China, and the lists of these and discussions about them were featured in the paper throughout the 1930s until the regiment departed China.
54. See Charles Grandison Finney, *Magician Out of Manchuria*, in *The Unholy City* (New York: Pyramid Books, 1968), 156, and *passim*; *The Sentinel*, October 12, 1929; Letters, Finney to General Frederick Mixon Harris, February 13 and September 29, 1965, in Folder 1/4, the Frederick Harris Collection.
55. See *The Sentinel*, December 12, 1924; March 13 [sic, 20], 27; April 3, 10, 17; May 1, 22, 29; June 26 and July 24, 1925.
56. Ibid., January 11 and October 18, 1930; June 20, 1931.
57. See for example ibid., March 5, 1932; April 1, 1933.

Chapter VI

1. *The Sentinel*, June 24, 1927.
2. Bantam paperback edition (New York, 1972), 123.
3. *The Sentinel*, April 3 and 10, 1925; October 17, 1931.
4. Ibid., January 14, 1921; December 6, 1930.
5. Ibid., March 28, 1924; June 25, 1926; April 13, 1928.

6. The snapshot books were published in Tientsin by the Peiyang Press. There is a copy of the 39-page *Snapshots of China*, no. 1 in the Frederick Harris Collection, folder 1/15, George C. Marshall Library, Lexington, Virginia. See also *The Sentinel*, February 9, 1929.
7. *The Sentinel*, February 23, 1929.
8. Ibid., April 20, 1928; July 6, 1929; April 16, 1932.
9. Ibid., March 22, 1930; October 5, 1935. Following the 15th's return to Fort Lewis, Washington, in 1938, the paper reappeared as the *Fort Lewis Sentinel*.
10. Ibid., November 18, 1921; January 11, 1924; October 16, 1925; December 17, 1926.
11. Ibid., March 13, September 25 and November 6, 1925; August 13 and December 3, 1926.
12. Ibid., May 20, 1921.
13. Ibid., July 21, 1922.
14. Ibid., January 20, 1922.
15. Ibid., March 4, September 9 and 16, 1921; January 20, February 17, April 21 and July 21, 1922; August 1, 1924.
16. Ibid., February 20, 1932.
17. Ibid., October 20, 1928.
18. Ibid., April 29, 1921; July 16, 1926.
19. But the editor grew tired of these, once declaring that "he'll commit mayhem and manslaughter on the first man who sends in again ... 'The Girl with the Blue Velvet Band.'" *The Sentinel*, July 16, 1926.
20. Ibid., April 23, 1926; May 18, 1928.
21. Ibid., Feb. 6, 1925; May 16 and December 19, 1931.
22. See issue of December 9, 1933, for example. Relevant documents on the limitations of advertising are in folder "461: *The Sentinel*," in entry 5960, RG 395. A list of advertisers that had to be dropped from *The Sentinel* was printed in the March 7, 1931, issue.
23. *The Sentinel*, June 30 and July 21, 1922. The June 16 issue was the first to cease listing personnel associated with the paper. The Philippine Department, following orders from Washington, instructed *The Sentinel*'s editor to forward copies of the paper "as soon as issued" through Manila for transmission to the Joint Committee on Printing, via the U.S. Quartermaster Corps and also to the adjutant general of the Army for examination as to compliance. See documents in folder "461 *The Sentinel*," in entry 5960, RG 395.
24. *The Sentinel*, May 2, 1931.
25. Ibid., March 15 and September 13, 1930.
26. Ibid., January 1 and March 19, 1926; January 23, 1932.

27. Ibid., September 19 and October 3, 1924.
28. Ibid., February 4 and 18, 1921.
29. Ibid., April 18, 1931.
30. Ibid., April 6, 1923, and other issues.
31. Ibid., February 20 and March 6, 1925; October 28, 1933. See Herbert O. Yardley, *The American Black Chamber* (Indianapolis, Indiana: Bobbs-Merrill, 1931). There is a discussion in *The Sentinel*, April 22, 1933.
32. *The Sentinel*, February 2 and March 2, 1923; August 8, 15, 22, 29; September 5 and 26, 1924.
33. Ibid., May 9, 1924.
34. There are good examples in ibid., August 24, 1923, and June 6, 1924.
35. Ibid., March 4, 1921; May 9, 1924.
36. Ibid., March 23, May 11, 1928; January 17, 1931. Thomason was well known for his book *Fix Bayonets* (New York: Charles Scribner's Sons, 1926), which, recounting incidents and Marine Corps operations in the World War, gained him some literary fame.
37. *The Sentinel*, August 25, 1928.
38. Ibid., January 1 and 15; February 19 and 26, 1926.
39. Ibid., August 28, 1925; October 20 and November 3, 1928; June 1, 1929; March 1, 1930.
40. Ibid., August 10, 1923.
41. Ibid., September 9, 1921.

Chapter VII

1. *The Sentinel*, March 11, 1921.
2. Ibid., February 10, 1922.
3. Flint, "The United States Army on the Pacific Frontier," 149; folder "Index and Post Regulations and G.O. 1-1937 HQ.U.S.A.T.C.— Tientsin, China," in entry 5963, RG 395; Article, "Lure of the East," in a regular column, "Things Chinese," *The Sentinel*, July 26, 1930; Ray et. al., "The United Sates 15th Infantry Regiment, 1915"; Tolley, *Yangtze Patrol*, 213.
4. *The Sentinel*, July 15, 1933.
5. The James E. Moore Papers, USAMHI. There were minor changes in the routine from time to time, some seasonal. See notice in *The Sentinel*, April 30, 1932. It did matter, though, that the prescribed formations be attended in a timely manner. New men were warned to "remember ... [that] reveille and retreat are important formations in the Regular Army. Better get up bright and early or Old Man Fatigue will catch you." See *The Sentinel*, October 22, 1926.
6. *The Sentinel*, December 24, 1932.
7. Ibid., August 22, 1924. On the subject of purchased discharges, see Vogel, *Soldiers of the Old Army*, 7.
8. *The Sentinel*, April 22, 1921; January 27, 1922; October 5, 1923.
9. Ibid., April 12 and 19, 1930.
10. Anonymous poem in ibid., July 15, 1921.
11. Ibid., October 6, 1928. There is a detailed discussion of guard duty at Tientsin in ibid., January 17, 1931, and a schematic plan of the compound with guard posts delineated in folder "353.5—Guard Duty," in entry 5960, RG 395. The men were frequently reminded that, at least in China, guard duty was officially recognized as the "most important duty of the soldier."
12. *The Sentinel*, January 27, 1922; March 9 and August 17, 1923; March 14, 1924; June 18, 1932.
13. Ibid., January 7, 1921; April 6 and May 11, 1923. One source of those "bugs" were melons, and the men were warned not to eat them as some deaths were recorded from failure to heed such exhortations. Melons were bad because of the conditions under which they are grown and "methods used in forcing them to ripen early," i.e., by injecting water—from impure sources—into them. The men could eat melons on their own mess tables "in comfort," however. Raw vegetables were also suspect and instructions were issued on how they might be prepared: radishes were to be thoroughly washed in clean water, then scalded and their skins removed; several outside layers of the skin of onions were to be removed and boiling water was to be poured over them. The eating of lettuce and water cress in a raw state was prohibited. See ibid., July 18 and August 22, 1931. On one occasion when Company K was in quarantine to relieve the monotony its commanding officer took his men out for a picnic and an afternoon of sports. Ibid., May 29, 1925.
14. Ibid., March 28 and April 4, 1924.
15. Ibid., January 21, 1921; July 28, 1922; and article, "An Observer Observes," by "Proff. Bojack," January 12, 1923, reprinted from *Shanghai Sports*.
16. *The Sentinel*, April 21, 1922, recorded that several new arrivals in China had recently been in German service. The American Forces in Germany (AFG) were withdrawn from the Rhine in 1923.
17. Ibid., March 28, 1924; October 1, 1926; April 29 and May 13, 1927; November 8, 1930; and folder "250.1: Narcotics, use of—," entry 5960, RG 395. This lists a few men involved in drug abuse and the disposition of their cases.

18. *The Sentinel* did not explain in its pages what the cryptic term "rate" meant, because the paper was read by families in the States as well as in China. Of course, there was little mystery among the Regiment's personnel.

19. Captain William Howard Arnold—later a lieutenant general—who was at Tientsin in the mid-1930s, later recalled that nearly all of the soldiers—perhaps 80 percent—"were all shacked up." But, "as long as they're shacked up, it's perfectly safe. What we were looking for were the ones who weren't shacked up." Therein lay the dangers. The William H. Arnold Papers, USAMHI. On Chinese concubinage, see the "Things Chinese" column in *The Sentinel*, October 11, 1930. For Lynch's comments see his "Address to Replacements Arriving on November 1935 Transport," in folder "Speech to Replacements Arriving at Tientsin, China, No. 1935," the George A. Lynch Papers, USAMHI.

20. See documents in folder "250.1: Houses of Prostitution," in entry 5960, RG 395.

21. *The Sentinel*, May 1, 1925. There also existed a pamphlet, the "Mukloo Gazette," describing this infamous street. It ran through several editions and obtained a wide circulation among the American troops. Its details were not revealed in the pages of the paper. See also poem, "The Mukloo Girl," in *The Sentinel*, October 13, 1922.

22. Ibid., January 28, 1927; June 26, 1925.

23. Ibid., May 11, 1928.

24. Ibid., June 3, 1927.

25. Memorandum from Headquarters, Fifteenth Infantry, October 4, 1924, to commanding officers of Companies G, K, and M. Ibid., October 10, 1924; August 20, 1926.

26. These matters were routinely discussed in annual reports. See examples in folder "Countries—American Forces in China, 123.61 to 333.3," in entry AGO 1917–25, RG 407.

27. See related documents in folder "Countries: American Forces in China, 350.03 to 726.1," entry AGO 1917–25, RG 407. See also the voluminous files in the regiment's records on VD, many in a series of folders "726.1," entry 5960, RG 395.

28. See documents pertaining to Sergeant Steely in folder "201.23—Complaints," and other relevant documents on VD in series of folders "721.5 to 726.1," entry 5960, RG 395.

29. *The Sentinel*, January 31, February 7, March 7, and April 4 and 11, 1931.

30. "The soldier owes it to himself, to his Commanding Officer and to his government, to KEEP FIT," *The Sentinel* declared. If he does not, "he has no right to call himself a 'soldier,' for a man is a soldier only when he is 'fit to fight.'" See cover cartoon of "Miss Chinwangtao" in ibid., July 1, 1927, and accounts in ibid., May 2 and 30, July 18, September 19 and November 21, 1931.

31. In addition, Arnold remembered, rather disgustedly, that "We used to have to give the [physical] inspection ourselves. I mean even the officers—line them up and give them a goddamn short arm inspection." The William H. Arnold Papers, USAMHI.

32. "Address to Replacements Arriving on November 1935 Transport," by Colonel George A. Lynch, in folder "Speech to Replacements Arriving at Tientsin, China, No. 1935," the George A. Lynch Papers, USAMHI.

33. *The Sentinel* often published running accounts of punishment averages company by company. *The Sentinel*, February 7, 1931. Not only were such publicity methods hoped to be salutary in keeping down offenses, competition was also encouraged for the Dinsmore Trophy, awarded to companies with the lowest incidence of disciplinary problems at any given time. Ibid., February 28, 1931. For a discussion of legal procedures in the Army in these years see Major William Henry Waldron, *The Infantry Soldier's Handbook*, (1917; reprint, New York: Lyons Press, 2000), 190–212.

34. See Vogel, *Soldiers of the Old Army*, 7–8; *The Sentinel*, April 20, 1928.

35. *The Sentinel*, September 9 and 30, 1921; May 19 and June 2, 1922; and October 12, 1923; Memorandum 26, China Expedition Headquarters, Tientsin, September 1, 1921.

36. *The Sentinel*, September 30, 1921.

37. Ibid., December 14, 1923; January 4 and 18, 1924. Because liquor was freely available in China, the repeal of Prohibition by act of Congress on March 22, 1933, was not a momentous event there, though sale of alcoholic beverages in post exchanges and officers clubs was then authorized on posts throughout the military establishment. Folder "250.1—Intoxicants and Liquor use and sale of in Army," entry 5960, RG 395.

38. *The Sentinel*, October 19, 1929.

39. Flint, "The United States Army on the Pacific Frontier," 149.

40. Letter, Marshall to John C. Hughes, July 18, 1925, in Bland, *The Papers of George Catlett Marshall*, 281; The James E. Moore Papers, USAMHI.

41. The James E. Moore Papers, USAMHI.

42. The Tientsin clubs are noted in "Conditions of Service in China," 173.

43. *The Sentinel*, April 9, 1926; February 11, 1927. There is a discussion of "wonks" in F.A. Sutton, *One-Arm Sutton* (New York: Viking Press, 1933), 238.

44. *The Sentinel*, April 1, 1921; August 11, 1922; July 11, 1924; and folder "400.134 — Periodicals, Subscriptions to," entry 5960, RG 395.

45. See *The Sentinel*, December 16 and 30, 1921; October 20 and 27, 1922; October 31, 1924; January 30 and July 17, 1925, for typical announcements of its activities. See in Richard C. Lancaster, *Serving the U.S. Armed Forces, 1861–1986* (Schaumburg, Illinois: Armed Services YMCA of the USA, 1987), 108.

46. *The Sentinel*, September 25, 1925.

47. Ibid., April 4, 1931.

48. Ibid., March 4, 1921; March 24, 1922; January 18, 1924; January 2, 1925. The Red Cross was also actively engaged in famine and flood relief in China in these years. See article by Major M.F. Waltz, of the 15th Infantry, in ibid., March 4, 1921, describing these activities in northern China. The Red Cross also saw to it that men of the regiment maintained ties with interested people and chapters in the United States from which the troops received Red Cross Christmas kits and other gifts.

49. The Century was inaugurated on Monday evening, October 31, 1927. Ibid., November 4, 1927. For discussions of other activities of the lodge, see ibid., February 10 and 24, 1928; March 16, 1929.

50. Ibid., March 4, 1927; April 2, 1932; October 14, 1933.

51. Ibid., March 4, April 1, October 21, and November 18, 1921; December 28, 1923. Fischer was transferred to Camp Meade, Maryland in December, 1923.

52. Ibid., October 23, 1925. See also ibid., April 22, 1927 for article by H.C. Connette of the *North China Star*, which recounted the history of the chapel's construction and its furnishing by Miller's efforts.

53. *The Sentinel*, December 17, 1926; May 4, 1928.

54. On Miller's career, see Caspar Nannes, "A Visit with Chaplain Luther D. Miller," *The Chaplain*, vol. 26, no. 2 (March–April 1969), 9–12. There is additional information in the document "Chaplain Luther D. Miller — Marshall Bio," George C. Marshall Research Library Research File, folder "Tientsin, China, 1924–1927."

55. Cover photo of Fisher in *The Sentinel*, July 9, 1932. See also ibid., February 4, 1933. Fisher's Catholic parishioners were ministered to by visiting speakers.

56. There are accounts of Cohee's career in ibid., May 3, October 11 and 18, 1930. Several of the chaplains so engaged availed themselves of the expertise of the "Y" secretary serving the Peking Legation Guard, A.C. Ellis, widely recognized for his knowledge of Peking and the Great Wall. He was also the author of a popular, widely-circulated book, "Guide to Peking." Ibid., January 17 and February 28, 1931.

57. Ibid., July 29, 1921.

58. Ibid., November 25, 1926.

59. Ibid., November 30, 1923.

60. Ibid., July 22 and 29, 1921. Lyndale and his buddies also visited Shankaikwan, Peking and other sites.

61. Ibid., October 9, 1925.

62. Ibid., November 13, 1925. See a memorandum on the camp issued by Headquarters, American Barracks, in ibid., October 8, 1926.

63. Ibid., October 14, 1933.

64. Ibid., March 5, 1926; June 25 and July 2, 1932. A soldier of Company G — or "Galloping G" as it was sometimes called — R.A. "Bud" Finney, making his way home to California on the *Thomas* in January 1923, graphically described in detail his voyage home in a letter back to *The Sentinel*. See in ibid., May 18, 1923. These transports normally published a shipboard paper for the entertainment of the troops which often included interesting details of the voyage. See issues of *The Sentinel* for March 15 and 22, 1930, for discussions of *The Breeze*, shipboard paper of the *Grant*.

65. *The Sentinel* regularly published ship schedules. See also ibid., April 28 and November 3, 1922; May 4, 1928. George Hopkins, one of the ship's bath stewards, proudly stated that he was on all of the voyages made by the *Thomas*. The *Thomas* was sold to the American Iron and Metal Company of San Francisco and broken up. See accounts in ibid., May 11, 1928 and June 8, 1929.

66. Ibid., August 29, 1931. See article in June 18, 1932 issue by Hal C. Head, an Army chaplain recounting the *Republic*'s maiden voyage.

67. Ibid., July 22, 1921. Money changers were also present to give "rates regulated by Compound authorities." Ibid., April 20, 1929; June 27, 1931; March 5, 1932.

68. See also the anonymous poem, "The Transport in the Harbor," in ibid., January 21, 1921. Labeled "A Parody on the Original," it recalls the poem. "Troopin'" by Kipling. Beinke's poem is in ibid., May 1, 1925.

69. Poem: "Farewell," by "Beejo," ibid., January 14, 1927.

70. Ibid., March 15, 1930.
71. Anonymous "Ode to the Rambler," from "With the Poets" page in ibid., September 26, 1924.
72. Ibid., May 13, 1927.
73. See numerous photographs of one such event in ibid., May 13, 1927. Another soldier who had earlier returned to the States noted along the same lines that "the Army is filled with friendships formed by the Great brotherhood of Soldiery." Specifically, he missed the 15th, asserting that "No other outfit in Service has the same general high type of soldiers, so one must feel a bit sad at leaving,..." and he hoped eventually to return to China. See in ibid., May 24, 1930, letter to the editor from Corporal William A. Lomasney, then with Company E, First Tank Regiment, at Ft. Benning, Georgia. Lomasney had been a *Sentinel* correspondent for "H" Company when he was in China.
74. Ibid., April 23, 1926; September 29, 1928.
75. Ibid., May 6, 1927, and September 9, 1933.
76. *The Sentinel* often published ads for local auto establishments. See also "Conditions of Service in China," 173.
77. Nonetheless, the Sunday night offerings perhaps left something to be desired, as one soldier-poet suggested in his "Lines Sung on Sunday Night": "Oh, Sergeant, my Mess Sergeant / My heart is cold and stony / I know, no matter how you slice / That stuff, it's still boloney." *The Sentinel*, January 21, 1921; October 9, 1925; and November 15, 1930. See also the column "K Keeps Kool," in *The Sentinel*, March 6 and July 3, 1925, for accounts of that company's excellent mess hall and listings of typical menus.
78. Ibid., July 9, 1926.
79. Ibid., January 1, 1926; January 3, 1931.
80. The areas judged, among other things, included the maintenance of the lowest venereal ratio, the least number of company punishments, the fewest convictions by courts-martial, the cleanest barracks and most orderly arrangement of clothing and equipment, and the best appearance at drill, on guard, at roll calls and before the public. In later years, this cup was superseded by other awards. See ibid., December 16, 1921, for the details of one such presentation. Any company winning the cup three times retained it permanently.
81. Details are in *Customs of the 15th Infantry*, 11. See also *The Sentinel*, April 18, 1924 and November 8, 1930.

82. *The Sentinel*, October 5, 1923; October 23 and December 11, 1925; and February 4, 1927. There is an example of both the regular banner and the miniature banner in folder "424 — Banners ("Banner Blue")," entry 5960, RG 395. The banners were woven of a deep blue silk with a dragon in gold and red thread embroidered thereon. The regular banner was about a yard square; the miniature about a foot square. Along the same lines, another cup award recognized units for "having [the] best cared for trees and flowers planted around the barracks."
83. *The Sentinel*, June 3, 1921.
84. Ibid., June 17, 1921.
85. Ibid., June 10 and July 1, 1921.
86. Ibid., September 23 and 30, 1921; February 3, 1922. Even a decade later, in 1931, the pass system, based on red, white and blue cards denoting various levels of privilege and trust, was still being tinkered with. Ibid., November 7, 1931.
87. Ibid., July 21, 1922; October 19, 1923.
88. See humorous article "Meet Readem and Weep," a history of dicing in ibid., May 18, 1923, and others on gambling in ibid., April 22, 1921, and February 13, 1925. See also ibid., December 7, 1923, for an article borrowed from the *5th Corps News*.
89. *The Sentinel*, February 8, 1930, regarding Standing Orders No. 615-500 dated January 30, 1930. In an interesting commentary on the regiment's level of literacy — and imagination — it was suggested that *The Sentinel* publish from time to time a sample missive which was to be "used as a possible model for soldiers who find it hard to compose a suitable monthly letter." See in ibid., November 12, 1932.
90. See poem "A Warning," in ibid., March 14, 1924, which explained. Rickshawmen were often those who extended "jawbone" to the troops, in one instance one holding a soldier's chit until he returned to China for a second tour of duty. The trooper only then paid up, justifying the coolie's patience. Ibid., November 23, 1929; March 14, 1924.
91. Folder "242.4 — Indebtedness of Enlisted men," entry 5960, RG 395.

Chapter VIII

1. *The Sentinel*, April 25, 1924.
2. Ibid., July 23, 1926.
3. Ibid., December 2, 1927.
4. See discussion of Field Service Regulations 1923 and other doctrinal developments in Odom, *After the Trenches*, especially 43–46,

and *passim*. For details of range firing, instruction and training, and lists of those qualifying at certain times, see numerous folders "353.1 to 353.5," entry 5960, RG 395. See also *The Sentinel*, December 26, 1924.

5. See, for instance, *The Sentinel*, July 9, 1932, which printed a copy of Training Order No. 8, July 6, 1932, noting that shooting pay for 52 experts and 88 sharpshooters and first class machine gunners was authorized for that shooting season, with no pay for pistol shooters.

6. Ibid., June 16, 1922; September 26, 1924; June 11 and 18, 1926.

7. Ibid., June 3, 1927. See also Vogel, *Soldiers of the Old Army*, 40, for discussion of the bolo.

8. *The Sentinel*, June 19, 1925; June 21, 1930.

9. Ibid., August 31, 1929. There was no extra firing pay for qualifying on the B.A.R., however.

10. Anonymous, poem: "A Richochet's Relapse," *The Sentinel*, September 1, 1928.

11. Passailaigue's article was originally published in *The Bullet*, a troop paper of the 25th Infantry; this was reprinted in *The Sentinel*, April 20, 1923; March 30, 1928; July 19, 1930.

12. As reprinted in *The Sentinel*, April 20, 1923.

13. The 15th Infantry's team fired a score of 2,964, the Marines 2,950. As of early March 1924, the Legation Guard numbered 347 men and 17 officers, the 15th almost three times that number. See accounts in ibid., August 3 and 24, 1923; March 28 and May 30, 1924.

14. Ibid., May 27, 1921; March 21, 1924. See also the spoof of a certain "Training Guide No. 13013," the subject of which was "Manual of the Riding Crop for Regimental Staffs."

15. Ibid., May 24, 1930; June 6, 1931.

16. Ibid., August 11 and 18, September 1, and October 20, 1928.

17. A small target range was also maintained at Tangshan through the courtesy of the Kailan Mining Administration and the Chee Hsin Cement Company, which permitted the use of the land for this purpose. See Annual Report, Headquarters, United States Army Forces in China to The Adjutant General, Tientsin, China, August 24, 1925 in folder "Countries—American Forces in China, 123.61 to 333.3," entry AGO 1917–25, RG 407.

18. *The Sentinel*, July 8 and 22, August 19 and 26, and September 9, 1921; June 30, 1922; August 20, 1932.

19. Bland, *The Papers of George Catlett Marshall*, vol. I, 267; Annual Report, Headquarters, American Forces in China, Tientsin, China, August 24, 1923, to the Adjutant General, folder "Countries—American Forces in China, 123.61 to 333.3," entry AGO 1917–25, RG 407; *The Sentinel*, June 15, 1923; August 6, 1926. Donkeys were used to transport men from the camp to Chinwangtao. The marines also maintained a firing range nearby.

20. *The Sentinel*, July 6 and August 3, 1923.

21. "Conditions of Service in China," 169. Certainly, the soldiers who had to construct and maintain the rest camp were sometimes less than enthusiastic about it. Ordered to clean up the beach to be used by the officers and their dependents, one soldier responded: "Poor girls we sure do feel sorry for your little feet. You should bind them like the Chinese do. Make your feet smaller and beyond a doubt you will sure miss all the burrs on the beach." Company L's column, *The Sentinel*, August 3, 1923. There was more bitching and grousing in the "Indiscreet Letters from Nicky Erdap to Nanty Zoo" (Nan Ta Ssu), in ibid., July 6, 1923.

22. Ibid., August 3, 1923.

23. Ibid., August 17, 1923. For a detailed, well-written feature article on a typical excursion, see ibid., August 5, 1927. These trips were often guided by the chaplain. Shankaikwan was an elaborately fortified gate in the Great Wall build in the Ming dynasty (1368–1644). It was famous for the inscription *Tianxia diyi guan*, or "First Barrier Under Heaven." There, the east end of the wall meets the sea at the "Old Dragon's Head" (*laolongtou*), "a picturesque group of gates, pavilions, and temples that descend right down to the water; to the west the wall meets the mountains, along whose ridges it continues." See discussion in Waldron, *From War to Nationalism*, 92, 103.

24. *The Sentinel*, August 13, and October 15, 1926.

25. Ibid., June 18, July 16, August 13 and 27, 1926. Jim Crow and Company was a Tientsin firm, listed as U.S. Army Contractors for fresh beef and native forage. Ralph S. Freeman, who also owned the Stag Bar of Tientsin, as well as the temporary beer palace in Nan Ta Ssu, was a former member of "H" Company. His remaining in Tientsin after his discharge to go into business catering to his old regiment was typical of several former 15th troopers.

26. Ibid., August 20, 1926; August 1, 1931.

27. Ibid., August 6 and 13, 1926.

28. Ibid., August 20, 1926; August 16, 1930.

29. See articles "Fishermen" and "Fisherfolk" in ibid., June 7 and September 13, 1930.
30. Ibid., August 6 and September 17, 1926; August 30, 1930; July 25 and August 29, 1931; folder "353.141—Anti-Aircraft Firing," entry 5960, RG 395.
31. Each member was authorized to wear a distinctive sleeve patch following year. It became the custom in the 15th for the winning squad to receive a silver cup bought by regimental funds, and for individual members to receive cash prizes. See *The Sentinel*, October 21, 1927, for cover photo of the winning squad for that year: "This is an intelligent looking group of men," one commentator playfully acknowledged. "They all have high foreheads and other superior anthropological qualities." *The Sentinel* devoted considerable space to this annual selection process.
32. Ibid., June 13, 20, and 27 and July 11, 1924. The march was well sustained, and despite the fact that the only water to be had ran in the ditches beside the road, after four days of these conditions the entire company arrived in Tientsin without the loss of a single man from sickness or fatigue. The march revealed that for service in China, the smaller Chinese-bred mules were superior to the larger traditional Army mules brought in from the United States.
33. Ibid., September 17, 1926.
34. Ibid., July 1, August 12, September 9, October 21, 1927; March 30, 1928; May 30, 1931; August 20, 1932. The camp was steadily improved. A hospital was constructed as was a road along the beach lined by newly planted trees. New quarters and facilities were built, including athletic fields, and by the early 1930s, the camp was a permanent installation.
35. Ibid., February 17 and April 27, 1928; August 20, 1932; folder "354.9—Outpost Detachments—Camp Borrowes," entry 5960, RG 395. In March of 1938, following the withdrawal of the 15th from China, Camp Borrowes was taken over by the marines and renamed "Camp Holcomb," in honor of Major General Thomas Holcomb, the Marine Corps commandant at the time. See Biggs, *The United States Marines in North China*, 182.
36. *The Sentinel*, December 2, 1927; October 6, 1928.
37. Ibid., October 26, 1923. The paper kept close tabs on the scores of each company, categorizing all who participated as either expert or disqualified. See for example ibid., October 24 and 31, 1931. Official U.S. Army doctrine as set forth in the *Field Service Regulations* of 1923 stated categorically that the infantry's "principal offensive weapon is the rifle and bayonet." Interestingly, in their own doctrine, the Japanese shared with the Americans the emphasis on the rifle and bayonet—as well as the primacy of people in battle. See discussions in Odom, *After the Trenches*, 43–46, 186–89. First Lieutenant William H. Arnold, with the 15th in the mid-1930s, recalled that the Japanese were "extremely good" with the bayonet and he once arranged a demonstration with some of their troops at the American compound. See the William H. Arnold Papers, USAMHI.
38. *The Sentinel*, November 26, 1932.
39. Flint, "The United States Army on the Pacific Frontier," 150. See also the Charles L. Bolte Papers, USAMHI, and *The Sentinel*, August 12, 1927.
40. *The Sentinel*, September 16, 1921; October 19 and 26, 1923.
41. Ibid., September 16, 1921.
42. Ibid., November 20, 1925. A copy of the map was published in ibid., April 23, 1926. The men were urged to mount the maps for posting and study.
43. Ibid., May 7, 1926.
44. Ibid., March 18, 1927.
45. Ibid., November 6, 1925; October 31, 1931.
46. Ibid., November 15, 1930. By late 1931, during Colonel Taylor's regime, the Regiment competed for some 29 trophies in sports, shooting, and in other areas. See listing of these in ibid., November 21, 1931.
47. See for example ibid., May 27, 1921.
48. See for example ibid., January 26, 1929; November 22, 1930; January 23, 1932; and folders "350.05 to 352.31," containing data pertaining to such training, garrison schools and related matters in entry 5960, RG 395. NCOs of the command were also welcomed to many of these presentations.
49. Examples with names of men involved and their final scores are available in *The Sentinel*, January 24, 1931, and other information in folders "352.9 to 353.1," in entry 5960, RG 395.
50. His articles had not been published in English until appearing in *The Sentinel*. These began in the February 11, 1933 issue. For the U.S. Army's interest in foreign armies in this period, especially regarding doctrine, see Odom, *After the Trenches*, 168–98.
51. *The Sentinel*, February 5 and 19, 1926. The tournament was held from February 8 through 13.

52. See the relevant documents and a description of the course in ibid., March 11 and 18, 1927.
53. See various memoranda and other information in ibid., March 26 and April 2, 1926. All the events were governed by the Spalding's Official Track Guide.
54. See Training Memorandum No. 6, Headquarters, American Barracks, Tientsin, China, April 30, 1926, and other documents in ibid., May 13, 1926. There were also on occasion interesting Inter-Allied Rifle Shoots at Tientsin, as the one on May 11, 1926, held on the Japanese target range. Teams from the Japanese, British, French and American garrisons fired. See accounts in ibid., May 21, 1926.
55. Ibid., May 11 and 18, 1923.
56. Vogel, *Soldiers of the Old Army*, 116.

Chapter IX

1. *The Sentinel*, July 8, 1933.
2. Ibid., April 29, 1927.
3. Ibid., February 4, 1921; January 21 and 28, 1927; and April 29, 1927, for this Service Company column bon mot: "First Goof, what is the thirteenth general order? Second Ditto. BEAT THE MARINES." (There were 12 standing general orders that guards had to memorize.)
4. See article on athletics in the Army during the World War by Steven W. Pope, "An Army of Athletes: Playing Fields, Battlefields, and the American Military Sporting Experience, 1890–1920," in *The Journal of Military History*, vol. 59, no. 2 (July 1995), 435–56.
5. See AG 353.8 (10-7-24) Misc. M-C, October 18, 1924, by order of the secretary of war, reprinted in *The Sentinel*, December 5, 1924.
6. "Address to Replacements Arriving on November 1935 Transport," by Colonel George A. Lynch, in folder "Speech to Replacements Arriving at Tientsin, China, No. 1935," The George A. Lynch Papers, USAMHI.
7. *The Sentinel*, December 21, 1923; July 9 and December 3 and 10, 1926.
8. Ibid., March 14 and August 15, 1924.
9. Ibid., June 12, 1925; May 28, 1926; May 27, 1927; August 4, 1931.
10. Ibid., December 16, 1921; July 14, 1922. For the regiment's sports and entertainment see folders "353.5 to 354.7," entry 5960, RG 395.
11. For typical meets, see *The Sentinel*, April 15, 1921, and May 22, 1925.
12. Ibid., August 29, 1924.
13. Ibid., October 14, 1921; September 25, 1925.
14. Ibid., March 21 and 28, 1924.
15. Ibid., January 21, 1921; February 20, 1925.
16. Ibid., June 30, 1922.
17. Ibid., February 27, 1932. *The Sentinel* once suggested a "Sportsman's Code" valid for daily living as well as for sports, which stated in part: "Thou shalt not quit," "Thou shalt not be a rotten loser," and "Thou shalt not gloat over winning." Ibid., March 19, 1932.
18. Ibid., November 28, 1924; Feb. 6, 1925.
19. The categories stipulated were 100 yard dash, broad jump, high jump, shot put, leaning rest, grenade throw, pullups and wall scale. Ibid., August 24 and November 23, 1923; April 18 and 25, May 16, October 24 and November 7, 1924; April 10, 1925. It should be noted that education was rarely emphasized by the 15th's E. and R. officers.
20. Ibid., April 13, 1923; April 11, 1924.
21. Ibid., October 24, 1924. The emphasis on sports was in keeping with the U.S. Army's official doctrine in these years which noted that the human element was one of the essentials in battle, and indeed, "war is decided by man rather than armament." This necessitated high morale and the ability of all combatants to exercise initiative in all situations to which sports skills could contribute. There is a discussion in Odom, *After the Trenches*, 41–43.
22. Ibid., December 26, 1924; January 2 and 9, 1925; February 5, 1926. The "Can Do" athletic field was built and maintained under the orders of Colonel Taylor. Ibid., January 23 and June 25, 1932.
23. "Golf in North China," by Eileen O'Brien Leonard, in the John William Leonard Papers, USAMHI; The James E. Moore Papers, USAMHI. "Putt Putt" golf—also called Wee Golf, or Tiny Golf—was popular in the 1930s and numerous courses dotted the city of Tientsin. *The Sentinel*, May 23, 1931.
24. *The Sentinel*, January 11, 1924.
25. Ibid., March 21, 1924.
26. Ibid., March 14 and 21, 1924, reprinting an article from the *Peking Leader*, March 14, 1924.
27. Ibid., February 6, 13, 20 and March 3, 6, 13, 1925. *Goofus Feathers III* followed the next year and was also a success. Its director was Captain Frank J. Pearson. Brought up in the atmosphere of the theater, his parents were members of the original "Bostonians." He had also actively participated in Army theatricals such as the So-Journers Minstrels at Fort Benning, an Army post with its own substantial theatrical history. His assistant director was

Lieutenant Morris B. DePass, who for two seasons was with the Augersten's Minstrels in New Orleans. See in ibid., March 18, 1927; April 15, 22 and 29, 1927.

28. Ibid., January 22 and December 31, 1926; January 7, 1927; March 30, 1928. Company H also won in 1927 with its skit "Topsy and Eva." To assist in the productions, six permanent sets were available for use of the performers: a jungle scene, a railroad station drop, a hotel interior, a street drop, and a log cabin set.

29. While Burt was in command, *The Sentinel* felt obliged to inform its readers of various aspects of the theater world and the playwright's craft. Anne H. Braun, wife of Captain Gustav J. Braun, both of whom were active thespians, took the lead in developing some of the plays. Anne also wrote a series of articles on dramatics for the paper. Another officer prominent in regimental theatrical productions during this time was Captain David D. Barrett, "perhaps the most polished and experienced actor in the 15th," as one account noted. Ibid., September 24, October 8 and 15, and November 19, 1932; February 18 and 25 and March 4, 1933.

30. Ibid., December 24, 1932.

31. Ibid., January 28, 1933.

32. Ibid., April 8, 1921. Warrant Officer Francis E. Lee was a graduate of the Army Music School, Class of 1916, when it was under the direction of the famous Dr. Frank Damrosch of the Institute of Musical Art of New York City. The band took pride in the fact that, though the men were primarily musicians, in 1925 every bandsman qualified on the rifle range. In 1929, the band also qualified 100 percent, though with the pistol rather than the rifle. See ibid., April 8, 1921; December 25, 1925; July 27, 1929. On occasion the band performed "The United States Volunteers March," written by Colonel William K. Naylor, the regimental commander, Colonel Burt not being the only composer to lead the 15th.

33. This was reprinted in ibid., November 3, 1922. See also an account of bands in the U.S. Army in the U.S. Army's *United States Army in the World War, 1917–1919*, vol. 12 (Washington, D.C.: Center of Military History, 1991), 238–40.

34. Bon mot borrowed from the *Baltimore Sun* by *The Sentinel*, January 14, 1921; General Headquarters: "G.H.Q. 'Blabber,'" ibid., October 9, 1925.

35. Anonymous poem, "JAZZ!" *The Sentinel*, June 2, 1922.

36. Ibid., September 26, 1924.

37. Ibid., June 29 and November 9, 1929; January 3 and September 26, 1931.

38. Ibid., December 1, 1928; April 13, 1929; November 22, 1930. Orthophonic Victrolas, the hi-fis of their day, employed electrical recording and other techniques.

39. Ibid., May 18, 1923; March 14 and May 2, 1924. See also the clever poem "Mah Jongg," by Edgar A. Guest, reprinted in ibid., March 28, 1924, for further insight into this phenomenon. See also a witty, rhymed editorial, "The Mah Jong [sic] Mother," describing the sad case of an unkempt child neglected because its mother was addicted to the game, in ibid., September 5, 1924.

40. Ibid., February 27, 1925; October 27, 1928.

41. Ibid., February 1, 1930; May 30 and June 13, 1931. See also Andrews, *Under a Lucky Star, passim*.

42. Ibid., December 26, 1931.

43. Ibid., December 26, 1931; January 16, 1932. Gibbons had lost his eye in action while covering American troops in the Great War.

44. Ibid., March 24 and June 16, 1922.

45. Ibid., May 7, 1926.

46. Ibid., October 14, 1921; March 21 and May 2, 1924.

Chapter X

1. *The Sentinel*, March 25, 1921.

2. Ibid., April 21, 1922. This poem was by Martha J. Opie, an aunt of Major G.F. Humbert of the regiment. She was a newspaper columnist contributing to many Eastern dailies as well as a published poet. Several of her poems were published in *The Sentinel*.

3. Ibid., March 16 and 23, 1929; October 25, 1930. It is necessary to observe that there were Americans other than the soldiers of the 15th in contact with the Chinese. These included missionaries and representatives of the YMCA. Regarding the latter, see the extensive holdings, especially the Annual and Quarterly Reports and Correspondence files in the Kautz Family YMCA Archives, located in the Elmer L. Anderson Library at the University of Minnesota in Minneapolis. These other Americans adopted a much more sympathetic attitude toward the Chinese than did the average American serviceman. See, for example, a speech, "Identifying Oneself with Another Civilization," delivered at the North China Union Language School in Peking on March 30, 1920, by Fletcher Sims Brockman, of the

Notes — Chapter X

YMCA and on the faculty at the University of Nanking. Therein he asserted that no one has give up one's own nationality to properly relate to the Chinese: "The first thing to do if we would adjust ourselves to the Chinese civilization is to make up our minds that we are going to be a part of the nation and not live apart from it." Notions that the Chinese were merely "semi-civilized" must be given up. What was needed was "an attitude of admiration, of sympathy," and if one could not "learn to love and admire the Chinese people," then one should take the next boat home. He confessed that when he himself first arrived, "the people were repulsive to me." But he had gotten to the point where he could not be happy away from them. "I am homesick when I get away from China," he declared. See folder 105A: "China: March–1920," in box 154: "China: Correspondence and Reports, Nov–1919 thru July–1920."

4. *The Sentinel*, September 2, 1921.

5. Ibid., October 27, 1922; December 5, 1924; October 30, 1925; and March 18, 1927. See also Annual Report, Headquarters, United States Army Forces in China, to the Adjutant General, Tientsin, China, August 25, 1924, in folder "Countries—American Forces in China, 123.61 to 333.3," entry AGO 1917–25, RG 407. For the period of 1930 to 1938, see also folder "350.03—Language, Chinese, Study of, Proficiency in (USATC)," in entry 5960, RG 395. By 1927, new Standing Orders No. 350–2505, American Barracks, Tientsin, China, dated March 9, 1927, by command of Brigadier General Castener, provided for refinements in the Chinese language course. See *The Sentinel*, March 18, 1927. The officer-students were informed that the "Chinese instructors are cultured gentlemen. They are loath to correct officers and very sensitive according to our standards. Officers will govern themselves accordingly." Some of the instructors supplemented their income by offering instruction outside of regular hours. See ibid., February 11, 1933, for a photograph of some of the Chinese instructors.

6. Officers within six months of departure from China were excused from further instruction or tests in Chinese. As a further requirement, during his first three months in China, every officer-student was to read Smith's *Chinese Characteristics* and *A Sketch of Chinese History*.

7. *The Sentinel*, April 23, 1926. See also ibid., March 12, 1926, for details of the textbook then being issued.

8. For a discussion of the interest that the study of the Chinese language created among officers and men of the regiment and some aspects of its importance see the William H. Arnold Papers, USAMHI, and Annual Report, Headquarters, United States Army Forces in China, to the Adjutant General, Tientsin, China, August 24, 1925, folder "Countries—American Forces in China, 123.61 to 333.3," entry AGO 1917–25, RG 407. See also *The Sentinel*, April 2, 1926; June 23, 1928; October 28, 1933.

9. The "Chung" was a puzzle to the Chinese who did not readily make the connection of a bare notation of "Chinese" with any tie with knowledge of the language. *The Sentinel*, December 2, 1927. One of the nurses, Miss Jeanette Blech, was awarded a Chung after completing the 250-hour course in Chinese language prescribed by headquarters for the honor. Ibid., April 8, 1933. See also ibid., August 11 and 18, 1928; January 26 and November 30, 1929.

10. Flint, "The United States Army on the Pacific Frontier," 149.

11. *The Sentinel*, December 31, 1926; April 1, 1927; September 29, 1928; April 13, 1929; February 18 and December 2, 1933.

12. Ibid., October 2, 1925.

13. Ibid., October 14, 1921; March 31 and April 7, 1922; April 6, 1923; September 5, 1931; March 12 and April 16, 1932; July 29, 1933.

14. See article, Harry P. Bibson, "A Boost Into Eternity," ibid., November 6, 1925.

15. Ibid., July 15, 1927.

16. Li San's death was the subject of regimental General Orders No. 23, June 19, 1928. See ibid., June 23 and 30, 1928; November 8, 1930. See also ibid., February 28, 1931 for article, "'Sammy' Checks Out," about the death of a coolie employed by *The Sentinel*.

17. Ibid., June 23, 1922.

18. Ibid., May 30 and July 25, 1924. The men of the regiment were routinely asked to contribute to Red Cross and Salvation Army fund drives to assist the Chinese. See, for example, ibid., February 25, 1927, for a sad description of "Coolie Conditions" asking for donations to the Salvation Army.

19. Ibid., March 4, 1921; article, "Red Crossing in China," by Ruby M. Sepulveda, in ibid., August 19, 1921.

20. For floods see articles in ibid., July 27 and August 17, 1929; for famine an article, "The Scourge of Famine," ibid., August 22, 1931.

21. Ibid., October 17, 1931; and February 13

Notes—Chapter X

and 20, 1932. See also Anne Morrow Lindbergh's book, *North to the Orient* (New York: Harcourt, Brace and World, Inc., 1935; paperback edition, 1963), 112–32.

22. *The Sentinel*, January 19, 1923.

23. See in Confidential Report, "English Language Newspapers in Tientsin," by the American consul in Tientsin, Jay C. Huston, prepared for Julean Arnold, the American commercial attaché in Peking, Tientsin, China, December 1, 1923, copy to Headquarters, The American Forces in China, in folder "000.71—Interviews and giving out Information," entry 5960, RG 395.

24. Signed by "Someone" of the Service Company, in *The Sentinel*, June 11, 1926.

25. Ibid., January 16, 1925. Significantly, Hunan was the birthplace of Mao and he went to school and taught there. In 1920s, this part of China was a hotbed of Communism. The YMCA's archives, discussed in note 4 above, contain numerous documents relating to the Anti–Christianity stance and other attitudes of many Chinese in the 1920s, and the reaction and response of the YMCA to these developments. See especially box 158: "China: Correspondence and Reports 1924"; box 159: "China: Correspondence and Reports January, 1925 thru August, 1925"; and box 160: "China: Correspondence and Reports October, 1925–Sept., 1926."

26. There is a list of the "Humiliation Days" in folder "C-103.8 China: Humiliation Days," in box 3, entry 38, "U.S. Marine Corps General Correspondence," RG 127: "Records Relating to Marine Activities in China, 1927–1938."

27. *The Sentinel*, October 25, 1930; February 7, 1931.

28. Ibid., April 27, 1929.

29. Ibid., December 8, 1928. For the Red Spears and other related matters see also Elizabeth J. Perry, *Rebels and Revolutionaries in North China, 1845–1945* (Stanford: Stanford University Press, 1980).

30. *The Sentinel*, May 13, 1927.

31. Ibid., March 23, 1928. See also Ball, *Things Chinese*.

32. *The Sentinel*, October 14, 1921; January 27, 1922; January 3 and 10, 1931. See also a series in ibid., January 17, 1931, on "Household Customs During the Twelfth Month," which in 1931 extended from January 17 to February 17.

33. Ibid., October 20, 1922; February 16, 1923; June 6 and October 3, 1924; January 19, 1929.

34. Ibid., April 10, 1923; November 14, 1924; May 3, 1930.

35. Ibid., February 10, 1928; November 23, 1929; July 19 and August 30, 1930; and May 23, 1931. Rats were also often revered. See article in ibid., March 28, 1931.

36. *The Sentinel* often published short "Festival Days" notices. See ibid., May 25, 1928; December 7, 1929; April 4, 1931; June 11, 1932.

37. Sutton, *One-Arm Sutton*, 141–42. George E. Sokolsky, a correspondent for *The New York Times* and an avowed expert on China, also recognized the centrality of "face" in the Orient. See his lengthy article in *The Sentinel*, May 7, 1932, and the issue of April 18, 1931, for another feature on the subject.

38. *The Sentinel*, September 8 and October 20, 1928.

39. Ibid., June 9, 1928; November 8, 1930; January 21 and March 18, 1933.

40. Ibid., April 6, 1928.

41. Ibid., April 13 and 20, 1928; January 26, June 15, and September 7, 1929. See Tolley, 268 quoting William Edgar Geil, *A Yankee on the Yangtze* (London: Hodder and Stoughton, 1904) for a passage on bamboo and also *The Sentinel*, April 27, 1928.

42. Ibid., May 18 and June 9, 1928; May 25, August 24 and September 28, 1929; April 4 and 11, October 24, 1931; March 19 and May 21, 1932. There are fine examples of Chinese iron pictures in the General Forrest Harding Memorial Museum in Franklin, Ohio.

43. Ibid., October 24, 1931.

44. Ibid., March 9 and April 20, 1929; July 5, 1930.

45. Ibid., September 28 and October 12, 1929.

46. Ibid., August 17, September 7, October 19 and 26, 1929; October 10, 1931. Among the familiar products for sale on the streets was a sweetened, whitish, refreshing beverage made from apricot kernels and also the ubiquitous doughballs, one of China's staffs of life. The many occupations or professions attracting notice included those who cared for fighting crickets or those who maintained the more familiar cages of songbirds.

47. Ibid., September 9, 1927; August 17 and October 26, 1929; July 12, 1930; and September 10, 1932.

48. Ibid., September 9, 1927.

49. Ibid., December 27, 1922; February 14, 1931.

50. Ibid., August 10, 1929.

51. Tolley, *Yangtze Patrol*, 254; *The Sentinel*,

December 16, 1927; October 6, 1928; July 12, 1930.
52. See Ball, *Things Chinese, passim*; and *The Sentinel*, August 18, 1928; June 22 and September 28, 1929; and June 6, 1931.
53. Column, "Chinese Tales," in *The Sentinel*, June 1, 1929. This feature also ran for some time, supplementing "Things Chinese."
54. Ibid., August 3 and 24, 1929.
55. Ibid., November 12, 1926; February 7 and 28, 1931; March 19, 1932. To assist the men desiring to travel, *The Sentinel* often published guides and lists of "must-see" sites, as well as suggestions for the purchase of souvenirs or for the more serious shoppers interested in Chinese antiques. See for example ibid., April 4, 1924, and an account of the Ming tombs, near Peking, in ibid., October 30, 1925.
56. Ibid., September 21, 1929; May 20, 1933.
57. Ibid., December 12 and 19, 1931.
58. Ibid., November 14 and 21, 1931.
59. Ibid., June 4 and 11, and December 24, 1932.
60. Ibid., July 9 and 16, 1932. One American officer in the regiment in the mid–1930s, First Lieutenant William H. Arnold, was especially struck by the intense aggressiveness of the Japanese in conducting their war against the Chinese. See his comments and some analysis in the William H. Arnold Papers, USAMHI.
61. *The Sentinel*, March 5, 1932.
62. Ibid., October 25, 1930.
63. Ibid., May 23, 1924.
64. Ibid., February 24, 1928.
65. Ibid., October 27, 1922.

Chapter XI

1. *The Sentinel*, August 6, 1932. "Meguaping" *(Meiguo bing)* was Chinese for "American soldier."
2. Anonymous poem, ibid., August 19, 1921.
3. Ibid., August 5 and October 14, 1921; January 19, 1923.
4. Ibid., April 14, 1922, poem by "J.T.," "The Flapper (As Kipling would see her)."
5. Ibid., August 3, 1923.
6. Anonymous poem, "A Flapper," ibid., October 27, 1922.
7. Ibid., January 14, 1921.
8. Ibid., January 6, 1922.
9. Ibid., October 5, 1923.
10. Ibid., August 3, 1923; October 13, 1928; Ball, *Things Chinese*, 113 and 715–19. Following the dictates of Confucianism regarding filial piety, sons carried on the family name and were charged with caring for their parents in their old age as well as observing ancestor worship and maintaining family graves. This explains, to a degree, the primacy of sons in Chinese society.
11. *The Sentinel*, October 11, 1930.
12. Ibid., August 3, 1923. See also the article "Chinese Women: Out for New Fields," by Caroline Singer, wife of book illustrator Cyrus LeRoy Baldridge, in the "Things Chinese" column in ibid., July 16, 1932. The role of Chinese women has also been explored in a contemporary novel, *The Red Cord*, by Thomas Grant Springer, published in 1925.
13. *The Sentinel*, January 31, 1931; February 20 and August 6, 1932; Tolley, *Yangtze Patrol*, 94. So as to be prepared to at least entice one of these lovely creatures one soldier had some advice for his buddy: "Hutch, why don't you get a visa all prepared and carry it around in your pocket so when you meet one of the MARRY AMERIKA PASSPORTSKI you will be prepared for the emergency?" Ibid., May 21, 1926.
14. Tolley, *Yangtze Patrol*, 95. For more on the White Russians see *One-Arm Sutton*, 172–77. See also the article by Randall Gould, "The Wildest Town in [the] Far East," containing observations on Harbin, Manchuria, where many Russian refugee ladies took up their abode, though from there "these seductive creatures all seem to have gravitated down to Peking, Tientsin and Shanghai." *The Sentinel*, April 16, 1926.
15. *The Sentinel*, March 14, 1924; February 18, 1927; and January 3, 1931.
16. Ibid., March 4, 1927; February 4, 1933.
17. Ibid., December 16, 1921; October 13, 1922; October 12, 1923.
18. Ibid., December 31, 1926. For a number of years, Mrs. Kingman also directed the base chapel's choir.
19. Ibid., June 23, 1922; July 24, 1925; January 13, 1934. Rather elaborate regimental protocol surrounded such weddings. See *Customs of the Fifteenth U.S. Infantry*, 4–5.
20. *The Sentinel*, December 31, 1926; February 18, 1927.
21. Ibid., January 13, 1934.
22. Ibid., January 2, 1932; *Customs of the Fifteenth U.S. Infantry*, 5.
23. *The Sentinel*, July 15, 1927.
24. Ibid., June 17, 1927.
25. Ibid., June 8, 1923.

Chapter XII

1. Column by Jake Striker entitled "Jake's Letters to LuLu" (borrowed from *The Bridgehead Sentinel* published in Montabaur, Germany, for the First Division serving in the American Forces in Germany, which included this poem, apparently by "Jake," *The Sentinel*, January 14, 1921.
2. Anonymous, *The Sentinel*, February 4, 1927, poem about "Corporal Mason's Army Mule."
3. This pride was perhaps more keenly felt in foreign stations such as China, where there was a clear sense of being exposed to vicissitudes, threats and dangers. Accordingly, *The Sentinel's* editor was dismayed by public signs in Tientsin's Russian Park appearing in 1924, well after the Armistice in 1918, reading "No soldiers in uniform allowed." See in the May 30, 1924, issue.
4. Poem, "Soldiers' Side of It," ibid., February 16, 1923.
5. Poem, "The Soldier," anonymous, ibid., May 25, 1923.
6. See Joseph Crosby Lincoln, *Cape Cod Ballads and Other Verse* (Trenton, New Jersey: Albert Brandt, 1902), 173-77, reprinted in *The Sentinel*, May 5, 1922. John S. Madden, a former captain in the Seventh Infantry in France and who also served on occupation duty with the American Forces in Germany, was even more certain of the Regulars' significance on an even larger stage as he elaborated in his poem "The Regular":

But I'm somewhat of a dreamer, so I picture some great day,
When Gabriel sounds his trump for me and you,
And all the hosts of Freedom march past the Great White Throne,
The Regulars will head that last review.

This was published originally in the *The Watch on the Rhine*, a troop paper published by the Third Division at Andernach, Germany, part of the American Forces in Germany, and reprinted in *The Sentinel*, April 15, 1921.
7. Anonymous poem, "Soldier and Gentleman," ibid., July 29, 1921.
8. Editorial in ibid., October 12, 1923. This emphasis on the prime position of the infantry followed official U.S. Army doctrine as stated in the *Field Service Regulations* of 1923, for example. This asserted that "The coordinating principle which underlies the employment of the combined arms is that the mission of the infantry is the general mission of the entire force." As quoted in Odom, *After the Trenches*, 47.
9. *The Sentinel*, September 22, 1922; December 7, 1929; October 18 and November 22, 1930.
10. Ibid., March 25, 1927; reprinted from the *Recruiting News* in *The Sentinel*, June 30, 1922.
11. *The Sentinel*, June 29 and September 28, 1923.
12. Ibid., April 21, 1922.
13. Article and poem, "The American Soldier," reprinted from the *U.S. Recruiting News* in *The Sentinel*, July 8, 1921.
14. *The Sentinel*, October 25, 1930. A surprisingly large number of soldiers noted that the haunting strain of taps had a strong appeal for them. John S. Madden acknowledged this each evening he appreciatively listened to its music, "Sweetest mortal ever wrote." He could then sleep in peace until "Reveille says, 'Awake.'" See his poem "Taps," ibid., April 15, 1921.
15. This poem first appeared in the *Recruiting News* and was reprinted in *The Sentinel*, January 7, 1921.
16. *The Sentinel*, October 30, 1925.
17. This was first published in *The Watch on the Rhine*, and reprinted in *The Sentinel*, January 21, 1921.
18. *The Sentinel*, August 29, 1924.
19. Ibid., January 14 and October 14, 1921; October 26, 1929; June 6, 1931; April 1, 1933.
20. Ibid., August 17, 1929; July 9 and 23, November 26, 1932; February 25, 1933.
21. Ibid., January 14, 1921; October 16, 1925; July 26, 1930; June 6, 1931.
22. Ibid., December 8, 1922; May 4, 1923; May 30, 1931; September 3, 1932. Henry had joined the Army in 1892, and enrolled in the 15th at Fort Huachuca, Arizona, in 1897. In his memoir, *The Old China Hands*, Charles Finney devoted an illuminating chapter entitled "The Old Fogies" to those remaining in China following their discharges. Unlike GIs World War II and the Korean War, there was no inclination to bring foreign women home as war brides. General William H. Arnold who served in the 15th in the mid-1930s explained, "...they were a totally different breed of cats. They were old soldiers. They had no desire to bring anybody back [to the U.S.] at all." See in the William H. Arnold Papers, USAMHI.
23. Poem, "A Small but Adequate Regular Army" in ibid., December 1, 1922.
24. Ibid., May 8, 1925.
25. Article, "Value of Polo to the Army," by Major A.G. Rudd in ibid., November 3, 1922. See also ibid., April 7, 1922. Tied in with the love of cavalry was nostalgia for the old tradi-

tional U.S. Army cavalry posts which dotted the American West in particular. For example, *The Sentinel* published several articles on this subject in the series "History of Old Army Posts," by Captain Donald A. Young, Second Cavalry, reprinted from the *Recruiting News*. For example, Fort Riley, Kansas, was featured in an article in *The Sentinel*, May 18, 1923. See also ibid., January 28, 1927. One scholar has maintained that "like the infantryman with rifle and bayonet, the horse-mounted cavalryman represented the human element so central to idealistic American conceptions of warfare." Odom, *After the Trenches*, 146.

26. Mounts selected for racing were about five years old, 13½ hands high, and able to gallop a quarter mile in 33 seconds. The price of a good racing steed delivered at Tientsin as of 1925 was about $280 Mex, with polo horses costing about half that ($50 to $60 gold). The premier racing pony in north China in the mid-1920s was "Bengal," owned by Major-General "One-Arm" Sutton of Marshal Chang Tso-lin's staff, and worth over $17,000 Mex. This animal had won every race in which he was entered. For details as to how the horses were procured see "[The] Fifteenth Inf. Polo Herd," in *The Sentinel*, November 20, 1925.

27. See *The Sentinel*, October 19, 1923, for "What is a China Pony," by Arthur de C. Sowerby, a clear discussion of the Mongolian horse. See also ibid., July 25 and August 1, 1931, for articles by Private John T. Fox of the Service Company, "In Praise of the Native Mount." On training, see articles by Lieutenant Colonel E.D. Miller of the British Army. Ibid., March 26 and April 9, 1926. For a discussion of riding and march discipline see ibid., February 19, 1926.

28. Ibid., October 16 and 23, 1925.

29. Ibid., October 1, 1926.

30. Ibid., October 13, 1928; Ibid., January 21 and February 11, 1927.

31. Ibid., February 12, 1926, which also featured a photo of the detachment on its cover. See also ibid., May 13, 1927; June 16 and 23, 1928; and March 31, 1934. *The Sentinel* often recounted details of the detachment's activities in the *Currycomb Column*. See, for example, the issue of January 23, 1932. See article by Ray, "The United States 15th Infantry Regiment, 1925," 19, and Pogue, *George C. Marshall, Education of a General, 1880–1939*, 240.

32. *The Sentinel*, March 5, 1926; January 2 and 16 and February 13, 1932.

33. Ibid., June 13 and October 31, 1924.

34. Poem, "Wild-Eyed Dementia," ibid., June 24, 1927.

35. See her photograph on the cover of ibid., May 20, 1927. For "Jerry," see ibid., November 2, 1929; April 26, 1930; April 16, 1932. "Jerry" lost his life in a stable fire in April of 1930.

36. Ibid., December 12, 1931; April 26, 1930.

37. Captain William B. "Wild Bill" Tuttle, largely because of his flair as a horseman — as perhaps befitted a Texan — was judged the best all-around performer of the show, carrying off individual honors. Ibid., October 16, 23, 30, and November 6, 1925. Horseshows were common throughout the U.S. Army between the wars, those in China being typical of such events.

38. Ibid., April 29, 1927. Ibid., November 15, 1930. *The Sentinel* often admonished soldiers with animals in their care to treat them as "partners and friends." Horses would perform most willingly if they were not subjected to a "lash of hate" and were similarly treated "as a living being, not as a machine." They only asked for kind and considerate treatment, and a recognition that "a good grooming is equivalent to half a feed." See "The Army Horse's Prayer," ibid., April 28, 1922, and a poem, "The Heart of a Horse," ibid., December 30, 1927.

39. Ibid., February 22, June 7 and 14, and July 15, 1930.

40. For details on these trials and experiments see Annual Tactical Inspection Reports, Headquarters, American Forces in China, to the Adjutant General of the Army, Tientsin, China, December 19, 1923, January 5, 1925 and December 4, 1925, and attached documents, in folder "Countries—American Forces in China, 123.61 to 333.3," entry AGO, 1917–25, RG 407.

41. *The Sentinel*, June 13, 1924.

42. Ibid., February 10, 1922; August 8 and September 26, 1931.

Chapter XIII

1. Anon., in *The Sentinel*, February 11, 1927.

2. Ibid., November 14 and 21, 1931. For a substantive analysis of crucial Chinese and Japanese relations in the 1930 see Parks M. Coble, *Facing Japan: Chinese Politics and Japanese Imperialism, 1931–1937* (Cambridge: Harvard University Press, 1991). For the United States involvement see the older but still important studies by Akira Iriye, *Across the Pacific: An Inner History of American–East Asian Relations* (New York: Harcourt, Brace and World, 1967); and Dorothy Borg, *The*

United States and the Far Eastern Crisis of 1933–1938 (Cambridge: Harvard University Press, 1964).

3. For details of the deployment and activities of the 31st in Shanghai see *The Sentinel,* June 4 and 18, July 9, 16, and 23, and August 6, 1932. At this time, the 31st's executive officer was George A. Lynch, who was to return to China in command of the 15th in 1935. The men of the 15th were envious that the troops of the 31st were authorized to wear a marine decoration, the Yangtze Service Medal, awarded for their service in the beleaguered city. The medal was established by the Navy Department and approved by the War Department for presentation to Army troops who served with the Fourth Marines in Shanghai from February 5 to July 1, 1932. See folder "220.31–220.48 — Medals and Decorations," entry 5960, RG 395.

4. Secret Memorandum, Headquarters, U.S. Army Troops in China, Lieutenant Colonel Karl Truesdell, Executive Officer, 15th Infantry, to Colonel Walter S. Drysdale, the American Military Attaché in Peiping, September 26, 1933, in folder "370.22 — U.S. Army Troops in China," entry 5960, RG 395. Drysdale had been the American Military attaché in Peking in the early 1920s, and in the late 1920s and early 1930s, before his being dispatched to Peiping in March 1932, had been the 15th's executive officer under Colonel James Taylor. *The Sentinel,* April 11, 1931; March 5 and 12 and April 23, 1932. Also for the 15th's situation in China in the 1930s, and the debates concerning it, see Morton, "Army and Marines on the China Station," 66–73.

5. Thomas, "The United States Army Troops in China," 25–28, 45–49.

6. Iriye, *Across the Pacific,* 171–99.

7. See the James E. Moore Papers, USAMHI, and documents in folder "250.1, Disturbances," entry 5960, RG 395.

8. John Alexander White, *The United States Marines in North China* (Millbrae, California: N.p., 1974), 2.

9. Memorandum of a conversation by Secretary of State Cordell Hull with the Chinese Ambassador, Washington, February 7, 1938, in *Foreign Relations of the United States: Diplomatic Papers, 1938,* vol. III, *The Far East* (Washington, D.C.: Government Printing Office, 1954), 74–75. The decision to withdraw caused a stir in Britain and France, though the Chinese were less perturbed. The French, in particular, were fearful that "the decision of the American Government may strengthen the position of the Japanese," and asked for "consultation between the interested Powers." See communication, French charge d'affaires to United States Under Secretary of State Sumner Welles, February 8, 1938, in ibid., 77–78.

10. See account of a letter Hull sent to Congress on January 10, 1938, in *The North-China Herald and Supreme Court and Consular Gazette,* January 19, 1938, and *The New York Times,* February 5, 1938. There is further discussion in *The China Weekly Review,* Shanghai, February 12, 1938. This paper viewed the withdrawal of the 15th as a triumph of American isolationists.

11. See Manny T. Koginos, *The Panay Incident: Prelude to War* (Lafayette, Indiana: Purdue University Studies, 1967), 127. See also Frank Dorn, *The Sino-Japanese War, 1937–41: From Marco Polo Bridge to Pearl Harbor* (New York: Macmillan, 1974), 96.

12. The following record of events is derived from Strength Return of the 15th Infantry, as of Midnight, February 28, 1938, and Special Strength Return, March 2, 1938, in box containing the Regular Army Organization Returns, Monthly Strength Returns, 1921–1939, 13th–15th Infantry Regiments, in RG 407; *The New York Times,* February 5, 1938. The State Department also noted that the withdrawal had "long been committed to," and would be accomplished "whenever and as the situation so develops as to warrant the view that withdrawals can be effected without detriment to American interests and obligations in general." At the War Department, the chief of infantry, Major General George Arthur Lynch, who had earlier commanded the 15th in China and knew the situation there quite well, may have been involved in making the final decision to extricate the regiment from its increasingly exposed position. See also Morton, "Army and Marines on the China Station," 72–73.

13. *The North-China Herald and Supreme Court and Consular Gazette,* Shanghai, March 9, 1938. This British paper was the weekly edition of *The North-China Daily News* and was published every Wednesday in Shanghai. The paper erroneously referred to Colonel McAndrew as Colonel "Grew."

14. Accounts in *The Peking Chronicle,* Peking, March 1, 4 and 7, 1938, and Biggs, *The United States Marines in North China,* 180.

15. Dorn, *The Sino-Japanese War,* 96.

16. *The New York Times,* February 5, 1938; White, *The United States Marines in North China*; Biggs, *The United States Marines in North China,* 180.

17. Vogel, *Soldiers of the Old Army*, 116. Following the 15th's return to Fort Lewis, it was reequipped and retrained to take its place in a more modern U.S. Army. Trading in its Mongolian ponies for jeeps and its Springfields for Garands, there were no special uniforms now and it was successfully melded into the "New Army" that was to fight World War II. See details in the *Army Day Program* for April 8, 1939, Fort Lewis, Washington, and article, "15th 'Can Do' Infantry, Fort Lewis, Washington," in the *Fort Lewis Sentinel*, vol. I, no. 6, 1941, n.p. Copies are in the Fort Lewis Military Museum, Fort Lewis, Washington.

Chapter XIV

1. An anonymous poem in *The Sentinel*, May 4, 1923, dedicated to the 15th Regiment.
2. The William H. Arnold Papers, USAMHI.
3. Secret Memorandum, Headquarters, U.S. Army Troops in China, Lieutenant Colonel Karl Truesdell, Executive Officer, 15th Infantry, to Colonel Walter S. Drysdale, the American military attaché in Peiping, 26 September 1933, in folder "370.22 — U.S. Army Troops in China," entry 5960, RG 395.
4. The engraving included the carved signatures of 15 prominent local citizens, to which were added those of the Yu Yuen Cotton Mills and the Pei Yang First Commercial Cotton Mill (see map p. 149). Naturally, the degree to which the Chinese on this occasion were sincere or intent only upon currying favor with a Western power cannot be accurately ascertained.
5. *The Sentinel*, May 1, 1925. See also ibid., September 1, 1928, for a picture of the monument. There is a good discussion of the civil strife and other circumstances that resulted in the Chinese presentation in a chapter called "The Gate" in Finney, *The Old China Hands*.
6. The monument weighed over a ton and was shipped in three cases. For Gallagher's career in the 15th, see *The Sentinel*, September 24, 1926. He was later a major general. See a series of documents regarding the monument's shipment and final disposition in folder "AG 619.1—15th Inf.," entry AGO 1917-25, RG 407.
7. Max Boot, *The Savage Wars of Peace: Small Wars and the Rise of American Power* (New York: Basic Books, 2002), 253–78; John King Fairbank, *The Great Chinese Revolution: 1800–1985* (New York: Harper and Row, 1986), 41, 47.
8. Connor to Jacob Gould Schurman, Tientsin, August 20, 1924, in folder "091—Foreign Countries-China-Political," entry 5960, RG 395.
9. Connor to MacMurray, January 25, 1926, in folder "370.22 — U.S. Army Troops in China," entry 5960, RG 395. Useful discussions can be found in Fairbank, *The Great Chinese Revolution*, 182–83, 204, and *passim*.
10. Schmidt, *Maverick Marine*, 179.
11. Flint, "The United States Army on the Pacific Frontier," 150.
12. Letter to the editor, *The Sentinel*, March 2, 1929; Secret Memorandum, Headquarters, U.S. Army Troops in China, Lieutenant Colonel Karl Truesdell, Executive Officer, 15th Infantry, to Colonel Walter S. Drysdale, the American military attaché in Peiping, 26 September 1933, in folder "370.22 — U.S. Army Troops in China," entry 5960, RG 395.
13. In a column, "News from Old Timers" in *The Sentinel*, was a notice that Lieutenant Colonel Marshall, the assistant commandant of the Infantry School at Fort Benning, had written that he was following the military situation in China through Major Stilwell's articles in the paper, and also "that there are about thirty old Tientsiners at Benning." A bit later, readers of the paper were informed that many of these Old China Hands, including Marshall and Major Edwin Forrest Harding, had organized a club at Fort Benning "to get together and talk over old times." See in *The Sentinel*, April 6 and June 9, 1928.
14. The William H. Arnold Papers, USAMHI; *The Sentinel*, January 8, 1926; March 31, 1934; October 5, 1935.
15. Letter, Marshall to Pershing, January 30, 1925, in Bland, *The Papers of George Catlett Marshall*, vol. I, 273–74; *The Sentinel*, May 6 and May 13, 1927.
16. Letters, Marshall to Pershing, December 26, 1926, and Marshall to Major General John L. Hines (Hines became the Army's chief of staff on September 14, 1924), June 6, 1925, in Bland, *The Papers of George Catlett Marshall*, vol. I, 276–77 and 293–97.
17. See account of Marshall's Organization Day address on May 4, 1927, in *The Sentinel*, May 13, 1927.
18. Ibid.
19. Ibid., November 20, 1925.
20. Merle Miller, *Ike the Soldier* (New York: G.P. Putnam's Sons, 1987), 306. During this period, for much of 1940, Lieutenant Colonel Dwight David Eisenhower was the commanding officer of the 15th's First Battalion and the executive officer of the regiment,

before departing to become chief of staff of the Third Division, and then soon on to even greater things. Just as was the case with Marshall, Eisenhower coveted the time with "men and weapons," the "two fundamental elements of military effort," and hated to leave them once more for a desk, which he did after a few months. The 15th's World War II record can be followed, as part of the Third Division, in the relevant volumes of the *U.S. Army in World War II* series. See also Shelby L. Stanton, *World War II Order of Battle* (New York: Galahad Books, 1991), 202. In addition, some of the details of its operations can be ascertained in the memoirs of its most famous member, Audie Murphy's *To Hell and Back* (New York: Henry Holt and Company, 1949). The regiment is currently represented by the lively 15th Infantry Regiment Association with an active Web page and a quarterly newsletter, which, recalling the unit's Chinese heritage, is appropriately called *The Dragon*. Web pages are also maintained by both battalions.

Selected Bibliography

Primary Sources

The principal documentary sources used, in addition to the microfilmed files of *The Sentinel*, located in the New York City Public Library, include the following from the National Archives, Washington, D.C.:

Entry 5960: "U.S. Army Troops in China, 1912–38, General Records," in Record Group 395: "U.S. Army Overseas Operations and Commands, 1898–1942, U.S. Army Troops in China, 1912–38."
Entries 38 and 245, in Record Group 127: "Records Relating to Marine Activities in China, 1927–1938."
Various entries from Record Group 407: "Office of the Adjutant General Central Files, 1926–39."
Entry 5963: "General Orders, 1914–29 and 1936–38," in Record Group 395: "U.S. Army Overseas Operations and Commands, 1898–1942, U.S. Army Troops in China, 1912–38."

Additional pertinent documents are located in the Archives, U.S. Army Military History Institute, Carlisle Barracks, Pennsylvania and the George C. Marshall Library, Lexington, Virginia. Further information on the Fifteenth Regiment's return to the United States and its subsequent activities are located in the Fort Lewis Military Museum, Fort Lewis, Washington.

Books and Articles

Abend, Hallett Edward. *My Life in China, 1926–1941.* New York: Harcourt, Brace, 1943. Abend was a correspondent for the New York *Times*.
Anders, Leslie. "The Watershed: Forrest Harding's *Infantry Journal*, 1934–1938." *Military Affairs* vol. XXXX, no. 1 (February 1976), 12–16.
———. "Retrospect: Four Decades of American Military Journalism." *Military Affairs* vol. XLI, no. 2 (April 1977), 62–66.
Andrews, Roy Chapman. *Under a Lucky Star: A Lifetime of Adventure.* New York: Viking, 1943.
Ball, James Dyer. *Things Chinese.* 2nd revised edition, London: Sampson Low, 1893; 4th edition, London: John Murray, 1904. A fifth edition, revised by Edward Chalmers Werner and published in 1925 following Ball's death, was

reissued in 1989 by Graham Brash Limited of Singapore. Quite knowledgeable about China, Ball (1847–1919) was chief interpreter for the Hong Kong Civil Service.

Bicker, Robert. *Britain in China: Community, Culture and Colonialism, 1900–1949.* Manchester: Manchester University Press, 1999.

Biggs, Chester M., Jr. *The United States Marines in North China, 1894–1942.* Jefferson, North Carolina: McFarland, 2003.

Bland, Larry I., and Sharon R. Ritenour, eds. *The Papers of George Catlett Marshall.* Vol. I: *"The Soldierly Spirit," December 1880–1939.* Baltimore: The Johns Hopkins University Press, 1981.

Boot, Max. *The Savage Wars of Peace: Small Wars and the Rise of American Power.* New York: Basic Books, 2002.

Borg, Dorothy. *American Policy and the Chinese Revolution, 1925–1928.* New York: Octagon Books, 1968.

_____. *The United States and the Far Eastern Crisis of 1933–1938.* Cambridge: Harvard University Press, 1964.

Brinkerhoff, Captain H.R. "The Fifteenth Regiment of Infantry." In *The Army of the United States: Historical Sketches of Staff and Line with Portraits of Generals-in-Chief,* edited by Theophilus Francis Rodenbough and William L. Haskin. New York: Maynard, Merrill and Company, 1896, 610–28.

Brooks, Barbara. *Japan's Imperial Diplomacy: Consuls, Treaty Ports, and War in China, 1895–1938.* Honolulu: University of Hawaii, 2000.

Butler, Brig. Gen. Smedley D. "American Marines in China." *Annals of the American Academy* (July 1929), 128–34. Butler commanded the marine detachment in China from 1927.

Chang, Raymond, and Margaret Scogin Chang. *Speaking of Chinese: A Cultural History of the Chinese Language.* New York: W.W. Norton and Company, 1978.

Coble, Parks M. *Facing Japan: Chinese Politics and Japanese Imperialism, 1931–1937.* Cambridge: Harvard University Press, 1991.

Coffman, Edward M. "The American 15th Infantry Regiment in China, 1912–1938: A Vignette in Social History." *The Journal of Military History* vol. 58 (January 1994), 57–74.

_____. *The Old Army: A Portrait of the American Army in Peacetime, 1784–1898.* New York: Oxford University Press, 1986.

Cohen, Paul A. *History in Three Keys.* New York: Columbia University Press, 1998.

Dorn, Frank. *The Sino-Japanese War, 1937–41: From Marco Polo Bridge to Pearl Harbor.* New York: Macmillan, 1974.

Esherick, Joseph W. *The Origins of the Boxer Uprising.* Berkeley: University of California, 1987.

Fairbank, John King. *The Great Chinese Revolution: 1800–1985.* New York: Harper and Row, 1986.

_____. *U.S. and China.* 4th edition. Cambridge: Harvard University Press, 1979.

Farnsworth, Robert M. *From Vagabond to Journalist: Edgar Snow in Asia, 1928–1941.* Columbia: University of Missouri Press, 1996.

15th Infantry Regiment. *Customs of the 15th U.S. Infantry.* Tientsin, China: Peiyang Press, (c. 1930).

Finney, Charles Grandison. *The Old China Hands.* New York: Doubleday, 1961.

_____. *The Circus of Dr. Lao.* New York: Viking Press, 1935.

Flint, Roy Kenneth. "The United States Army on the Pacific Frontier, 1899–1939,"

Selected Bibliography

The American Military and the Far East: The Proceedings of the Ninth Military History Symposium, United States Air Force Academy (October 1980). Joe C. Dixon, ed. Washington, D.C.: Government Printing Office, 1981. 139–59.
Harding, Edwin Forrest. *Lays of the Mei-Kuo Ying-P'an*. Tientsin: N.p., N.d. There is a copy in the Frederick Harris Collection, folder 1/15, George C. Marshall Library, Lexington, Virginia.
Hart, John N. *The Making of an Army "Old China Hand": A Memoir of Colonel David D. Barrett*. Berkeley, California: Institute of East Asian Studies, 1985.
Hart, Robert. *"These from the Land of Sinim": Essays on the Chinese Question*. London: Chapman and Hall, 1901.
Hershatter, Gail. *The Workers of Tianjin, 1900–1949*. Stanford: Stanford University Press, 1986.
Hutchings, Graham. *Modern China: A Guide to a Century of Change*. Cambridge, Massachusetts: Harvard University Press, 2001.
Iriye, Akira. *Across the Pacific: An Inner History of American–East Asian Relations*. New York: Harcourt, Brace and World, 1967.
Kates, George N. *The Years That Were Fat: Peking, 1933–1940*. New York: Harper, 1952.
Koginos, Manny T. *The Panay Incident: Prelude to War*. Lafayette, Indiana: Purdue University Studies, 1967.
Krausse, Alexis Sidney. *China in Decay: The Story of a Disappearing Empire*. London: Chapman and Hall, 1900.
Kwan, Man Bun. *The Salt Merchants of Tianjin: State-Making and Civil Society in Late Imperial China*. Honolulu: University of Hawai'i Press, 2001.
La Forte, Robert S., and Ronald E. Marcello, eds. *Remembering Pearl Harbor: Eyewitness Accounts by U.S. Military Men and Women*. New York: Ballantine Books, 1992.
Lancaster, Richard C. *Serving the U.S. Armed Forces, 1861–1986*. Schaumburg, Illinois: Armed Services YMCA of the USA, 1987.
Lau Shaw. *Rickshaw Boy*. Trans. Evan King. New York: Reynal and Hitchcock, 1945.
McCullers, Carson Smith. *Reflections in a Golden Eye*. Boston: Houghton Mifflin, 1941.
Morton, Louis. "Army and Marines on the China Station: A Study in Military and Political Rivalry," *Pacific Historical Review* vol. 29, no. 1 (February 1960), 51–73.
Murphy, Audie. *To Hell and Back*. New York: Henry Holt, 1949.
Nayor, Colonel William K. "Christmas in China During the Boxer Rebellion, 1900." Memoir note. *The Military Collector and Historian* vol. 54, no. 4, edited by Alfred E. Cornebise. 169–73.
Noble, Dennis L. *The Eagle and the Dragon: The United States Military in China, 1901–1937*. Westport, Conn.: Greenwood Press, 1990.
_____, ed. *Gunboat on the Yangtze: The Diary of Captain Glenn F. Howell of the U.S.S. Palos, 1920–1921*. Jefferson, North Carolina: McFarland, 2002.
Odom, William O. *After the Trenches: The Transformation of U.S. Army Doctrine, 1918–1939*. College Station: Texas A&M University Press, 1999.
Perry, Hamilton Darby. *The Panay Incident: Prelude to Pearl Harbor*. New York: Macmillan, 1969.
Pogue, Forrest C. *George C. Marshall: Education of a General, 1880–1939*. New York: Viking Press, 1963.

Power, Brian. *The Ford of Heaven*. New York: Michael Kesend, 1984.
Preston, Diana. *The Boxer Rebellion*. New York: Walker, 2000.
Rasmussen, O.D. *Tientsin: An Illustrated Outline History*. Tientsin: Tientsin Press, 1925.
Reinsch, Paul S. *An American Diplomat in China, 1913–1919*. New York: Doubleday, Page, 1922.
Rickey, Don G., Jr. *Forty Miles a Day on Beans and Hay*. Norman: University of Oklahoma Press, 1963.
Ridgway, Matthew Bunker. *The Korean War*. New York: Doubleday, 1967.
_____. *Memoirs*. New York: Harper and Brothers, 1956.
Rogers, Paul P. *The Bitter Years: MacArthur and Sutherland*. Westport: Praeger, 1991.
_____. *The Good Years: MacArthur and Sutherland*. Westport: Praeger, 1990.
Schmidt, Hans. *Maverick Marine: General Smedley D. Butler and the Contradictions of American Military History*. Lexington: The University Press of Kentucky, 1987.
Sheridan, James E. *China in Disintegration: The Republican Era in Chinese History, 1912–1949*. New York: The Free Press, 1975.
_____. *Chinese Warlord: The Career of Feng Yu-hsiang*. Stanford: Stanford University Press, 1966.
Smith, William Jay. *Army Brat: A Memoir by William Jay Smith*. New York: Penguin Books, 1982.
Springer, Thomas Grant. *The Red Cord*. New York: Brentano's, 1925.
Stanton, Shelby L. *World War II Order of Battle*. New York: Galahad Books, 1991.
Sutton, F.A. *One-Arm Sutton*. New York: Viking Press, 1933.
Thomason, John W. "Approach to Peiping," *National Geographic* magazine vol. 29, no. 2 (February 1936), 275–308.
Tolley, Kemp. *The Yangtze Patrol: The U.S. Navy in China*. Annapolis, Maryland: Naval Institute Press, 1971.
Tuchman, Barbara W. *Stilwell and the American Experience in China, 1911–45*. New York: Macmillan, 1971.
Venzon, Anne Cipriano, ed. *General Smedley Darlington Butler: The Letters of a Leatherneck, 1898–1931*. Westport, Conn.: Praeger, 1992.
Vogel, Victor. *Soldiers of the Old Army*. College Station: Texas A&M University Press, 1900.
Waldron, Arthur. *From War to Nationalism: China's Turning Point, 1924–1925*. New York: Cambridge University Press, 1995.
Waldron, Major William Henry. *The Infantry Soldier's Handbook*. 1917. Reprint, New York: Lyons Press, 2000.
Wedemeyer, Albert Coady. *Wedemeyer Reports!* New York: Henry Holt, 1958.
White, John Alexander. *The United States Marines in North China*. Millbrae, California: N.p., 1974.

Index

Aguinaldo, Emilio (Filipino insurrectionist) 53, 65
All Quiet on the Western Front (movie) 162
American Army Dramatic Club 160
American Army Polo Club 124
The American Black Chamber (Yardley) 107
American China Expedition 27, 28
The American Embassy Guard News 108
American Forces in China (AFC) 32, 37, 59, 148
American Legion 125, 164
The American Legion Weekly 109
American Red Cross 43, 123, 125, 173
Amos and Andy 160
Ander, Red Cross Captain A.S. 20
Andrews, Roy Chapman (Gobi explorer) 43, 50, 163
Arlington, Lewis Charles (author) 170
The Army and Navy Journal 91
The Army News 98
"Army News" (*Sentinel* column) 108
Army Service Club 119, 122
Arnold, Captain William Howard 121, 217
Arrasmith, Major James M. 27, 28
The Asheville Skyline (paper of USS *Asheville*) 109
"Asia for the Asiatics" 34
"At Random" (*Sentinel* column by Roger Jones) 105
Austrians 14, 22, 29, 54

Ball, James Dyer (author) 178, 191
Banner Blue 135
Barrett, Captain David D. 216, 217, 225; attitudes towards Chinese 87; attitudes towards Japan 87; language studies of 86-87, 170; military career of 86-88
bayonet 146-147
Beach, Rex (writer) 124
Beardsley, Staff Sergeant James H. 97
Becker, Private George R. "China" (*Sentinel* columnist) 105, 130
Beery, Noah (movie star) 162
Beinke, Private Otto (*Sentinel* columnist) 7, 9, 20, 94-95, 130
Belgian House, 149
Belgians 12, 14, 15, 22
Bell, Captain R.D. (*Sentinel* editor) 97, 99
The Best People (play) 88
Big Swords (Chinese religious cult) 177
"Bill Howitzer" (Chinese waif) 172-173
Biograph (Tientsin cinema) 162
bolo 138-139
Bolshevik Revolution 43
Bolte, Captain Charles Lawrence 56, 68, 147, 170, 221-222
Borodin, Mikhail (communist organizer) 43
Bowles, Corporal John Henry "Major" (*Sentinel* columnist) 95
Boxer Indemnity Funds 173
Boxer Protocol of September 7, 1901 15, 23, 26, 27, 30, 33, 37, 41, 48
Boxer Uprising 1, 14, 25-27, 186, 173

"'Boy'—The Call of the East" (*Sentinel* article by von Eltz) 174–175
Boy Scouts 125
Boyles, Lieutenant Cliff H. 158, 159
Bradley, General Omar Nelson 76
Brann, First Lieutenant Donald W. 90
Breckinridge, Colonel J.C. (United States Marine commander, Peking) 156
Bristol, Rear Admiral Mark (commander, United States Asiatic fleet) 47
British 3, 12, 14, 15, 22, 25, 26, 28, 29
British Municipal Council 215
Browning Automatic Rifle (B.A.R.) 138, 139
Buddhist Brotherhood of Sacred Soldiers of the Virtuous Way 177
The Bullet (25th Infantry Regiment troop paper) 109
Burrowes, First Lieutenant Robert M. 91, 146
Burt, Colonel Reynolds J. 121–122, 147; Chinese language and 170; military career of 67–68; music and 67–68; theater and 160
Butler, Brigadier General Smedley Darlington "Old Gimlet Eye" (commander, United States Marine Third Brigade) 45, 46, 47, 50, 58, 71–72, 221
Butterworth, Suzane (lecturer) 190
"By Anonymous Request" (*Sentinel* column) 101
"By Request" (*Sentinel* column) 101
"By the Movie Editor" (*Sentinel* column) 106

Calhoun, W.A. (American minister in Peking) 27, 28
Camp Burrowes (firing range site) 91, 146
Camp Dabney (firing range site) 91, 146
Camp Spoerry (Nan Ta Ssu) 143
Can Do Players 160
Canton (Guangzhou) 22, 43
Castner, Brigadier General Joseph C. (commander, American Forces in China) 45, 48, 49, 60, 146, 211, 223, 227; attitudes of 71–74; military career of 70–71; personality of 71–72
Castner, Lieutenant Lawrence 223

Catholics 24
"Caught on the Fly" (*Sentinel* column) 108
Century of Cornelius 125
Chang Tso-lin (Zhang Zuolin) (warlord) 32, 35, 36, 37, 38, 84
Chapultepec 51, 55
Chateau Thierry, USAT 7
Chaumont, USS 45
Chen Hua (*Sentinel* photographer) 97
Cheney, Colonel S.A. (American military attaché, Peking) 159
Chestefield, Lord 136
Chiang Kai-shek 1, 22, 30, 43, 47, 48, 59, 83, 84, 87, 183, 225
Chief of Infantry's Combat Squad (15th Infantry Regiment) 145
Chihli, Gulf of 8, 142
Chihli (Zhili) Province of (now Hebei) 13, 35, 47
Child, Richard Washburn (American ambassador to Italy) 99
China: American policy toward 33, 40–43, 45–49; atmospherics in 3, 8, 9, 10, 11; culture of 178–181, 182, 184–185, 186–187; currency of 2, 18; description of, 8, 9–11, 13; extraterritoriality and 24, 48; foreign concessions in 14–15, 22–23, 28; health concerns in 13, 17; history of 21–50; institutions of 181–182; military service and 2; missionaries in 24; nationalism in 26, 34, 35, 38, 176–178; railroads and 8; servants in 18–19; shopping in 19; treaty ports in 14, 22–23; warlordism and 30–31, 32–33, 35–36, 37–38
China-Burma-India Theater (CBI) 223
China Review 34, 171
"China Versus Japan: A Clash of Tempos" (*Sentinel* article) 185
Chinese: American attitudes toward 3, 4, 8–11, 48–49, 69–70; attitudes of 9–11, 35, 41, 42; attitudes toward foreigners 23–24, 29, 34, 43; character of 9–11; military attributes of 184–186; personal characteristics of 182–183, 184–187; strategic concepts of 34, 184–186; students 29, 34, 173, 176–178; tactics of 34–35; vices of 183

Index 265

"Chinese Fighting Men" (*Sentinel* article, Magruder) 184
Chinese New Year 9, 178
Chinese stone gateway (Fort Benning, Georgia) 82, 218–220
Chinwangtoa (CWT — Qinhuangdao) 8, 27, 31, 49, 121, 128, 131–132, 137, 142, 146, 171, 213, 216, 221
Chinwangtao Club 146
"Chit on a Chingle" (*Sentinel* column) 105
Chung 57, 170
Chungking (Chongqing) 13, 87
Churchill, Winston 4
The Circus of Dr. Lao (novel, Finney) 94
Civilian Conservation Corps (CCC) 211
Cobb, Irvin S. (syndicated columnist) 105–106
Cocke, Brigadier General William H. (superintendent, VMI) 78, 92
Cohee, Chaplain Ora J. 127
Coldstream Guards (British) 44
Communist International (Comintern) 43
Communists 26, 44, 87–88, 177, 192–193, 213, 225
Confucianism 24
Congressional Medal of Honor 227
Connor, Brigadier General William Durward (commander, American Forces in China) 32, 33–34, 37, 39, 40, 41, 42, 43, 48, 60, 119, 120, 143, 158, 170, 217, 219, 221; Chinese language and 168; military career of 70, 74
Coolidge, President Calvin 46, 173
Cope, Captain Jesse D. 38, 39, 40, 128, 228
Council of the United Russian Public Organizations 192
Croix de Guerre 57
Cummins, Mrs. Joseph M. 206
Cunningham, Private Willis E. (*Sentinel* assistant editor) 171–172
"Currycomb Column" (*Sentinel* column) 105
Customs of the 15th U.S.Infantry 66, 218

Dabney, Major Henry Harold 90–91, 146
"Damned China Crowd" 3, 86, 222–228
Dapp, Warrant Officer S.A. 68
Davis, Stewart G. (*Sentinel* artist) 97
Denning, Staff Sergeant Henry H. 169
Dix, USS 129
Doings in Grain (journal) 106
Dorn, Brigadier General Frank 216
Drysdale, Colonel Walter S. (American military attaché, Peking) 211–212
Dunlap, Colonel R.H. 144
Dutch Annie (Tientsin madam) 118–119, 222

Egan, Captain Gerald 200
Eisenhower, General Dwight David 76
Eltz, Eleonore von (writer) 174
Empire Theater (Tientsin) 159, 162, 194
Enlisted Mens' Club 123
Estimating Distance Competitions 149–150
Eyster, Lieutenant G.S. (*Sentinel* columnist) 108

Fairbank, John King (Harvard Sinologist) 220, 221
Fantasy and Science (magazine) 94
Farnsworth, Major General Charles S. (U.S. Army chief of infantry) 110
Feng Yu-shiang (Feng Yuxiang) (warlord) 35, 37, 38, 39–40, 77, 84, 88
Field Service Regulations (U.S. Army, 1923) 69
15th Infantry Gymkhana and Horse Show 207–208
15th Infantry Stock Company (theater group) 160
The Fifteenth Tank Battalion Weekly (Fort Benning, Georgia) 109
Finney, Private Charles Grandison (soldier-author) 1, 66, 71, 74, 80–81, 93, 94
First Chihli-Fengtien War 32
Fisher, Chaplain Orville E. (*Sentinel* editor) 99, 126, 143
Fisher, Chaplain William L. 127
Flappers 188–190, 195
"For All Who Would Make Expert Shots" (article, Passailaigue) 139–141
Ford, Henry 107
Ford, Lieutenant Homer P. 223

Index

Ford, Brigadier General Stanley H. (Philippine Department) 223
Fort Benning (Georgia) 37, 81–82, 86, 87, 218–220, 222, 224
Fort Benning News 109
Fort Douglas (Utah) 27, 53
Fort Lewis (Tacoma, Washington) 74, 109, 215, 219, 226
Fort William McKinley (Manila) 8, 27, 28, 59, 60
The 14th Infantry Dragon (troop paper, Fort Davis, Canal Zone) 109
Fox, Private First Class John T. (*Sentinel* columnist) 95, 202
France 14, 15, 24, 25, 26, 29, 155
Freeman, Ralph 138
Fuqua, Major General Stephen Ogden (U.S. Army chief of infantry) 223
Fuqua, Lieutenant Stephen Ogden, Jr. 223
Fusiliers, Royal Tunskilling (British) 28

Gallagher, Lieutenant Philip E. 39, 79, 159, 220
Gardiner, Private (*Sentinel* columnist) 105
Gauss, Clarence E. (U.S. consul-general, Tientsin) 37
Germans 2, 10–11, 14, 22, 25, 26, 29
Gettysburg 150
The Ghosts of Manacle (short stories, Finney) 94
Gibbons, Floyd (foreign correspondent) 164
Gibson, Private Harry P. 203
Goofus Feathers (15th regimental musical) 158, 159
Goofus Feathers II (15th regimental musical) 159, 160
Goofus Feathers III (15th regimental musical) 80
Gordon, Colonel Walter H. 55
Green Gang (Ch'ing-pang) (Chinese radical group) 44
Grey, Zane 124
Guest, Edgar A. 101
Gullion, Major Walter C. 155
Gump, Andy 107

Hai Ho River 13, 45, 66–67, 128, 129, 158
Hale, Colonel Harry C. 54
Hankow 87
Hanson, G. C. (U.S. vice consul, Tientsin) 29
Happy Days (15th minstrel show) 160
Harant, Lieutenant Louis J. 141
Harding, Major Edwin Forrest (15th poet laureate) 19, 40, 80, 88, 89, 228
Harper's 94
Harris, Lieutenant Frederick M. 83–84
Hart, Sir Robert (Chinese expert) 23–24
Haydock, Private (*Sentinel* writer) 105
Hayne, Captain Frank B. 78
Healy, Private First Class L. M. (*Sentinel* artist) 97, 131, 133
Hei-Niu-Cheng (village) 148
Helmick, Major General Eli A. (U.S. Army inspector general) 56–57, 170
Henry P'u-i, Emperor 210
Here and There with the 31st Infantry 190
Hines, Major General John L. (U.S. Army chief of staff) 78, 150, 224
Hirohito, Emperor (Japanese emperor) 49
"His Belle of the Orient" (*Sentinel* short story, Haydock) 105
Hope, Bob 164
Hopei Province (Chihli, now Hebei) 47
Horse and Transportation Show 208
"Hot Stove League" (*Sentinel* column) 108
How Kee (soldier-poet) 167
Hsin Ho (village) 45
Hughes, Charles Evans (U.S. secretary of state) 32
Hull, Cordell (U.S. secretary of state) 214
Human Bullets (book, Colonel Sakurai) 109
Hunan 35
The Huron Flashlight (paper of USS *Huron*) 109

imperialism 3, 4
"In the Realm of the Philatelists" (*Sentinel* column) 105
In Worldly Clutches (*Sentinel* novella, Roger Jones) 105
Infantry Drill and Combat Regulations (American Expeditionary Forces, France) 69
The Infantry Journal 67–68, 69, 84, 109, 135
Infantry School Journal (Fort Benning, Georgia) 104
International Track and Field Meet (Tientsin) 155
international trains 38–39, 40
Iriye, Akira (historian) 213
Italians 3, 14, 15

Jacobs, Captain Fenton S. 205
Japan 1, 3, 183; army of 164; military operations of 184–186, 210–215, 228; U.S. policy toward 46–47, 49
Japanese 14, 15, 22, 25, 26, 29, 34; military attributes of 185–186
jawbone (credit) 51, 136
jazz 102, 107, 161–162
The Jazz Singer (movie, Al Jolson) 162
Jesuits 24
Jim Crow's Place 144
Johnson, General Hugh S. (NRA head) 69
Jolson, Al 162
Jones, Roger (*Sentinel* columnist and writer) 105

Kailan Mining Administration 138, 142
Kaiping (village) 28
Kalgan 170
Kearney, Captain (*The Tattler* editor) 109
Kellogg, Frank B. (U.S. secretary of state) 46
King, Colonel Campbell 62–63, 74, 144, 154
Kingman, Ruth 194
Kipling, Rudyard 4, 20, 80, 88, 101, 167, 175, 189, 197, 202, 221
Knights of Columbus 125
Knox, Captain Dudley W. (author) 184
Koenig Wilhelm II (ship) 129

Kokki ("Glory of Empire," Japanese troop paper, Colonel Sakurai editor) 109
Korea 49, 183
Korean War 92, 216
Ku Hung-Ming (writer) 175
Kuang-hsu, Emperor (Manchu dynasty) 25–26
Kuominchun (Feng Yu-shiang's forces) 77, 88
Kuomintang (KMT or Nationalist Party) 43–44

Lao Tzu 181
Lee, Warrant Officer Francis E. (15th's band leader) 160
Legation Guard News 108
Lehr, First Lieutenant Howard W. (*Sentinel* editor) 96, 157
Leichuang (firing range site) 28, 31, 142
Leonard, Eileen O'Brien 158
Leonard, Major John William 158
"A Letter" (*Sentinel* column) 106
Lewis, Captain H.B. 79–80
Lewis, Sinclair 105
Li-Chi-Chuang (village) 149
Li Ching-Lin (Lin Jinglin) (warlord) 38, 39–40
Li Hung-Chang (Li Hongzhang) (Chinese official) 175
Li San (U.S. government employee) 172
Liao Chia (Chinese fairy tales) 181
Liberty, USAT 129
Lin Tse-hsu (Chinese official) 22
Lincoln, President Abraham 52
Lincoln, Joseph Crosby (writer) 198–199
Lindbergh, Anne Morrow 174
Lindbergh, Charles 174
Linsi (village) 28
Liscum, Colonel Emerson H. 123
Lloyd's Weekly 110, 163
Lomasney, Private John "Chin a Loo" (*Sentinel* columnist) 109
Loyola, Ignatius 66
Lynch, Colonel George Arthur 117, 121–122, 154, 219–220, 227; attitudes of 69–70; military career of 68–69, 74
Lystad, Lieutenant Helmer W. 144

Index

The Machine Gunners' Burst (15th regimental show) 160
MacMurray, John Van Antwerp (American minister to China) 40, 44, 46, 47, 48
Madawaska, USS 129
The Magician Out of Manchuria (novella, Finney) 94
Magruder, Major John 184
Mah Jongg 9, 107, 125, 163, 193
Main Street (Sinclair Lewis) 105
Manchu Dynasty (Qing) 1, 13, 22, 175
Manchukuo 210
Manchuria 29, 32, 35, 36, 49, 164, 183, 184, 185, 192, 210
Manual of Courts-Martial 141
Manual of Interior Guard Duty 141
Margetts, Lieutenant Colonel Nelson E. (U.S. military attaché, Peking) 155, 156
Marne Miracle (Naylor) 63
Marshall, Lieutenant Colonel George Catlett (15th Regiment executive officer) 36, 39–40, 61, 123, 144, 145, 193, 206; attitudes of 15th's soldiers toward 79–81; attitudes toward the Chinese 78, 79; China experiences and 77–79, 224–225, 227, 228; Chinese language and 170; as commander of the 15th 77; 15th Infantry Regiment and 77–81, 86, 92; Marshall Plan and 82, 224, 225; military career of 76–77, 86; music and 79, 80; personality of 79–80; policies of 82, 223– 225; recreation and 78, 79–80; theatricals and 80, 160; training views of 81–82
Martin, Colonel William F. 55, 61–62, 135, 227
Mason, Walt 101
Masons 125
May Fourth Movement 29
May Thirtieth Movement 38, 43
McAndrew, Colonel Joseph A. 70, 215, 219–220
McCarthy, Senator Joseph (Wisconsin) 88, 225
McCormick, Elsie (*Sentinel* columnist) 181

McCoskrie, Major Frank U. (*Sentinel* editor) 96
McCunniff, Major Dennis E. 79, 90
McIlroy, Lieutenant Colonel James (U.S. military attaché, Tokyo) 184
McNally, Thomas J. 123
Meigs, Major General Montgomery C. 129
Meigs, USS 129
Meiji Period (Japan) 49
Merritt, USAT 164
Messiah (Handel) 194
Mexico 31, 51, 55, 173
Miller, Chaplain Luther D. 78, 80, 125, 126–127
Miller, Mrs. Luther D. 193
Ming Dynasty 13, 183
missionaries 2, 43, 173, 220
Mongolia 54, 164, 192, 205, 207
Moore, Captain James Edward 158
Morrison, Colonel John F. 54
Morrison, the Reverend Robert 24
Moseley, Major General George Van Horn (U.S. Army Fourth Corps Area commander) 223
Moseley, George Van Horn, Jr. 223
Mother's Day 107–108
"Movie Chats" (*Sentinel* column) 106
Mukloo (Mucklu) (Tientsin street) 118, 165
Murphy, Lieutenant Audie 227, 228
Mutshuhito, Emperor (Japan) 49
"My Favorite Stories" (Irvin S. Cobb) 105

Nan Ta Ssu (firing range site) 79, 142–146, 167
"Nan Ta Ssu Zephyrs" (*Sentinel* column, Barbara Spoerry) 143
Nankai, University of (Tientsin) 149, 155
Nanking (Nanjing) 13, 44, 47, 48, 214
Nanking, Treaty of 22, 24
National Recovery Administration (NRA) 69
Naylor Colonel William K. 61, 63–64, 77, 90, 138, 154
Neighbors, G.S. (soldier-poet) 163
Nestorians 24

Index 269

New Deal 211
The New York Times 170, 185
The New Yorker 94
Newell, Colonel Isaac 64, 65, 71, 77, 80, 81, 117, 178, 193
Newell, Mrs. Isaac 193
North China Baseball League 155
North China Star 32, 170
Northern Expedition 43, 44, 48

O'Connor, Private William A. 200
Officers' Reserve Corps (ORC) 92, 150, 151
Olympic Theater (Tientsin) 159, 162
Opium War 22
Oriental Real Estate Company 10–11
Orthophonic Victrola, 162–163
The Outlook 174

Panay, USS 214
Paris Review 94
"Pass in Review" (*Sentinel* column) 108
Passailaigue, Lieutenant 139–141
Past the End of the Pavement (novel, Finney) 94
Pasteur, Louis 163
Pecos, USS 142
Pei Ho River 13, 25,
Peiping 47, 48, 86, 87; Japanese operations against 213; U.S. Marines and 216
Peitaiho (Beidaihe) (resort) 142, 144
Peking 8, 13, 21, 25, 26, 28, 29, 30, 35, 36, 37, 44, 45, 47; travel to 170; Chinese language and 170; theaters in 159, 162; U.S. Marines in 96, 45, 58, 144, 153, 183, 215–216
The Peking and Tientsin Times 47, 96, 175
Peking-Hankow railway 173
Peking Leader 159
Peking-Mukden (Beijing-Shenyang) railway 1, 12, 14, 26, 30, 36, 38, 134, 142, 169
Peking Pavilion 162
Peking-Tientsin-Pukow railway 134
Pershing, General John "Black Jack" 77, 78, 81, 199–200, 224
Philippines 2, 3, 8, 56, 164

Philippines Department (Division) 27, 32, 57, 59, 150
Phillips, Lieutenant Colonel Albert E. 209
Pierce, Second Lieutenant James R. 90
Pinkerton Detective Agency 107
Ping Ting Chow 173
"Pistol Shots, Like Other Shots Are Made—Not Born" (article by Harant) 141
Portugal 22
"Princess and the Pea" 158
Principles of Strategy (Naylor) 63
Principles of War (Naylor) 63
Privates' Club 123, 130
Prohibition 2, 15, 115
prostitution 117–122
P'u-i (Manchu emperor) 27

The Quartermaster Gadget (troop paper, Fort Bragg, North Carolina) 95

The Radionews (*Sentinel* daily publication) 97
"Ramblings" (*Sentinel* column, Becker) 105
Rasmussen, O.D. (author) 170
Recreation Hall 123, 129, 157–158, 159, 163
Red Spears (Chinese religious cult) 177
Rees, Miss G.M. (writer) 170–171
Reeves, Corporal Raymond R. 93–94, 228
Regulars 197–204
Republic, USAT 66–67, 129
rickshaws 9, 10, 12, 18, 134, 182, 208
Ridgway, Captain Matthew Bunker 92, 216, 225
Riley, James Whitcomb 101
Rinehart, Mary R. (writer) 124
"Roaming Round the Town" (*Sentinel* column by "Hiker") 102
Rock of the Marne (Third Division troop paper, Fort Lewis, Washington) 109
Rogers, Will 164
Roosevelt, President Franklin Delano 211

Root, Lieutenant Colonel Edwin A. (15th's executive officer) 28
Rotary Club 125
The Rough Riders (film) 162
Russian Emigrants' Committee 192
Russians 14, 15, 17, 22, 25, 26, 29, 36, 49, 192–193
Russo-Japanese War 49

Saint Germaine, Treaty of 29
Sakurai, Colonel (Japanese writer and editor) 109
San Antonio Military Review 104
Sand Pebbles (novel) 2
"Sayings of Mrs. Solomon" (*Sentinel* column) 105
Schaick, Colonel Louis I. Van (U.S. Army inspector general) 72–73
"School Days" (skit) 159–160
Schurman, Dr. Jacob Gould (U.S. minister to China) 33, 144
"Scribbled by Scribes" (*Sentinel* column) 108
Scott, General Winfield 51
Second Chihli-Fengtian War 32, 35
Section House 22 149
"See If You Can Laugh" (*Sentinel* column) 106
The Sentinel 4; advertising in 101–105; analysis of 110; censorship and 99–100; circulation of 4, 96–97; columnists of 99, 105, 106, 107, 108, 109; crossword puzzles in 107; cryptograms in 107; debates and contests in 107–108; editorials in 100–101, 154; fads in 106–107; humor in 105-106; origins of 97–98; poetry in 101; racism in 105–106; reporters of 98; revenues of 98
The Sentinel "Dry Diving" trophy 208
The Sentinel, Snapshots of China 97
Sepulveda, Ruby M. (journalist) 173
Sergeants' Club 123, 144
Service, Robert (poet) 101
Shakespeare, 201–202
Shanghai 14, 29, 43, 44, 127, 170; military operations and 185, 186, 210, 213–214; United States Marines in 45, 47

"Shanghai Sayings" (*Sentinel* column, Elsie McCormick) 181
Shankaikwan (Shanhaiguan) 14, 36, 39, 54, 142, 144
Shansi Province 173
Shantung (Shandong) 29, 35, 149
Shiomoto Brigade (Japanese) 185–186
Showa Period (Japan) 49
Shriners 125
Sian (Xi'an) 26
Siberia 54, 192
Sigerfoos, Colonel Edward F. 55
Sino-Japanese War 49
Slam Door Alley 165
Sloan, Lieutenant Colonel Albert Brevard 127–128, 135–136
Snodgrass, Second Lieutenant Edgar H. 90
Snow, Edgar 171, 174
"Social Notes" (*Sentinel* column) 193
Sokolsky, George E. (*New York Times* correspondent) 170, 185
The Soldier 104
Sonderegger, General Emile (Swiss military expert) 150
Sousa, John Philip 161
Soviet Union 15, 38, 39, 40, 43, 44
Spanish War Veterans 125
Spoerry, Barbara (*Sentinel* columnist) 143
Spoerry, Lieutenant Gottfried W. 143
Springer, Thomas Grant (writer) 34
squeeze 18, 19
Stag Cafe 144
The Standard (Fort Riley, Kansas) 109
Standard Oil Company 8, 43, 45, 203
The Stars and Stripes 97
Stilwell, Major Joseph Warren 170, 216, 217, 223, 225; attitudes toward the Chinese 84–85; as China expert 83–85, 171; military career of 82–83, 86, 87
Stilwell, Lieutenant Joseph Warren, Jr. 223
Stilwell and the American Experience in China (Tuchman) 96
Sun Yat-sen, Dr. 27, 43, 54
Sutherland, Captain Richard Karens 92, 225
Sutton, F.A. (soldier-author) 179–180

Ta Fang (*Sentinel* photographer) 97
Taisho Period (Japan) 49
Taiwan 87
Taku (Dagu) 13, 25, 26, 128
Taku Road (Tientsin) 15–16, 102, 148
Tangku (Tanggu) 13, 25, 142
Tao Kuang (Manchu emperor) 22
The Tattler (Kearney) 109
Taylor, Colonel James D. 118, 119, 121, 123, 134, 136, 150, 156, 184, 193, 210, 227; Chinese language and 170; military career of 65–67
Taylor, Mrs. James D. 193
Things Chinese (Ball) 178
"Things Chinese" (*Sentinel* column) 168, 178, 182
The Thistle (Royal Scots troop paper) 109
Thomas, USAT 8, 129
Thomason, Captain John W., Jr. (author) 108
Through the Dragon's Eyes (Arlington) 170
Tientsin (Tianjin) 1, 2, 7, 8, 9, 10, 11, 12–13, 14, 15; American operations around 219; athletics and 155; Boxer Uprising and 123; business in 13–14, 15; clubs in 17, 123, 124, 194, 205, 215; defense and maneuver area of 147–150; description of 15, 16, 17; hotels in 17; industry in 13–14; international forces in 110; military operations and 184; prostitution in 118–122; riots in 210; Russians in 192–193; schools and colleges in 19–20, 155; theaters in 159, 162; U.S. Marines and 45, 47, 58, 221; U.S. Navy and 109, 141
Tientsin: An Illustrated Outline History (Rasmussen) 170
Tientsin Anglo-Christian College 155
Tientsin Club 215
Tientsin Country Club 123
Tientsin Golf Club 124
Tientsin Junior Athletic Association 155
Tientsin Press 96
Tientsin-Pukow railway 134, 149
Tientsin Race Club 123, 205
Tientsin Rotary Club 194
Tientsin Women's Club 194

Tillson, Colonel J.C.F. 28, 54
Tongshan (Tangshan) 12, 28, 37, 49, 90, 145, 169, 172, 183
Tracy, USS 144
Training Manuals 141
Training Regulations 145–6, Musketry (U.S. Army) 145
Triangle Service League 125
Trianon, Treaty of 29
Truesdell, Lieutenant Colonel Karl (15th executive officer) 211–212, 222
Tsing Hua College (Peking) 173
Tsingtao (Qingdao) 54
Tso Kuhn (Cao Kun) (Chinese Republic president) 35, 36
Tuan Chi-jui (Duan Qirui) (Chinese Republic president) 36
Tu-cheng (village) 39, 148–149
Tuchman, Barbara 96
Tunghsien 20
Tuttle, Captain William B. "Wild Bill" 40, 228; cartoon ad and 103; horses and 89–90; military career in China of 89–90
24 "Humiliation Days" 177
Twenty-One Demands 29, 49
The Typhoon (U.S. Navy shipboard paper) 108
Tz'u-hsi (Manchu empress dowager) 25–26

The Unholy City (novel, Finney) 94
United States Army Air Corps 60
United States Army, doctrine of 138, 145, 150, 200
United States Army 15th Infantry Regiment: alcoholism and 94–95, 117, 119; armed confrontations and 38–40, 213; attitudes of troops of 92–93, 115, 134– 136; attitudes toward Chinese of 30– 31, 35, 130, 132, 166–187, 217, 219, 220, 221, 222; chaplains and 125–127; China legacy of 83, 221–228; Chinese language and 39, 42, 57, 70, 78, 81, 83, 84, 86, 87, 88–89, 167–170, 219; Civil War campaigns of 51–52, 56; compound of 9, 10–12; coolies and 57, 69, 113, 114, 171–172; courts-martial and 120–122; deaths in 114, 115, 144,

195; deployment to China of 27–28; discipline and 65, 66, 67, 69–70, 71–74, 120–122, 132, 135–136; films and 162; firing ranges and 138–146; First Battalion of 27, 52, 54, 59; gambling and 136; Great War and 54, 55, 57; guard duty and 114; health and 114–115, 117–122; history in China of 21–55; history of 51–60; holidays and 134; horses and 204–206, 207, 208, 209; hunting and 127–128; Indian campaigns of 52, 53; maneuvers and 147–150; motto of 55–56, 227; mounted detachment of 81, 206; mules and burros and 207, 208; music and 160–162; operations in 31; organization day of (May 4, 1861) 55, 77, 82, 150, 155, 164, 219; organization of 54–55, 59–60, 97; pass systems and 135–136; Philippine operations and 53; policy toward China 48–49; post–World War II operations of 226–227; recreation and 122–128, 153–165; regimental coat of arms of 55–56, 227; regimental pride and 66, 69–70; research and development programs of 208–209; retirement in China and 203; routine of 111–114; Second Battalion 148; service conditions in 17–20, 61, 111–117; sources for study of 4; Spanish-American War and 52–53; sports and 62–63, 66, 74, 151, 153–158; sportsmanship and 153, 156; strategic policy of 48–49, 211–212, 213, 217, 218, 219, 220, 221, 222; theater and 158–160; Third Battalion of 28, 145, 148; training schedule and 137–152; travel and 127–128, 130–132, 133–134, 183; troop ships and 128–132, 215, 216; trophies and 154–155; uniforms and 56–57, 58; weapons of 138, 139–141, 146–147, 148; withdrawal from China and 214–216, 220; women's activities and 124, 143–145, 192–194, 195–196, 206; World War II operations in 226

United States Army Infantry School (Fort Benning, Georgia) 81–82, 86, 87, 218–219, 222, 224

United States Army Ninth Infantry Regiment 123
The U.S. Army Recruiting News 109
United States Army Third Infantry Division 226, 228
United States Army 35th Infantry Regiment 52
United States Army 31st Infantry Regiment ("Polar Bears") (Philippines) 31, 54, 69, 210, 214
United States Army Troops in China (USATC) 7, 21, 59–60, 70, 96, 211, 222
United States Army 24th Infantry Brigade (Philippines) 31–32
United States Disciplinary Barracks, Alcatraz 132
United States foreign policy 219, 220, 221, 222, 227
United States Marine Corps Fighter Squadron Three 45
United States Marine Corps Fourth Regiment 44–45, 47, 210
United States Marine Corps Legation Guard (Peking) 45, 58, 144, 153, 183, 215–216
United States Marine Corps Scouting Squadron One 45
United States Marine Corps Sixth Regiment 45
United States Marine Corps Tenth Regiment 45
United States Marine Corps Third Brigade 45, 47, 58
United States Military Academy 61, 64, 67, 68, 70, 74, 76, 82
United States Navy 2; China policy of, 46, 47
United States Penitentiary, McNeil Island 132
United States State Department 1, 2, 21, 27, 32, 43, 44, 211, 212, 214
United States War Department 2, 25, 27, 32, 43, 51, 55, 59, 60, 104–105, 108, 145, 153, 156–157, 209, 211, 212

venereal disease 117–122
Vera Cruz 51
Versailles, Conference of 29
Versailles, Treaty of 29

Index 273

Virginia Military Institute 65, 76, 92
Vogel, Victor (author) 151–152, 216
Volsted Act 9, 80, 117

Wali, 28
Walker, Major Walton Harris 91–92, 216, 225
Walter Reed General Hospital 67
Waltz, Major M.F. 173
Wampoa, Treaty of 24
Wanghsia, Treaty of 24
War of 1812 51
Warren, Senator Francis E. (Wyoming) 199
Waseda, University of (Japan) 155
Washington Conference 30
Washington, General George 126
Washington, Treaty of 33
Wedemeyer, First Lieutenant Albert Coady 88, 91, 216, 225
Weeks, John W. (U.S. secretary of war) 32
West Newark USS 129
Whitcomb, Captain John C. (*Sentinel* editor) 186–187
Whittier, Greenleaf 189

"Who's Who in the Chinese Situation" (*Sentinel* column, Stilwell) 84
"Why I Like Service in China" (*Sentinel* article) 203
Wiley, Major Noble J. 59
Williams, Rear Admiral Clarence S. (commander United States Asiatic fleet) 44, 47
Williams, Lieutenant Laurin L. (*Sentinel* editor) 154, 157, 158, 159
Woodbridge, Captain Woodrow W. 170
Woodrow Wilson Field 45, 184
"Writing Chinese" (*Sentinel* column, Barrett) 87
Wu Pei-fu, Marshall (Wu Peifu) (warlord) 32, 35, 36, 37, 40
Wuhan 13

Yangtsun 38–39
Yangtze River 13, 36, 44, 127, 174
Yardley, Herbert O. (writer) 107
Yellow River 34, 173
Yenan 87
YMCA 43, 119, 124, 125, 163, 168, 177, 183, 194
Yoshihito (Japanese emperor) 49
"You Can Hang It on a Hook" (*Sentinel* column, Roger Jones) 105

www.ingramcontent.com/pod-product-compliance
Lightning Source LLC
Chambersburg PA
CBHW051212300426
44116CB00006B/544